FOOD RESEARCH

**Research Methods for Anthropological Studies
of Food and Nutrition**

Published in Association with the Society for the Anthropology of Food and
Nutrition (SAFN) and in Collaboration with Rachel Black and Leslie Carlin

Volume I
Food Research: Nutritional Anthropology and Archaeological Methods
Edited by Janet Chrzan and John Brett

Volume II
Food Culture: Anthropology, Linguistics, and Food Studies
Edited by Janet Chrzan and John Brett

Volume III
Food Health: Nutrition, Technology, and Public Health
Edited by Janet Chrzan and John Brett

Food Research

Nutritional Anthropology and Archaeological Methods

Edited by
Janet Chrzan and John Brett

berghahn
NEW YORK · OXFORD
www.berghahnbooks.com

Published in 2017
Berghahn Books
www.berghahnbooks.com

Library of Congress Cataloging-in-Publication Data

Names: Chrzan, Janet, editor. | Brett, John A., editor.
Title: Food research : nutritional anthropology and archaeological methods / edited
    by Janet Chrzan and John Brett.
Other titles: Food research (Berghahn Books : 2017)
Description: New York : Berghahn Books, 2017. | Series: Research methods for
    anthropological studies of food and nutrition ; volume I | Includes
    bibliographical references and index.
Identifiers: LCCN 2016047231 (print) | LCCN 2016048886 (ebook) | ISBN
    9781785332876 (hardback : alk. paper) | ISBN 9781785332883 (ebook)
Subjects: LCSH: Nutritional anthropology—Research—Methodology. | Food
    habits—Research—Methodology. | Public health—Research—Methodology. |
    Archaeology—Methodology.
Classification: LCC GN407 .F684 2017 (print) | LCC GN407 (ebook) | DDC
    394.1/20721—dc23
LC record available at https://lccn.loc.gov/2016047231

British Library Cataloguing in Publication Data

A catalogue record for this book is available from the British Library.

ISBN 978-1-78533-287-6 hardback
ISBN 978-1-78920-526-8 paperback
ISBN 978-1-78533-288-3 ebook

Contents

Figures and Tables

Figures

Tables

SECTION

I

Introduction and Research Ethics

Introduction to the Three-Volume Set *Research Methods for Anthropological Studies of Food and Nutrition*

Janet Chrzan

These three volumes provide a comprehensive examination of research design and methods for studies in food and nutritional anthropology. Our goal is to provide a resource that bridges the biocultural or biological focus that traditionally characterized nutritional anthropology and the broad range of studies widely labeled as the anthropology of food, and food studies. The dramatic increase in all things food in popular and academic fields over the last two decades, accompanied by vast changes in technology, has generated a diverse and dynamic set of new methods and approaches to understanding the relationships and interactions people have with food. Earlier methods books tended toward the biocultural perspective of nutritional anthropology (e.g., Pelto, Pelto, and Messer 1989; Quandt and Ritenbaugh 1986) while more recent volumes have focused on food studies (e.g., MacBeth and MacClancy 2004; Belasco, 2008; Miller and Deutsch 2009) and applied work (e.g., den Hartog, Van Staveren and Brouwer 2006). The rapidly evolving field of food studies has generated a host of new perspectives and methods from a wide variety of academic backgrounds, many of which include anthropological theories and research designs. Because of the expansion of the field and the recent rise of food studies, we saw a need for a comprehensive reference volume to guide design and research across the full spectrum of food, diet, and nutrition studies.

The set has eight sections, each of which can almost stand alone as a food methods volume for a particular subdiscipline of anthropology. Just as nutritional anthropology and studies in the anthropology of food benefit from a four-field, contextualized approach, this volume assumes that research in food systems and nutrition relies upon four subdisciplines in order to effectively study the importance of food within human societies. Therefore, in addition to sections covering biological/nutritional, sociocultural, linguistic, and archeological anthropology methods, we have included sections on public health/applied nutrition, food studies, technology, and statistics. Each section is anchored by an introductory chapter that chronicles the history of the study of food within that area of research or practice and provides a comprehensive discussion of previous studies that have helped to define current work. By examining where we have been in relation to what we are doing and where we are going, each section seeks to define how current and future research can choose, adopt, and adapt the best methods to ensure high-quality outcomes. Each section is designed to provide readers with the background sources necessary for a fully comprehensive understanding of the use of methods for that area of study—a "pointing to" of studies and practitioners that have defined the field so that the reader has a good understanding of what is necessary to conduct respectable food research using methods germane to that area of anthropology. The individual chapters provide case studies and examples of how these methods have been used by other social scientists.

The chapters within each section form a complementary packet covering most of the major methods generally used by practitioners within each subdiscipline. We have included what might be called standard methods in the various subdisciplines (e.g., participant observation, ethnographic interviewing, excavation techniques, site surveying, etc.) but have expanded this focus with specialized techniques and approaches that have emerged or become popular more recently, such as digital storytelling, GIS, bone chemistry, and the use of biomarkers. The authors write about the methods and research design for their topics from their own research experience, outlining how they thought through their research questions, designs, data collection, and in some cases analysis. These volumes are meant to be a primary resource for research about food for not only the beginning student but also graduate students as well as research and teaching professionals who desire a better understanding of how their peers have tackled specific questions and problems. Each author follows a similar outline, with a short introduction to the method and its antecedents (covering key background/historical literature and essential readings where applicable) followed by current discussions and uses of the method, including the gray literature where applicable (e.g., material from the FANTA projects, FAO, Gates Foundation, etc.) and then discussion of analysis and research design considerations, concluding with the references cited and further readings. The sections on further reading include key historical volumes, reviews, monographs, software links, and so on for background or more in-depth exploration.

The eight sections were divided into three volumes by clustering areas of anthropological research that are linked conceptually and methodologically. The first volume contains ethics, nutritional anthropology and archeological methods, studies that are often biological in focus. The second volume is mostly sociocultural, covering classic social anthropology, linguistic anthropology, and food studies. We felt that research in food studies was more frequently rooted in social processes and disciplines such as history, journalism, and sociology and thus belonged amongst the allied anthropological fields. The final volume folds the more applied research paradigms together with public health anthropology and finishes with a section on technology and statistical analysis. Clearly, this last volume could be paired with one or the other volumes to provide a comprehensive overview of allied methods, as applied anthropology and technology are utilized in biological/archeological fields as well as socio-cultural, linguistic, and food studies research and practice. By breaking these three volumes into sections we hope to provide a comprehensive overview of methods related to food research, one that allows faculty, students, and researchers to purchase the volume(s) best suited to their subdiscipline and research interests.

A final word concerns research design. These volumes have no chapter dedicated to research design for two reasons: one, the topic is far too large to be adequately covered in one or even two chapters, and two, each chapter includes some aspect of research design. Clearly, research design will differ between biological and sociocultural studies, even if the philosophy of each is derived from classic anthropology theory. However, each author was asked to provide foundational examples of research design in their field in order to create a comprehensive core bibliography for research design and methods in food and nutritional anthropology and food studies. That bibliography is given here, along with a second bibliography for Rapid Assessment Procedures and Focused Ethnographic Studies.

Food/Nutritional Anthropology and Food Studies: Research Design and Methods

Albala, Ken, ed. 2013. *Routledge Handbook to Food Studies*. New York: Routledge.

Axinn, William, and Lisa Pearce. 2006. *Mixed Method Data Collection Strategies*. Cambridge: Cambridge University Press.

Belasco, Warren. 2008. *Food: The Key Concepts*. New York and Oxford: Berg.

Bernard, H. Russell. 2011. *Research Methods in Anthropology: Qualitative and Quantitative Approaches,* 5th ed. Lanham, MD: AltaMira Press.

den Hartog, Adel P., Wija A. van Staveren, and Inge D. Brouwer. 2006. *Food Habits and Consumption in Developing Countries*. Wageningen, The Netherlands: Wageningen Academic Publishers.

Dufour, Darna L., and Nicolette I. Teufel. 1995. Minimum Data Sets for the Description of Diet and Measurement of Food Intake and Nutritional Status. In *The Comparative Anal-*

ysis of Human Societies: Toward Common Standards for Data Collection and Reporting, ed. Emilio F. Moran, 97–128. Boulder, CO: Lynne Rienner.

Edge, John T. 2013. *The Larder: Food Studies Methods from the American South*. Athens, GA: University of Georgia Press.

Gibson, Rosalind. 2005. *Principles of Nutritional Assessment*, 2nd ed. Oxford: Oxford University Press.

Johnston, Francis, ed. 1987. *Nutritional Anthropology*. New York: Alan R. Liss.

Kedia, Satish, and John van Willigen. 2005. *Applied Anthropology: Domains of Application*. Westport, CT: Praeger.

Kiefer, Christie W. 2006. *Doing Health Anthropology: Research Methods for Community Assessment and Change*. New York: Springer.

Macbeth, Helen, and Jeremy MacClancy. 2004. *Researching Food Habits: Methods and Problems*. New York: Berghahn Books.

Margetts, Barrie, and Michael Nelson. 1997. *Design Concepts in Nutritional Epidemiology*, 2nd ed. Oxford: Oxford University Press.

Mead, Margaret. 1945. *Manual for the Study of Food Habits*. Washington, DC: National Research Council.

Miller, Jeff, and Jonathan Deutsch. 2009. *Food Studies: an Introduction to Research Methods*. Oxford and New York: Berg.

Murcott, Anne, Warren Belasco, and Peter Jackson, eds. 2013. *The Handbook of Food Research*. London and New York: Bloomsbury.

Pellett, P. L. 1987. Problems and Pitfalls in the Assessment of Human Nutritional Status. In *Food and Evolution: Toward a Theory of Human Food Habits*, ed. Marvin Harris and Eric Ross, 163-180. Philadelphia: Temple University Press.

Pelto, Gretel, Pertti Pelto, and Ellen Messer. 1989. *Research Methods in Nutritional Anthropology*. Tokyo: United Nations University.

Pelto, Pertti. 2013. *Applied Ethnography: Guidelines for Field Research*. Walnut Creek, CA: Left Coast Press.

Pelto, Pertti, and Gretel Pelto. 1978. *Anthropological Research: The Structure of Inquiry*. Cambridge: Cambridge University Press.

Quandt, Sara, and Cheryl Ritenbaugh, eds. 1986. *Training Manual in Nutritional Anthropology*. Washington, DC: American Anthropological Association.

Scrimshaw, Susan C. M., and Elena Hurtado. 1987. *Rapid Assessment Procedures for Nutrition and Primary Health Care: Anthropological Approaches to Improving Programme Effectiveness*. Tokyo: United Nations University and New York: UNICEF.

Shamoo, A., and D. Resnik. 2009. *Responsible Conduct of Research*, 2nd ed. New York: Oxford University Press.

Sobo, Elisa J. 2009. *Culture and Meaning in Health Services Research*. Walnut Creek, CA: Left Coast Press.

Sutton, Mark Q., Kristin D. Sobolik, and Jill K. Gardner. 2010. *Paleonutrition*. Tucson: University of Arizona Press.

Thursby, Jacqueline S. 2008. *Foodways and Folklore*. Westport, CT: Greenwood Folklore Handbooks.

Ulijaszek, Stanley. 2005. *Human Energetics in Biological Anthropology*. Cambridge Studies in Biological and Evolutionary Anthropology 16. Cambridge: Cambridge University Press.

Ulijaszek, Stanley, and S. S. Strickland. 1993. *Nutritional Anthropology: Biological Perspectives.* Littlehampton: Smith-Gordon.

VanderWerker, Amber M., and Tanya M. Peres. 2010. *Integrating Zooarchaeology and Paleoethnobotany: A Consideration of Issues, Methods and Cases.* New York: Springer.

Weiss, William, and Paul Bolton. 2000. *Training in Qualitative Research Methods for NGOs and PVOs: A Trainer's Guide to Strengthening Program Planning and Evaluation.* Baltimore, MD: Center for Refugee and Disaster Studies, Johns Hopkins University School of Public Health. http://www.jhsph.edu/research/centers-and-institutes/center-for-refugee-and-disaster-response/publications_tools/publications/_pdf/TQR/tg_introduction.pdf.

Rapid Assessment Procedures and Focused Ethnographic Studies

Beebe, James. 2001. *Rapid Assessment Process: An Introduction.* Lanham, MD: AltaMira Press.

———. 2014. *Rapid Qualitative Inquiry: A Field Guide to Team-Based Assessment.* Lanham, MD: Rowman and Littlefield.

Blum L., P. J. Pelto, G. H. Pelto, & H. V. Kuhnlein. 1997. *Community Assessment of Natural Food Sources of Vitamin A.* Boston: International Nutrition Foundation.

Catholic Relief Services. n.d. *Rapid Rural Appraisal/Participatory Rural Appraisal Manual.* http://www.crsprogramquality.org/storage/pubs/me/rrapra.pdf.

Catley, Andrew, John Burns, Davit Abebe, and Omeno Suji. 2008. Participatory Impact Assessment: A Guide for Practitioners. Feinstein International Center, Friedman School of Nutrition Science and Policy, Tufts University (in English, Spanish, or French). http://fic.tufts.edu/assets/Part_Impact_10_21_08V2.pdf.

Chaiken, Miriam S. 2011. Using Qualitative Methods in Save the Children Programs and Research: A Training Manual. Washington, DC: Save the Children.

Chaiken, Miriam S., J. Richard Dixon, Colette Powers, and Erica Wetzler, 2009. Asking the Right Questions: Community-Based Strategies to Combat Hunger. *NAPA Bulletin* 32(1): 42–54.

GERANDO: Community Based Disaster Risk Management; Facilitator's Manual. 2011. http://www.wvi.org/disaster-risk-reduction-and-community-resilience/publication/gerando-community-based-risk-reduction.

Gittelsohn, J., P. J. Pelto, M. E. Bentley, K. Bhattacharyya, and J. Russ. 1998. *Ethnographic Methods to Investigate Women's Health.* Boston: International Nutrition Foundation.

Gove, S., and G. H. Pelto. 1994. Focused Ethnographic Studies in the WHO Programme for the Control of Acute Respiratory Infections. *Medical Anthropology* 15: 409–24.

Pelto, Gretel H., and Margaret Armar-Klemesu. 2014. *Focused Ethnographic Study of Infant and Young Child Feeding 6–23 Months: Behaviors, Beliefs, Contexts and Environments. Manual for Conducting the Study, Analyzing the Results, and Writing a Report.* Global Alliance for Improved Nutrition (GAIN). http://www.hftag.org/resources/all-resources/ (select "Demand Generation for Home Fortification", then "Focused Ethnographic Study").

Pelto, G. H., M. Armar-Klemesu, J. Siekmann, and D. Schofield. 2013. The Focused Ethnographic Study: Assessing the Behavioral and Local Market Environment for Improving the Diets of Infants and Young Children 6 to 23 Months Old and Its Use in Three Countries. *Maternal & Child Nutrition* 9: 35–46.

Pelto, G. H., and S. Gove. 1994. Developing a Focused Ethnographic Study for the WHO Acute Respiratory Infection Control Programme. In *Rapid Assessment Procedures: Qualitative Methodologies for Planning and Evaluation of Health Related Programmes,* ed. N. S. Scrimshaw and G. R. Gleason, 215–26. Boston: International Nutrition Foundation.

Scrimshaw, Nevin S., and Gary R. Gleason, eds. 1992. *Rapid Assessment Procedures: Qualitative Methodologies for Planning and Evaluation of Health Related Programmes.* Boston: International Nutrition Foundation for Developing Countries (INFDC). http://archive.unu .edu/unupress/food2/UIN08E/UIN08E00.HTM.

Scrimshaw, S., and E. Hurtado. 1987. *Rapid Assessment Procedures for Nutrition and Primary Health Care.* Tokyo: UNU.

Smith, Madeleine, Geoff Heinrich, Linda Lovick, and David Vosburg. 2010. *Livelihoods in Malawi: A Rapid Livelihoods Assessment Using the Integral Human Development Conceptual Framework.* http://www.crsprogramquality.org/storage/pubs/general/Malawi-Assessment-low.pdf.

Introduction to *Food Research: Nutritional Anthropology and Archaeological Methods*

Janet Chrzan

Volume and Section Overviews: Introduction and Sections I and II

Section I: Introduction and Ethics

This volume, the first in the three-volume set *Research Methods for Anthropological Studies of Food and Nutrition,* begins with a discussion of the volume followed by a chapter on research ethics by Sharon Devine and John Brett. Their chapter will be reproduced in all three volumes because all researchers must understand ethics, and consideration of the ethics of methods used to collect, analyze, store, and publish must be an essential and initial element of the planning of any project. In their chapter they expand the idea of research ethics beyond publication and permissions to include the ethics of study design, recruitment, enrollment, and obtaining informed consent. They present a brief history of the research problems that led to current ethics regulation requirements as well as a primer on the principles that guide ethical research: respect for persons, beneficence, and justice. They conclude with two short case studies highlighting application of these ethical principles in hypothetical food studies.

Section II: Nutritional Anthropology

Section II covers nutritional anthropology using a biocultural approach that can be considered the historical "mother" framework of nutritional anthropology and underlies almost all basic and applied research. Though new frameworks and perspectives have emerged over the last two decades, the biocultural perspective continues to influence much of the research in food and nutritional anthropology. The chapters in this section cover classic topics within the field, including anthropometry, biological measurements, physical activity and energy expenditure, and dietary analyses on the individual and group levels. Darna Dufour and Barbara Piperata provide an overview of this section along with an introduction to nutritional anthropology methods and study design. They explicitly situate such research as biocultural: it seeks to understand how biological and cultural forces work together to channel human food use and nutritional status. They review the design of three studies, considering the kinds of questions asked, the type of data needed to answer the questions, and the methods used, and then evaluate the strengths and weakness of each design. Study design—as the conceptual starting point and first potential stumbling block—is probably one of the most difficult aspects of research, so this chapter will be a valuable addition to the canon on biocultural research.

In the next chapter, Leslie Sue Lieberman addresses that other mainstay of nutritional anthropology: body composition and anthropometry. She discusses the background theory and design protocols for composition studies and provides a comprehensive overview of how to assess nutritional status, growth and developmental patterns in body mass, composition, size, and shape. Lieberman also discusses the use of composition studies in nutritional anthropology for surveillance and monitoring of populations, assessing the impact of nutritional and other types of health, sanitation, economic, and educational interventions, and describes their use in predicting risk for acute and chronic illnesses and death. Finally, she reviews the many websites and materials that provide instruction on these methods as well as the use of reference data sets and standards in interpreting measurements for both individuals and populations. Mark Jenike then focuses on measuring energy expenditure. While this has long been a favorite and even foundational focus in nutritional anthropology, technological advances have introduced a wealth of possible devices and analytical options that make measuring physical activity and energy use both easier and more perplexing. Jenike presents an overview of key concepts and established methods for measuring total daily energy expenditure in humans, and reviews currently available devices for recording physical activity and energy expenditure among free-living populations.

As a rational companion piece to those two assessment methods, the following chapter by Andrea Wiley examines dietary analysis methods. Dietary data are a core part of almost all research in nutritional anthropology, whether biological or biocultural, yet inaccuracies in data collection and analysis are common and caused by both random error and collection bias. Wiley describes likely sources of error with self-report methods for measuring food intake as well as effective observational methods for field and/or community-based research, and compares the benefits of each method and the kinds of research questions to which each is suited. She tackles food frequency questionnaires and compositional tables, and reviews methods for assessing nutritional status, including biomarkers, anthropometric indices, and reference standards. This chapter, when paired with Leslie Sue Leiberman's, provides researchers at all levels with up-to-the minute reviews of the latest incarnations of core methods for dietary health assessment.

The final three chapters in this section cover applied nutritional assessment, primate studies, and measurement of commensality. Sera Young and Emily Tuthill contribute a chapter on using ethnography for evaluation in public health nutrition. While it may be natural for an anthropologist to use ethnographic techniques, it is not natural for many people who practice public health, public health nutrition or community nutrition. In this chapter they describe why and how to bring ethnographic methods into program planning and assessment. They describe how ethnography can be incorporated into public health projects, and discuss doing so with a case study on infant feeding. They then analyze how core concepts of ethnographic work, such as ecology, biocultural modeling and an emic/etic framework, can bring new insights to programs for infant and young child feeding practices. Their conclusion provides examples of application and evaluation using ethnographic and mixed methods in programming for public health nutrition as well as a set of questions that researchers and program designers will want to ask prior to beginning a new protocol. Their methodological look at public health ethnography is destined to be core reading for anyone planning to implement a program for nutrition improvement, especially in infants and children.

In a departure from human studies but still within biological/biocultural nutritional anthropology, the next chapter, contributed by Jessica Rothman and Caley Johnson, is about methods for collecting data on primate diet. They discuss the assessment of primate diets, focusing on how to collect and process primate foods and measure the content of macro- and micronutrients as well as secondary compounds. To conclude, they reappraise the methodologies that inform the various frameworks for understanding primate diets and foraging patterns. The section's final chapter explores how anthropologists and others have measured commensality in relation to health, well-being, and social function variables. Here Janet Chrzan outlines the theory, methods, and history of research about social eating, discussing how different disciplines conceive of the variables that contextualize commensality, and what outcomes each deems important. She divides the studies into three broad categories—social facilitation, correlation, and direct connections between commensality and dependent outcome—and discusses the strengths, weaknesses and methods of each. She concludes with a case study from her own research of maternal and child health and provides tables that itemize the methods used in current research in this area. Together, these seven chapters cover almost the entire range of methods used to collect and analyze the human and nonhuman primate diets that are the basis of most biocultural research. They thus serve as an excellent and up-to-date primer on conducting food and nutritional research in the field.

Section III: Archaeological Study of Food and Food Habits

The study of past food use and habits has changed greatly in the last two decades as new discoveries and technologies have enhanced our understanding of the archaeology of food and increased the means by which to collect, analyze, and understand past diet. The essays in this section cover all aspects of past diet retrieval and analysis, from identification of food remains (through taphonomy, zooarchaeology, archaeobotany, lithic analysis, and palynology) to analysis of the indirect evidence of diet, such as bone chemistry, structural analysis, dental microwear, and population health.

At the outset of Section III, Patti Jo Wright provides an introduction to methods in archeological research, highlighting that compared to past studies, current research benefits from greater sophistication in research methods and from a holistic, integrated approach that allows for analysis of many lines of evidence. She describes the kinds of evidence that can now be collected, from old standards (bones, seeds, etc.) to trace residuals of lipids, DNA, and isotopes, and discusses the methods and techniques used to sample, collect, process, identify, and quantify these remains. She also includes a discussion of research design and several case studies to encourage readers to think about how they "think through" their research. In the next chapter Wright focuses her attention on the retrieval of plant remains and the various approaches (macroscopic, microscopic, chemical, and molecular) to analysis of these data. She then examines research design, consideration of research questions, and biases in preservation, and concludes with a discussion of current perspectives on research fundamentals for the study of plant remains.

Bethany Turner and Sarah Livengood contribute a chapter on diet reconstruction via bioarchaeology and human osteology, providing a philosophical approach to the subject and a thorough overview of current methods and research design. They point out that these methods are direct—they indicate exactly what past humans ate and how their health was affected by diet—rather than indirect, that is, reliant on inferred relationships between human eating patterns and environmental evidence such as pollen, soil, or artifact assemblages. Situating their focus in microscopic and chemical studies, they cover the theoretical issues involved in these analyses as well as practical concerns and basic methodologies for dental microscopy, stable isotope analysis, and trace element analysis. They assert that when bioarcheological studies of this sort are analyzed in relation to other (direct and indirect) data, a wide range of questions about social organization and resource use can be inferred. Alan Goodman next tackles a difficult task: the assessment of nutritional status in past populations. He reviews current issues in the study of nutritional stress in archeological studies and examines how stress indicators in bone and teeth (linear bone growth, linear enamel hypoplasias, and porotic hyperostosis) indicate the functional consequences of nutritional deprivation. He reminds us that stress indicators linked to bone and teeth can be difficult to interpret because they are amorphous in timing, duration, and cause and may obscure the reasons for morbidity and mortality. Regardless, paleo-nutritional studies have provided many insights into human social changes including the transition from gathering-hunting to horticulture.

In the following chapter, Katherine Moore also examines bones, but in this case those of animals found in the assemblages associated with past human diet. She highlights that transitions in human social organization have been identified via analysis of animal and food remains, including the domestication of animals, changes in foraging patterns, and the origins of stratified societies. In her chapter she describes how bones and other animal remains are used to understand past cuisine and the nutritional consequences of past diets, and examines how taphonomy, the changes that occur to bones and other assemblages after death, can affect interpretation. She also discusses how zooarchaeologists infer dietary intake from animal remains using models from social anthropology, ecology, and veterinary anatomy. She concludes with an analysis of how archeologists can use the full archeological assemblage—what is present, what is missing, how the bones were butchered and cooked—to derive a picture of past human diet, especially in reference to the social habits of our species.

In the next chapter of this section, Janet Monge discusses how evolution and foodways are connected and how they can be studied together to better understand how food use may have influenced evolutionary change. She identifies a central question: "Can an understanding of the diet of our ancestors give us insights into modern human diets and the adequacy of these diets for the maintenance of long-term health?" To answer this question, she provides background on five stages of human evolution: generalized omnivory, shifts in food types due to hominid ancestors' movement into novel environments, the development of social eating and cooking in conjunction with the integration of higher quality protein from animal sources, the expansion of agriculture and the domestication of animals, and the now globalized food trade that introduces human populations to a larger range of potential comestibles. She details the evidence for each stage and points the reader to studies that define good practices for research in these areas.

The final chapter in this section, by Karen Bescherer Metheny, pulls together how we know what we think we know, how we found the evidence, how it has been analyzed, and appropriate inferences that can be drawn about diet and evolution. It is a fitting conclusion, allowing us to think through the various processes that are used to create, analyze, and report our biocultural data. Metheny points out that research in past foodways is informed by experimental archeology as well as ethnoarcheology; the former shifts research paradigms from inductive to deductive methods of reasoning. Past archeological methods more typically relied on the description of observations to lead to inferences about behavior, the classic inductive model. Newer archeological methods propose specific hypotheses which are tested using the evidence uncovered. Similarly, ethnoarcheology allows researchers to propose specific questions about behavior and to test if living human groups (with cultures presumed similar to those of the past) create similar assemblages of artifacts. Metheny then provides examples of research using experimental archeology and ethnoarcheology, and analyzes how such studies lead to increased understanding of past foodways.

Volume One of Research Methods for Anthropological Studies of Food And Nutrition is designed to provide readers with a grounding in the research, theory and methods that allow for data collection and analysis in the biocultural anthropology of food. This approach allows for students and advanced researchers to think through the full range of anthropological query relating to biological and archaeological studies; Volumes Two and Three cover sociological, linguistic, and applied research.

Research Ethics in Food Studies

Sharon Devine and John Brett

Why Ethics Are Important

Imagine that someone approaches you at a shopping center and asks if you would mind answering a few questions about what you eat. You answer the questions—what time you usually eat; how many meals you typically eat in a day; the types of foods you eat; and whether you consider yourself of average weight. Later you find out a research study has published your answers together with your photograph. The analysis suggests that you are overweight and that your nutritional intake could explain your deviation from ideal weight. Most people in this situation would be surprised and perhaps angry that by answering a few generic questions they wound up enrolled in a research study, and that personally identifiable information was in the public domain as a result.

Our research results are only as good as the information provided by those we study, and a trusting and respectful relationship is the basis for obtaining indepth and nuanced information. Therefore compliance with ethical principles and the regulatory structures that support them should be a professional virtue of researchers (DuBois 2004). The question is, how do we ensure that research is conducted ethically? First, we must be aware of the historical background of ethical lapses that led to the development of principles embodied in research regulations. Second, we must incorporate ethical principles into our research designs from the very beginning.

History of Ethical Lapses in Research

A lengthy history of research studies raising ethical concerns led up to the adoption of federal regulations for protection of human subjects in the United States.

A favorite argument of social scientists is that federal regulations governing research were designed to curb biomedical researchers (Heimer and Petty 2010; Hammersley 2009; Hamilton 2005). However, the impetus for ethical principles and regulations is not solely a result of ill-advised medical studies. A brief description of key episodes in the history of ethical lapses makes clear that ethical concerns apply as much to social science as to medical studies. Each of the examples described in this chapter has been explored in depth, and at the end of the chapter references are provided for those who wish to learn more. In hindsight concerns with these studies might appear obvious, but the facts, context, and nuances of each are often complex, sometimes contradictory, and documentation may be sketchy or lost to history. The purpose of this list is not to condemn so much as to present a number of studies, done over a long period of time, from which lessons for contemporary ethics have been extracted.

- Reed Commission/Yellow Fever (1900–1901). This research occurred as part of the U.S. occupation of Cuba after the Spanish-American War. Yellow fever was devastating occupation forces at the time, and it was unclear how it was transmitted. Suspected modes included contact with an infected person, contact with infected objects such as clothing or blankets, and transmission via mosquitoes. Army personnel and other volunteers were offered $100 in gold to participate in the study and be exposed to blankets used by infected persons, transfused with blood from an infected person, or bitten by mosquitoes. The study was carefully designed and implemented at great expense. Notes of Major Walter Reed, who conducted the study, state that written informed consent was obtained from the volunteers (Lederer 2008; Baxby 2005).
- Tuskegee Syphilis Study (1932–1972). The U.S. Public Health Service, working with the Tuskegee Institute, investigated the natural history of syphilis to justify treatment programs for blacks. Six hundred men volunteered for the study: 399 with syphilis, 201 without. The volunteers were poor, most were illiterate, and none knew anything about syphilis. The study included routine blood tests, spinal taps, as well as autopsies. The men were told they were being treated for "bad blood." They were offered free hot meals, clinic visits, and burial insurance, which was of great importance to this group. In 1943 penicillin was accepted as curative for syphilis, but it was not offered to the men in the study, which continued to observe the study participants without treating them until 1972 (Katz and Warren 2011; Reverby 2009; Jones 1993).
- Radiation Experiments (1944–1994). People were intentionally exposed to fallout from nuclear bomb testing events and told that the fallout was not harmful, even though scientists involved in the testing knew differently.

In some instances people were injected with plutonium to see what would happen (U.S. Department of Defense 1994a, 1994b).

- Willowbrook Study (1956). Willowbrook was a school for the intellectually challenged. Healthy children were injected with a virus causing hepatitis to study the natural history of the disease and eventually test a vaccine. Parental consent was obtained (Robinson and Unruh 2008; Rothman 1982).

- Milgram Obedience Study (1961). Milgram wanted to investigate the psychology of people who follow the directions of an authority figure, even when they are told to do cruel and unethical things. Participants were told the study was investigating learning and memory. They were asked to give what appeared to be increasingly harmful electric shocks to a fake "subject" if the subject performed incorrectly on a memory test. Participants were not told the real purpose of the study (how long people would follow orders) or that the shocks were fake until their participation was over. At this debriefing, many experienced extreme psychological distress (Nicholson 2011; McArthur 2009).

- Tearoom Trade Study (1970). A graduate student conducted a study of homosexual behavior in public restrooms. While functioning as a "watch queen" outside the restroom to sound the alert at any police presence, he recorded car license numbers to locate names and addresses of subjects. He then went to their homes and misrepresented himself to interview subjects about their lives (Warwick 1973).

- Zimbardo Prisoner Study (1971). College students were recruited for a two-week experiment to determine whether personality or situational differences cause conflict between guards and prisoners. The students took the California Personality Inventory and interviewed with the study team. The most normal, average, and healthy students on all dimensions were invited to participate and divided into guards and prisoners. The guards met for a general orientation and to formulate rules for proper prisoner behavior. The prisoners were arrested by the local police and brought to the site in handcuffs. The study was stopped after six days when the simulation seemed real and the guards became abusive. About half of the prisoners left the study before it ended due to severe emotional or cognitive reaction (McLeod 2008; Savin 1973; Zimbardo 1973).

- Havasupai Origins Study (1990–2003). Members of the Havasupai tribe provided DNA samples to researchers from Arizona State University beginning in 1990 for studies of diabetes. Other researchers at the university later used these samples to study mental illness and theories about the tribe's geographical origins. The results of the study about origins conflicted with the tribe's origin beliefs. The scope of the informed consent was disputed. Ultimately unused samples were returned to the tribe, and the university paid $700,000 to settle a lawsuit brought by the tribe (Garrison and Cho 2013; Reardon and TallBear 2012).

Types of Ethical Concerns in Food Studies

Many involved in food studies might argue that ethical concerns, especially of the type that led to the creation of the regulations applicable to human subject research, are unlikely to arise in their work. And yet, because food is so central to life—and in many cases to our sense of identity and place in the world—study topics can easily raise ethical issues if they are not appropriately addressed.

- Stigma can attach to studies of overweight, obesity, and eating disorders, as noted in the scenario that introduces this chapter.
- Belief systems of certain groups of people may conflict with the taking of blood samples or body measurements.
- Cultural norms may be offended by judgments about body image.
- Communities may be negatively impacted by studies of action anthropology such as advocating breastfeeding or studies of food security.

In short, almost any study can raise ethical issues. Therefore, ethical principles should be the foundation of the design and operation of all studies so as to minimize ethical lapses, protect human subjects, and obtain valid research results.

What Makes a Study Ethical?

Nuremberg Code

The Nuremberg Code and the Helsinki Declaration are international statements of aspirational principles for ethical research. The Nuremberg Code was proposed as a result of the war crimes trials held in Nuremberg, Germany, after the end of World War II (Nuremberg Military Tribunals1949). The trial verdict against one of the doctors accused of unlawfully conducting medical experiments during the war incorporated ten principles that were later labeled the Nuremberg Code. These ten principles address the record in the trials of experiments done on captives who were not able to consent to or dissent from participation in experiments, many of which had little if any scientific value when weighed against the risk to subjects. A common defense was that the experimenter was following orders of superiors. The ten principles in the code are:

1. Each subject must give voluntary consent, based on comprehension of the study, its procedures, and the risks associated with participation in the

experiment. This is a personal duty of any researcher involved in obtaining informed consent—it cannot be delegated.

2. The experiment should be designed to produce results for the good of society and not be random or unnecessary.
3. The experiment should be based on scientific knowledge and previous animal studies, if appropriate.
4. The experiment should avoid unnecessary physical and psychological suffering and injury.
5. No experiment should be done if there is reasonable belief that death or disabling injury would occur.
6. The degree of risk should never exceed the potential humanitarian benefit.
7. Researchers must prepare for and provide facilities to address even remote possibilities of injury, disability, or death.
8. Only scientifically qualified persons may conduct experiments on humans.
9. A human subject must have the liberty to refuse to continue with an experiment.
10. The scientist in charge of the experiment must terminate any experiment, at any stage, if the scientist has probable cause to believe that the experiment might lead to injury, disability, or death of any human subject.

Declaration of Helsinki

In 1947, representatives of twenty-seven medical associations from around the world created the World Medical Association, an open forum for discussions about medical ethics, medical education, and socio-medical topics with the purpose of reaching international consensus and guidance. In 1964, the World Medical Association adopted the Declaration of Helsinki—Ethical Principles for Medical Research Involving Human Subjects (World Medical Association 1964). It incorporates the same principles as the Nuremberg Code and adds others that broaden interests to be protected and provide procedural safeguards:

1. It is the right of human subjects to protect their privacy and confidentiality of private information.
2. Research proposals should address funding, sponsors, institutional affiliations, conflicts of interest, and incentives to subjects.
3. Research proposals must be reviewed and monitored by an independent committee.
4. Research on a vulnerable population or community may be justified only if it is responsive to the needs and priorities of the population or community and there is a reasonable likelihood that the vulnerable group stands to benefit from the results of the research.

5. Clinical trials must be registered in a publicly accessible database before recruitment of any subject.
6. Ordinarily, subjects must consent to collection, analysis, storage, or reuse of identifiable human materials or data. Waiver of consent may be granted only by the independent review committee.
7. The welfare of animals used for research must be respected.
8. Research must respect harm to the environment.
9. Authors, editors, and publishers have ethical duties regarding the publication of results of human subjects research.

Belmont Report and Federal Regulations

Certain states and countries adopted the Nuremberg Code into law, but neither it nor the Declaration of Helsinki has the authority of federal law in the United States. However, in 1974, prompted largely by revelations about the Tuskegee Syphilis Study, Congress authorized the National Commission for the Protection of Human Subjects of Biomedical and Behavioral Research, as part of the National Research Act, to recommend ethical principles for research with human subjects. In 1979, the predecessor of the Department of Health and Human Services published the report of the national commission. Called the Belmont Report, this document organizes its discussion of ethics in research around three principles: respect for persons, beneficence, and justice (U.S. Department of Health and Human Services 1979). It draws heavily from both the Nuremberg Code and the Declaration of Helsinki. These principles were embodied in federal regulations in the 1980s. In 1991, fourteen other federal agencies adopted the same federal regulations, codified as 45 C.F.R. Part 46 and known today as the "Common Rule" (U.S. Department of Health & Human Services 2009, n.d. [List]). The regulations also established a requirement for independent review by an institutional review board (IRB) in many circumstances. A study may need permission from multiple IRBs—university, tribe, and country (or regional IRBs if the study is international). IRBs in the United States apply the regulations that are based on the Belmont Report and any other regulations applicable to the study under review. All researchers should use the Belmont principles as their touchstone for ethical research whether or not they are required to get approval from an IRB.

Respect for persons

Respect for persons requires that research involving human subjects must protect their autonomy, privacy, and confidentiality; avoid coercion; and provide additional protection for vulnerable populations. Autonomy demands that a person be in control of her or his life and not suffer from diminished self-worth and independence as a result of participating in research. Thus respect requires that human subjects provide informed consent to research that is not obtained through coercion or undue influence. This principle of respect requires that subjects receive sufficient information about a study—its purpose, why they are being recruited, what they will be asked to do, potential harms, potential benefits, alternatives to being in the study, and information about confidentiality—so that they can understand what is being asked and their consent is truly voluntary. Although these elements of informed consent are usually embodied in a document, informed consent is a process. Different methods of communication may be used and should accommodate subjects' levels of understanding. The informed consent process should include methods to test each subject's comprehension of the study.

Respect for persons requires that any compensation for study participation be compensatory for the time of participation and not unduly influence the decision to participate. If the payment constitutes an inducement, then consent is not voluntary. Therefore payment is not considered a benefit for participation in a study and may not be considered in the analysis of risk and benefit.

Consent may be waived by the IRB if full waiver of consent is necessary to accomplish the goals of the research, risks are no more than minimal, and there is an adequate plan to debrief subjects if appropriate, including when deception is involved (45 CFR 46.116). The regulations require a showing that the waiver is necessary for the validity of the research; waivers are not granted simply because it is inconvenient or more expensive to obtain informed consent. Waiver of consent may be appropriate for the review of pre-existing medical records when it is impracticable to reach all subjects to ask for their consent or when study design requires information from consecutive medical records. Waiver of signature may be appropriate in cultures where signing a document is culturally inappropriate under the circumstances, when the signature is the only link identifying the subject to the study and identification of participation in the study could increase risk, or when the study collects information for which written consent is not normally obtained (45 CFR 46.117).

Some individuals may have diminished autonomy and therefore receive additional protections against coercion or undue influence. Certain groups are specifically addressed as "vulnerable" in the federal regulations: minors (45 CFR 46.401–409); pregnant women, fetuses, and neonates (45 CFR 46.201–207); and prisoners or other institutionalized persons (45 CFR 46.301–306). Other groups that may be considered vulnerable to coercion include decisionally challenged persons and those in other situations subject to coercion or undue influence. Situational and institutional coercion can occur when someone is asked to be in a study by their treating physician or professor, or when a person feels obligated to participate because the community feels that participation is important. There are mechanisms for obtaining consent from appropriate third parties when the subject is not capable of giving his or her own consent. These mechanisms, such as parental consent, legally authorized representatives, and proxies, can be complex because they are governed by federal regulation and sometimes also by state law.

Protection of privacy and confidentiality originates in the concept of respect for persons. The harm that results from an invasion of privacy or breach of confidentiality is a social harm because it can compromise reputation, financial status, employability, or insurability. Although often conflated, privacy and confidentiality address different concepts. Privacy is the desire to control access to oneself and comes into play when considering methods to contact and recruit subjects, the research setting, and methods of data collection. Confidentiality applies to the way information is handled, managed, and stored once a person is enrolled in a study. Here researchers should consider how information is protected, what limitations affect access to information, and how to collect the least amount of information necessary for the study.

Beneficence

Ethical research maximizes benefits and minimizes risks, as researchers have an obligation to protect subjects from harm. The principle of beneficence comes from the Hippocratic Oath: "I will do no harm or injustice." Harm in the context of research includes not just physical harm, but also psychological and social harm, which may apply to the individual or the community. Brutal or inhumane treatment of human subjects is never morally justified.

Application of the principle of beneficence requires an assessment of potential risks and benefits to assure that the balance is always in favor of potential benefits. Subjects may participate in studies that will provide no direct or immediate benefit to them so long as the risks are minimal and there is the potential for societal benefit. The higher the risk and the more remote the benefit, the harder the questions of balancing risks and benefits. When assessing risk, it is important to consider both probability and magnitude of risk. A risk may be common but low or very uncommon but very damaging. Studies need not be risk free, but researchers should design their studies to minimize risk. The principle of beneficence necessarily implicates study design. A poorly designed study that is unlikely to generate data to answer the research question posed has no benefit to subjects or to society. Researchers should always consider whether human subjects are necessary. And if the study proposes to include vulnerable subjects, the researcher should justify why they are necessary for the study.

Justice

The principle of justice requires that the benefits and burdens of research be distributed equitably in society. Injustice occurs when one group is unduly burdened with research risks and another group receives benefits. One of the reasons prisoners are identified as a vulnerable population and given additional regulatory protections, aside from the potential for coercion as a captive population, is that historically they have borne unequal burdens of research with no prospect of enjoying the benefits. Selecting classes of subjects because they are convenient, compromised, marginalized, or easily manipulated raises questions of justice. Injustice also occurs when one group is denied access to benefits to which they are entitled, as in the Tuskegee Syphilis Study. Another example of injustice includes the groups of people who are selected for study. For many years most pharmaceutical research was conducted using Caucasian males. Women and people of color were not routinely included in research. Today federally funded studies prohibit researchers from excluding subjects on the basis of gender, race, or ethnicity unless exclusion is required based on the question being studied, so that benefits of the research may accrue to all groups.

Other Sources of Ethical Principles and Rules

The Common Rule, as embodied in federal regulations, is not the only source of ethical rules for research. The Department of Health and Human Services administers the Health Insurance Portability and Accountability Act (HIPAA) (U.S. Department of Health and Human Services n.d. [Health Information Privacy]), which protects personal health information. HIPAA is complex and applies to "covered entities." The Food and Drug Administration, Department of Veterans Affairs, Department of Education, and Department of Defense all have regulations governing aspects of research under their auspices (U.S. Department of Health & Human Services n.d. [List]). In addition, many professional associations, such as the American Anthropological Association (American Anthropological Association 2012), Society for Applied Anthropology (Society for Applied Anthropology n.d.), and the American Sociological Association (American Sociological Association n.d.), have codes of conduct that include ethical standards for research. In general, all of these bodies apply principles consistent with or based on the principles in the Belmont Report, but they may have more protective requirements or specific processes that apply to research within their domains. Researchers should familiarize themselves with all applicable sources of ethical principles before designing their studies.

Application of Principles

There is usually little disagreement on the ethical principles for research, but their application in practice is often much more nuanced than a mere recitation of the rules. The following two case studies raise various ethical questions. Each is followed by a brief identification of ethical issues and considerations.

Case 1

Researchers wish to study the dietary practices of a community of Native Americans living on a tribal reservation in the United States. The study is designed to identify attitudes and understanding of the healthfulness of foods in the diet; journal actual consumption by individuals and families; collect weight, height, and medical histories; and correlate the findings with concerns about BMI and diabetes. Some information will be confirmed by comparing it with Indian Health Service medical records of subjects. The study is exploratory and will inform interventions designed to reduce obesity and diabetes among those living on the reservation. The tribal council is enthusiastic about the study and wants it to be in the nature of community-based participatory research including the use of tribal research assistants, data collectors, and analysts.

Issues

Respect for persons
- There is the potential for coercion of individuals in light of tribal support. Can individual members safely exercise their autonomy and say no? Will the tribal council demand to know who has agreed to participate and who has not? What if the tribe has a long history of communal decision making that binds the group? Do you impose Western ideals of individual autonomy? First, it is important to understand the cultural values of the tribe or group and discuss all proposed procedures with the community and the IRB to identify any nuances in their application. Then consider whether you need to institute procedures to reduce the potential for coercion. For example, researchers might make clear that they will not provide any information about the identity of those who enroll or decline to participate to the tribal council to protect the privacy of individual participants.
- There is the potential for inadvertent release of confidential information. As part of the community-based approach, research assistants and data collectors will be members of the community. Procedures to train assistants and data collectors should emphasize the need for absolute confidentiality of information obtained. Personally identifiable data should be entered immediately into encrypted databases and recorded in such a way that data cannot be linked back to individuals or coded in a way that makes identification without the code very difficult. Any paper records should be destroyed as soon as possible.

Beneficence
- All researchers should be trained in cultural sensitivity, including respect for cultural norms around body image to assure appropriate interaction with

subjects and reporting of findings in a nonjudgmental, nonstigmatizing manner.

Justice
• Concerns about justice could arise if there is divergence of understanding about the scope of the research between the researchers and the community. For example, the community may expect that interventions will be immediately forthcoming while researchers understand that the current study is a pilot and that there is no funding for interventions at this time.

Process
• There may be multiple IRB stakeholders: researchers' institutions, the tribe, and the Indian Health Service. HIPAA may apply. Community-based research is, by definition, fluid and dynamic, requiring lots of work, time, and patience to manage the review process.

Case 2

Researchers wish to conduct action research into breastfeeding in a lesser-developed country. The study wishes to catalog women's decision making around breastfeeding to identify cultural norms and tie breastfeeding to infant and child health outcomes. The community where this is to occur is poor and has a variety of breastfeeding practices. Women come to live with their husband's family; the culture is strongly patriarchal.

Issues

Respect for persons
• When looking at women's decision making, the very process of getting informed consent may influence choices. If women choose not to breastfeed, they may not want to discuss it or may feel that they are "bad mothers." In this situation, researchers might consider requesting permission from the IRB to engage in minor deception, for example by describing the study as one of infant/child heath generally, without mentioning that the focus of the study is breastfeeding (technically, this is a request to waive consent to omit the true purpose of the study). This type of waiver for minor deception is justifiable if telling people about the focus of the study would tend to skew the results.
• In a patriarchal society it may be appropriate to assure that men understand and approve of the research, even if men will not be subjects. Knowing the culture and its norms is key.

Beneficence
- Women who face or have experienced sexual abuse may have strong emotional attitudes, unknown to the researcher. As with all research, it is important to know the culture and its norms so that appropriate probes and safeguards can be used to protect vulnerable subjects, so as not to cause additional harm from participation in the study.
- If it is reasonable to expect that the researcher may identify cases of neglect from inadequate or inappropriate breastfeeding, the team should consider how to handle such instances in advance.

Sharon Devine, PhD, JD is Research Assistant Professor at the University of Colorado Denver, where she teaches, conducts research, and co-chairs the social and behavioral panel of the Colorado Multiple Institutional Review Board. Before joining academia, she practiced corporate and compliance law.

John Brett is retired faculty in the Department of Anthropology, University of Colorado Denver. He received his PhD from the Joint Program in Medical Anthropology at the University of California San Francisco and Berkeley in 1994. His primary research interests focus on food systems, food security and food justice, and microfinance as a development enterprise.

References

45 C.F.R. 46.116.
45 C.F.R. 46.117.
45 C.F.R. 46.201–207.
45 C.F.R. 46. 301–306.
45 C.F.R. 46.401–409.
American Anthropological Association. 2012. AAA Statement on Ethics-Principles of Professional Responsibility. http://ethics.aaanet.org/category/statement/. Accessed 30 August 2016.
American Sociological Association. n.d. ASA Code of Ethics. http://www.asanet.org/about/ethics.cfm. Accessed 30 August 2016.
Baxby, Derrick. 2005. Walter Reed and Yellow Fever. *Epidemiology & Infection* 133(Supp. 1): S7–8.
DuBois, James M. 2004. Is Compliance a Professional Virtue of Researchers? Reflections on Promoting the Responsible conduct of Research. *Ethics & Behavior* 14(4): 383–395.
Garrison, Nanibaa' A., and Mildred K. Cho. 2013. Awareness and Acceptable Practices: IRB and Researcher Reflection on the Havasupai Lawsuit. *American Journal of Bioethics Primary Research* 4(4): 55–63.
Hamilton, Ann. 2005. The Development and Operation of IRBs: Medical Regulations and Social Science. *Journal of Applied Communication Research* 33(3): 189–203.
Hammersley, Martyn.2009. Against the Ethicists: On the Evils of Ethical Regulation. *Journal of Social Research Methodology* 12(3): 211–225.

Heimer, Carol A., and JuLeigh Petty. 2010. Bureaucratic Ethics: IRBs and the Legal Regulation of Human Subjects Research. *Annual Review of Law and Social Science* 6: 601–626.

Jones, James H. 1993. *Bad Blood: The Tuskegee Syphilis Experiment.* New York: Free Press.

Katz, Ralph V., and Reuben Warren, eds. 2011. *The Search for the Legacy of the USPHS Syphilis Study at Tuskegee.* Lanham: Lexington Books.

Lederer, Susan E. 2008. Walter Reed and the Yellow Fever Experiments. In *Oxford Textbook of Clinical Research Ethics,* ed. Ezekiel J. Emanuel and Christine Grady et al., 9–18. Oxford: Oxford University Press.

McArthur, Dan. 2009. Good Ethics Can Sometimes Mean Better Science: Research Ethics and the Milgram Experiments. *Science and Engineering Ethics* 15: 69–79.

McLeod, Saul. 2008. Zimbardo-Stanford Prison Experiment. *Simply Psychology.* http://www.simplypsychology.org/zimbardo.html. Accessed 30 August 2016.

Nicholson, Ian. 2011. "Torture at Yale": Experimental Subjects, Laboratory Torment and the "Rehabilitation" of Milgram's "Obedience to Authority." *Theory & Psychology* 21(6): 737–761.

Nuremberg Military Tribunals. 1949. Trials of War Criminals before the Nuremberg Military Tribunals under Control Council Law No. 10, V.2, 181–182. https://history.nih.gov/research/downloads/nuremberg.pdf. Accessed 30 August 30 2016.

Reardon, Jenny, and Kim TallBear. 2012. "Your DNA Is *Our* History": Genomics, Anthropology, and the Construction of Whiteness as Property. *Current Anthropology* 53(S5): S233–S245.

Reverby, Susan M. 2009. *Examining Tuskegee: The Infamous Syphilis Study and Its Legacy.* Chapel Hill: University of North Carolina Press.

Robinson, Walter M., and Brandon T. Unruh. 2008. The Hepatitis Experiments at the Willowbrook State School. In *Oxford Textbook of Clinical Research Ethics,* ed. Ezekiel J. Emanuel and Christine Grady et al., 80–85. Oxford: Oxford University Press.

Rothman, David J. 1982. Were Tuskegee & Willowbrook "Studies in Nature"? *Hastings Center Report* 12(2): 5–7.

Savin, H. B. 1973. Professors and Psychological Researchers: Conflicting Values in Conflicting Roles. *Cognition* 2(1): 147–149.

Society for Applied Anthropology. n.d. Statement of Ethics and & Professional Responsibilities. http://www.sfaa.net/about/ethics/. Accessed 30 August 2016.

U.S. Department of Defense. 1994a. Report on Search for Human Radiation Experiment Records 1944-1994, V.1. http://archive.defense.gov/pubs/dodhre/Narratv.pdf. Accessed 30 August 2016.

U.S. Department of Defense. 1994b. Report on Search for Human Radiation Experiment Records 1944-1994, V.2. http://archive.defense.gov/pubs/dodhre/Volume2.pdf. Accessed 30 August 2016.

U.S. Department of Health and Human Services. 1979. Ethical Principles and Guidelines for the Protection of Human Subjects Research (The Belmont Report). http://www.hhs.gov/ohrp/humansubjects/guidance/belmont.html. Accessed 30 August 2016.

———. 2009. Federal Policy for the Protection of Human Subjects ("Common Rule"). 45 C.F.R. 46. http://www.hhs.gov/ohrp/humansubjects/guidance/45cfr46.html. Accessed 30 August 2016.

———. n.d. Health Information Privacy. http://www.hhs.gov/ocr/privacy/hipaa/understanding/index.html. Accessed 30 August 2016.

————. n.d. List of U.S. federal agencies that have signed onto the Federal Policy for the Protection of Human Subjects ("Common Rule"). http://www.hhs.gov/ohrp/humansubjects/commonrule/index.html. Accessed 30 August 2016.

Warwick, Donald P. 1973. Tearoom Trade: Means & Ends in Social Research. *Hastings Center Studies* 1(1): 27–38.

World Medical Association. 1964, as amended. WMA Declaration of Helsinki-Ethical Principles for Medical Research Involving Human Subjects. http://www.wma.net/en/30publications/10policies/b3/. Accessed 30 August 2016.

Zimbardo, Philip G. 1973. On the Ethics of Intervention in Human Psychological Research: With Special Reference to the Stanford Prison Experiment. *Cognition* 2(2): 243–256.

SECTION
II

Nutritional Anthropology

CHAPTER 1

Design in Biocultural Studies of Food and Nutritional Anthropology

Section Introduction

Darna L. Dufour and Barbara A. Piperata

Introduction

Biocultural approaches in nutritional anthropology are concerned with understanding the interrelationships of biological and social forces that shape human food use and the nutritional status of individuals and populations (Pelto, Dufour, and Goodman 2013). Because they focus on interrelationships, they occupy a middle ground along the broad continuum from purely biological studies of food and nutritional status to purely cultural studies of food. For example, a study investigating the effects of dietary nitrates on blood pressure would be on the biological end of the continuum, and a study of artisanal cheese production would be on the cultural end of the spectrum. By comparison, biocultural studies of similar topics might focus on the kind of food-related behaviors that result in high dietary nitrate intake, or the linkages between artisanal cheese production and the adequacy of dietary intake in the local population.

The kinds of questions that bioculturally oriented anthropologists ask are emblematic of their approach (Pelto, Dufour, and Goodman 2013). They might ask, for example, what is the impact of a particular cultural belief on diet and nutrition? The belief could be the idea that green leafy vegetables are "too strong" for young children. Or, they might ask, what is the effect of a given socioeconomic change on diet and nutrition? The change could be broad in scale, like the change from an agricultural subsistence base to a market economy, or the kind of rapid increase in food prices that occurs in a food crisis, or any number of things. They might also focus on a nutritional condition like undernutrition and ask, what are the sociocultural and socioeconomic correlates of this condition? In these studies diet is typically measured as actual food intake, and nutrition refers to nutritional status—the outcome of diet—measured in terms of child growth, fatness, serum vitamin C levels, et cetera.

In this chapter our goal is to think through the design of biocultural studies in food and nutritional anthropology by looking at examples of specific studies. By design here we are referring to the basic structure, or architecture, of the study. The goal is to reveal the connections between the researchers' biocultural question(s) and the study design and methods. Our selection of studies is based on personal experience and not meant to be exhaustive.

Examples of Study Design

In each of the three examples below we will consider the rationale behind the question(s) asked, the data needed to answer the question(s), the basic design and sampling strategy required, and the methods used. For each we will also comment on strengths and weaknesses of the design and methods.

Cultural Beliefs Shaping Intake and Their Consequences

One fundamentally biocultural question is the effect of cultural beliefs on human nutrition. The example here is a study of the universal human practice of classifying certain edible substances as nonfoods. Every human group has its own food taboo system that can include both permanent and transient taboos. An example of the former is the taboo against consumption of dog meat, a potential source of dietary protein, in the United States. Transient food taboos are equally common and include the avoidance of specific foods but only during certain periods of time.

Considering how common transient food taboos are during the immediate postpartum, and knowing that during this period women need greater amounts of both energy and protein due to breastfeeding, anthropologists have been interested in how adherence to food taboos affects women's abilities to meet their dietary needs, and what logic and meaning lie behind it (Aunger 1994; Laderman 1981: Harris 1987; Messer 1981; Santos-Torres and Vasquez-Guribay 2003). However, few studies have documented the actual effects of food taboos on dietary intake, and none have considered the joint effects of dietary restrictions and other postpartum practices like restrictions on physical activity. To illustrate how a biocultural approach can be used to address questions regarding food taboos, we use the work of Barbara Piperata (2008), who studied transient food taboos in rural Amazonian communities where women avoid foods classified as taboo, or *reimoso*, as well as certain activities during the first forty days postpartum, a period locally referred to as *resguardo* (Piperata 2008).

Question

Piperata's research question centered on answering how adherence to the food taboos and activity restrictions associated with *resguardo* affected maternal energy balance (dietary intake minus energy expenditure = energy balance).

Key Measures Needed

To address her question, Piperata needed the following data.

1. A clear understanding of the local taboo system, in other words, the rules, local logic and meaning behind the practice.
2. Qualitative and quantitative data on the actual dietary intakes and energy expenditure of the women during the restricted period.
3. Data on women's individual energy and protein needs in order to assess the adequacy of the women's intakes and calculate energy balance.
4. Diet and activity data on the same women outside of the restricted period.

Study Design and Sampling Strategy

The study was longitudinal in design and followed a cohort of women from the birth of their infant and the period of *resguardo* through approximately one year postpartum. This design was selected to help control for confounding variables like individual food preferences and work responsibilities, and household economic status, size, and composition, to better elucidate the degree to which adherence to taboos affected energy balance. Also, in a longitudinal design participants are compared to themselves, allowing the minimum sample size for statistical purposes to be smaller than in other designs.

Given the highly dispersed settlement pattern of the population, Piperata's sampling strategy was to include all women in their second and third trimester of pregnancy living within a geographic zone that was reasonably accessible using local boat transportation.

Methods

Piperata used a variety of methods, qualitative and quantitative, to collect the data required for the study. For data on the beliefs and rules of the taboo system, she used participant observation and focus groups to generate a list of all foods consumed in the communities, including all species of fish, game, and fruit as well as purchased foods such as coffee, sugar, beans, rice, and cooking oil. A similar list was made for women's work responsibilities. Once the lists were created she interviewed adult men and women individually and, for each food and work item, asked if it was taboo or not during the postpartum period. She used these lists to identify the most agreed-upon taboo foods and work restrictions, and then used a series of semistructured interviews to focus on the meaning behind the taboo system, including why different foods and different kinds of work were avoided. Continuing participant observation allowed Piperata to understand the broader significance of these practices for women in the study.

To assess the actual effects adherence to taboos had on energy balance during the postpartum period, Piperata collected data on dietary intake and energy expenditure in physical activity over a three-day period. For dietary data she used the weighed-inventory method (Gibson, 2005) for its accuracy. The method also included qualitative data on the foods consumed (name, species, part of animal, etc.) as well as information on the source (local, purchased, gifted) of the food. For composite dishes, entire recipes were recorded and weighed, and the weight of the portion a woman consumed was then measured to the nearest gram. To calculate the nutritional composition of the women's diets, nutritional information on the individual food items was taken from published sources and from new nutritional analyses conducted using Nutribase, a dietary software program, as part of the study .

Physical activity data were collected using the activity diary or factorial method (see Ulijaszek 1992), in which activities were recorded continuously, nine hours per day. Daily energy expenditure was estimated by using standard equations (FAO/WHO/UNU 1985) for basal metabolic rate and published energy expenditure values (Ainsworth et al. 1993; FAO/WHO/UNU 1985) for individual activities. Energy balance was calculated as total dietary intake (kcal) minus total daily energy expenditure (kcal), including the costs of breastfeeding (Prentice et al. 1996). To determine whether women's energy balance was different in *resguardo* compared to the other stages of lactation, a general linear model that compared individual women's energy balance over time was used.

Strengths and Weaknesses of the Design

Together, the cultural and biological data allowed Piperata to demonstrate that the food taboos during *resguardo,* while culturally significant, impacted nutritional status (i.e., energy balance) less than did the activity restrictions, which effectively removed the new mother from food production. This was a valuable new insight. The study had the strengths of a case study that permitted close examination of a research question combined with a longitudinal design that controlled for major confounders associated with variation between women. A weakness of the design was the small sample size (n = 23 women) and nonrandom sampling method, which limited generalization to the larger population.

The Effects Of Socioeconomic Changes on Diet and Nutrition

Questions about how shifts in a society's economic structure have shaped human nutrition have a long history in anthropology. For example, understanding the nutritional consequences of the transition from hunting and gathering to agricultural production has been a central question in the field of bio-archaeology (Larsen 2006). The more recent shift away from food production and toward dependence on the market for accessing food has also been of interest to anthropologists. Much of the literature on this shift and the accompanying increase in overweight and obesity, referred to as the nutrition transition (Popkin 2001), comes from economics and public health, where the focus has been on national and even global shifts in food consumption patterns and the prevalence of associated chronic diseases. There is a dearth of local-level studies designed to confront the nutrition transition model with real-world examples.

In considering the contribution a biocultural approach can make to understanding the nutrition transition, we focus on research conducted by Barbara Piperata and colleagues in the Brazilian Amazon (Piperata et al. 2011a; Piperata et al., 2011b). The idea for this research stemmed from a 2007 visit Piperata made to the Amazonian communities where she had conducted her dissertation research in 2002. It was during this visit that she observed what appeared to be significant changes in dietary practices and work patterns. Further, these changes appeared to be associated with increases in household incomes resulting from the Brazilian government's initiation of a conditional cash transfer program, *Bolsa Família*. In essence, what Piperata found was a natural experiment.

Question

The question was, what biosocial consequences of the recent increases in income were associated with the implementation of *Bolsa Família*?

Key Measures Needed

Answering this kind of question requires data on current conditions that can be compared to a previous baseline condition. Piperata had data on the baseline condition, including a large anthropometric survey, detailed data on household economics and women's dietary intake and energy expenditure for a small sample, and ethnographic observations over a two-year period. The needed data on the current condition included:

1. Measures of household economic activities in 2009 that could be compared to the baseline 2002 data.
2. Measures of diet and activity patterns in 2009 that could be compared to the baseline 2002 data.
3. Measures of nutritional status (i.e., body size and composition) of adults and sub-adults of both sexes in 2009 that could be compared to the baseline 2002 data.

To provide an understanding of the changes and to document the current status of the population, Piperata also included the following data:

4. Participant observations and interview data from participants regarding household economics, diet, and activity patterns.
5. A food security assessment to provide additional documentation of the nutritional context in 2009.

Study Design and Sampling Strategy

Clearly, the ideal study design would have been longitudinal, so that the same households and individuals could be compared to themselves over time relative to variables measured in the same manner. Further, the sample at baseline would have been randomly selected based on study criteria. However, it had not been possible in 2002 to select a random sample, as there were no census data available to use as a sampling frame. Hence in 2009 Piperata again selected samples using the same procedures she had used at baseline: she visited all communities within 1.5 hours' travel (by speedboat) from a central location and invited all households to participate in an anthropometric survey. This zone held a population of approximately 1,200 people, of which some 469 individuals participated in the 2002 survey and 429 in the 2009 survey. Some 43 percent of those surveyed at baseline were re-measured in 2009. Detailed dietary and energy expenditure data were available for $n = 30$ women at baseline. In 2009, 20 of the 30 were re-contacted, and an additional 22 who met the 2009 study criteria of having a child between four and sixteen years old were recruited from the households visited during the anthropometric survey. The study then used two samples—a smaller longitudinal subsample nested within a larger cross-sectional sample.

Methods

In both 2002 and 2009, anthropometric data were collected on adults and sub-adults of both sexes following the same standardized procedures (Lohman, Roche, and Martorell 1988). In 2009, data on household economics were collected in structured interviews using an interview instrument that was based heavily on the one used in 2002 and Piperata's ethnographic knowledge of the socioeconomic context of the rural households but was modified in the field to accommodate recent economic changes, specifically the importance of funds from *Bolsa Família*. In both 2002 and 2009, dietary data were collected over a three-day period at both the individual and household level using the weighed-inventory method (Gibson 2005), chosen because of its accuracy. Because of time constraints in 2009, data on activity patterns were collected using spot observations instead of the activity diaries used in 2002. In 2009, a series of semistructured interviews were designed to engage men and women in discussions of changes in economic strategies, nutrition, and ideal foods. In addition, Piperata's participant observation was crucial to her collection of data on attitudes and worldviews that allowed her to gain greater insight into the local meaning of and driving factors behind the observed economic, diet, and health changes. In 2009 a validated food security questionnaire was used to provide additional information on perceptions of diet.

Strengths and Weaknesses

A major strength of the study was its semi-longitudinal design, where a cohort of those measured at baseline was re-measured by the same methods after the economic change. The exception was the method used to collect the activity data in 2009, which limited comparisons to data gathered by the detailed factorial method used in 2002. An additional strength was Piperata's in-depth ethnographic understanding of the population, which allowed her to trace the pathways by which the economic changes impacted households and individuals.

Sample size was a clear limitation, especially for the dietary data. This was due, in part, to the decision in 2009 to use the same time-intensive weighed-inventory method that had been used in 2002, in order to make the data comparable. The lack of true longitudinal data limited the ability to determine causal relationships, and the nonrandom sampling strategy made it difficult to generalize to the larger population. Finally, the food security questionnaire used in 2009 had not existed in 2002, meaning that there were no data on perceptions of food security at baseline. This was unfortunate, as perceptions of food security appear to have shifted significantly.

Nutritional Conditions and Their Sociocultural Correlates

In the 1970s and 1980s, poverty in developing countries was assumed to be associated with undernutrition in adults as well as children. Based on that assumption and the literature available at the time, we (Darna Dufour and GB Spurr) designed a large study of the energy-nutrition of economically impoverished urban women in Colombia, a focus of which was the effect of undernutrition on physical activity. At the beginning of the study in the late 1980s, we conducted an anthropometric survey and were surprised to find a low prevalence of undernutrition in impoverished women. Indeed, the average BMI (body mass index) was in the normal range—indeed, in the middle of the normal range—and there were a surprising number of overweight and even obese women. In order to understand how women were able to maintain normal nutritional status under the conditions of poverty, we refocused part of the research on the phenomenon of coping strategies.

Question

The main question was what coping strategies urban women living in poverty in a developing country like Colombia use to maintain normal nutritional status. A second question was, are the coping strategies hierarchically ranked as theory predicts?

Key Measures Needed

To address the main question we needed to understand the "how," that is, the women's coping strategies. To do that, we needed several kinds of data.

1. Measures to define what we meant by "poverty."
2. One or more measures of economic constraint on food access.
3. Information on the behaviors that could be considered coping strategies.
4. An understanding of dietary intake and a way to demonstrate that it actually reflected economic constraints.
5. A way to link dietary intake to nutritional status measured as BMI.

Study Design and Sampling Strategy

The design was a case study nested within the larger study of the energy-nutrition of women living in economically impoverished neighborhoods in Cali, Colombia. The sample was a subsample of all nonpregnant, nonlactating women from the larger study, which used a snowball sampling strategy in selected neighborhoods that the city of Cali classified as among its most economically disadvantaged. The snowball sampling strategy (participants refer their friends) seemed the best alternative given the lack of any data on individuals, or even street maps, that could have allowed selection of a random sample. Further, the high degree of insecurity in the city due to drug trade–associated violence in the 1980s and 1990s made it very difficult to gain any kind of entrance to the neighborhoods except through social networks. Indeed, we had to rely on research team members from the targeted neighborhoods to get the snowball started. By the end of the study we had generated our own maps and found that study participants were distributed quite evenly throughout the targeted neighborhoods. The sample size was 85, large enough to adequately assess usual diet (Quandt 1986).

Methods

To effectively and convincingly answer the question posed, we needed a variety of different kinds of methods, some qualitative and some quantitative. To define what we were referring to as poverty we focused on economic disadvantage and used observational and interview data on housing conditions and ownership as measures of relative wealth.

To determine whether or not economic conditions negatively affect food intake, at least potentially, we used a very short structured interview focused on the availability of monetary resources to obtain food and developed from indicators of hunger in Radimer, Olson, and Campbell (1980). As a second measure we used focus group interviews to probe the issue of monetary constraints on food consumption in the neighborhood and the kinds of coping strategies women used. We chose the focus group format because women were often ashamed to admit they did not have money to buy food and hence justifiably reluctant to discuss it or admit to using the kind of coping strategies we were hoping to identify. Focus groups have the advantage of allowing participants to discuss a sensitive topic without having to expose their own position/status regarding that topic. We began the focus group interviews with a discussion of ideal meals, that is, the kinds of meals women thought were the best and would like to serve if they could. That easily led into a discussion of the kinds of meals that might be served when it was not possible to achieve the ideal.

To document actual dietary intake we used observational food records kept by carefully trained research assistants from the same neighborhoods as the participants. Gibson (2005) describes food records in detail. We chose food records, rather than the commonly used method of food recalls, because we were concerned with the accuracy of food recalls in this context and the possibility that participants would underreport less socially acceptable foods or overreport amounts to avoid embarrassment. We used research assistants to maintain the food records because we felt they would be more accurate than records kept by the participants themselves. In addition, we were using the same research assistants to maintain records of physical activity as part of the larger study, and they were able to record diet at the same time. Since the research assistants were young women from the same neighborhoods as the study participants, they were also able to provide valuable observations of coping strategies.

Food energy intakes were calculated using a software program written for the project and compositional data from published food composition tables, analysis of local recipes, and proximate analyses of common foods. To assess adequacy of the energy intake of each participant we used the ratio of 24-hour food energy intake to 24-hour BMR (basal metabolic rate). We considered a ratio of less than 1.27, the survival requirement (FAO/WHO/UNU 1985), as evidence of low energy intake. We measured BMR using standard techniques (Spurr et al. 1994), but BMR can also be estimated using the Schofield equations, which are available in FAO/WHO/UNU (1985).

We examined the diet records of participants with low energy intakes, as well as those with normal intakes, for evidence of the kinds of modifications to meals (coping strategies) that the focus groups had identified. This allowed us to demonstrate that the frequency of these kinds of modifications were more prevalent in the records of women with low energy intakes. To assess the potential impact of these modifications on nutrition we considered two things. First, did they affect macronutrient (carbohydrate, protein, fat) intake? For example, substituting egg for beef at the main meal, while socially significant, would not change animal protein intake or the adequacy of protein in the diet, unless of course the portion size of the egg was less than the typical portion size of beef. Second, did the modifications affect total energy intake? This would be the case if portion sizes were reduced, or meals eliminated.

Strengths and Weakness

The study had the strengths of a case study design in that it provided a much deeper understanding of diet in the context of urban poverty. It provided a reasonable answer to the question of "how" women were able to maintain normal nutritional status (or even overweight) by documenting the range of coping strategies available and demonstrating that they were generally able to maintain adequate energy intake by manipulating meal composition. The relatively large size of the sample and its even geographic distribution in the target neighborhoods ensured that the diet data were representative. The design also allowed us to test adaptive models' assumption that coping strategies would be hierarchically ranked, even though testing against theoretical explanations had not been one of the original goals. The study had three significant weakness: (1) we could not establish solid linkages between individuals' diet and their nutritional status as measured by BMI; (2) we were not able to demonstrate the representativeness of the coping strategies identified, although we assumed they were representative given the sample size and reasonable geographic coverage of the neighborhoods targeted; (3) the measures of wealth were not useful because dietary intake was driven by short-term economic circumstances.

Summary and Concluding Thoughts

The three studies described above illustrate biocultural approaches that provided both a detailed understanding of particular research questions, and in-depth analyses of the interplay between biological and cultural variables. Importantly, the biocultural approach allowed the researchers to assess the actual effects of selected dietary practices on nutritional status. The researchers employed various methods, some qualitative and some quantitative. The qualitative methods generated a rich understanding of the local context, allowing the researchers to provide more satisfying explanations of the quantitative data than is possible with survey-type research designs.

All three examples used non-randomly selected samples because the realities of the field situations rendered random sampling neither feasible nor practical. Indeed, all three examples were from what are called difficult-to-sample or difficult-to-reach populations (Faugier and Sargeant 1997; Lepkowski 1991). Non-random sampling does, however, make it more difficult to ensure that the sample is representative and can therefore limit the ability to generalize from the sample to the population. Representativeness was not a major concern in the three examples discussed above because the researchers had sufficient expert knowledge of the populations to feel comfortable that the samples were reasonably representative. Generalization to the larger population was not a primary research goal in any of the studies. Rather, the goals were more focused on understanding real-life situations in order to add to our general knowledge, and to test the applicability of theoretical expectations against real life.

Darna L. Dufour is Professor of Anthropology at the University of Colorado Boulder. She has conducted long-term field research on food and nutrition with Tukanoans in the northwest Amazon and economically disadvantaged women in urban Colombia. Her current research is on the nutrition transition in Latin America.

Barbara Piperata is Associate Professor of Anthropology at The Ohio State University. She has conducted field research on human reproductive energetics (dietary intake, energy expenditure, and body composition), child growth, and the nutrition transition in the eastern Brazilian Amazon, as well as on food security and maternal-child health in rural and urban communities in Nicaragua.

References

Ainsworth, Barbara E., W. L. Haskell, A. S. Leon, D. R. Jacobs, H. J. Montoye, J. F. Sallis, and R. S. Paffenbarger. 1993. Compendium of Physical Activities-Classification of Energy

Costs of Human Physical Activities. *Medicine and Science in Sports and Exercise* 25(1): 71–80.

Aunger, Robert. 1994. Are Food Avoidances Maladaptive in the Ituri Forest of Zaire? *Journal of Anthropological Research* 50: 277–310.

Dufour, Darna L., Lisa K. Staten, Julio C. Reina, and Gerald B. Spurr. 1997. Living on the Edge: Dietary Strategies of Economically Impoverished Women in Cali, Colombia. *American Journal of Physical Anthropology* 102(1): 5–15.

FAO/WHO/UNU (Food and Agricultural Organization/World Health Organization/United Nations University). 1985. Energy and Protein Requirements. WHO Technical Report Series 724. Geneva: World Health Organization.

Faugier, Jean, and Mary Sargeant. 1997. Sampling Hard to Reach Populations. *Journal of Advanced Nursing* 26(4): 790–797.

Gibson, Rosalind S. 2005. *Principles of Nutritional Assessment.* New York: Oxford University Press.

Harris, Marvin. 1987. Foodways: Historical Overview and Theoretical Prolegomenon. In *Food and Evolution: Toward a Theory of Human Food Habits,* ed. Marvin Harris and Eric B. Ross, 57–90. Philadelphia: Temple University Press.

Laderman, Carol. 1981. Symbolic and Empirical Reality: A New Approach to the Analysis of Food Avoidances. *American Ethnologist* 8(3): 468–493.

Larsen, Clark S. 2006. The Agricultural Revolution as Environmental Catastrophe: Implications for Health and Lifestyle in the Holocene. *Quaternary International* 150: 12–20.

Lepkowski, James M. 1991. Sampling the Difficult-to-Sample. *Journal of Nutrition* 121(3): 416–423.

Lohman, Timothy G., Alex F. Roche, and Reynaldo Martorell, eds. 1988. *Anthropometric Standardization Reference Manual.* Champaign, IL: Human Kinetics Books.

Messer, Ellen. 1981. Hot–Cold Classification: Theoretical and Practical Implications of a Mexican Study. *Social Science & Medicine Part B-Medical Anthropology* 15(2B): 133–145.

Pelto, Gretel H., Darna L. Dufour, and Alan H. Goodman. 2013. The Biocultural Perspective in Nutritional Anthropology. In *Nutritional Anthropology: Biocultural Perspectives on Food and Nutrition,* 2nd ed., ed. Darna L. Dufour, Alan H. Goodman, and Gretel H. Pelto, 1–6. New York: Oxford University Press.

Piperata, Barbara A. 2008. Forty Days and Forty Nights: A Biocultural Perspective on Postpartum Practices in the Amazon. *Social Science and Medicine* 67(7): 1094–1103.

Piperata, Barbara A., Sofia A. Ivanova, Pedro da Gloria, Gonçalo Veiga, Analise Polsky, Jennifer E. Spence and Rui S.S. Murrieta. 2011a. Nutrition in Transition: Dietary Patterns of Rural Amazonian Women during a Period of Economic Change. *American Journal of Human Biology* 23(4): 458–469.

Piperata, Barbara A., Jennifer E. Spence, Pedro da Gloria, and Mark Hubbe. 2011b. The Nutrition Transition in Amazonia: Rapid Economic Change and Its Impact on Growth and Development in Ribeirinhos. *American Journal of Physical Anthropology* 146(1): 1–13.

Popkin, Barry. 2001 The Nutrition Transition and Obesity in the Developing World. *Journal of Nutrition* 131: 871S–873S.

Prentice, Andrew M., C. J. K. Spaaij, G. R. Goldberg, S. D. Poppitt, J. M. A. van Raaij, M. Totton, D. Swann, and A. E. Black. 1996. Energy Requirements of Pregnant and Lactating Women. *European Journal of Clinical Nutrition* 50(1): S82–S111.

Quandt, Sarah A. 1986. Nutritional Anthropology: The Individual Focus. In *Training Manual in Nutritional Anthropology*, ed. Sara A. Quandt and Cheryl Ritenbaugh, Special Pub. #20, 3–20. Washington, DC: American Anthropological Association.

Radimer, K. L., C. M. Olson, and C. C. Campbell. 1980. Development of Indicators to Assess Hunger. *Journal of Nutrition* 120(11S): 1544–1548.

Santos-Torres, M. I., and E. Vasquez-Garibay. 2003. Food Taboos among Nursing Mothers of Mexico. *Journal of Health, Population and Nutrition* 21(2): 142–149.

Spurr, Gerald B., Darna L. Dufour, Julio C. Reina, R. G. Hoffman, Carol I. Waslien, and Lisa K. Staten. 1994. Variation of the Basal Metabolic Rate and Dietary Energy Intake of Colombian Women during One Year. *American Journal of Clinical Nutrition* 59(1): 20–27.

Ulijaszek, Stanley J. 1992. Human Energetics Methods in Biological Anthropology. *Yearbook of Physical Anthropology* 35: 215–242.

Key Resources

Bernard, H. Russell. 2011. *Research Methods in Anthropology: Qualitative and Quantitative Approaches,* 5th ed. Plymouth, UK: Altima Press.

Dufour, Darna L., and Nicolette I. Teufel. 1995. Minimum Data Sets for the Description of Diet and Measurement of Food Intake and Nutritional Status. In *The Comparative Analysis of Human Societies: Toward Common Standards for Data Collection and Reporting,* ed. Emilio F. Moran, 97–128. Boulder: Lynne Rienner.

Gibson, Rosalind S. 2005. *Principles of Nutritional Assessment.* New York: Oxford University Press.

Moran, Emilio F., ed. 1995. *The Comparative Analysis of Human Societies: Toward Common Standards for Data Collection and Reporting.* Boulder: Lynne Rienner.

Quandt, Sarah A., and Cheryl Ritenbaugh, eds. 1986. *Training Manual in Nutritional Anthropology.* Special Pub. #20. Washington, DC: American Anthropological Association.

CHAPTER 2

Nutritional Anthropometry and Body Composition

Leslie Sue Lieberman

Introduction

Anthropometric techniques are one approach to assessing the nutritional status of individuals or groups through the standardized measurement of the absolute and relative size and shape of the human body, and are a non-invasive way of assessing body composition. Nutritional anthropometry uses standardized measurement techniques and protocols, specialized instrumentation, and international and national reference data. Individual measurements may be combined to produce ratios (e.g., waist-to-hip ratio) and indices (e.g., body mass index [BMI] = weight [kg]/height [m]^2). Individual values and aggregate data often are expressed as z-scores (i.e., the individual value minus the reference population mean for the age and sex, divided by the corresponding standard deviation) or as percentiles between the 3rd or 5th percentiles and the 95th or 97th percentiles (Himes 1991; Preedy 2012).

Uses of Anthropometric Data for Assessing Nutritional Status

There are many caveats regarding the use of anthropometric data to assess nutritional status. Anthropometric data do not necessarily reflect food consumption or energy adequacy per se because they are influenced by other determinants, some internal (e.g., the intestinal microbiome) and some external or environmental (e.g., temperature). Comparative analyses of data derived from dietary energy intake and anthropometric approaches indicate a lack of correlation between the estimates of under- and overnutrition in children and adults. However, these two approaches provide complementary information that can be used to monitor populations and evaluate nutritional and other health-related interventions. Different methods have greater or lesser sensitivity and specificity. Anthropometric measurements or indices (e.g., weight-for-height) have high sensitivity and are very useful in screening, surveillance, or interventions because they allow detection of small, repeated changes in energy balance that affect nutritional status. However, anthropometric measurements generally cannot specify or distinguish among genetic, nutritional, infectious, and chronic disease, or behavioral etiologies. A complete nutritional assessment incorporates measures summarized by the mnemonic "ABCD": anthropometric measurement, biochemical or laboratory tests, clinical indicators, and dietary assessment (Shetty 2003; World Health Organization (WHO) Expert Committee 1995).

References and Standards

Anthropometric references are statistical summaries of anthropometric measurements of representative samples of a population. References are descriptions of how things are. Widely used examples are the Anthropometric Reference Data for Children and Adults: United States, based on the National Health and Nutrition Examination Survey (NHANES) data (*Vital and Health Statistics*, Series 11, No. 252, 2012; Vital and Health Statistics, Series 3, No. 39, 2016). In contrast, anthropometric standards are statistical summaries of anthropometric measurements of selected segments of a population and represent how children should grow or healthful body dimensions and weights for adults. One widely used example is the WHO Multicentre Growth Reference Study (MGRS), conducted from 1997 to 2003, which examined children from Brazil, Ghana, India, Norway, Oman, and the United States (www.who.int/growthref/en/). The new growth curves provide a single international standard that represents the best description of physiological growth for all well-nourished children from birth to five years of age (Eveleth and Tanner 1990; de Onis et al. 2012). In April 2011 the WHO reported that 125 countries had adopted the WHO Child Growth Standards *www.who.int/childgroth/standards/en/* (de Onis et al. 2012). The Centers for Disease Control and Prevention (CDC) growth charts are used as standards, but these charts are references and identify how typical children in the United States grow during a specific time period. Typical growth patterns may not be ideal growth patterns, for example, the current high prevalence of overweight and obesity among children in many countries (Cameron and Bogin 2011; Hermanussen 2013).

Hermanussen (2013) presents the choice of appropriate data sets and the most recent statistical techniques. He delineates the requirements for reference samples, noting the importance of correctly assigning age to each subject by birth date. Since it is unlikely that measurements can be done at exact ages, for example, on one's birthday, then age classes need to be defined and documented. As an example, "three years old" may indicate children age 2.0–2.99, that is, in the third year of life; or aged 2.50–3.49; or children who have already had their third birthday, 3.0-3.99 (Hermanussen 2013: 159). Age classes are particularly important in infancy, when growth rates decline quickly. In addition, the circumstances of ascertaining a sample may introduce age bias, as with school samples that overrepresent the second half of the age class.

To interpret anthropometric data from individuals or groups, measurements are compared with references and standards generally as percentiles or z-scores and with cutoff points (e.g., 2 standard deviations above or below the mean) and categorical labels such as "overweight," "mild/moderate malnutrition," et cetera. Growth charts—graphic representations of growth references by age and sex—are usually presented as centiles and are widely used in clinical medicine for tracking individual children, for example: *www.cdc.gov/growthcharts//2000growthchart-us .pdf* (Hermanussen 2013). These charts are based on cross-sectional data but are used to track children longitudinally over time with repeated measuring of both cumulative changes (i.e., size or amplitude) and velocity (i.e., tempo).

Nutritional Anthropometry: Protocols for Taking the Measurements

The following descriptions and illustrations are accepted protocols for taking standardized measurements for comparisons with reference data. Brief information on application of measurements is also noted. There are many videotapes (some on YouTube), Power Point slide presentations, and books that include details of measurement techniques and common problems encountered in field situations. Some useful websites and training materials are listed below. Ideally, two researchers are involved in measuring, one the primary anthropometrist and the other the recorder. Both paper forms and computer forms (e.g., from National Center for Health Statistics (NCHS) and WHO publications) are available or can be developed for specific purposes. With large samples it is advantageous for both the scale and stadiometer to have wireless links to a computer where the individual measurements are recorded and checked for outliers. NHANES uses the Integrated Survey Information System (ISIS) for recording data.

General Guidelines

1. Calibrate all equipment before a measurement session and periodically throughout the day. The number of times will depend on the circumstances: movement of the equipment, number of individuals, large temperature changes throughout the measurement period, frequent extreme values, etc.

2. Always explain what you are going to do (e.g., locating the top of the hip [iliac crest] for waist circumference measurement). Maintain professionalism at all times while adjusting clothing, hair, etc.

3. Measure the right side of the body unless there is an abnormality.

4. Generally turn the subjects in the direction needed for a given measurement. Depending on the measurement you may be in front, at the side or behind the subject.

5. With respect to circumference measures, do not take any measurement readings with the zero end of the tape placed above the section of the tape with the result of the measurement.

6. Avoid parallax when taking measurement readings. Parallax is a common cause of data error, especially for measurements obtained using the skinfold calipers and measurement tape. The examiner should read the measurement with his or her line of sight directly in front of the value.

7. Record all linear and circumferences measurements to the nearest tenth of a centimeter (0.1 cm).

8. Always verify the result before advancing to the next measure. Computerized systems reduce data entry time and errors. The NHANES ISIS has data entry screens in the correct sequence based on the age of the participant. If a recorded value falls outside the pre-programmed edit range, the ISIS system will alert the recorder. http://webapp1.dlib.indiana.edu/cgi-bin/virtcdlib/index.cgi/3725325/FID1/speakers/binzer.pdf.

9. Analyses are possible through standard statistical packages (e.g., Statistical Package for the Social Sciences, [SPSS], Statistical Analysis System [SAS]) and through specialized applications such as Epi Info 7, which has nutritional anthropometry tools for collecting, analyzing and graphing child growth data. Among these tools are a data entry form used to calculate z-scores and percentiles as data are entered, growth charting capabilities in the Visual Dashboard, and several functions in Classic Analysis that you can use to add z-scores and percentiles to existing sets of data: CDC/WHO 1978, CDC 2000, WHO Child Growth Standards, and the WHO Reference 2007. Epi Info 7 allows selection of reference sets of interest. (Epi Info Users Guide: Nutritional Anthropology *http://wwwn.cdc.gov/epiinfo/user-guide/Nutritional-Anthropometry/introduction.html*)

Measurement Error

Anthropometrists should be carefully trained to reduce both intra- and inter-measurement error. There are two types of measurement error: The first type is in reliability or repeatability of the measures. The second type concerns departure from the true value. Both may be due to instrumentation or technique. A commonly used measure of imprecision is the technical error of measurement (TEM). For example, stature has both high reliability and validity, whereas skinfolds have much lower reliability and validity, in part because of adipose tissue's compressibility. An acceptable level of measurement error has a coefficient of reliability (R) > 0.95, indicating that 95% of the variance in measurements is due to factors other than measurement error. A detailed discussion of measurement errors and the calculations of TEM and R can be found in Hermanussen (2013) and Ulijaszek and Lourie (1994).

Anthropometric Measurements

Stature or Height

This vertical measurement is made from the floor or standing surface to the vertex (highest point) on the top of the head. The preferred instrumentation is a portable or wall-fixed stadiometer (Figure 2.1). Measurements in centimeters are made to the nearest millimeter for subjects age 2 years and older. Three consecutive measurements are made and the median is used. If an anthropometer (Figure 2.2) is used, extra care is taken with the alignment of the body since there is no surface behind the subject. Subjects should wear light clothing with nothing in the pockets and no shoes. Subjects are positioned with their heels, buttocks, shoulders (scapula) and back of the head (posterior cranium) touching the stadiometer. The head is adjusted in the Frankfurt Horizontal Plane (i.e., the lower border of the eye orbit is in the same horizontal plane as the superior border of the ear canal (the porion) (Figures 2.1, 2.2, 2.3). Subjects are asked to maintain this position while the head board of the stadiometer or the horizontal blade of the anthropometer is lowered to meet the most superior part of the head. There is circadian variation in height with greater height in the morning and decreasing height throughout the day. When it is possible, the time of day should be standardized. A digital measurement device can be connected to the head board and interfaced with a computer.

Recumbent Length

Length rather than stature is measured for infants from birth to two years of age. This horizontal measurement is made from the bottom of the feet to the most superior point on the top of the head, using a length board. Two consecutive measurements are made in centimeters to the nearest millimeter (Figure 2.2), and the median is used. The infant with minimal clothing is positioned supine on the board, arms by the sides and the crown of the head touching the vertical, stationary head board. The head is gently held in the Frankfurt Horizontal Plane. A

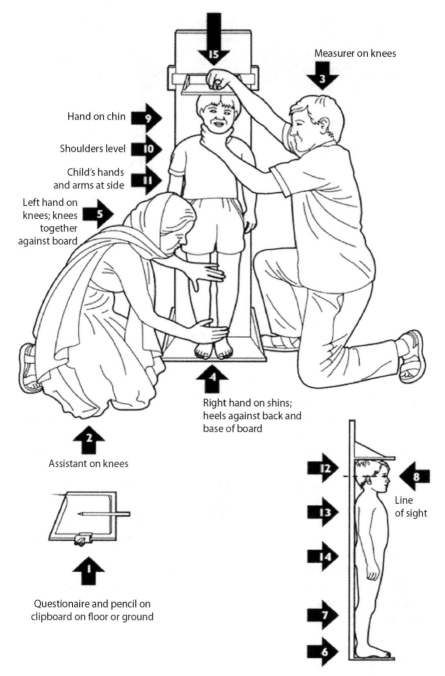

Figure 2.1. Stature/Height with a Stadiometer

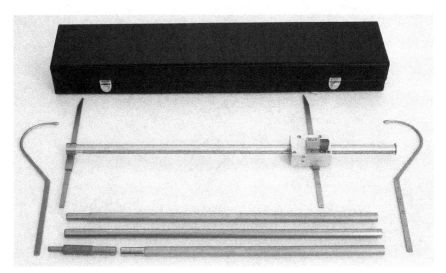

Figure 2.2. Anthropometer

second anthropometrist places one hand on the knees to ensure that the legs are extended and then moves the foot board to press against the soles of the flexed feet.

Weight (Children and Adults)

Adults and children should be weighed with minimal clothing. If individuals must be weighed wearing "street clothing," similar clothing should be weighed and standard correction factors applied to the weight. In some instances these correction factors are available (Centers for Disease Control 2007)). The NHANES ISIS computer system is also able to correct for casts and prostheses. Subjects are directed to stand in the center of the digital or balance scale platform facing the anthropometrist, hands at sides, weight equally distributed on both feet and looking straight ahead. The reading is taken when the measurement becomes stable. Replicate readings are made to the nearest 0.1 kg. When infants and toddlers cannot stand alone on the scale, either the guardian or the examiner stands on the scale while the recorder records the weight. The child is then handed to the adult on the scale and the resulting difference (adult's + child's weight - adult's weight = child's weight) is recorded as the child's weight. Some computerized systems have programs to calculate the child's weight.

Weight (Infant)

Many infant scales are available, most with a capacity of approximately 0–13 or 0–24 kg. Two consecutive replicate measures to the nearest 0.01 kg should be

Measurer on knees

Assistant on knees

Arms comfortably straight

Hand on knees or shins; legs straight

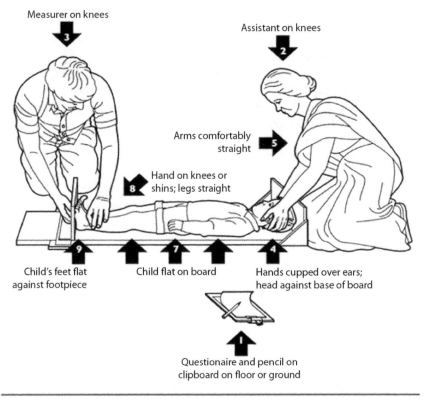

Child's feet flat against footpiece

Child flat on board

Hands cupped over ears; head against base of board

Questionaire and pencil on clipboard on floor or ground

Line of sight perpendicular to base of board

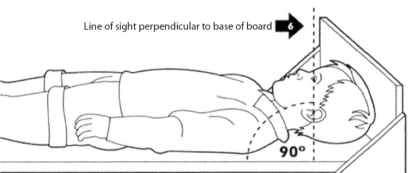

90°

Figure 2.3. Recumbent Length

taken with the infant relatively still. Diapers may be weighed separately. If breast milk intake is to be estimated, babies should be weighed immediately before and after a feeding with the same clothing and diapers/nappies. Difference in pre- and post-feeding weights gives an estimate of the net amount of milk consumed (1.06 g = 1.0 ml milk).

Circumferences

A retractable, flexible steel measuring tape or other tape that does not stretch is used to take length and circumference measurements. The accuracy of the circumference measurements depends on the tightness of the measuring tape. The tape should be snug but not constricting. The tape should be positioned parallel to the floor at the level at which the measurements is taken (WHO Expert Consultation 2008). Generally, two replicate measures should be taken unless they are widely divergent (> 0.5 cm to > 1.0 cm depending on the subject's size) whereupon a third measurement is taken and the median reported.

Head circumference

Head circumference is taken with a tape positioned above the eyebrows and placed posteriorly to give the maximum circumference. It is pulled sufficiently tight to compress the hair. The measurement is read to the nearest 0.1 cm and should be repeated. An infant or young child may be seated on the lap of the mother or caregiver. This is a useful measure for infants from birth to 24 months and young children up to 60 months.

Mid-upper arm circumference

A retractable tape measure is used to measure the mid-upper arm circumference (MUAC) to the nearest 0.1 cm. The measurement is taken midway between the lateral tip of the scapula (the acromion process) and the tip of the elbow (the olecranon process of the ulna) with a tape measure that does not stretch. The arm may be bent at a 90° angle to ascertain the olecranon but is in a relaxed, normal position for the measurement (Lohman, Roche, and Martorell 1988). Mei et al. (1997) provide references of MUAC-for-height (Table 2.1) listing the median and ± 2 standard deviations and MUAC-for-age (Table 2.2) for children 6 months to 5 years of age. The mid-upper arm circumference is commonly used as an estimate of a child's nutritional status and a proxy for low weight-for-height. Initially fixed cut-off values were used, but now the use of MUAC-for-age and MUAC-for-height are recommended. MUAC-for-height can be used when age is unknown. In therapeutic feeding programs MUAC shows advantages over weight-for-height z-scores, and the WHO recommends it as an independent criterion for nutritional status screening for children 6–59 months old.

Waist circumference

A retractable tape measure is used to measure the waist circumference in 0.1 cm at the level of the top of the iliac crest. The crest may be difficult to locate in overweight people. Subjects should stand relaxed with weight equally distributed on both feet. Other protocols indicate that measurement be made at the level of the umbilicus, but this may give a smaller circumference (WHO, 2008; WHO Expert Consultation 2008). Waist circumference should be measured at the end of a normal expiration and care taken not to compress the soft tissue (Table 2.3) (Fredriks 2004). Waist circumference is a good indicator of abdominal fat in adults, and large waist circumferences are associated with increased risk for diabetes, cardiovascular diseases and mortality (http:whqlibdoc.who.int/publications/2011/9789241501491eng.pdf.). The National Cholesterol Education Program's Adult Treatment Panel III identified a waist circumference cutoff of ≥ 102 cm for males and ≥ 88 cm for females as criteria for metabolic syndrome. However, the International Diabetes Federation cutoffs are ≥ 94 cm for males and ≥ 80 cm for females in Europid and African populations, ≥ 90 cm for males and ≥ 80 cm for females among South Asians, Chinese, and Japanese populations (http://www.idf.org/webdata/docs/MetSyndrome_FINAL.pdf; Grundy, Cleeman, Smith, and Lenfant 2004).

Hip circumference

A retractable tape measure is used to take the hip circumference in 0.1 cm at the widest portion of the buttocks. Subjects should stand relaxed with weight equally distributed on both feet. The anthropometrist measures from the side of the subject so that the maximum extension of the buttocks can be observed. A helper may be needed to stand at the other side of the subject to adjust the tape so that it is parallel to the floor.

Skinfolds: General Comments

Skinfold measurements require practice and skill because of the great variation in amounts of skin, subcutaneous fat, and muscle thicknesses as well as compressibility, which is affected by disease, hydration, and aging. They are taken on the right side of the body with a skinfold calipers (Figure 2.4). Prior to the measuring of the skinfold, the appropriate site is carefully marked with a washable marker.

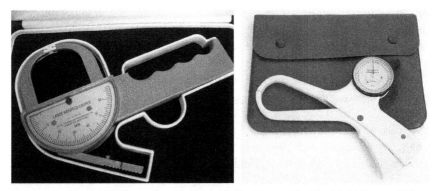

Figure 2.4. Skinfold Calipers. Lange calipers (left) photographed by M. McIntyre. Holtain Calipers (right) Permission obtained from Holtain. http://www.holtain.com/anth.php

A right-handed measurer will use the thumb and index finger of the left hand to pull up a double fold of skin with the underlying layer of fat about 2 cm above the mark. The fold should glide over the underlying muscle. With the calipers held in the right hand, the jaws of the calipers are placed on the mark about 2 cm from the fingers of the left hand, which continues to hold the fold of skin. The trigger of the calipers is released so that the entire force of the jaws is on the skinfold. The fingers of the left hand should not be released while readings are taken. The calipers will "creep" a little, so a fixed time (3 or 4 seconds) should be allowed to pass before taking the measurement. Measurements are recorded to the nearest 0.5 mm (Lange calipers) and 0.2 mm (Holtain calipers). The reading on the scale is noted before release of the calipers. A replicate measure is taken and the median reported. A third measurement may be done if the first two have a difference greater than the TEM's for intra-observer measurement error.

Triceps skinfold
The triceps skinfold is taken at the level of the midpoint between the acromial process (i.e., bony tip of the shoulder) and the olecranon process of the elbow on the midline of the posterior (back) surface of the arm (over the triceps muscle). This is the same level at which the MUAC is measured. The arm should be relaxed with the palm of the hand supinated (facing forward). A vertical pinch, parallel to the long axis of the arm, is made about 2 cm above the mark. The calipers are placed perpendicular to the skinfold and parallel to the floor at the marked midpoint. The skinfold protocol outlined above should be followed.

Biceps skinfold
The biceps skinfold measurement is taken on the center of the front of the upper arm following the general skinfold protocols outlined above.

Subscapular skinfold
The subscapular skinfold is made on the back below the shoulder blade or subscapular. The skinfold is taken at a 45-degree angle to the horizontal plane following the inferior angle of the scapular. The caliper jaws are applied 1 cm infero-lateral to the fold. The same general skinfold protocols are followed. This skinfold and the suprailiac skinfold may be more difficult to obtain because people must be partially undressed.

Suprailiac skinfold
The waist or suprailiac skinfold is located 1 cm above the anterior superior iliac crest or the top of the hip bone. Finding the iliac crest will require palpating the hip area and is especially difficult in obese individuals. Grasp the skin that follows the natural fold, which will follow a line approximately from the suprailiac to the umbilicus at an angle of approximately 30 degrees. The same general skinfold protocols are followed.

Indices and Equations

Indices are routinely used in surveillance and monitoring as sensitive indicators of children's nutritional status, growth and development, overall health, and risk for illnesses and conditions (e.g., high weight-for-age and hypertension) and mortality. They are useful in assessing the impact of nutritional interventions (e.g., provision of nutritional supplements, school-based weight reduction programs) and other health-related interventions (e.g., provision of clean drinking water, intestinal worm pharmacotherapies, infant vaccination programs).

Height-for-Age

Low height-for-age is an indicator of stunting and often chronic undernutrition. The conventional categories used by the WHO, United Nations International Children's Emergency Fund (UNICEF), and other organizations are: Normal ± 2 SD, Moderately Stunted > -2 < -3 SD, Severely Stunted > -3 SD (Table 2.5). (See WHO references for girls 5–19 years: http://www.who.int/growthref/ sft_hfa_girls_z_5_19years.pdf?ua=1; and boys 5–19 years: http://www.who .int/growthref/sft_hfa_boys_z_5_19years.pdf?ua=1). WHO also has tables of percentiles.

Weight-for-Age

Low weight-for-age is indicative of chronic or acute undernutrition, whereas high weight-for-age is indicative of overnutrition leading to overweight and obesity. Some heavily muscled athletes have high weights-for-age and weights-for-height and low levels of body fat. The conventional categories used by the WHO, UNICEF, and other organizations are: Normal ± 2 SD, Moderately Under/Overweight > ± 2 < ± 3 SD, Severely Under/Overweight > ± 3 SD.

Weight-for-Height

Low weight-for-height is indicative of wasting and acute undernutrition. High weight-for-height is indicative of overnutrition. The conventional categories used by the WHO, UNICEF, and other organizations are: Normal ± 2 SD, Moderately Wasted/Overweight > ± 2 < ± 3 SD, Severely Wasted/Overweight > ± 3 SD (Table 2.4).

Body Mass Index (Adults)

The BMI (BMI = weight [kg]/height [m]^2) is universally used to categorize individuals from severely underweight (< 16.5) to morbidly obese (> 40). In general it correlates well with percentage of body fat, but it is not a measure of body composition. Unfortunately, the public has widely assumed it to be a direct measure of body fatness, and clinicians and public health professionals have treated it as such. High BMI is a risk factor for many metabolic and cardiovascular diseases.

Body Adiposity Index (Adults)

The body adiposity index (BAI = (hip circumference [cm]/height [m]$^{1.5}$) - 18), an alternative to BMI, has had very mixed results with different populations and generally is less well correlated with percent body fat than BMI, compared to measurements with dual-energy X-ray absorptiometry (DXA), a laboratory technique. It was developed by Bergman and colleagues (2011).

Body Mass Index Percentiles (Children)

In contrast to adults, whose BMI categories are not distinguished by age or sex, the BMI percentiles used for children are age- and sex-specific. In general, children at or below the 3rd (WHO) or d 5th (CDC) percentiles are classified as underweight, children at or above the 85th percentile as overweight, and those at or above the 95th (CDC) or 97th (WHO) percentiles as obese. The WHO, CDC, International Obesity Task Force, or local references often will give widely different percentages of children classified as overweight or obese (Cole et al. 2000; de Onis et al., 2012; Gonzalez-Casanova et al. 2013; Quelly and Lieberman 2011).

Frame Index

The frame index (frame index = [elbow breadth (mm)/stature (cm)] x 100) is a measure of relative skeletal mass or robusticity. The reference data are disaggregated by age and sex (Frischano 1984, 1990).

Percent Body Fat

Estimates of body fat percentages in the field are generally calculated from skinfold measurements, circumferences, height, weight, and body density. Many equations are available for specific populations, with well over a hundred skinfold formulae (Shepard 1991: 57). Most fail to have high predictive value across populations (Deurenberg, Pieters, and Hautvast 1990). Below are some of the most commonly used equations:

Calculation of Body Density (D)

$D = 1.1765-0.0744 \ (\log_{10} \Sigma_4 S)$ (males 20–69 years)
$D = 1.1567-0.0717 \ (\log_{10} \Sigma_4 S)$ (females 20–69 years)
(S = the sum of the biceps, triceps, subscapular, and suprailiac skinfolds)

Estimation of Percent Body Fat for Adults

Percent body fat = [(495/body density) − 450] * 100 (Siri 1961)
Percent body fat = [(4.570/body density) − 4.142] * 100 (Brozek 1963)

Estimations of Body Density (D) for Children

$D = 1.660\text{-}0.0070^* (\log\Sigma_4 S)$ for boys
$D = 1.144\text{-}0.060^* (\log\Sigma_4 S)$ for girls
(S = the sum of the biceps, triceps, subscapular, and suprailiac skinfolds)

Estimations of Percent Body Fat for Children

Percent body fat = [(530/Density) − 489] * 100 (Lohman et al. 1984), for prepubescent children. This equation takes into account the lower bone mineral and higher water content of children's bodies compared to those of adults.

Slaughter and colleagues (1988) provide a series of equations to estimate body fatness for normal weight. For white prepubescent boys (0–12 years), white pubescent boys (13–15 years), white post-pubescent boys (16–18 years), black boys, and all girls, and for overweight boys and girls based on the sum of the triceps and subscapular skinfolds, < 35 mm = normal and > 35 mm = overweight. Hermanussen (2013: 272–273) lists a number of other equations used to calculate body density and body fat in children and adolescents. Table 2.6 lists the body composition for fat mass, fat free mass, and components of the fat-free body mass for children based on Fomon et al. (1982). Table 2.7 provides reference data for the sum of 4 skinfolds (biceps, triceps, subscapular, and suprailiac) by age and sex after Durnin and Womersly (1974). Addo and Himes (2010) provide reference curves for United States children and adolescents.

More recently, portable bioelectrical impedance devices have become popular as either handheld devices or scales (Figure 2.5) that give information on weight and calculate BMI, percent body fat, pounds of body fat, and lean body mass using formulae based on bioelectrical impedance (resistance), age, sex, height, and overall self-assessed fitness level. Bioelectrical impedance is a technique that involves conducting an imperceptible electrical current through the body, with contacts made by either the hands or feet via sensors (electrodes) in the instrument or scales. Muscle conducts electricity better than fat, so the greater the resistance, the more body fat one has. Some devices and scales can send this information via wireless transmission to a computer. Healthy ranges of body fat percentages have been suggested for categories of adults, including men (9–15%) and women (14–21%) under 30; men (11–21%) and women (15–33%) aged 30–50 years, and men (12–24%) and women (16–33%) over 50 (Lawrenson 2012; Shephard 1991). In older individuals internal fat increases at a faster rate that subcutaneous fat (Shephard 1991).

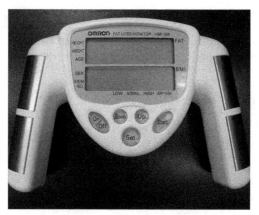

Figure 2.5a. Handheld Bioelectrical Impedance Instruments. Photographed by M. McIntyre.

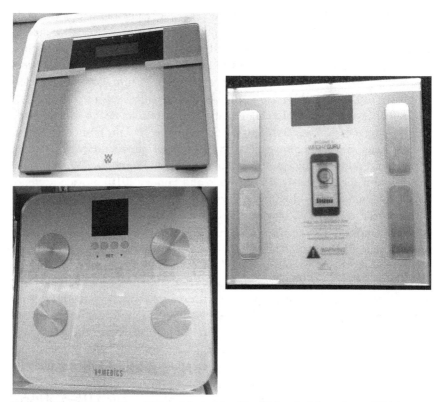

Figure 2.5b–d. Examples of Digital Scales that Use Bielectrical Impedance. Weight, Body Fat Percentage, BMI, and other features. Photographed by L. S. Lieberman.

Waist/Hip Ratio

The waist/hip ratio is a good indicator of abdominal fat and useful in determining risk for coronary heart disease and metabolic syndrome. The WHO Clinical Criteria for Metabolic Syndrome include a waist/hip ratio of > 0.9 for men and > 0.85 for women (Grundy et al. 2004).

Other Measurements

Many other measurements have proven useful in nutritional anthropology, such as sitting height and leg length, but the measurements presented in this chapter have proven most useful, and there are thousands of published examples of their application. Useful websites are listed below:

1. Online calculator to predict childhood obesity from biosocial risk factors: maternal and paternal BMIs, birth weight, maternal smoking behavior, maternal occupational category, household size. *http://files-good.ibl.fr/childhood -obesity/*
2. CDC growth charts: *www.cdc.gov/growthcharts//2000growthchart-us.pdf*
3. NCHS growth curves: *www.cdc.gov/nchs/data/series/sr_11/sr11 _*
4. References for child and adolescent body composition: *www.bcm.edu/bodycomlab*
5. World Health Statistics: http://www.who.int/gho/publications/world_health_statistics/EN/_
6. Series 11. Data From the National Health Examination Survey, the National Health and Nutrition Examination Surveys, and the Hispanic Health and Nutrition Examination Survey http://www.cdc.gov/nchs/products/series/series11.htm
7. WHO Child Growth Standards, birth to 5 years: *www.who.int/childgrowth/standards/en/* (Length/Height-for-Age, Weight-for-Age, Weight-for-Length/Height, BMI-for-Age, Head Circumference-for-Age, Mid-upper Arm Circumference-for-Age, Subscapular Skinfold-for-Age, Triceps Skinfold-for-Age for Females and Males)
8. WHO growth references for 5–19 years: *www.who.int/growthref/en* (Height-for-Age, Weight-for-Age, Weight-for-Height, BMI-for-Age, etc. for Females and Males)
9. CDC Growth Charts, birth to 36 months: *http://www.cdc.gov/growthcharts/clinical_charts.htm* (Length-for-Age, Weight-for-Age, Weight-for-Length, Head Circumference-for-Age for Females and Males)
10. National Center for Health Statistics. 2016. Anthropometric Reference Data for Children and Adults: United States, 2011–2014. Vital and Health Statistics, Series 3, No. 39. Age Birth to over 60 years (Stature/Length,

Weight, Body Mass Index, Waist Circumference, Upper Arm Circumference, Mid-Thigh Circumference, Upper Arm Length, Upper Leg Length, Subscapular Skinfold, Triceps Skinfold; all measurements disaggregated by age and sex) *http://www.cdc.gov/nchs/data/series/sr_03/sr03_039.pdf6.*

11. MMWR: Use of World Health Organization and CDC Growth Charts for Children Aged 0–59 Months in the United States: *http://www.cdc.gov/mmwr/preview/mmwrhtml/rr5909a1.htm*

12. Using the WHO Growth Charts to Assess Growth in the United States Among Children from Birth to 2 Years (an online training course): *http://www.cdc.gov/nccdphp/dnpao/growthcharts/who/index.htm*

13. Food and Nutrition Technical Assistance III Project (FANTA) Anthropometric Indicators Measurement Guide (2003): http://www.fantaproject .org/publications/anthropom.html
This is an excellent field guide used internationally with the United States Agency for International Development (USAID) and other projects.

14. Centers for Disease Control (CDC) 2012 Epi Info Users Guide: Nutritional Anthropology: *http://wwwn.cdc.gov/epiinfo/user-guide/Nutritional-Anthropometry/introduction.html*
Epi Info 7 contains nutritional anthropometry tools used to collect, analyze, and graph child growth data. Among these tools are a data entry form used to calculate z-scores and percentiles as data are entered, growth charting capabilities in the Visual Dashboard, and several functions in Classic Analysis that can be used to add z-scores and percentiles to existing sets of data: CDC/WHO 1978, CDC 2000, WHO Child Growth Standards, and the WHO Reference 2007. Epi Info 7 allows easy selection of the reference of interest.

Dr. Lieberman specializes in biomedical anthropology. She received her MA in Anthropology from the University of Arizona and her PhD in Behavior Genetics from the University of Connecticut. Her research interests include nutritional anthropology, obesity, diabetes, women's health and child growth and development. Research with Native American, Puerto Rican, Samoan, African American and Croatian communities was supported by NSF, NIH, national and local foundations and corporations. She was a faculty member at the University of Florida (1976–2001), the University of Central Florida (2001–2011) and a European Union Visiting Scholar at Vilnius University, Lithuania (2010–2014). She has over 200 publications and has served as President of the National Association of Academies of Science/American Association for the Advancement of Science (AAAS), Society for the Anthropology of Food and Nutrition and the Biological Anthropology Section of the American Anthropological Association and the Florida Academy of Science. She is a fellow of AAAS and has received numerous awards for professional leadership.

Appendix of Tables

Table 2.1. U.S. Reference for MUAC-for-Height

Height cm	Girls Median cm	Girls -2 SD	Boys Median cm	Boys -2 SD
66	14.2	12.3	14.7	12.8
68	14.5	12.5	15	12.9
70	14.8	12.7	15.1	13.1
72	15	12.9	15.3	13.2
74	15.2	13	15.4	13.3
76	15.4	13.2	15.6	13.4
78	15.5	13.3	15.7	13.4
80	15.6	13.4	15.8	13.5
82	15.8	13.5	15.9	13.6
84	15.9	13.6	15.9	13.7
86	15.9	13.7	16	13.7
88	16	13.7	16.1	13.8
90	16.1	13.8	16.2	13.9
92	16.2	13.9	16.3	14
94	16.3	14	16.4	14.1
96	16.4	14.1	16.5	14.2
98	16.5	14.2	16.6	14.3
100	16.6	14.3	16.7	14.4
102	16.7	14.4	16.9	14.5
104	16.9	14.5	17	14.6
106	17	14.6	17.1	14.8
108	17.1	14.8	17.3	14.9
110	17.3	14.9	17.4	15
112	17.5	15	17.5	15.1
114	17.7	15.2	17.7	15.2
116	17.9	15.3	17.9	15.4
118	18	15.5	18	15.5
120	18.3	15.7	18.2	15.6
122	18.5	15.8	18.4	15.7
124	18.8	16	18.6	15.8
126	19.1	16.2	18.8	15.9
128	19.4	16.4	19.1	16.1
130	19.7	16.6	19.3	16.2
132	20.1	16.8	19.5	16.3
134	20.4	17	19.9	16.5
136	20.8	17.2	20.3	16.7
138	21.3	17.5	20.7	16.9
140	21.7	17.8	21.1	17.1
142	22.2	18	21.6	17.4
144	22.8	18.4	22.1	17.7

Mei et al., 1997

Table 2.2. U.S. Reference for MUAC-for-Age for Infants and Children

Age years	Girls mean	Girls -2 SD	Boys mean	Boys -2 SD
0.5	13.9	11.5	14.9	12.6
0.75	14.6	12.2	15.4	12.9
1	15.1	12.6	15.7	13.2
1.5	15.7	13.1	16	13.4
2	16	13.4	16.2	13.6
2.5	16.2	13.5	16.4	13.7
3	16.4	13.6	16.6	13.8
3.5	16.6	13.8	16.8	13.9
4	16.8	13.9	17	14.1
4.5	17.1	14	17.2	14.2
4.9	17.3	14.1	17.4	14.2

Mei et al., 1997

Table 2.3. References for Waist Circumference, Hip Circumference, and Waist-to-Hip Ratio

	Age	Waist circumference			Hip circumference			WHR		
	years	-2 SD	mean	+2 SD	-2 SD	mean	+2 SD	-2 SD	mean	+2 SD
	0.25	32.1	38.4	44.2	31.4	36.8	43.7	0.885	1.031	1.174
	0.5	35	41	47	35.3	41.1	48.4	0.868	0.997	1.128
	0.75	36.4	42.3	48.5	37.2	43.1	50.4	0.863	0.982	1.105
	1	37.4	43.2	49.6	38.5	44.4	51.6	0.863	0.973	1.091
	2	40.9	46.4	53	42.3	48.4	55.8	0.864	0.959	1.063
	3	43.5	49.2	56.6	45.4	52	60.1	0.856	0.946	1.047
	4	44.6	50.6	58.7	47.6	54.8	63.9	0.835	0.923	1.028
	5	45.1	51.3	60.4	49.2	57	67	0.809	0.899	1.008
	6	45.9	52.5	62.7	51	59.6	70.9	0.788	0.879	0.993
	7	47.1	54	65.5	53	62.4	75.3	0.772	0.863	0.981
	8	48.3	55.7	68.5	55.1	65.5	80	0.757	0.849	0.97
	9	49.6	57.3	71.4	57.6	69	85	0.743	0.834	0.958
	10	50.9	59	74.2	59.9	72.1	89.4	0.73	0.82	0.946
	11	52.3	60.6	76.9	62.2	75.2	93.2	0.716	0.806	0.934
	12	53.8	62.4	79.3	65.1	79	97.2	0.703	0.792	0.922
	13	55.3	64.1	81.4	68.5	83.2	101.2	0.691	0.779	0.911
	14	56.6	65.6	83.2	71.4	86.6	104.3	0.681	0.768	0.903
	15	57.8	66.8	84.6	73.5	89	106.4	0.673	0.76	0.898
	16	58.8	67.9	85.7	74.9	90.6	107.9	0.667	0.755	0.897
	17	59.6	68.8	86.7	76.1	91.9	109.1	0.664	0.752	0.898
	18	60.3	69.5	87.5	77.1	93	110.3	0.662	0.75	0.9
	19	60.9	70.2	88.3	77.8	93.8	111	0.661	0.75	0.904
	20	61.4	70.8	88.9	77.9	93.9	111.2	0.661	0.75	0.908
	21	61.9	71.3	89.5	78.5	94.5	111.7	0.66	0.75	0.912
Boys	0.25	33	39.4	45.4	31.6	37.3	43.9	0.899	1.041	1.196
	0.5	35.9	42	48	35.5	41.4	48.3	0.885	1.013	1.152
	0.75	37.4	43.4	49.5	37.6	43.4	50.4	0.879	0.998	1.128
	1	38.3	44.3	50.6	39.1	44.7	51.6	0.875	0.988	1.111
	2	41.1	46.9	53.7	42.9	48.5	55.6	0.869	0.968	1.077
	3	44	49.7	56.9	45.5	51.4	59	0.866	0.962	1.07
	4	45.5	51.2	59	47.8	54.2	62.5	0.849	0.945	1.053
	5	46.3	52.1	60.7	49.8	56.7	66	0.827	0.923	1.032
	6	47.2	53.3	62.9	51.5	59	69.6	0.81	0.905	1.015
	7	48.4	54.8	65.5	53.2	61.3	73.2	0.796	0.891	1.002
	8	49.7	56.5	68.5	55.3	64.2	77.5	0.784	0.878	0.99
	9	51	58.2	71.4	57.8	67.4	81.7	0.773	0.866	0.978
	10	52.3	59.9	74.3	60.2	70.4	85.2	0.763	0.855	0.966
	11	53.8	61.8	77.2	62.4	73.3	88.4	0.755	0.846	0.957
	12	55.4	63.9	80	64.7	76.3	91.7	0.748	0.838	0.949
	13	57.2	66.1	82.8	67.4	79.8	95.5	0.741	0.831	0.942
	14	59.1	68.2	85.2	70.7	83.7	99.1	0.735	0.825	0.937
	15	60.9	70.3	87.4	74.2	87.1	102	0.73	0.821	0.933
	16	62.6	72.3	89.4	76.9	89.6	104	0.729	0.82	0.934
	17	64.1	74	91.9	78.6	91.3	105.4	0.729	0.821	0.936
	18	65.4	75.6	92.6	79.8	92.3	106.3	0.731	0.824	0.941
	19	66.6	77	94	80.6	93.1	107	0.733	0.827	0.946
	20	67.7	78.3	95.4	81.2	93.6	107.5	0.735	0.831	0.951
	21	68.8	79.6	96.6	81.6	94.1	107.9	0.738	0.834	0.956

Fredriks, 2004

Table 2.4. WHO Classification for Protein-Energy Malnutrition

	Moderate Malnutrition	Severe Malnutrition
Symmetric oedema	No	Yes*
weight-for-height	SD -2 to -3 70-90% of median (moderate wasting)	SD < -3 <70% of median (severe wasting)
height-for-age	SD -2 to -3 85-89% of median (moderate stunting)	SD < -3 <85% of median (severe stunting)
MUAC	<12.5 - 11.5 cm	<11.5 cm

* This includes kwashiorkor and marasmic kwashiorkor

WHO, 2011

Table 2.5. Combined BMI and Waist Circumference Cutoff Points for Adults and Association with Disease Risk

	BMI	Disease risk relative to normal BMI and waist circumference	
		Men <102 cm Women< 88 cm	Men >102 cm Women>88 cm
Underweight	<18.5		
Normal	18.5-24.9		
Overweight	25.0-29.9	increased	high
Obesity	30.0-34.9 35.0-39.9 >40.0	high very high extremely high	very high very high extremely high

WHO, 2011

Table 2.6. References for Body Composition

	Age	Length	Weight	Fat	Fat	FFBM	Protein	Components of FFBM % body weight					
								TBW	ECW	CW	OS	NOS	CARB
	years	cm	kg	kg	%	g	%	%	%	%	%	%	%
Girls	0	50.5	3.33	0.50	14.9	2.83	12.8	68.6	42	26.7	2.6	0.6	0.5
	0.083	53.4	4.13	0.67	16.2	3.46	12.7	67.5	40.5	26.9	2.5	0.6	0.5
	0.167	56.7	4.99	1.05	21.1	3.94	12.2	63.2	37.1	26.1	2.4	0.6	0.5
	0.25	59.6	5.74	1.37	23.8	4.38	12	60.9	35.1	25.8	2.3	0.6	0.5
	0.33	61.9	6.30	1.59	25.2	4.72	11.9	59.6	33.8	25.8	2.3	0.5	0.4
	0.5	65.8	7.25	1.92	26.4	5.34	12	58.4	32.4	26	2.2	0.5	0.4
	0.75	70.4	8.27	2.07	25	6.20	12.5	59.3	32	27.3	2.3	0.5	0.4
	1	74.3	9.18	2.18	23.7	7.01	12.9	60.1	31.8	28.3	2.3	0.5	0.5
	1.5	80.2	10.78	2.35	21.8	8.43	13.5	61.3	31.5	29.8	2.4	0.6	0.5
	2	85.5	11.91	2.43	20.4	9.48	13.9	62.2	31.5	30.8	2.4	0.6	0.5
	3	94.1	14.10	2.61	18.5	11.49	14.4	63.5	31.3	32.2	2.5	0.6	0.5
	4	101.6	15.96	2.76	17.3	13.20	14.8	64.3	31.2	33.1	2.5	0.6	0.5
	5	108.4	17.66	2.95	16.7	14.71	15	64.6	31	33.6	2.5	0.6	0.5
	6	114.6	19.52	3.21	16.4	16.31	15.2	64.7	30.8	34	2.6	0.6	0.5
	7	120.6	21.84	3.66	16.8	18.18	15.2	64.4	30.3	34.1	2.5	0.6	0.5
	8	126.4	24.84	4.32	17.4	20.52	15.2	63.8	29.6	34.2	2.5	0.6	0.5
	9	132.2	28.46	5.21	18.3	23.25	15.1	63	28.9	34.1	2.5	0.6	0.5
	10	138.3	32.55	6.32	19.4	26.23	15	62	28.1	33.9	2.5	0.6	0.5
Boys	0	51.6	3.55	0.49	13.7	3.06	12.9	69.6	42.5	27	2.6	0.6	0.5
	0.083	54.8	4.45	0.67	15.1	3.78	12.9	68.4	41.1	27.3	2.6	0.6	0.5
	0.167	58.2	5.51	1.10	19.9	4.41	12.3	64.3	38	26.3	2.4	0.6	0.5
	0.25	61.5	6.44	1.50	23.2	4.94	12	61.4	35.7	25.8	2.3	0.6	0.5
	0.33	63.9	7.06	1.74	24.7	5.32	11.9	60.1	34.5	25.7	2.3	0.5	0.4
	0.5	67.6	8.03	2.04	25.4	5.99	12	59.4	33.4	26	2.3	0.5	0.4
	0.75	72.3	9.18	2.20	24	6.98	12.4	60.3	33	27.2	2.3	0.6	0.5
	1	76.1	10.15	2.29	22.5	7.86	12.9	61.2	32.9	28.3	2.3	0.6	0.5
	1.5	82.4	11.47	2.38	20.8	9.09	13.5	62.2	32.3	29.9	2.5	0.6	0.5
	2	87.2	12.59	2.46	19.5	10.13	14	62.9	31.9	31	2.6	0.6	0.5
	3	95.3	14.68	2.58	17.5	12.10	14.7	63.9	31.1	32.8	2.8	0.6	0.5
	4	102.9	16.69	2.66	15.9	14.03	15.3	64.8	30.5	34.2	2.9	0.6	0.5
	5	109.9	18.67	2.72	14.6	15.95	15.8	65.4	30	35.4	3.1	0.6	0.5
	6	116.1	20.69	2.80	13.5	17.90	16.2	66	29.6	36.4	3.2	0.6	0.5
	7	121.7	22.85	2.93	12.8	19.92	16.5	66.2	29.1	37.1	3.3	0.6	0.5
	8	127	25.30	3.29	13	22.01	16.6	65.8	28.3	37.5	3.4	0.6	0.5
	9	132.2	28.13	3.72	13.2	24.41	16.8	65.4	27.6	37.8	3.5	0.6	0.5
	10	137.5	31.44	4.32	13.7	27.12	16.8	64.8	26.7	38	3.5	0.6	0.5

Fomon et al., 1982
FFBM fat free body mass
TBW total body water
ECW extracellular water
CW cellular water
OS osseus
NOS non osseus
CARB carbohydrate

Table 2.7. Percentage of Body Fat Based on the Sum of the Triceps, Biceps, Subscapular, and Suprailiac Skinfolds

Sum in mm	Males			Females		
	Age 16-29	Age 30-49	Age 50+	Age 16-29	Age 30-49	Age 50+
14				9.4	14.1	17.0
16				11.2	15.7	18.6
18				12.7	17.1	20.1
20	8.1	12.1	12.5	14.1	18.4	21.4
22	9.2	13.2	13.9	15.4	19.5	22.6
24	10.2	14.2	15.1	16.5	20.6	23.7
26	11.2	15.2	16.3	17.6	21.5	24.8
28	12.1	16.1	17.4	18.6	22.4	25.7
30	12.9	16.9	18.5	19.5	23.3	26.6
35	14.7	18.7	20.8	21.6	25.2	28.6
40	16.3	20.3	22.8	23.4	26.8	30.3
45	17.7	21.8	24.7	25.0	28.3	31.9
50	19.0	23.0	26.3	26.5	29.6	33.2
55	20.2	24.2	27.8	27.8	30.8	34.6
60	21.2	25.3	29.1	29.1	31.9	35.7
65	22.2	26.3	30.4	30.2	32.9	36.7
70	23.2	27.2	31.5	31.2	33.9	37.7
75	24.0	28.0	32.6	32.2	34.7	38.6
80	24.8	28.8	33.7	33.1	35.6	39.5
85	25.6	29.6	34.6	34.0	36.3	40.4
90	26.3	30.3	35.5	34.8	37.1	41.1
95	27.0	31.0	36.5	35.6	37.8	41.9
100	27.6	31.7	37.3	36.3	38.5	42.6
110	28.8	32.9	38.8	37.7	39.7	43.9
120	29.9	34.0	40.2	39.0	40.8	45.1
130	31.0	35.0	41.5	40.2	41.9	46.2
140	31.9	36.0	42.8	41.3	42.9	47.3
150	32.8	36.8	43.9	42.3	43.8	48.2
160	33.6	37.7	45.0	43.2	44.7	49.1
170	34.4	38.5	46.0	44.6	45.5	50.0
180	35.2	39.2	47.0	45.0	46.2	50.8
190	35.9	39.9	47.9	45.8	46.9	51.6
200	36.5	40.6	48.8	46.6	47.6	52.3

Lawrenson, D. *How to Measure Your Body Fat % Using Calipers.*
www.muscleandstrength.com/how-°©-to-°©-measure-°©-body-°©-fat-°©-using–calipers.html

References

Addo, O.Y. and John H. Himes. 2010 Reference curves for triceps and subscapular skinfold thickness in US children and adolescents. *American Journal of Clinical Nutrition* 91: 35–642.

Bergman, R. N., D. Stefanovski, T. A. Buchanan, A. E. Sumner, J. C. Reynolds, N. G. Sebring, A. H. Xiang, and R. M. Watanabe. 2011. A Better Index of Body Adiposity. *Obesity (Silver Spring)* 19(5): 1083–1089.

Brozek, Josef, F. Grande, T. Anderson, and Ancel Keys. 1963. Densitometric Analysis of Body Composition: Revisions of Some Quantitative Assumptions. *Annals of the New York Academy of Sciences* 110: 113–140.

Cameron, Noel, and Barry Bogin, eds. 2011. *Human Growth and Development*, 2nd ed. London: Academic Press.

Centers for Disease Control (CDC). 2007. National Health and Nutrition Examination Survey (NHANES): Anthropometry Procedures Manual. *http://www.cdc.gov/nchs/data/nhanes/nhanes_07_08/manual_an.pdf*. Accessed 14 April 2013.

Cole, Tim J., M. C. Bellizzi, K. M. Flegal, and William H. Dietz. 2000. Establishing a Standard Definition for Child Overweight and Obesity Worldwide: International Survey. *British Medical Journal* 320: 1240–1243.

de Onis, M., A. Onyango, E. Borghi, A. Siyam, M. Blossner, C. Lutter, and the WHO Multicenter Growth Reference Study Group. 2012. Worldwide Implementation of the WHO Child Growth Standards. *Public Health Nutrition* 5(9): 1603–1610.

Deurenberg, Paul, John J. Pieters, and Joseph G. A. J. Hautvast. 1990. The Assessment of the Body Fat Percentage by Skinfold Thickness Measurements in Childhood and Young Adolescence. *British Journal of Nutrition* 63: 293–303.

Durnin J. V., and J. Womersley. 1974. Body Fat Assessed from Total Body Density and Estimation from Skinfold Thickness Measurements on 481 Men and Women Aged 16–72 Years. *British Journal of Nutrition* 32: 77–96.

Eveleth, Phyllis B., and James M. Tanner. 1990. *Worldwide Variation in Human Growth*, 2nd ed. Cambridge: Cambridge University Press.

Fomon, S. J., F. Haschke, E. E. Ziegler, and S. E. Nelson. 1982. Body Composition of Reference Children from Birth to 10 Years of Age. *American Journal of Clinical Nutrition* 35 (5): 1169–1175.

Fredriks, A. M. 2004. "Growth Diagrams: Fourth Dutch Nation-Wide Survey, 1997." Ph.D. dissertation. Leiden University, Netherlands.

Frisancho, A. Roberto. 1984. New standards of weight and body composition by frame size and height for assessment of nutritional status of adults and the elderly. *American Journal of Clinical Nutrition* 40(4): 808–819.

Frisancho, A. Roberto. 1990. *Anthropometric Standards for the Assessment of Growth and Nutritional Status*. Ann Arbor: University of Michigan Press.

Gonzalez-Casanova, Ines, O. L. Sarmiento, J. A. Gazmararian, S. A. Cunningham, Reynaldo Martorell, M. Pratt,. Comparing Three Body Mass Index Classification Systems to Assess Overweight and Obesity in Children and Adolescents. *Revista Panamericana de Salud Pública* 33(5): 349–355.

Grundy, Scott, James Cleeman, Sidney Smith Jr., and Claude Lenfant. 2004. NHLBI/AHA Conference Proceedings: Definition of Metabolic Syndrome. *Circulation* 109: 433–438.

Hermanussen, Michael, ed. 2013. *Auxology: Studying Human Growth and Development.* Stuttgart: Schweizerbart.

Himes, John H. 1991. *Anthropometric Assessment of Nutritional Status.* New York: Wiley-Liss.

Lawrenson, D. 2012. How to Measure Your Body Fat % Using Calipers. *http://www.musc leandstrength.com/tools/how-to-measure-bodyfat-using-calipers.html.* Accessed 1 May 2013.

Lohman, Timothy G., Alex F. Roche, and Reynaldo Martorell. 1988. *Anthropometric Standardization Reference Manual.* Champaign, IL: Human Kinetics Books.

Lohman, Timothy G., M. H. Slaughter, R. A. Boileau, J. C. Bunt and L. Lussier. 1984. Bone Mineral Content Measurements and Their Relation to Body Density in Children, Youth and Adults. *Human Biology* 56: 667–679.

Mei, Z., L. M. Grummer-Strawn, M. de Onis, and R. Yip. 1997. The Development of a MUAC for Height Reference, Including Comparison to Other Nutritional Status Screening Indicators. *Bulletin of the World Health Organization* 75: 333–341.

National Center for Health Statistics. 1999. National Health and Nutrition Examination Survey Integrated Survey Information System (ISIS). http://www.cdc.gov/nchs/data/nhanes/nhanes_07_08/manual_an.pdf. Accessed 22 April 2013.

National Center for Health Statistics. 2016. Anthropometric Reference Data for Children and Adults: United States, 2011–2014. *Vital and Health Statistics,* Series 3, No. 39. National Center for Health Statistics.

National Health and Nutrition Examination Survey (NHANES) Anthropometry Procedures Manual. 2007. *http://www.cdc.gov/nchs/data/nhanes/nhanes_07_08/manual_an.pdf.* Accessed 7 April 2013.

Preedy, Victor R. 2012. *Handbook of Anthropometry: Physical Measures of Human Form in Health and Disease.* New York: Springer.

Quelly, Susan B., and Leslie S. Lieberman. 2011. Global Prevalence of Overweight and Obesity in Preschoolers. *Anthropologischer Anzeiger: Journal of Biological and Clinical Anthropology* 68(4): 437–456.

Siri, William E. 1961. Body Composition from Fluid Spaces and Density. In *Technique for Measuring Body Composition,* ed. Josef Brozek and Austin Henschel, 108–117. Washington, DC: National Academy Press.

Shepard, Roy J. 1991. *Body Composition in Biological Anthropology.* Cambridge: Cambridge University Press.

Slaughter M.H., T.G. Lohman, R.A. Boileau, C.A. Horwill,, R.J. Stillman, M.D. van Loan and D.A. Bemben. 1988 Skinfold Equations for the Estimation of Body Fatness in Children and Youth. *Human Biology* 60: 709–723.

Shetty, Prakash. 2003. Measures of Nutritional Status from Anthropometric Survey Data. Keynote Paper presented at the Measurement and Assessment of Food Deprivation and Undernutrition, Rome, 26–28 June 2002. *http://www.fao.org/docrep/005/Y4249E/y4249E00.HTM.* Accessed 24 April 2013.

Slaughter, M. H., T. G. Lohman, R. A. Boileau, C. A. Horwill, R. J. Stillman, M. D. van Loan, and D. A. Bemben. 1988. Skinfold Equations for the Estimation of Body Fatness in Children and Youth. *Human Biology* 60: 709–723.

Ulijaszek, Stanley J. and Deborah A. Kerr. 1999 Anthropometric measurement error and the assessment of nutritional status. *British Journal of Nutrition* 82: 165–177.

Ulijaszek, Stanley J., and John A. Lourie. 1994. Intra and Inter-Observer Error in Anthropometric Measurement. In *Anthropometry: The Individual and the Population,* ed. Stanley

Ulijaszek and C. G. Nicholas Mascie-Taylor, 30–55. Cambridge: Cambridge University Press.

World Health Organization. 2008 Training Course on Child Growth Assessment. Geneva: WHO. *http://www.who.int/childgrowth/training/en/* Accessed April 13, 2013.

WHO Expert Committee on Physical Status. 1995. Physical Status: The Use and Interpretation of Anthropometry. WHO Technical Report Series 854. Geneva: WHO.

WHO Expert Consultation. 2008. Waist Circumference and Waist-Hip Ratio: Report of a WHO Expert Consultation. Geneva: WHO. *http://whqlibdoc.who.int/publications/2011/9789241501491_eng.pdf.* Accessed 12 April 2013.

World Health Organization Expert Consultation. 2008 Waist Circumference and Waist-Hip Ratio: Report of a WHO Expert Consultation. Geneva: WHO. *http://whqlibdoc.who.int/publications/2011/9789241501491_eng.pdf.* Accessed April 12, 2013.

CHAPTER 3

Measuring Energy Expenditure in Daily Living
Established Methods and New Directions

Mark Jenike

Introduction

The measurement of physical activity and energy expenditure has a long and distinguished history in anthropology, particularly in the areas of cultural ecology, human biology, and nutritional anthropology (Dufour and Piperata 2008; Leonard 2003; Sackett 1996; Ulijaszek 1995). Estimates of energy expenditure during daily living have been used to describe the nature and dynamics of energetic trade-offs (e.g., between work effort, pregnancy or lactation, growth, and immune function) in food-limited populations (Madimenos et al. 2011; Pontzer et al. 2015; Rashid and Ulijaszek 1999). They have also revealed equity, inequity, and complementarity in the distribution of workloads within households and communities (Kashiwazaki et al. 2009; Madimenos et al. 2011; Meehan, Quinlan, and Malcom 2013; Panter-Brick 1996). The measurement of daily energy expenditure has been an important tool in studies of health outcomes associated with modernization, rural-to-urban migration, and other forms of social and economic transition (Kashiwazaki et al. 2009; Spurr, Dufour, and Reina 1996; Wilson et al. 2014; Yamauchi, Umezaki, and Ohtsuka 2000); and analysis of variation in daily energy expenditure over time and between population subgroups has provided a window onto seasonal patterns of nutritional stress, gendered division of labor, changing patterns of work effort and physical exertion with age, and the economic and nutritional implications of residence in neighboring geographic zones (Brun 1992; Jenike 1996; Kashiwazaki et al. 2009; Panter-Brick 1996; Yamauchi et al. 2000).

Early methods emphasized the collection of expired air, imposing severe constraints on the measurement conditions and requiring both expensive equipment and considerable investigator training. Current methods have substantially reduced the invasiveness, cost, and difficulty of assessing physical activity and energy expenditure in free-living humans in both more developed and less developed field settings while posing new challenges to the validity of results. As a result, measurement of physical activity and energy expenditure is now more accessible for inclusion in mixed-methods research designs.

Dimensions and Indices

Human energy budgets are usefully divided into three broad categories: (1) the baseline energy that is needed even at rest to support minimal vital functions, (2) the energy that is needed to digest, transform, and store the nutrients in our food, and (3) the energy that is expended above and beyond these on physical activity, reproduction, and other functions. Baseline expenditure, defined as either basal or resting metabolism (see Snodgrass 2012 for the distinction), is most often assessed in anthropological work as resting energy expenditure (REE). It can be measured for individuals (DeLany 2012; Leonard 2012) but is more commonly estimated using a prediction equation that requires the input of stature, weight, gender, age, and sometimes other variables as well (e.g., Harris and Benedict 1918; Mifflin et al. 1990; Schofield 1985). The validity of a prediction equation for basal metabolism or resting metabolism is greatest when applied to the populations for which it was designed.

The thermic effect of food (TEF) is the energy used by the digestive system to process food and make its nutrients available to the body. It can be estimated as 10 percent of the overall energy content of food but is known to vary with the composition of the diet, increasing with the proportion of protein in the diet (Snodgrass 2012) and generally decreasing with the intensity of external processing of food items (e.g., grinding, cooking, refining) prior to ingestion (Carmody and Wrangham 2009). TEF is also sometimes referred to as diet-induced thermogenesis or the specific dynamic action of food.

Activity energy expenditure (AEE), the energy expended to support voluntary and nonvoluntary physical activity, is estimated by subtracting REE (and sometimes TEF) from total energy expenditure (TEE) (Snodgrass 2012). This framework allows other important components of energy expenditure such as growth, immune system activation, pregnancy, and lactation to be separated out if indicated by research conditions, but ignored or subsumed within REE in studies of healthy, nonpregnant, nonlactating adults. Total daily energy expenditure (TDEE) is TEE summed over a 24-hour period.

Measurement of TDEE: Behavioral Observation, Heart Rate Monitoring, and the Doubly Labeled Water Method

Most anthropological studies of energy expenditure have focused on individual energy budgets and targeted free-living TDEE for measurement or estimation (Leonard 2012). Prior to the advent of the small wearable devices discussed below, studies of TDEE in free-living conditions relied primarily on three methodologies: the factorial method, the flex heart rate (flex-HR) method, and the doubly labeled water method.

The factorial method combines estimates of time allocated to different activities and to different resting postures with independently derived estimates of the rate of energy expenditure for those activities (see Leonard 2012 for a detailed description). Though subject to significant sources of bias and error (Kashiwazaki et al. 2009; Leonard, Galloway, and Ivakine 1997; Leonard, Katzmarzyk, and Ross 1995), the factorial method remains an important tool because it requires no specialized equipment or laboratory. It requires only published estimates of the energy cost of activities, and daily logs of the amount of time spent in different activities and postures. It generates both an estimate of TDEE and estimates of how much time and energy is devoted to different activities and postures throughout the period of observation.

The flex-HR method (Spurr et al. 1988) also has the potential to generate both an estimate of TDEE and a picture of variation in the intensity of energy expenditure throughout the day. Because heart rate (HR) increases in proportion to the intensity of physical exertion and the rate of energy expenditure, it can be used an indirect indicator of TEE. However, the relationship between HR and energy expenditure is not consistent across individuals. It also breaks down at low rates of energy expenditure, such as those experienced at rest. G. B. Spurr and colleagues used these findings and late twentieth-century advances in ambulatory heart rate monitoring and data storage to develop the flex-HR method for estimating TDEE. Flex-HR relies on the calculation of a threshold HR for each participant—the flex HR—and on collection of minute-by-minute records of HR during the measurement period, which may last from one to several days. For intervals during which HR is below the flex HR, TEE is estimated with a constant that corresponds to the REE. For intervals when HR is above the flex HR, TEE is estimated with an individually calibrated linear equation relating HR to EE. With the development of inexpensive, reliable, durable heart-rate monitors capable of storing several days of minute-by-minute heart rates, the flex-HR method became a very important tool for estimating TDEE during normal daily activities (Leonard 2003). The minute-by-minute heart-rate log generated with flex-HR also constitutes a fine-grained record of the intensity of energy expenditure throughout the day. When combined with an activity log or recall interview, it can provide estimates of the energy expended on specific activities or in different locations.

An important limitation of the flex-HR method is its dependence on access to laboratory facilities to derive the individual HR-TEE calibration curves for each participant. This is typically done by measuring respiratory gas exchange (indirect calorimetry) at varying levels of exertion while simultaneously recording heart rate. Though it is possible to carry out these calibration measurements in a field laboratory, they require a means of measuring the volume of expired air (e.g., a flow meter) and a gas analyzer. While these capabilities are now available in the form of portable, miniaturized metabolic carts, their use can add significantly to the cost and invasiveness of TDEE research relative to the factorial method or the newer methods discussed below (Jenike and Crofut 2004; Snodgrass 2012).

The doubly labeled water method (Schoeller 1988, 1999) has the advantage of not requiring participants to visit a laboratory or undergo any respiratory testing. This method requires only the administration of a dose of isotopically labeled water and subsequent collection of urine samples from participants. It relies on the fact that whereas humans shed both hydrogen and oxygen through the loss of body water, they shed oxygen (in the form of CO_2), but not hydrogen, through respiration. The ratio of oxygen turnover to hydrogen turnover is, therefore, an index of carbon dioxide production, and therefore of energy metabolism. The decline in the ratio of labeled oxygen to labeled hydrogen from the ratio in the original dose of doubly labeled water is assessed in periodic urine samples and used as an index of CO_2 production and energy metabolism. Samples are collected at the end of the study period (up to three weeks for one dose) or at intervals over the duration of the study (Delaney 1997).

The doubly labeled water method is well validated and considered a "gold standard" method for measuring TDEE. It does, however, require purchase of the labeled water and access to laboratory equipment or collaborators for measurement of the isotope concentrations in urine samples. Its cost, therefore, typically exceeds that of the other methods. The doubly labeled water method also does not provide the fine-grained picture of changing rates of energy expenditure throughout the day that can be obtained with flex-HR or the factorial method. It provides only TEE for the time between sample collections (Colbert and Schoeller 2011).

Leonard (2012) offers a thorough review of established field and laboratory methods not discussed here. Readers interested in a more detailed discussion of the fundamental science, empirical evidence, and assumptions underlying these methods should consult McLean and Tobin (1987) or a current exercise physiology textbook (e.g., McArdle, Katch, and Katch 2014).

Measurement of TEE: Small, Wearable Devices

The past two decades have seen a proliferation of small, wearable devices for measuring TDEE. These devices are either strapped on the arm or leg, clipped at the waist to a belt or other tight-fitting article of clothing, mounted on a shoe, or attached to the chest with adhesive electrodes or an elastic belt. They weigh less than fifty grams and are designed to be worn for several days or more at a time. Designed primarily for health care and fitness applications, these devices feature the benefits of low cost, integrated software applications, and the ability to produce a rich picture of the varying intensity of energy expenditure throughout the day. They are relatively noninvasive and require little technical expertise to use.

All of the devices are based on measurement of one or more variables that, like heart rate, have a predictable relationship with energy expenditure. While some include only one sensor (typically an accelerometer that detects movement in space), others make use of multiple sensors, each recording a different variable. Most also rely on proprietary equations to derive energy expenditure from the sensor data. Only two types of device are discussed here, but others have been reviewed elsewhere (Anastasopoulou et al. 2014; Butte, Ekelund, and Westerterp 2012; Dannecker et al. 2013).

Standalone accelerometers measure movement and can be worn on the wrist, ankle, or belt. Actical (Philips Respironics) and ActiGraph are two of the accelerometers that anthropologists have adopted for use in fieldwork settings (Madimenos et al. 2011; McGarvey et al. 2011; Wilson et al. 2014), in part because of their durability, waterproof casing, and unobtrusiveness. One weakness of standalone accelerometers is that they can over- or underestimate energy expenditure depending on which part of the body is moving more. When cycling, for example, an ankle-mounted accelerometer will be in constant motion and might overestimate energy expenditure relative to a hip- or wrist-mounted device, which will move around less during the same activity. Advances in data analysis algorithms, the addition of gyroscopes, or the use of multiple devices can reduce this source of error (Intille et al. 2012; Schneller et al. 2015). In addition, accelerometers cannot detect energy expenditure related to resistance rather than movement, such as the added exertion associated with load-carrying (Snodgrass 2012). Nonetheless, accelerometry is a proven technology that has been widely studied and validated with diverse populations (Chen and Basset 2005; Plasqui and Westerterp 2007). It is also the technology that underlies consumer activity trackers such as Fitbit, Jawbone, and Nike Fuelband. Current versions of many of these devices, though widely available, inexpensive and noninvasive, may not produce sufficiently valid estimates of TDEE for research purposes (Ferguson et al. 2015; Lee, Kim, and Welk 2014; Sasaki et al. 2015).

Actiheart (CamNtech) is a multi-sensor device that combines accelerometry with heart-rate monitoring (Assah et al. 2009; Brage et al. 2005; Crouter, Churilla, and Basset 2008). In principle, the combination of multiple methods makes it possible to overcome some of the weaknesses each has when applied on its own. Worn on the chest, Actiheart is attached to adhesive electrodes or mounted on an elastic belt. Because of its small size and flat design, Actiheart is very unobtrusive when participants are not bare-chested or wearing tight-fitting clothing. Male participants with chest hair may be reluctant to use the adhesive mounts, as they must either shave two patches of skin prior to wearing the device, or risk pulling out chest hair when the adhesive patches are removed. Some participants also find the electrodes to be itchy or distracting during sleep. With any heart-rate method, the investigator needs to be cognizant of the widespread use of beta-blockers and other medications that affect heart rate and could therefore influence the estimates of energy expenditure (Butte et al. 2012).

Actical accelerometers, Actiheart monitors, and most other small wearable devices for measuring TDEE come with user-friendly software or web applications that manage data download and report generation. Reports typically present both quantitative results and graphical output as well as the ability to integrate dietary intake and body composition data. Fine-grained reports that show minute-by-minute variation in the intensity of energy expenditure can be useful as prompts for and checks of behavioral or dietary recall interviews, helping to reduce error when the day is reconstructed in an interview focused on food-related behavior, or any kind of behavior.

Two drawbacks associated with the use of small, wearable devices are the absence of universal, transparent standards for calibration and validation (Butte et al. 2012), and the devices' reliance on proprietary algorithms. Regardless, for many research applications, trading off access to the basic data and algorithms for lower cost, less invasiveness, and greater ease of use may be worthwhile. When relying on output from proprietary algorithms, it is particularly important to choose a device that has been well validated with a population whose growth status, reproductive state, and health are similar to those of the population to be investigated. The most useful validation studies will also evaluate the device with respect to a gold standard method such as doubly labeled water or a metabolic chamber rather than indirect calorimetry, and will focus on the outcome variable of interest, such as TDEE in free-living conditions, rather than TEE while at rest or while engaged in a specific activity such as riding an exercise bicycle in a lab. When assessing devices via validation studies, it is important to remember that even the gold standard doubly labeled water method has a precision (the standard deviation of the % difference) of 2–8 percent relative to measurement under laboratory controlled conditions (Schoeller 1988). Slightly higher rates of error for wearable devices, particularly if their estimates are unbiased, will be acceptable for most research applications in the anthropology of food and nutrition.

Conclusion

There is considerable potential for broadening the scope of research in the anthropology of food and nutrition by incorporating activity monitoring and energy expenditure assessment into mixed-methods research designs. The lived experience of physical activity and energy expenditure can be incorporated, empirically and quantitatively, into understandings of food-related behavior, cognition, and culture. Reviewing the record of the day's physical activity with a fine-grained activity log provides an opportunity to probe for food-related behavioral motivations, meanings, and habits. Time-stamped records can reveal temporal behavioral patterns related to food with less recall bias.

Mixed-methods designs, made possible by the increased accessibility of energy expenditure measurement to scholars with only limited expertise in the field of exercise physiology, also have the potential to advance research in applied human energetics. In a world where the default pattern of physical activity for a significant number of people is sedentarism, and where an active lifestyle often requires intentionality, it is essential to understand how we construct meaning around physical activity, how we cognitively model physical activity and energy expenditure, and ultimately why people choose to be active or not. Research designs that include measurement of physical activity and energy expenditure will promote achievement of this goal and the application of findings to advancing public health.

For those who choose to pursue measurement of activity or energy expenditure, the choice of method will involve assessing trade-offs between cost, invasiveness, and the documented validity of the methods in the context of the constraints imposed by the specific research application.

Mark R. Jenike is Associate Professor of Anthropology and Environmental Studies at Lawrence University in Appleton, WI. He received a BA from Harvard University and a PhD from the University of California, Los Angeles. He carried out field research on physical activity and seasonal hunger in the Ituri Forest, Congo, from 1984 to 1990; studied methods of energy expenditure assessment and the nutritional ecology of college students in Claremont, CA, from 1997 to 2004 and in Appleton, WI, between 2007 and 2009; and has been focused on community-based applied nutritional anthropology in Appleton, WI, since 2004. He is currently director of the Office of Community-Based Learning and Research at Lawrence University.

Further Reading

Leonard, W. R. 2010. Measuring Human Energy Expenditure and Metabolic Function: Basic Principles and Methods. *Journal of Anthropological Science: Rivista Di Antropologia* 88: 221–230. http://www.isita-org.com/jass/Contents/ContentsVol88.htm

Medicine & Science in Sports & Exercise 44 (Supplement 1): Objective Measurement of Physical Activity: Best Practices and Future Directions (2012).
Snodgrass, J. J. 2012. Human Energetics. In *Human Biology: An Evolutionary and Biocultural Perspective,* ed. S. Stinson, B. Bogin, and D. O'Rourke, 2nd ed., 325–384. Hoboken, NJ: John Wiley & Sons.

References

Anastaspoulou, Panagiota., Mirnes Tubic, Steffen Schmidt, Ranier Neumann, Alexander Woll, and Sascha Härtel. 2014. Validation and Comparison of Two Methods to Assess Human Energy Expenditure during Free-Living Activities. *PLoS One* 9(2): e90606. doi: 10.1371/journal.pone.0090606
Assah, Felix K., Ulf Ekelund, Soren Brage, Kirsten Corder, Antony Wright, Jean C. Mbanya, and Nicholas J. Wareham. 2009. Predicting Physical Activity Energy Expenditure Using Accelerometry in Adults from sub-Sahara Africa. *Obesity* 17(8): 1588–1595.
Brage, S., N. Brage, P. Franks, U. Ekelund, and N. Wareham. 2005. Reliability and Validity of the Combined Heart Rate and Movement Sensor Actiheart. *European Journal of Clinical Nutrition* 59(4): 561–570.
Brun, Thierry 1992. The Assessment of Total Energy Expenditure of Female Farmers under Field Conditions. *Journal of Biosocial Science* 24(3): 325–333.
Butte, Nancy F., Ulf Ekelund, and Klaas R. Westerterp. 2012. Assessing Physical Activity Using Wearable Monitors: Measures of Physical Activity. *Medicine & Science in Sports & Exercise* 44: S5–S12.
Carmody, Rachel N., and Richard W. Wrangham. 2009. The Energetic Significance of Cooking. *Evolutionary Anthropology* 57(4): 379–391.
Chen, Kong, and David Bassett. 2005. The Technology of Accelerometry-Based Activity Monitors: Current and Future. *Medicine & Science in Sports & Exercise* 37: S490–S500.
Colbert, Lisa H., and Dale A. Schoeller. 2011. Expending Our Physical Activity (Measurement) Budget Wisely. *Journal of Applied Physiology* 111(2): 606–607.
Crouter, Scott E., James R. Churilla, and David R. Bassett Jr. 2008. Accuracy of the Actiheart for the Assessment of Energy Expenditure in Adults. *European Journal of Clinical Nutrition* 62(6): 704–711.
Dannecker, Kathryn L., Nadezhda A. Sazonova, Edward L. Melanson, Edward S. Sazonov, and Raymond C. Browning. 2013. A Comparison of Energy Expenditure Estimation of Several Physical Activity Monitors. *Medicine & Science in Sports & Exercise* 45(11): 2105–2112.
DeLany, James P. 1997. Doubly Labeled Water for Energy Expenditure. In *Emerging Technology for Nutrition Research,* ed. Sydne J. Carlson-Newberry and Rebecca B. Costello, 281–296. Washington, DC: National Academy Press.
DeLany, James P. 2012. Measurement of Energy Expenditure. *Pediatric Blood & Cancer* 58(1): 129–134.
Dufour, Darna L., and Barbara A. Piperata. 2008. Energy Expenditure among Farmers in Developing Countries: What Do We Know? *American Journal of Human Biology* 20(3): 249–258.
Ferguson, Ty, Alex V. Rowlands, Tim Olds, and Carol Maher. 2015. The Validity of Consumer-Level, Activity Monitors in Healthy Adults Worn in Free-Living Conditions: A

Cross-Sectional Study. *International Journal of Behavioral Nutrition and Physical Activity* 12: 42. doi:10.1186/s12966-015-0201-9.

Harris, J. Arthur, Francis G. Benedict. 1918. A Biometric Study of Human Basal Metabolism. *Proceedings of the National Academy of Sciences USA* 4: 370–373.

Intille, Stephen S., Jonathan Lester, James F. Sallis, Glen Duncan. 2012. New Horizons in Sensor Development. *Medicine & Science in Sports & Exercise* 44: S24–S31.

Jenike, Mark R. 1996. Activity Reduction as an Adaptive Response to Seasonal Hunger. *American Journal of Human Biology* 8(4): 517–534.

Jenike, Mark R., and April E. Crofut. 2004. Alternatives to Flex-HR in Longitudinal Studies of Daily Energy Expenditure: Unrecalibrated Flex-HR and % Flex. *American Journal of Human Biology* 16(2): 210.

Kashiwazaki, Hiroshi, Kazuhiro Uenishi, Toshio Kobayashi, Jose O. Rivera, William A. Coward, and Antony Wright. 2009. Year-Round High Physical Activity Levels in Agropastoralists of Bolivian Andes: Results from Repeated Measurements of DLW Method in Peak and Slack Seasons of Agricultural Activities. *American Journal of Human Biology* 21(3): 337–345.

Lee, Jung-Min, Yongwon Kim, and Gregory J. Welk. 2014. Validity of Consumer-Based Physical Activity Monitors. *Medicine & Science in Sports & Exercise* 46(9): 1840–1848.

Leonard, William R. 2003. Measuring Human Energy Expenditure: What Have We Learned from the Flex-Heart Rate Method? *American Journal of Human Biology* 15(4): 479–489.

Leonard, William R. 2012. Laboratory and Field Methods for Measuring Human Energy Expenditure. *American Journal of Human Biology* 24(3): 372–384.

Leonard, William, Victoria Galloway, Evgueni Ivakine. 1997. Underestimation of Daily Energy Expenditure with the Factorial Method: Implications for Anthropological Research. *American Journal of Physical Anthropology* 103(4): 443–454.

Leonard W. R., P. T. Katzmarzyk, M. A. Stephen, and A. G. P. Ross. 1995. Comparison of the Heart Rate-Monitoring and Factorial Methods: Assessment of Energy-Expenditure in Highland and Coastal Ecuadoreans. *American Journal of Clinical Nutrition* 61(5): 1146–1152.

Madimenos, Felicia C., J. Josh Snodgrass, Aaron D. Blackwell, Melissa A. Liebert, and Lawrence S. Sugiyama. 2011. Physical Activity in an Indigenous Ecuadorian Forager-Horticulturalist Population as Measured Using Accelerometry. *American Journal of Human Biology* 23(4): 488–497.

McArdle, William D., Frank I. Katch, and Victor L. Katch. 2014. *Exercise Physiology: Nutrition, Energy, and Human Performance,* 8th ed. Baltimore, MD: Lippincott Williams & Wilkins.

McGarvey, Stephen T., Gabriel Heiderich, Benjamin Rome, Don Vargo, Dale A. Schoeller, Lara Dugas, and Amy Luke. 2011. Exploratory Studies of Doubly-Labeled Water (DLW) and Accelerometry in American Samoan Children. *American Journal of Physical Anthropology* 144(S52): 211.

McLean, J. A., and G. Tobin. 1987. *Animal and Human Calorimetry.* Cambridge: Cambridge University Press.

Meehan, Courtney L., Robert Quinlan, and Courtney D. Malcom. 2013. Cooperative Breeding and Maternal Energy Expenditure among Aka Foragers. *American Journal of Human Biology* 25(1): 42–57.

Mifflin, M., S. St Jeor, L. Hill, B. Scott, . Daugherty, and Y. Koh. 1990. A New Predictive Equation for Resting Energy-Expenditure in Healthy Individuals. *American Journal of Clinical Nutrition* 51(2): 241–247.

Panter-Brick, Catherine. 1996. Seasonal and Sex Variation in Physical Activity Levels among Agro-pastoralists in Nepal. *American Journal of Physical Anthropology* 100(1): 7–21.

Plasqui, Guy, Klaas R. Westerterp. 2007. Physical Activity Assessment with Accelerometers: An Evaluation against Doubly Labeled Water. *Obesity* 15(10): 2371–2379.

Pontzer, Herman, David A. Raichlen, Brian M. Wood, Melissa E. Thompson, Susan B. Racette, Audaz Z. P. Mabulla, and Frank W. Marlowe. 2015. *American Journal of Human Biology* 27(5): 628–637.

Rashid, M., and Stanley J. Ulijaszek. 1999. Daily Energy Expenditure across the Course of Lactation among Urban Bangladeshi Women. *American Journal of Physical Anthropology* 110(4): 457–465.

Sackett, Ross D. 1996. Time, Energy, and the Indolent Savage. PhD thesis. University of California, Los Angeles.

Sasaki, Jeffer E, Amanda Hickey, Marianna Mavilia, Jacquelynne Tedesco, Dinesh John, Sarah K. Keadle, and Patty S. Freedson. 2015. Validation of the Fitbit Wireless Activity Tracker for Prediction of Energy Expenditure. *Journal of Physical Activity and Health* 12(2): 149–154.

Schoeller, Dale 1988. Measurement of Energy-Expenditure in Free-Living Humans by Using Doubly Labeled Water. *J Nutr* 118(11): 1278–1289.

Schoeller Dale 1999. Recent Advances from Application of Doubly Labeled Water to Measurement of Human Energy Expenditure. *Journal of Nutrition* 129(10): 1765–1768.

Schofield, W. N. 1985. Predicting Basal Metabolic Rate, New Standards and Review of Previous Work. *Human Nutrition. Clinical Nutrition* 39C: 5–41.

Schneller, Mikkel B., Mogens T. Pedersen, Nidhi. Gupta, Mette Aadahl, and Andreas Holtermann. 2015. Validation of Five Minimally Obstructive Methods to Estimate Physical Activity Energy Expenditure in Young Adults in Semi-standardized Settings. *Sensors* 15(3): 6133–6151.

Snodgrass, J. Josh 2012. Human Energetics. In *Human Biology: An Evolutionary and Biocultural Perspective,* ed. S. Stinson, B. Bogin, and D. O'Rourke, 2nd ed., 325–384. Hoboken, NJ: John Wiley & Sons.

Spurr, G. B., D. L. Dufour, and J. C. Reina. 1996. Energy Expenditure of Urban Colombian Women: A Comparison of Patterns and Total Daily Expenditure by the Heart Rate and Factorial Methods. *American Journal of Clinical Nutrition* 63: 870–878.

Spurr, G. B., A. M. Prentice, P. R. Murgatroyd, G. R. Goldberg, J. C. Reina, and N. T. Christman. 1988. Energy Expenditure from Minute-by-Minute Heart-Rate Recording: Comparison with Indirect Calorimetry. *American Journal of Clinical Nutrition* 48(3): 552–559.

Ulijaszek, Stanley J. 1995. *Human Energetics in Biological Anthropology.* Cambridge: Cambridge University Press.

Wilson, Hannah J., William R. Leonard, Larissa A. Tarskaia, Tatiana M. Klimova, Vadim G. Krivoshapkin, and J. Josh Snodgrass. 2014. Objectively Measured Physical Activity and Sedentary Behaviour of Yakut (Sakha) Adults. *Annals of Human Biology* 41(2): 180–186.

Yamauchi Taro, Masahiro Umezaki, and Ryutaro Ohtsuka. 2000. Energy Expenditure, Physical Exertion and Time Allocation among Huli Speaking People in the Papua New Guinea Highlands. *Annals of Human Biology* 27(6): 571–585.

CHAPTER 4

Dietary Analyses

Andrea S. Wiley

Introduction

A fundamental question in nutritional anthropology concerns the determinants and consequences of peoples' dietary choices. Yet obtaining a correct and sufficiently precise account of what and how much people eat turns out to be notoriously difficult. As Marion Nestle and Malden Nesheim wrote recently, "we consider finding out what people eat the greatest intellectual challenge in the field of nutrition today" (Nestle and Nesheim 2012: 86). In this chapter I outline the methods available to ascertain dietary intake along with their benefits and shortcomings, highlighting those that are of greatest use to anthropologists working with contemporary humans, and in field settings with minimal technology. Collecting high-quality dietary intake data is the only the first step; those data must then be analyzed for the nutrients or food components of interest (e.g., calories, macro- and micronutrients, or phytochemicals), or to assess dietary diversity or adequacy. Alternatively, biomarkers can be used in some cases if the research questions center around nutritional status rather than diet per se.

Before proceeding with any of the methods described below, researchers should carefully consider what kind of analysis they will pursue with the data collected. Most importantly, they should clearly determine their interest: foods or categories of foods; nutrients and other constituents of foods; evaluation of diet in relation to existing dietary guidance or in relation to nutritional status. If the goal is to document nutrient intake or link it to a biological outcome, then dietary intake data must be converted into nutrients and it becomes especially important to accurately quantify intake. This is done using food composition databases. For other constituents of food such as phytochemicals in plants (e.g., carotenoids, isoflavones, or specific secondary compounds), the available extant data are limited, and laboratory analysis may be necessary. Alternatively, broad patterns of consumption of food may be of interest. In this case, having a reasonably complete inventory of foods is necessary so that the focus can be on the frequency of their consumption over a defined period.

Researchers must also be clear on what they wish to know about diet in a population. Is it overall patterns? Is it documenting variability within the population? Or is it uncovering links between diet and a biological outcome (e.g., a health condition)? Each of these may require a different method or combination of methods, along with different sampling strategies. Depending on the research question, analysis of food groups, foods, and nutrients may be advisable, especially if the goal is to associate intake with a given biological outcome (Willett and Buzzard 1998). Multiple methods also provide a check on the shortcomings of a narrow focus on nutrients (Scrinis 2013). Ultimately, however—and as is the case with most aspects of anthropological research—decisions about methods will be based on what is "practical and feasible in a given situation with limited resources" (Buzzard 1998: 55).

Regardless of which method or combination is used, it is essential to know the dietary context before data collection on individual diets takes place. Although the methods discussed here can be used to gain initial insight into this context, using them effectively to gather accurate data in relation to a specific research question requires some basic ethnographic understanding of the local diet situation, which may stem from preliminary surveys or participant observation. Furthermore, although on the surface a method such as the 24-hour dietary recall might seem "culture free," in fact it requires appropriate prompting for recall of likely moments or items of consumption. These methods have been developed and most widely applied in the United States and other Western industrialized countries. Food frequency questionnaires in particular are culture-bound, as they include lists of foods that are typically consumed by members of a given society as well as typical serving units and utensils. Researchers must have a good idea of what foods are commonly available for consumption as well as those that might be used on special occasions before embarking on detailed surveys of dietary behavior.

Dietary Self-Reports

Self-reported food intake methods are by far the most commonly used means to ascertain food intake in individuals. When used in a sufficiently representative sample, they provide a dietary snapshot of the population of interest. These methods are widely employed because they are relatively cheap in terms of both time and materials required. However, data collected by these methods are vulnerable to error, both patterned and random. There are three basic methods: the 24 hour (24-h) recall, the food record, and the food frequency questionnaire. Ideally the food record is filled out concurrently with consumption, but in practice these are all retrospective methods. A neutral, nonjudgmental attitude on the researcher's part is also essential, as is "buy in" from research participants. For a detailed overview of these methods, see Gibson (1993, 2005), Lee and Nieman (1995), and Willett (1998a); comparisons of the methods can be found in Bingham et al. (1994, see also Bingham 1991). Depending on the research question and resources available, methods can be validated with biomarkers such as urinary nitrogen or doubly labeled water (for protein and energy, respectively).

24-h Recall

Of the three, this method is the simplest and quickest, although it can take around a half hour, especially if the foods consumed contained multiple ingredients and/or were prepared using several different techniques. An individual is asked to report all foods and drinks consumed over the past twenty-four hours, which may proceed from the past to the present or vice-versa, or can instead be a determined time frame—for example, midnight to midnight. The potential shortcomings are twofold: (1) individuals may not remember everything they have consumed, or may be unwilling to report items that they feel the researcher would judge negatively (i.e., foods considered "unhealthy" or inappropriate), resulting in underestimates; and (2) one 24-h window is unlikely to accurately represent an individual's "average" diet. An individual's diet is likely to vary daily, monthly, and seasonally, according to activity and myriad other factors, and these axes of variation themselves differ across groups. For example, seasonality may be a much larger determinant of variability in diet for individuals who produce or forage for most of their food locally, compared to those living in an urban industrialized context. Thus an attempt must be made to cover these sources of variation. In the United States, 24-h recall often generates underestimates of intake by around 30 percent (ranging from 10% to 45% across studies), and the underestimation is greater among older individuals, women, those who are overweight, and those with low income and education. On the other hand, "healthy" foods are often overreported (Buzzard 1998). The 24-h recall also offers advantages, in that respondents need not be literate and dietary behavior is not altered by this activity (although recall of it certainly can be), as it is retrospective.

A 24-hour recall is not simply asking a person to recall everything eaten or drunk over the past twenty-four hours; rather, it involves a series of prompts for contexts in which a person would be likely to eat or drink. A multi-pass method is recommended. First a quick list of foods consumed is generated, followed by a probe for forgotten foods and the time and setting for eating/drinking. Next is the "detail cycle," wherein each food is queried regarding method of preparation (e.g., eaten raw, steamed, sautéed, or deep fried), ingredients, or specific names of commercially prepared foods, amount consumed, and mode of consumption (e.g., whether condiments were used), and the 24-hour period is reaffirmed. The interview ends with a final probe for any items that might have been forgotten (Raper et al. 2004). When children's intake is of interest, usually the primary caretaker answers on behalf of the child.

The 24-h recall requires a priori knowledge about the daily rhythms of consumption common to the group being investigated in order to know what kinds of prompts or context will yield the most accurate accounting. Do people consume foods at discrete "mealtimes" or snack throughout the day? It may be helpful to pair this inquiry with an activity recall to facilitate associations of consumption with activities. It is essential to be as precise as possible about quantities consumed. Consumers generally do not translate amounts eaten into common standard weight or volume units, so it is more appropriate to use local serving-size models that have been calibrated. Cups, bowls, plates, or even models of foods of different sizes can be used to more accurately quantify intake.

For researchers working in the United States and/or with a population that has access to the internet, the National Cancer Institute developed ASA 24, an automated self-administered 24-h diet recall (National Cancer Institute 2012). The anonymity associated with this method (and with an unanticipated telephone interview) may increase accuracy, as recall bias due to the interviewer's presence is diminished. In the U.S. National Health and Nutrition Examination Surveys (NHANES), a 24-h recall is done in person, with a second conducted by telephone 3–10 days after the first one, using the multi-pass method described above. The protocol and measuring guides can be found at: http://www.cdc.gov/nchs/nhanes/measuring_guides_dri/measuringguides.htm.

The question of how many repeated 24-h recalls should be conducted to approach "average" intake is an open one, and depends on the variability in an individual's diet. If the research goal is to describe food or nutrient intake at the population level, collecting one or two 24-h recalls on a large, representative sample may be sufficient, as long as they are collected along the major axes of dietary variation in the population (e.g., each of the seven days of the week). The goal of ascertaining the distribution of intake within a population warrants more 24-h recalls per individual, and they should be distributed (and nonconsecutive) across the relevant time frame. If the research question concerns the relationship between individual intake and a biological outcome, then more 24-h recalls per person are needed to ensure that the estimates are reflective of total diet. If the food or nutrient has high variability in the individual's diet, more days are ideal; however, they are often impractical. In this case, food records or a food frequency questionnaire may provide more appropriate data.

Food Record/Diary

Unlike the retrospective 24-h recall administered by an interviewer, the food record is filled out by respondents themselves. As such it is less vulnerable to memory lapses and bias caused by the presence of the interviewer, and can be used to cover periods of greater length, although it requires a high level of participant motivation. That said, knowing that someone is going to evaluate the record may prompt alterations in eating patterns during the period covered by the records, and there may in fact be lapses between consumption and recording in any case. Further, respondents must generally be literate, and provided with sufficient instructions and training as to the necessary level of detail, especially regarding quantities and ingredients. It may be desirable to provide measuring guides and descriptions, and, to increase accuracy, a scale for the participant to weigh foods on before eating (and after, if the whole portion was not consumed). The investment of time that this requires, as well as any equipment, limits the number of individuals who can be engaged in this exercise simultaneously. Furthermore, this method is subject to the same problem of underestimation as the 24-h recalls, with even motivated subjects underreporting their energy intake by 20 percent or more due to modifications in eating behavior or omissions of foods (Buzzard 1998).

There currently exist numerous ways that individuals can keep records. Traditionally these records were in written form, with participants writing down the foods and quantities consumed as they went along. Food record software is now widely available for computers, PDAs, and smartphones. The increasing use of smartphones in particular has had a dramatic influence on the use of this method. Individuals can take pictures of what they consume, record an oral description, or in many applications, they can record what they eat by choosing from a standardized list of foods. These lists can be customized to reflect favorite foods; in some, new foods can be entered and the software developers will attempt to find nutrient analyses for those. See Rusin, Arsand, and Hartvigsen (2013) for a current review of these options, which have been used in scientific research most frequently with individuals who have health conditions that require close monitoring of their diets, although many individuals use them as an aid to meeting health goals.

Food Frequency Questionnaire

The food frequency questionnaire (FFQ) is useful for ascertaining longer-term dietary patterns of individuals and groups, and although the data an FFQ generates may be cruder than that from 24-h recalls or food records, it is more likely to reflect patterns than episodes of food intake. It uses a predetermined list of foods, usually grouped according to a common theme. Long established food groups are often used in the United States, and FFQs are used to ascertain adherence to food groups established in national dietary guidelines (e.g., Dietary Guidelines for Americans and its visual representation, MyPlate [www.choosemyplate.gov]). Whatever grouping is used should reflect local cognitive categories, or specific research questions (e.g., food might be grouped by density of a specific nutrient of interest), but specific foods and beverages rather than categories should be used in the questions. Again, this list should reflect whether the researcher seeks to give an overall account of dietary patterns that are of interest, or focus on the intake of specific foods or nutrients. The list of foods is usually accompanied by multiple-choice options for frequency of consumption, rather than using an open-ended option. An FFQ must be developed after the researcher has a reasonable understanding of the universe of foods likely to be in the diet, and a basic sense of their importance in the diet. This can be accomplished in various ways, including by using pooled 24-h recalls. The list of foods need not include every possible edible substance: indeed, going through a questionnaire with every possible food, however unusual, is a recipe for participant burnout. Even more focused FFQs require a significant investment of time (over an hour to administer a relatively short FFQ, esp. a semi-quantitative one; see below). Willett (1998b) provides an excellent overview of the benefits and potential pitfalls of FFQs.

The reference period for an FFQ is often one year, to account for seasonal variation, but if month-to-month variation is not high, it can be based on the past month, or any period that is relevant to the outcome of interest. Common options for frequency include never, less than once per month, one to three times per month, once per week, once per day, twice per day, and so forth. The scale should also be developed in relation to the research question—it may or may not be meaningful to know the difference between one or more times per day. For foods that are rarely consumed, it does not make sense to have multiple categories "per day." Conversely, for common foods, several "per day" categories might be appropriate. The FFQ scale should reflect the likely frequency of consumption in the population. Rather than specifying quantities, this form of FFQ shows overall patterns of what foods are consumed and how frequently they can be obtained. As such, it cannot be used to make claims about nutrient sufficiency, although it can be used to address questions related to dietary diversity.

More prevalent is the semi-quantitative FFQ, which combines both quantity and frequency. Units for consumption are usually predetermined and should be typical serving sizes that are easily conceptualized by respondents. Relative terms such as "small," "medium," or "large" should be avoided unless a reference item is used, as individuals may have different perceptions of these. Adding a serving size then allows researchers to calculate nutrient intake from the FFQ, using food composition tables.

Some widely used FFQs developed in the United States are (1) the Harvard School of Public Health's Semi-Quantitative Food Frequency Questionnaire (also known as the Willett FFQ), which has been validated for use in a number of settings (Willett et al. 1985, material available online: https://regepi.bwh.harvard.edu/health/nutrition.html); (2) the Health Habits and History FFQ, also known as the Block FFQ, developed by Gladys Block and colleagues for the National

Cancer Institute (Block et al. 1986; see online resources at http://www.nutri tionquest.com/assessment/); and (3) the Diet History Questionnaire (DHQ) currently used by the National Cancer Institute (http://epi.grants.cancer.gov/ dhq2/). A comparison of the three for use with the Eating at America's Table Study can be found in Subar et al. (2001). The Block and DHQ are available in web-based form, and all can be coupled with nutrient analysis.

Observational Methods and Food Availability Data

Additional observational methods from the participant-observation toolkit well known to anthropologists can also be profitably used to investigate diet. These methods are time-intensive and invasive, insofar as the researcher interacts directly with individuals during periods of food procurement, preparation, and consumption, which may result in deviations from "typical" behavior. This bias can be mitigated in the process of establishing relationships with the community under study, as is typical in ethnographic fieldwork. The intensive nature of this work precludes its use with a large sample size, and days of investigation must be chosen carefully for representativeness. This kind of research often takes the form of recording and/or weighing all foods coming into a household, weighing of amounts used in food preparation, weighing amounts of the final product before each individual consumes a portion, and weighing any food left uneaten. In this way it is possible to gather information on all household members simultaneously. If most consumption occurs within a household, this is an ideal, if cumbersome, method. Although weighed food intake can be part of a self-administered food record, direct observation ensures greater accuracy, assuming researcher bias is not in play.

If household members are absent for long periods during the day, researchers can engage in the same recording and weighing of foods consumed outside of the home by accompanying individuals as they go through their daily activities outside of the household. This method has most often been used among foraging populations (see Berbesque, Marlowe, and Crittenden 2011; Kaplan et al. 1984; Lee 1973). Christine Wilson pioneered this method for use with children, doing what she termed "child following" to gather direct data on food intake about children's consumption of foods outside the home and without adult caretaker oversight (Wilson 1974). Alternatively, at least for adults and possibly older children who are literate and highly motivated to participate in the research, a food record can be kept or the researcher can do a targeted recall covering the time period outside of the home.

As noted above, anthropological studies of foraging or subsistence-level populations have generally relied on observational and weighed food methods, since opportunities for food consumption outside of foraging trips or villages are limited or nonexistent. Depending on cultural norms about food sharing, individual consumption can be deduced from food availability data, collected from observation and weighing of food procured or produced for local consumption. Both spot scans of behavior and intensive observation of individual behavior can provide insight into the relative consumption levels of individuals, which can then be used as a basis for calculating individual intake, although this method is best used to generate community-level consumption estimates.

Food availability data are also available at much larger scales and can be used to calculate rough estimates of per capita consumption. The United States Department of Agriculture (USDA) Economic Research Service maintains a database on food availability in the past and present in the United States, which is adjusted for waste (USDA Economic Research Service 2016). For the past few decades the USDA Foreign Agricultural Service has maintained food production, supply, and distribution databases for other countries as well, although these are not adjusted for population size (USDA FAS 2016). The Food and Agricultural Organization (FAO) of the United Nations maintains a database of national food trends, including production, exports, imports, and consumption, including per capita (see http://faostat.fao.org/).

Diet Analysis

Once dietary data have been collected, the challenge of analyzing them ensues. Researchers often underestimate the effort involved, especially when undertaking nutrient analysis. If intake of specific foods or food groupings is of interest, descriptive analysis is fairly straightforward and consists of summing individual reports and running a variety of descriptive statistics (means, distributions, etc.). If the purpose is to evaluate food intake, reference dietary guidelines can serve as a comparison. The Dietary Guidelines for Americans (United States Department of Health and Human Services and United States Department of Agriculture 2016) are one such reference, but many countries maintain their own national food-based guidelines. The USDA provides links to many of these (USDA 2016), as does the Food and Agriculture Organization (FAO 2016), but as these are not necessarily the most recent versions, researchers should check to see if the country of interest has current guidelines. The Dietary Quality Index (Patterson, Haines, and Popkin 1994) and Healthy Eating Index (HEI; Guenther et al. 2013) are indices that researchers can use to evaluate diets in relation to chronic disease risk or public health nutrition programs, and there is also the Dietary Quality Index-International to facilitate cross-population comparisons of dietary quality (Kim et al. 2003). Indices also exist for the topic of dietary diversity; they can be the total number of different foods or food groups or include quantities as well (cf. Jayawardena et al. 2013; Katanoda, Kim, and Matsumura 2006).

Researchers often want to know about the nutrient composition of the diet, including energy, macronutrients (carbohydrates, fat, and protein, each of which provides energy), and micronutrients (vitamins and minerals). The amounts of these are calculated using food composition tables that are developed and overseen by governmental and private institutions and encompass locally consumed foods in their raw, prepared, or commercially produced forms. Importantly, given the expense of generating a full nutrient profile for any given food, these tables report on foods as they existed at the time of analysis, though there is evidence that nutrient composition among some commercially grown plant foods has changed over time (cf. Davis, Epp, and Riordan 2004). The U.S. Department of Agriculture Agricultural Research Service (USDA ARS 2016) maintains the standard reference for these. It also includes phytochemicals identified as important to human health and nutrition, and is regularly expanded and revised using an established sampling protocol (Pehrsson et al. 2000). The FAO provides a clearinghouse for international food composition tables, including national and regional tables, some of which exist only on hard copy (FAO 2013). If a particular food is not included in any available food composition table, it will need to be sent to an appropriate laboratory for content analysis. Nutrient composition data are made available for most commercially processed foods as mandated by law or subject to national or international guidelines such as the Codex Alimentarius (www.codexalimentarius.org). Those commonly consumed in the United States will likely have entries in the USDA ARS database.

Fortunately, food composition tables are embedded in many 24-h recall or food record software programs, so once the food and quantity consumed are entered, nutrient analysis is available immediately, usually with comparison to established dietary reference values, which vary by country or region. The University of Minnesota Nutrition Data System for Research, which is the research standard for 24-h recall and food record software, uses the USDA ARS database and augments it with foods not available in that database, although it is strongly U.S.-focused (see http://www.ncc.umn.edu/food-and-nutrient-database/). Another option is http://www.myfoodrecord.com/, formerly overseen by the University of Illinois and now available commercially. The USDA database can be used directly with results compared to the U.S. Dietary Guidelines (https://www .supertracker.usda.gov/).

Nutritional Status

The above methods are appropriate for assessing dietary *behavior*. A variety of other methods that are available for assessing the nutritional *status* of individuals can either be combined with dietary data (or correlated with dietary data stemming from the food intake methods described above) or used on their own as an indirect measure of nutrient intake. In the latter case, they are used to make inferences about dietary behavior, based on evidence of an individual's circulating levels, metabolites, or excreted levels or stores of nutrients. See Hedrick et al. (2012) and Potischman and Freudenheim (2003) and the articles in that issue for an assessment of serological or urinary biomarkers for specific nutrients. Such methods may be indirect with respect to dietary behavior, but they are biologically meaningful results of dietary behavior.

The most common of these used by anthropologists is anthropometry, literally the measurement of the body (Lohman, Roche, and Martorell 1988 and Frisancho 1990 provide the standards and rationale for measurements; see also Lieberman in this volume for a more detailed overview). Standard measures include height and weight, as well as various circumferences and skinfolds (subcutaneous fat), all of which are used as markers of energy status. They cannot be used to assess the status of any particular nutrient, but they may be symptoms of certain specific nutrient deficiencies (which themselves may stem from food insufficiency and hence low calorie intake). Height is often used as a measure of nutrient sufficiency in childhood, whereas weight is a marker of current energy stores. While weight and height are relatively easy to measure, taking circumference and skinfold measures requires considerable training, and intra- and inter-rater variability can be high among novices. These measures are used to get an estimate of energy stores (since energy is stored as weight, which can be parsed into lean body mass and fat mass). Body mass index (BMI: weight [kg]/height [m]^2) is a commonly used assessment of energy stores, as it correlates well with fatness, and waist circumference is currently in use to measure abdominal fat, which appears to be a good marker of risk for metabolic and cardiovascular disease. In otherwise healthy adults, weight gain over a period of time is marked by increased BMI and indicates that energy intake exceeds expenditure; obviously weight loss reflects an energy deficit. If doubly labeled water or another accurate assessment of energy expenditure is not available, then weight gain or loss (or changes in BMI) can be a proxy for caloric intake excess or deficit.

Among children, height- and weight-for-age are used to assess growth, with height used as a measure of long-term energy sufficiency/insufficiency, and weight (or weight-for-height) as a measure of current energy stores. An individual's height-for-age, weight-for-age, BMI-for-age, or weight-for-height can be converted to a z-score (deviation from the median) using a reference population or standard. Standards are normative—that is, they describe the range of sizes that are appropriate for healthy children—while references should be used for comparative purposes only. The World Health Organization has developed international standards for the assessment of child growth through 5 years of age, and uses the National Center for Health Statistics data as a reference for children up to 19 years old (WHO Multicentre Growth Reference Study Group 2006). Their software is freely available at: http://www.who.int/childgrowth/software/en/.

Conclusion

In sum, various methods exist for assessment of dietary behavior and nutritional status, but these require careful consideration of their respective utility in relation to research questions. As with any method, researchers are advised to pilot-test their protocols and hone their anthropometric measuring skills before using them in an active study. It is critical that any assessment of dietary behavior be conducted only after the researcher has established a basic understanding of the dietary context for the group under study and, in community studies, a good rapport and commitment from study participants.

Andrea S. Wiley is Professor of Anthropology and Director of the Human Biology Program at Indiana University, Bloomington. She received her PhD in medical anthropology from the University of California, Berkeley and San Francisco, an MA in demography from UC Berkeley, and a BA in the biological basis of behavior at the University of Pennsylvania. She is the author of four books: *Cultures of Milk: The Biology and Culture of Dairy Consumption in India and the United States* (Harvard University Press, 2014), *Re-imagining Milk* (Routledge Press, 2011 [2nd ed. 2016]), *Medical Anthropology: A Biocultural Perspective* (Oxford University Press [with John S. Allen, 3rd ed., 2017]), and *An Ecology of High-Altitude Infancy* (Cambridge University Press, 2004). Her current research focuses on the relationship between milk consumption and child health in the United States and in India. The two countries make an apt comparison as both are major producers of milk and both have cultural and/or religious traditions that privilege milk, yet the cultural and biological contexts in which each promotes and consumes milk are very different. Milk is designed to facilitate the growth and survival of juveniles within a particular mammalian species, yet cow's milk is now widely consumed by humans of all ages. Thus the question is how ongoing consumption of milk alters human life history trajectories. There is also well-described variation in the digestive physiology necessary to consume milk after infancy, yet milk is increasingly consumed in populations with little culinary history of milk. The causes and consequences of such dietary changes are a focus of my research.

References

Berbesque, J. Colette, Frank W. Marlowe, and Alyssa N. Crittenden. 2011. Sex Differences in Hadza Eating Frequency by Food Type. *American Journal of Human Biology* 23(3): 339–345.

Bingham, Sheila A. 1991. Limitations of the Various Methods for Collecting Dietary Intake Data. *Annals of Nutrition and Metabolism* 35(3): 117–127.

Bingham, Sheila A., et al. 1994. Comparison of Dietary Assessment Methods in Nutritional Epidemiology: Weighed Records v. 24 h Recalls, Food-Frequency Questionnaires and Estimated-Diet Records. *British Journal of Nutrition* 72(4): 619–643.

Block, G., A. M. Hartman, C. M. Dresser, M. D. Carroll, J. Gannon, and L. Gardner. 1986. A Data-Based Approach to Diet Questionnaire Design and Testing. *American Journal of Epidemiology* 124(3): 453–469.

Buzzard, Marilyn. 1998. 24-Hour Dietary Recall and Food Record Methods. In *Nutritional Epidemiology*, ed. W. Willett, 50–73. New York: Oxford University Press.

Davis, Donald R., Melvin D. Epp, and Hugh D. Riordan. 2004. Changes in USDA Food Composition Data for 43 Garden Crops, 1950 to 1999. *Journal of the American College of Nutrition* 23(6): 669–682.

FAO (Food and Agriculture Organization). 2016. Food Guidelines by Country. http://www .fao.org/nutrition/nutrition-education/food-dietary-guidelines/en/, accessed 1 September 2016.

———. 2013 International Network of Food Data Systems (INFOODS). http://www.fao .org/infoods/infoods/en/, accessed 1 September 2016.

Frisancho, A. Roberto. 1990. *Anthropometric Standards for the Assessment of Growth and Nutritional Status*. Ann Arbor: University of Michigan Press.

Gibson, Rosalind S. 1993. *Nutritional Assessment: A Laboratory Manual*. New York: Oxford University Press.

———. 2005. *Principles of Nutritional Assessment*. New York: Oxford University Press.

Guenther, P. M., et al. 2013. Update of the Healthy Eating Index: HEI-2010. *Journal of the Academy of Nutrition and Dietetics* 113(4): 569–580.

Hedrick, Valisa, et al. 2012. Dietary Biomarkers: Advances, Limitations and Future Directions. *Nutrition Journal* 11(1): 109.

Jayawardena, Ranil, et al. 2013. High Dietary Diversity Is Associated with Obesity in Sri Lankan Adults: An Evaluation of Three Dietary Scores. *BMC Public Health* 13(1): 314.

Kaplan, Hillard, et al. 1984. Food Sharing among Ache Hunter-Gatherers of Eastern Paraguay. *Current Anthropology* 25(1): 113–115.

Katanoda, K., H. S. Kim, and Y. Matsumura. 2006. New Quantitative Index for Dietary Diversity (QUANTIDD) and Its Annual Changes in the Japanese. *Nutrition* 22(3): 283–287.

Kim, Soowon, et al. 2003. The Diet Quality Index-International (DQI-I) Provides an Effective Tool for Cross-National Comparison of Diet Quality as Illustrated by China and the United States. *Journal of Nutrition* 133(11): 3476–3484.

Lee, Richard Borshay. 1973. Mongongo: The Ethnography of a Major Wild Food Resource. *Ecology of Food and Nutrition* 2(4): 307–321.

Lee, Robert D., and David C. Nieman. 1995. *Nutritional Assessment*. St. Louis, MO: Mosby.

Lohman, Timothy G., Alex F. Roche, and Reynaldo Martorell. 1988. *Anthropometric Standardization Reference Manual*. Champaign, IL: Human Kinetics.

National Cancer Institute. 2012. ASA 24. http://epi.grants.cancer.gov/asa24//. Accessed 1 September 2016.

Nestle, Marion, and Malden Nesheim. 2012. *Why Calories Count: From Science to Politics*. Berkeley: University of California Press.

Patterson, Ruth E., Pamela S. Haines, and Barry M. Popkin. 1994. Diet Quality Index: Capturing a Multidimensional Behavior. *Journal of the American Dietetic Association* 94(1): 57–64.

Pehrsson, P. R., et al. 2000. USDA's National Food and Nutrient Analysis Program: Food Sampling. *Journal of Food Composition and Analysis* 13(4): 379–389.

Potischman, Nancy, and Jo L. Freudenheim. 2003. Biomarkers of Nutritional Exposure and Nutritional Status: An Overview. *Journal of Nutrition* 133(3): 873S–874S.

Raper, Nancy, et al. 2004. An Overview of USDA's Dietary Intake Data System. *Journal of Food Composition and Analysis* 17(3): 545–555.

Rusin, M., E. Arsand, and G. Hartvigsen. 2013. Functionalities and Input Methods for Recording Food Intake: A Systematic Review. *International Journal of Medical Informatics* 82(8): 653–664.

Scrinis, Gyorgy. 2013. *Nutritionism: The Science and Politics of Dietary Advice.* New York: Columbia University Press.

Subar, Amy F., et al. 2001. Comparative Validation of the Block, Willett, and National Cancer Institute Food Frequency Questionnaires: The Eating at America's Table Study. *American Journal of Epidemiology* 154(12): 1089–1099.

United States Department of Health and Human Services, and United States Department of Agriculture. 2016. Dietary Guidelines for Americans. https://health.gov/dietaryguidelines/2015/. Accessed 1 September 2016.

USDA. 2016. Dietary Guidelines from Around the World. http://fnic.nal.usda.gov/professional-and-career-resources/ethnic-and-cultural-resources/dietary-guidelines-around-world. Accessed 1 September 2016.

USDA FAS (United States Department of Agriculture Foreign Agricultural Service). 2016. Production, Supply, and Distribution Online. http://www.fas.usda.gov/psdonline/psdHome.aspx. Accessed 1 September 2016.

USDA ARS (U.S. Department of Agriculture Agricultural Research Service). 2016. USDA National Nutrient Database for Standard Reference, Release 28. Nutrient Data Laboratory Home Page. https://www.ars.usda.gov/northeast-area/beltsville-md/beltsville-human-nutrition-research-center/nutrient-data-laboratory/docs/usda-national-nutrient-database-for-standard-reference/. Accessed 1 September 2016.

USDA Economic Research Service. 2016. Food Availability (Per Capita) Data System. http://www.ers.usda.gov/data-products/food-availability-%28per-capita%29-data-system.aspx#.Ud73Am3lfms. Accessed 1 September 2016.

WHO Multicentre Growth Reference Study Group. 2006. WHO Child Growth Standards: Length/Height-for-Age, Weight-for-Age, Weight-for-Length, Weight-for-Height and Body Mass Index-for-Age: Methods and Development. http://www.who.int/childgrowth/standards/technical_report/en/index.html. Accessed 1 September 2016.

Willett, Walter C. 1998a. *Nutritional Epidemiology.* New York: Oxford University Press.

Willett, Walter C. 1998b. Food Frequency Methods. In *Nutritional Epidemiology,* 2nd ed., ed. Walter C. Willett, 74–100. New York: Oxford University Press.

Willett, Walter C., and Marilyn Buzzard. 1998. Food and Nutrients. In *Nutritional Epidemiology,* 2nd ed., ed. Walter C. Willett, 18–32. New York: Oxford University Press.

Willett, Walter C., et al. 1985. Reproducibility and Validity of a Semiquantitative Food Frequency Questionnaire. *American Journal of Epidemiology* 122(1): 51–65.

Wilson, Christine S. 1974. Child Following: A Technic for Learning Food and Nutrient Intakes. *Journal of Tropical Pediatrics* 20(1): 9–14.

CHAPTER 5

Ethnography as a Tool for Formative Research and Evaluation in Public Health Nutrition

Illustrations from the World of Infant and Young Child Feeding

Sera Young and Emily Tuthill

Ethnography and Formative Research

"Ethnography" comes from Greek for "people" or "culture" (ethnos) and "writing" (grapho). The primary purpose of ethnography can thus be understood to be the written representation of a culture. Although a "culture" may be an entire ethnic group or nation, most ethnography focuses on a subset of such a culture (Emerson, Fretz, and Shaw 1995; Fetterman 2010; Bernard 2011), such as mothers and their children in a Brazilian favela (Scheper-Hughes 1992) or Gogo breastfeeding women in Dodoma, Tanzania (Mabilia and Ash 2005). An ethnographic description of a culture is usually developed through an individual's participation with and observation of that culture during prolonged contact. Traditionally, in anthropology, this has occurred over the course of a year or more, but in the 1980s strategies for "focused" or "rapid" ethnography began to be increasingly incorporated (Scrimshaw and Hurtado 1987; Bentley et al. 1988; Scrimshaw et al. 1991; Pelto and Pelto 1997).

"Formative research" is a term used across many disciplines, including public relations and marketing (Daymon and Holloway 2010), television production (Palmer 1973), and public health (Sussman 2001). Across all of these sectors, "formative research" broadly refers to the use of qualitative and quantitative methods to inform the development of some sort of product. That product may be an advertising campaign, a political candidate's stump speech, television program content, or research surveys. Any subsequent formative research conducted to understand how that product is received could also be considered evaluation (described below).

Standard ethnographic techniques have come to be used frequently in formative research (LeCompte and Schensul 2010). These techniques are well suited to formative research because of their emphasis on careful, objective observation and a paradigm centered on holism. Qualitative approaches such as participant observation, structured and unstructured interviews, focus group discussions (FGDs), and field notes are common (Bernard, 2011). Quantitative ethnographic techniques that help to describe a culture, such as surveys, behavioral checklists, and ranking or grouping exercises (ibid.), are also useful formative strategies, although qualitative ethnographic work is more common and will thus be the focus of this chapter. Mark Nichter (2004) and colleagues have developed a formative research schema that involves eight distinct but interactive stages. Their approach provides a very clear outline of how to develop, design, monitor, and evaluate public health programs.

Evaluation

Like "formative research," evaluation is a term used across many academic disciplines. Evaluation can be broadly defined as any effort to increase effectiveness through systematic, data-based inquiry (Patton 1990). In the social sciences, "evaluation" is often used more specifically to mean "program evaluation"—the activities directed at collecting, analyzing, interpreting, and communicating information about the workings and effectiveness of social programs (Rossi, Lipsey, and Freeman 2004).

The purposes of evaluations are numerous, but they can be broadly classified into five categories (Habicht, Victora, and Vaughan 1999; Rossi et al. 2004):

1. provision: to determine if services are available and accessible;
2. use: to determine if a program is being used by the target population;
3. impact: to determine if a program has resulted in changes to relevant indicators;
4. improvements: to understand how a program should be modified to better achieve its mission; and
5. to assess the cost-effectiveness of the program.

Ethnographic techniques are also well suited to evaluation. For one, ethnographic techniques can yield data that explain the more complex questions of why and how, better than the more "standard" types of data that explain who, where, when, and what. For example, information about community members' perceptions of a program's availability, accessibility, effect, and inadequacies can be more readily obtained from ethnographic techniques such as participant observation, interviews, and FGDs than from surveys or medical records. Secondly, ethnographic techniques are useful in evaluation because of their relatively simple design and application. As such, they may be less daunting than approaches such as epidemiological and econometric evaluation methods, and thus can be more easily implemented.

Although evaluation is the most reliable way to know if a public health intervention or program actually works, the attention and resources it receives have long been incommensurate with its importance. Instead, the development of new technologies (Leroy et al. 2007) and the implementation of public health interventions (Mantell, DiVittis, and Auerbach 1997) have typically been prioritized. Of late, however, the emphasis placed on evaluation appears to be increasing in both public health generally (Rabin et al. 2008) and public health nutrition specifically (WHO and UNICEF 2009). Ultimately the integration of intervention and program implementation with subsequent evaluation provides optimal public health outcomes.

Nutritional Anthropology and Infant and Young Child Feeding Practices

Although many approaches to nutritional and food anthropology are described throughout this volume, it is worth highlighting here what we consider to be four core concepts in nutritional anthropology, and how they are suited to guiding formative and evaluative research. Briefly, they are (1) a biocultural approach, (2) elucidation of emic versus etic understandings, (3) the use of an ecological framework, and (4) the central role of adaptation (Young and Pelto 2012). Rather than define these at length here, we will discuss each as applied to sub-optimal infant feeding behaviors.

Sub-optimal Infant and Young Child Feeding Practices: A Major Public Health Issue

Good nutrition is imperative for health, and optimal infant feeding begins at birth. The World Health Organization (WHO) infant and young child feeding (IYCF) recommendations state that infants should begin breastfeeding within one hour of delivery and be exclusively breastfed (meaning no other foods or liquids except medicines) for six months (WHO and UNICEF 2003). Complementary foods should be introduced in a timely (at 6 months of age), adequate (nutrient-dense, of sufficient quantity and frequency), safe (pathogen- and toxin-free), and fed in an appropriate (in terms of texture and parental responsiveness) manner (Pan American Health Organization 2003). It is also recommended that breastfeeding continue for two years of age or beyond. (For other global IYCF recommendations, see Badham 2013).

These recommendations are based on the short-term and long-term benefits of breastfeeding for both the mother and her infant. For infants, breastfeeding has an unequaled role in reducing morbidities and improving child growth, development, and survival in both resource-limited (WHO Collaborative Study Team 2000) and resource-rich (Stuebe 2010) countries. It reduces the burden of infectious and chronic diseases in infants (Ip et al. 2009) and is also associated with the reduction of a number of maternal health risks (Labbok 2001).

Despite the fact that optimal IYCF is recognized as a fundamental public health strategy for reducing child morbidity and mortality, child malnutrition remains a major public health problem (Jones et al. 2003). In developing countries, approximately 112 million children under five are underweight, and 178 million are stunted (Black et al. 2008). Furthermore, poor nutritional status accounts for roughly a third of deaths in children under five (Pelletier et al. 1995; Black et al. 2003). Much of this morbidity and mortality can be attributed to sub-optimal IYCF practices.

Nutritional Anthropology and Infant and Young Child Feeding Practices

Nutritional anthropology is fundamentally concerned with understanding the interrelationships of biological and social forces that shape human food use and the subsequent nutritional status of individuals and populations (Pelto, Dufour, and Goodman 2012). In other words, it is biocultural. Infant feeding practices are similarly biocultural in that they are shaped by both biological phenomena like maternal health, infant growth, and illness, and social factors such as cultural values, maternal employment, and family structure (van Esterik 2002; Cattaneo 2012; Fouts, Hewlett, and Lamb 2012; Tuthill, McGrath, and Young 2014). Therefore, by understanding both the biological and cultural determinants of IYCF, it becomes possible to understand why these practices often fall short of international recommendations (McElroy 1990; Dettwyler 1994; Fouts et al. 2012).

"Emic" and "etic" are key concepts in much of anthropology, including nutritional anthropology, and are also used by many other social scientists (Headland, Pike, and Harris 1990). "Emic" refers to the perspective of cultural insiders (i.e., definitions and interpretations of reality as seen through local eyes and ideas). The term "etic" is used to refer to the external, analytic perspective that scientists consider when studying cultural and social phenomena. Because people's beliefs about food are central to their nutrition-related behavior, an understanding of emic perspectives is usually an essential step in the design and development of interventions aimed at improving nutrition and thus reducing the burden of human disease. For example, the construction of emic understandings of maternal complementary feeding practices in Morelos, Mexico, is beautifully illustrated by Eva Monterrosa and colleagues (2012).

A third core concept in nutritional anthropology is the ecological framework (Jerome, Kandel, and Pelto 1980; also see Fig. 5.1). This heuristic tool is a guide to identifying the complex social, environmental, and biological determinants of human nutrition. Briefly, the physical, social, ideational, and technological environments are thought to act and be acted upon by individual biological and psychological needs, mediated through diet. (For a more in-depth description of what the various boxes represent, see Jerome et al. 1980 and Young and Pelto 2012).

Applying the ecological framework to understand infant feeding decisions of a hypothetical Mama Sharifa, an HIV-positive Tanzanian woman, and her HIV-uninfected son can help illuminate what may initially seem to be an inscrutable decision.[1] Having exclusively breastfed her son since birth, Sharifa decides to introduce cow's milk to his diet while continuing to breastfeed him (also known as mixed feeding) when he reaches three months of age. Although this decision conflicts with international and Tanzanian recommendations to breastfeed exclusively for six months and increases the infant's risk of becoming HIV-infected and malnourished (Young et al. 2011), this behavior "makes sense" to Sharifa in the context of her ecological model. Not only is she receiving messages from her husband, mother-in-law, and neighbors that she is "starving" her baby by feeding him only breast milk (microlevel social and ideational environments), but previous Tanzanian policy also encouraged HIV-infected mothers to breastfeed for only 3–4 months and then abruptly cease breastfeeding. This message about abrupt cessation continues to be conveyed to new mothers by some clinical staff

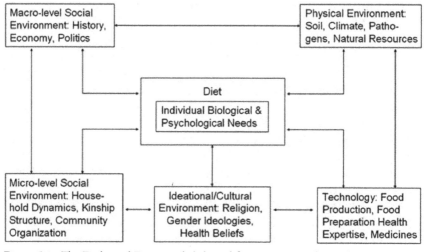

Figure 5.1. The Ecological Framework (adapted from Jerome et al. 1980)

as well as other mothers who were counseled to heed this message (technology and ideational environment). Sharifa is worried about transmitting HIV to her infant and would like to limit her infant's exposure to her breast milk (ideational environment), but she has not disclosed her HIV-positive status to her family, so she is unwilling to explain her concerns (microlevel social environment). Further, she is expected to help prepare the family's land for rice and cassava cultivation, which requires long hours in the fields away from her infant (technological environment), and this work is made more difficult by low rainfall in the past few years (physical environment). Sharifa feels that the stress that her insistence upon exclusive breastfeeding causes, together with her heavy workload and HIV status, is causing her milk to be insufficient to satisfy her baby. For all of these reasons, she decides to add cow's milk to her baby's diet.

Sharifa's responses to these various inputs, for example, how she adjusts her infant's diet to meet his and her needs in the given environments, are emblematic of the fourth core concept in nutritional anthropology: adaptation. Adaptation, or how humans cope and adjust to meet needs, material or otherwise, is of great interest to many nutritional anthropologists (Haas and Harrison 1977; Stinson 1992). Because IYCF practices are exceptionally dynamic and often shaped by myriad unexamined ecological factors, nutritional anthropology and ethnographic techniques are approaches well suited to their study.

Ethnographic Techniques for Formative Research on Infant and Young Child Feeding Practices

The most commonly used ethnographic techniques are (1) unstructured or semistructured interviewing, (2) observation, (3) FGDs, (4) visual techniques, and (5) focused ethnographic methodologies. Each of these will be discussed and applied to IYCF in turn below, with the exception of focused ethnographic methodologies, which is the subject of volume 3, chapter 3.

For all of these techniques, it is important to remember the critical role of the researcher in ethnography. To fully understand, for example, the culture of infant feeding in a particular area, a certain level of familiarity, even intimacy, with participants is requisite. Such knowledge takes time to develop and typically necessitates being physically present. For this reason, when using ethnographic techniques, the researcher him- or herself is seen as an instrument and plays a key role in analyzing and interpreting the ethnographic data collected.

The Ethnographic Interview

Ethnographic interviewing is a frequently used technique in formative research on infant feeding practices (e.g., Buskens, Jaffe, and Mkhatshwa 2007; Levy,

Webb, and Sellen 2010; Taylor et al. 2010). Generally, such interviews are conducted with those who are regularly feeding infants, as well as with key informants or representatives who have some knowledge about or connection with the culture (Spradley 1979). Examples of key informants about IYCF practices include infant feeding counselors; household members such as fathers, siblings, or grandmothers; and community leaders.

Such interviews may be completely unstructured, or they may be rather structured (Polit and Beck 2004). Examples of ways to begin unstructured interviews about infant feeding practices are as simple as "Tell me about your baby" or "Tell me about how you plan to feed your baby after you deliver." Indeed, an ethnographic interview need not always be formal; it can even sound like a casual conversation. As interviews become more structured, that is, guided by a topic list or even a set list of questions, it is important to remember that their purpose is to uncover important themes or experiences that often cannot be determined *a priori* (i.e., they may not be on the checklist). Thus, the researcher must become skillful at keeping the interview germane to the research question while following novel threads that will allow new findings to emerge. There are no rules about the duration of an interview, but ninety minutes seems to be the point at which fatigue or inconvenience begins to set in (Spradley 1979).

Ethnographic interviews may occur over multiple encounters, and the rapport between researcher and respondent will likely evolve over time. As the ethnographic researcher establishes rapport among members of the target culture, interviews may become more formal and more structured; however, if this is done too quickly it may cause informants to feel interrogated (Spradley 1979). Alternatively, a structured interview may feel more comfortable before the interviewer and interviewee know each other well. Follow-up conversations may then become more informal, expanding on what was already formally inquired about, with the respondent feeling more at ease and therefore able to provide richer insights.

Observation

Observation is another useful ethnographic technique in formative research (Spradley 1979). It may happen at a distance, in the form of sitting, observing, and writing notes on infant feeding behaviors, for instance at a prenatal clinic, in an open-air market, at a daycare center, or in a family's home (Levy et al. 2010; Buskens et al. 2007). It may also be more participatory, whereby the researcher both observes and does (Spradley 1979). One example of this transformation is captured in *The Blessings of Motherhood,* in which Anja Krumeich is transformed from observer to participant observer when she becomes a mother while conducting research on child health in Dominica (Krumeich 1994). Ethnographic observation can be labor-intensive, but the observations can be extremely valuable for exploring previous confusions or sparking additional lines of inquiry.

Focus Group Discussions

FGDs are an approach to formative research in which the researcher gathers together a group of people (usually 6–8) to discuss a common issue (Morgan 1997; Krueger and Casey 2009). A facilitator moderates the FGD, keeping participants focused on the topic of interest while promoting dialogue and discussion (Krueger and Casey, 2009).

There are a number of advantages to FGDs. Given that people commonly work and discuss in groups, FGDs can be a very comfortable mode for sharing ideas. They are also a method for hearing the opinions of many individuals in a very short period of time (Krueger and Casey 2009). Further, the group's responses to other participants' comments are often very informative; for example, they can be a metric of how resonant an experience is. For example, in a FGD conducted with HIV-infected mothers and infant feeding counselors about their experiences with breast-milk pasteurization, the dialogue and affirmations between mothers and clinic staff reflected how both parties agreed that HIV stigma had been a major barrier to the practice (Young et al. 2012).

However, FGDs may be less appropriate for sensitive issues or discussion of private matters. They can also be uncomfortable for individuals whose opinions or experiences differ from those of the majority of the group, potentially resulting in an individual remaining quiet. Nonetheless, FGDs have been conducted with many vulnerable populations and about many sensitive subjects. Ultimately, the research team determines how appropriate they are (Liamputtong 2010), and their success relies heavily on the skill of the facilitator. Finally, logistically, they can be difficult to organize.

Visual Techniques

Space precludes enumeration of all ethnographic techniques for studying infant feeding, but an overview would be incomplete without the mention of two visual techniques. One is Photovoice, a participatory technique in which participants photograph images relevant to the area of exploration. These photos are then discussed in one-on-one and then group settings, often with the purpose of eliciting some kind of social change (Wang and Burris 1997). For example, in the San Francisco Bay area Photovoice was successfully used in formative research by eliciting participation among community members to explore key issues in maternal and child health (Wang and Pies 2004).

Many other types of visual records can also provide ethnographic insights, including depictions of infant feeding in movies, commercials, print advertisements, and documentary film. For example, to explore how ecological conditions and cultural values shape infant feeding, Yovsi and Keller (2008) videotaped and coded breastfeeding episodes in rural Cameroon among two ethnic groups: the Fulani, who are pastoral; and the Nso, who are agricultural.

Applying Multiple Ethnographic Techniques in Formative Research

Levy and colleagues' work on infant feeding among HIV-positive women in Malawi is an excellent example of how multiple ethnographic techniques can be used in formative research (Levy et al. 2010). Their study design included participant observation, semistructured interviews (with 34 mothers), FGDs (4 FGDs with 4–6 women per group), and key informant interviews (8 nurses, 2 clinical officers, 3 program leaders, 3 health policy makers, and 4 participants from aid agencies). The purpose of their study was to better understand HIV-positive women's experiences with their infant feeding decisions.

They found that despite a new policy and increased resources for the promotion of exclusive breastfeeding, it had not become the predominant infant feeding practice. Their ethnographic work helped to highlight several reasons for this: (1) confusion about the definition of exclusive breastfeeding, (2) the challenges of weaning, (3) the role of HIV stigma, and (4) the psychosocial burden of "downloaded responsibility" (or the transfer of responsibility from health care providers at the government and clinic level, to the end-users, i.e., mothers, so that the initiation and continuation of exclusive breastfeeding falls solely to the mother; see Levy et al. 2010). Findings from this formative work could then be used to inform policy makers on the current behaviors, experiences, and decisions of HIV-positive women. With this increased understanding, policy makers could decide how to best allocate resources in HIV programs (e.g., staff for counseling, workload, funding) to reduce vertical transmission of HIV.

Ethnographic Techniques to Evaluate Infant and Young Child Feeding Practices

As discussed earlier, all programs should be evaluated, and ethnographic techniques are frequently a useful strategy for such evaluations. In this section, we discuss the utility of ethnography using the examples of evaluating (1) study instruments, (2) program impact of a completed intervention, and (3) an ongoing intervention using mixed-methods designs.

Ethnographic Evaluation of Instruments

There are countless instruments for measuring the impact of an intervention. In the realm of IYCF, for example, we have identified more than thirty scales, surveys, and instruments that assess such characteristics of infant feeding as knowledge, self-efficacy, attitudes, and behaviors among mothers, health care providers, and/or family members (Tuthill, et al. 2016, Casal et al. under review). It must be ascertained that an instrument is valid and data are reliable before they can actually be used in evaluation (McCoach, Gable, and Madura 2013).

Cognitive interviewing could be considered an ethnographic technique useful for refining and improving instrument validity and reliability of data (Willis 2005). In cognitive interviewing, participants are asked a survey question and then asked to describe what they believe the item is asking, how they might rephrase it, and so forth. Those interviews can then be coded and analyzed to identify inconsistent interpretations and more culturally consonant phrasing (e.g., Alaimo 1999; Fein et al. 2008).

Ethnographic Interviews to Evaluate Program Impacts

Ethnographic interviews used in evaluation are more formal than those used in formative work. This is because the researcher is seeking particular understandings (e.g., what works in a given program, what was disliked, what needs modification). Such interviews may therefore take on a more structured approach from the outset.

For example, in a study by Cricco-Lizza (2005), an ethnographic approach was used to better understand the Women, Infants and Children (WIC) program's impact on infant feeding decisions by black inner-city women. In this population, formula feeding was the norm and maternal relationships with health care providers were strained. Two or three semistructured interviews were conducted with eleven key informants (African American women willing to be followed through pregnancy and postpartum). Findings from these interviews highlighted barriers in several areas, from accessing WIC services to the impact services had in terms of influencing breastfeeding decisions. While key informants reported they had learned about the benefits of breastfeeding from WIC staff, some believed that breastfeeding was being promoted as a means to save money rather than provide what they considered to be optimal food (formula) to their infants. Others reported that because WIC distributed formula for free, they "might as well use it." This information was invaluable for explaining why mothers continued to favor formula despite the programmatic efforts; these data could then be used to modify subsequent WIC programs.

A second example comes from work in three southern African countries to evaluate the effectiveness of infant feeding counseling and to inform an intervention aimed at improving this counseling (Buskens et al. 2007). Ethnographic interviews were conducted over a seven-month period with 155 mothers, 31 relatives, 92 health care providers, and 7 traditional healers. The research team analyzed the data using a conceptual framework designed for health policy research by Ritchie and Spencer (1994). Findings highlighted that mixed feeding (i.e., the practice of feeding both breast milk and other foods or fluids to one's infant) was a common behavior among HIV-infected mothers. In addition, numerous barriers to exclusive breastfeeding emerged, including the knowledge and beliefs held by mothers and health care providers regarding HIV transmission risk, limited support from family, hurdles to HIV disclosure, and lack of appropriate complementary foods to follow the then current WHO recommendations about abrupt cessation of breastfeeding. These evaluative data could then be used to inform the development of an intervention aimed at addressing barriers to infant feeding through a counseling intervention.

Ethnographic Evaluation in Mixed-Methods Research

In addition to being conducted as the sole approach to evaluation, ethnographic evaluation can also be used in conjunction with other types of data collection in what is known as a "mixed methods" design. There are many options in mixed methods designs that this chapter will not address, but one option particularly relevant to ethnographic evaluation is an "embedded approach" (Creswell and Clark 2011). In the case of an experimental embedded design, researchers may incorporate the collection of ethnographic data to evaluate the reactions or impressions the target population experiences after participating in an intervention or program (ibid.). Thus applying ethnographic evaluation techniques (e.g., interviews or FGDs) following quantitative data collection denotes an embedded approach. In this scenario, ethnographic evaluation provides supplemental data to enhance the overall understanding of impact an intervention has among its target population. Such mixed-methods approaches are becoming more common in ethnographic evaluation techniques (Bamberger 2012).

For example, an embedded approach applying ethnographic evaluation was used to better understand the impact of the baby-friendly hospital initiative (BFHI) in Australia (Taylor et al. 2010). This ethnographic evaluation took place within the context of a larger study investigating the implementation of BFHI within one Health Service Area in Australia. The BFHI is an initiative of the WHO and UNICEF aimed at increasing breastfeeding; it has accredited more than 20,000 hospitals worldwide (WHO 2009).

Taylor and colleagues conducted five FGDs and forty-seven interviews to understand the perceptions, understandings, and experiences of maternity staff regarding the implementation of BFHI in the neonatal intensive care units (NICU) in four Australian hospitals. Embedded ethnographic techniques revealed staff perceptions of BFHI that were supportive, but suggested the need for increased education and resources as well as context specific guidelines for NICUs and maternity floors. These findings clearly explained the nature of the very real barriers the staff were confronting to other stakeholders in the BFHI. This was an important finding because it identified a structural issue rather than an attitude or belief system that needs changing.

Using Ethnographic Techniques in Your Own Formative or Evaluative Research

As you prepare to use ethnography in your own formative or evaluative research, there are many considerations during the design, implementation, and analytic phases. Space precludes a lengthy discussion of these, but we will leave you with some of the most important questions to consider.

Design

What is the purpose of the research—how would you like your findings to be used?

Will this be formative or evaluative research?

Who will be your audience—program stakeholders, policy makers, scientists, a grant review committee?

What type of data will they be more responsive to, and what type of data will they best understand?

What is the time frame for completion of data collection and analysis?

What are your methodological strengths and weaknesses?

Implementation

Who will conduct the ethnographic data collection?

Are they fluent in the language in which the research is to be conducted?

Are you a cultural insider or outsider?

Will interviews be transcribed (and translated)?

Where will data collection take place?

Analysis and Dissemination

What is your analytic plan?

Will transcripts and notes be coded by hand or using software?

Will study populations have opportunities for feedback on preliminary findings?

How will findings be disseminated to the target population as well as more widely?

Formative and evaluative ethnography is an exciting, valuable approach that permits a deeper understanding of the target population's experiences and the impact of programs and other interventions. The application of formative and evaluative techniques through the lens of nutritional anthropology is likely to lead to great improvements in public health, including in infant and young child feeding.

Dr. Young has an MA in medical anthropology (University of Amsterdam) and a PhD in international nutrition (Cornell University). She has had faculty and fellowship positions at the Universities of California Berkeley, Davis, and San Francisco and Cornell. Currently, she is an Assistant Professor in the Department of Anthropology at Northwestern University. Her work focuses on maternal and child undernutrition in sub-Saharan Africa, with an emphasis on HIV, infant feeding, food and water insecurity, and nonfood cravings (pica). Descriptions of her publications, including her recent book *Craving Earth,* for which she received the Margaret Mead award, can be found at www.serayoung.org.

Dr. Tuthill is a Registered Nurse and has a PhD in nursing (University of Connecticut) She is currently a postdoctoral fellow at the University of California, San Francisco. Her work focuses on maternal and child health in sub-Saharan Africa and domestically with an emphasis on infant feeding, HIV, food insecurity and mental health. Her current work, in sub-Saharan Africa, centers on mother-to-child transmission of HIV and its reduction through safer infant feeding methods.

Acknowledgements

We warmly acknowledge suggestions made by Gretel Pelto. Sera L. Young was supported by NIH K01MH098902. Emily L. Tuthill was supported by NIH F31MH099990. The content is solely the responsibility of the authors and does not necessarily represent the official views of the National Institute of Mental Health or the National Institutes of Health.

Notes

1. Although Mama Sharifa is not a real person, she is realistic in that she represents an amalgamation of women with whom we have worked in sub-Saharan Africa over the last few years.

Key Readings

Bamberger, M. 2012. Introduction to mixed methods in impact evaluation. InterAction and The Rockefeller Foundation. http://www.interaction.org/sites/default/files/Mixed%20Methods%20in%20Impact%20Evaluation%20%28English%29.pdf. Accessed 23 June 2014.

Creswell, J. W., and V. L. P. Clark. 2011. *Designing and Conducting Mixed Methods Research.* Thousand Oaks, CA: Sage.

Dettwyler, K. A. 1989. Styles of Infant Feeding: Parental/Caretaker Control of Food Consumption in Young Children. *American Anthropologist* 91(3): 696–703.

Dettwyler, K. 1994. *Dancing Skeletons: Life and Death in West Africa.* Long Grove, IL: Waveland Press.

LeCompte, M. D., and J. P. Goetz. 1982. Ethnographic Data Collection in Evaluation Research. *Educational Evaluation and Policy Analysis*: 387–400.

Patton M. 1990. *Qualitative Evaluation and Research Methods.* Thousand Oaks, CA: Sage.

Rossi, P. H., M. W. Lipsey, and H. E. Freeman. 2004. *Evaluation: A Systematic Approach.* Thousand Oaks, CA: Sage.

Spradley, J. P. 1979. *The Ethnographic Interview.* Belmont, CA: Wadsworth.

References

Alaimo, K. 1999. Importance of Cognitive Testing for Survey Items: An Example From Food Security Questionnaires. *Journal of Nutrition Education* 31: 269–275.

Badham, J. 2013. Ensuring Optimal Breastfeeding and Improvements in Complementary Feeding to Improve Infant and Young Child Nutrition in Developing Countries. *Maternal and Child Nutrition* 9(1): 1–5.

Bamberger, M. 2012. Introduction to Mixed Methods in Impact Evaluation. *InterAction* and The Rockefeller Foundation. http://www.interaction.org/sites/default/files/Mixed%20 Methods%20in%20Impact%20Evaluation%20%28English%29.pdf. Accessed 23 June 2014

Bentley, M. E., G. H. Pelto, W. L. Straus, D. A. Schumann, C. Adegbola, E. de La Pena, G. A. Oni, K. H. Brown, and S. L. Huffman. 1988. Rapid Ethnographic Assessment: Applications in A Diarrhea Management Program. *Social Science & Medicine* 27: 107–116.

Bernard, R. H. 2011. *Research Methods in Anthropology: Qualitative and Quantitative Approaches,* 5th ed. Lanham, MD: AltaMira Press.

Black R., L. Allen, Z. Butta, L. Caulfield, M. de Onis, M. Ezzati, C. Mathers, and J. Rivera. 2008. Maternal and Child Undernutrition: Global and Regional Exposures and Health Consequences. *The Lancet* 371: 243–260.

Black, R., S. Morris, and J. Bryce. 2003. Where and Why are 10 Million Children Dying Every Year? *The Lancet* 361: 2226–2234.

Buskens, I., A. Jaffe, and H. Mkhatshwa. 2007. Infant Feeding Practices: Realities and Mind Sets of Mothers in Southern Africa. *AIDS Care* 19(9): 1101–1109.

Casal C., A. Lei., S.L. Young, E.L. Tuthill. Under review. A Critical Review Of Instruments Measuring Breastfeeding Attitudes, Knowledge, And Social Support. *Journal of Human Lactation.*

Cattaneo A. 2012. Academy of Breastfeeding Medicine Founder's Lecture 2011: Inequalities and Inequities in Breastfeeding; An International Perspective. *Breastfeeding Medicine* 7: 3–9.

Creswell, J. W., and V. L. P. Clark. 2011. *Designing and Conducting Mixed Methods Research.* Thousand Oaks, CA: Sage.

Cricco-Lizza, R. 2005. The Milk of Human Kindness: Environmental and Human Interactions in a WIC Clinic that Influence Infant-Feeding Decisions of Black Women. *Qualitative Health Research* 15: 525–538.

Daymon. C., and I. Holloway. 2010. *Qualitative Research Methods in Public Relations and Marketing Communications.* New York: Routledge.

Dettwyler, K. 1994. *Dancing Skeletons: Life and Death in West Africa.* Long Grove, IL: Waveland Press.

Emerson, R. M., R. I. Fretz, and L. L. Shaw. 2011. *Writing Ethnographic Fieldnotes,* 2nd ed. Chicago, IL: The University of Chicago Press.

Fein, S. B., J. Labiner-Wolfe, K. R. Shealy, R. Li, J. Chen, and L. M. Grummer-Strawn. 2008. Infant Feeding Practices Study II: Study Methods. *Pediatrics* 122(2): 28–35.

Fetterman, D. M. 2010. *Applied Social Research Methods Series,* vol. 17. Thousand Oaks, CA: Sage.

Fouts, H. N., B. S. Hewlett, and M. E. Lamb. 2012. A Biocultural Approach to Breastfeeding Interactions in Central Africa. *American Anthropologist* 114: 123–136.

Haas, J. D., and G. G. Harrison. 1977. Nutritional Anthropology and Biological Adaptation. *Annual Review of Anthropology* 6: 69–101.

Habicht, J., C. Victora, and J. Vaughan. 1999. Evaluation Designs for Adequacy, Plausibility and Probability of Public Health Programme Performance and Impact. *International Journal of Epidemiology* 28: 10–18.

Headland, T. N., K. L. Pike, and M. Harris. 1990. Introduction: A Dialogue between Kenneth Pike and Marvin Harris on Emics and Etics. In *Emics and Etics: The Insider/Outsider Debate,* 1–2. Thousand Oaks, CA: Sage Publications.

Ip, S., M. Chung, G. Raman, T. A. Trikalinos, and J. Lau. 2009. A Summary of the Agency for Healthcare Research and Quality's Evidence Report on Breastfeeding in Developed Countries. *Breastfeeding Medicine* 4(1): 17–30.

Jerome, N., R. Kandel, and G. Pelto. 1980. An Ecological Approach to Nutritional Anthropology. In *Nutritional Anthropology: Contemporary Approaches to Diet and Culture,* ed. N. Jerome, R. Kangel, and G. H. Pelto, 13–45. Pleasantville, NY: Redgrave.

Jones, G., R. Steketee, R. Black, Z. Bhutta, and S. Morris. 2003. How Many Child Deaths Can We Prevent This Year? *The Lancet* 362: 65–71.

Krueger, R. A., and M. A. Casey. 2009. *Focus Groups: A Practical Guide for Applied Research.* Thousand Oaks, CA: Sage.

Krumeich, A. 1994. *The Blessings of Motherhood: Health, Pregnancy and Child Care in Dominica.* Amsterdam: Het Spinhuis.

Labbok, M. H. 2001. Effects of Breastfeeding on the Mother. *Pediatric Clinics of North America* 48: 143–158.

LeCompte, M. D., and J. J. Schensul. 2010. *Designing and Conducting Ethnographic Research.* Plymouth, MA: Altamira Press.

Leroy, J., J. Habicht, G. H. Pelto, and S. Bertozzi. 2007. Current Priorities in Health Research Funding and Lack of Impact on the Number of Child Deaths per Year. *American Journal of Public Health* 97: 219–223.

Levy, J. M., A. L. Webb, and D. W. Sellen. 2010. "On Our Own, We Can't Manage": Experiences with Infant Feeding Recommendations among Malawian Mothers Living with HIV. *International Breastfeeding Journal* 5: 15.

Liamputtong, P. 2010. *Infant Feeding Practices: A Cross-Cultural Perspective.* New York: Springer.

Mabilia, M., and M. S. Ash. 2005. *Breast Feeding and Sexuality: Behavior, Beliefs and Taboos among Gogo Mothers in Tanzania.* New York: Berghahn Books.

Mantell, J. E., A. T. DiVittis, and M. I. Auerbach. 1997. *Evaluating HIV Prevention Interventions.* New York: Springer.

McCoach, D. B., R. K. Gable, and J. P. Madura. 2013. *Instrument Development in the Affective Domain.* New York: Springer.

Mcelroy, A. 1990. Biocultural Models in Studies of Human Health and Adaptation. *Medical Anthropology Quarterly* 4: 243–265.

Monterrosa, E. C., G. H. Pelto, E. A. Frongillo, and K. M. Rasmussen. 2012. Constructing

Maternal Knowledge Frameworks: How Mothers Conceptualize Complementary Feeding. *Appetite* 59: 377–384.

Morgan, D. L. 1997. *Focus Groups as Qualitative Research.* Thousand Oaks, CA: Sage.

Nichter, M., G. Quintero, M. Nichter, J. Mock, and S. Shakib. 2004. Qualitative Research: Contributions to the Study of Drug Use, Drug Abuse, and Drug Use(r)-Related Interventions. *Substance Use & Misuse* 39: 1907–1969.

Palmer, E. L. 1973. Formative Research in the Production of Television for Children.

Pan American Health Organization. 2003. Guiding Principles for Complementary Feeding of the Breastfed Child. http://whqlibdoc.who.int/paho/2003/a85622.pdf. Accessed 10 June 2014.

Patton, M. 1990. *Qualitative Evaluation and Research Methods.* Thousand Oaks, CA: Sage.

Pelletier, D., E. Frongillo, D. Schroeder, and J. Habicht. 1995. The Effects of Malnutrition on Child Mortality in Developing Countries. *Bulletin of the World Health Organization* 73: 443–448.

Pelto, G. H., D. L. Dufour, and A. H. Goodman. 2012. The Biocultural Perspective in Nutritional Anthropology. In *Nutritional Anthropology,* ed. D. Dufour, A. H. Goodman, and G. H. Pelto, 1–8. New York: Oxford University Press.

Pelto, P. J., and G. H. Pelto. 1997. Studying Knowledge, Culture, and Behavior in Applied Medical Anthropology. *Medical Anthropology Quarterly* 11: 147–163.

Polit, D. F., and C. T. Beck. 2004. *Nursing Research: Principles and Methods,* 7th ed. Philadelphia: Lippincott Williams & Wilkins.

Rabin, B. A., R. C. Brownson, D. Haire-Joshu, M. W. Kreuter, and N. L. Weaver. 2008. A Glossary for Dissemination and Implementation Research in Health. *Journal of Public Health Management Practices* 14: 117–123.

Ritchie, J., and L. Spencer. 1994. Qualitative Data Analysis for Applied Policy Research. In *Analyzing Qualitative Data,* ed. A. Bryman and R. G. Burgess, 173–195. New York: Taylor & Francis.

Rossi, P. H., M. W. Lipsey, and H. E. Freeman. 2004. *Evaluation: A Systematic Approach.* Thousand Oaks, CA: Sage.

Scheper-Hughes, N. 1992. *Death Without Weeping: The Violence of Everyday Life in Brazil.* Berkeley and Los Angeles: University of California Press.

Scrimshaw, S. C., M. Carballo, L. Ramos, and B. A. Blair. 1991. The AIDS Rapid Anthropological Assessment Procedures: A Tool for Health Education Planning and Evaluation. *Health Education Quarterly* 18: 111–123.

Scrimshaw, S. C. M., and E. Hurtado. 1987. *Rapid Assessment Procedures for Nutrition and Primary Health Care.* Los Angeles, CA: University of California Press.

Spradley, J. P. 1979. *The Ethnographic Interview.* Belmont, CA: Wadsworth.

Stinson, S. 1992. Nutritional Adaptation. *Annual Review of Anthropology* 21: 143–170.

Stuebe, A. 2010. The Risks of Not Breastfeeding for Mothers and Infants. *Reviews in Obstetrics and Gynecology* 2: 222–231.

Sussman, S. Y. 2001. *Handbook of Program Development for Health Behavior Research and Practice.* Thousand Oaks, CA: Sage.

Taylor, C., K. Gribble, A. Sheehan, V. Schmied, and Dykes F. 2010. Staff Perceptions and Experiences of Implementing the Baby Friendly Initiative in Neonatal Intensive Care Units in Australia. *Journal of Obstetric, Gynecologic, and Neonatal Nursing* 40: 11.

Tuthill, E., J. McGrath, M. Graber, R. Cusson, S.L.Young. 2016. Breastfeeding Self-efficacy: A Critical Review of Available Instruments. *Journal of Human Lactation* 32(1): 35–40.

Tuthill, E., J. McGrath, and S. Young. 2014. Commonalities and Differences in Infant Feeding Attitudes and Practices in the Context of HIV in Sub-Saharan Africa: A Metasynthesis. *AIDS Care* 26(2): 214–225.

van Esterik, P. 2002. Contemporary Trends in Infant Feeding Research. *Annual Review of Anthropology* 31: 257–278.

Wang, C., and M. A. Burris. 1997. Photovoice: Concept, Methodology, and Use for Participatory Needs Assessment. *Health Education and Behavior* 24: 369–387.

Wang, C. C., and C. A. Pies. 2004. Family, Maternal, and Child Health through Photovoice. *Maternal and Child Health* 8: 95–102.

WHO Collaborative Study Team. 2000. Effect of Breastfeeding on Infant and Child Mortality due to Infectious Diseases in Less Developed Countries: A Pooled Analysis. WHO Collaborative Study Team on the Role of Breastfeeding on the Prevention of Infant Mortality. *The Lancet* 355: 451–455.

WHO. 2009. Baby-Friendly Initiative. *WHO Geneva.* http://www.who.int/nutrition/topics/bfhi/en/. Accessed 12 June 2014

WHO and UNICEF. 2003. *Global Strategy for Infant and Young Child Feeding.* Geneva: WHO.

———. 2009. Strengthening Action to Improve Feeding of Infants and Young Children 6–23 Months of Age in Nutrition and Child Health Programmes, Geneva, 6–9 October 2008: Report of Proceedings. Geneva: WHO. http://whqlibdoc.who.int/publications/2008/9789241597890_eng.pdf. Accessed 10 June 2014.

Willis, G. B. 2005. *Cognitive Interviewing.* Thousand Oaks, CA: Sage.

Young, S. L., S. Leshabari, C. Arkfeld, J. Singler, E. Dantzer, K. Israel-Ballard, C. Mashio, C. Maternowska, and C. Chantry. 2012. Barriers and Promoters of Home-Based Pasteurization of Breastmilk among HIV-Infected Mothers in Greater Dar es Salaam, Tanzania. *Breastfeeding Medicine* 8(3): 321–326.

Young, S. L., M. Mbuya, C. Chantry, E. P. Geubbels, K. Israel-Ballard, D. Cohan, S. Vosti, and M. Latham. 2011. Current Knowledge and Future Research on Infant Feeding in the Context of HIV: Basic, Clinical, Behavioral, and Programmatic Perspectives. *Advances in Nutrition* 2: 225–243.

Young, S. L., and G. H. Pelto. 2012. Core Concepts in Nutritional Anthropology. In *Nutritional Health: Strategies for Disease Prevention,* ed. N. Temple, T. Wilson, and D. R. Jacobs Jr., 523–537. Totowa, NJ: Humana Press.

Yovsi, R. D., and H. Keller. 2008. Breastfeeding: An Adaptive Process. *Ethos* 31: 147–171.

CHAPTER **6**

Primate Nutrition and Foodways

Jessica M. Rothman and Caley A. Johnson

Characterizing Primate Diets

Primates eat a diverse range of foods. These include fruits, leaves, seeds, flowers, gums, tubers, insects, and vertebrates. Most primates can be characterized as herbivores that eat vegetation and fruit, or omnivores that combine plants and animal matter in their diet. Within this assortment, some primates, such as baboons and humans, are generalists with greater flexibility in the types of foods they eat, although they are not especially efficient at eating any one type of food. Other primates are specialists that efficiently exploit a lesser range of foods, like the bamboo lemur, named for its food specialty. Primate diets can usually be predicted by body size and resultant metabolism. Small primates with a high metabolism usually consume more insects than larger primates do, as insects are a good source of energy although hard to gather in quantity. Large primates have a slower metabolism but need a larger amount of food overall. They therefore focus on leaves, which are not as high in energy but are more abundant (Kay 1984). Most primates tend to eat some fruit, which spans the continuum of abundance and nutrition.

Food is a selective force that affects all aspects of animal ecology. Since adequate energy and protein are necessary for survival and reproduction, examining primate diets in relation to their nutritional quality is an important goal of understanding primate population abundance, ecology, and sociality. Many models of primate social organization rely on knowledge of the nutritional properties of foods, and models of primate abundance (Oates 1990; Chapman et al. 2004) and primate social interactions within and between groups are, in part, related to dietary characteristics (Wrangham 1980; Koenig 2002). Examining the nutritional composition of foods is thus key to unraveling the intricacies of primate ecology and social behavior.

Primate nutrition in the wild can be characterized through observation and the collection of foods and feces. By observing primates, we can determine diet composition—the amounts and types of food eaten, including specific food items of specific species (e.g., leaves, fruits, insects). Some researchers have used the time an animal spends feeding on different items to describe diet; this is a measure of foraging effort. Diet composition can also be typified by quantifying the mass (i.e. grams) of food ingested. The best way to estimate nutrient intake is to quantify the amount of food eaten. In describing primate diets through observation, there exists a trade-off between the time spent observing an individual, and the number of individuals to be observed. It is important to consider the hypotheses and questions of interest before determining the methods to be used. The most accurate way to measure the total amount of nutrients a type of primate consumes in a day by is to observe one focal individual over the course of an entire day. To learn about diet diversity in a species or population, the best method would be to scan across individuals, each for a predetermined period of time, to capture food variety. When collecting foods to determine nutrient intake, it is important to record precisely the food species, part, maturation stage of the food item, and location of feeding, as all these elements may affect nutrition in the collected food. Feces can also be used to characterize diet, even in the absence of primate observation. For example, seeds or fibers from plants in dung can be used to identify food. Other methods include the use of DNA and isotopes in feces to determine the identity and types of food consumed (Blumenthal et al. 2012; Pickett et al. 2012).

Digestive Strategies

Primates use a wide variety of digestive strategies and systems to process the foods they eat. An understanding of primate digestion is essential for investigating primate feeding and nutrition because physiology determines how primates will digest foods. In primate diets, higher quality foods are considered those that provide energy and protein without fermentation by symbiotic bacteria. Lower quality foods, such as leaves and fibrous fruits contain higher quantities of difficult to digest plant cell wall (fiber), and require fermentation. To digest lower quality foods, a more extensive digestive system is needed.

In general, insectivorous and frugivorous primates have simple digestive tracts that contain an unsacculated stomach, a short small intestine, and small colon. They also have fast rates of passage through the gut. A fast passage time does not allow for extensive fiber fermentation, but more food can be processed. Conversely, primates that eat leaves must have digestive adaptations for doing so. Leaf-eating primates tend to have a slower passage time that maximizes nutrient efficiency and provides time for symbiotic bacteria to digest food. In a classic

Figure 6.1. Black-and-white colobus monkey (*Colobus guereza*) feeding on young tree leaves

study, Milton (1981) showed that the digestive strategies of the sympatric frugivorous spider monkey and folivorous howler monkey are very different, despite having similar body sizes. Compared to howler monkeys, spider monkeys have a short digestive transit time that is adaptive for quickly passing high-quality, easily digested food through the gut. Howler monkeys have a larger colon and cecum compared to spider monkeys, which allows them to better ferment lower quality, more fibrous leafy foods. However, howler monkeys prefer fruit and eat it whenever possible (Milton 1980). The colobines are also leaf-eating primates, but unlike howler monkeys they have extensive fermentation in a sacculated foregut that hosts fiber-digesting bacteria (Kay and Davies 1994). Other primates that eat mainly leaves and fruit, such as the old world monkeys, some lemurs, and apes, have a large colon or cecum that hosts symbiotic bacteria. Understanding a particular primate's digestive strategy helps to decipher how much energy they obtain from their food. Since fermentation leads to energy gain, a primate with digestive adaptations for fiber fermentation will acquire more energy from a high-fiber food than will a primate without these adaptations. For example, in a study where primates with different digestive strategies were fed the same diet of 30 percent fiber, the simple-stomached animals digested much less of their diet (42%) than the hindgut (61%) and foregut fermenters (81%) (Edwards and Ullrey 1999). This demonstrates the importance of considering primate digestive physiology in estimating the nutritional quality of wild primate diets.

The digestibility of wild primate diets can be estimated without controlled feeding experiments by using internal markers such as lignin, an indigestible component of the plant cell wall that passes through the gut unchanged. When primate diets contain more than 5 percent lignin on a dry-matter basis, it can be used as an internal marker to estimate the diet digestibility, whereby the amount of lignin intake is related to the amount of lignin output (Fahey and Jung 1983; Rothman, Chapman, and van Soest 2012). This requires detailed observations of food intake and the collection of fecal samples (Rothman, Dierenfeld, et al. 2008). Similarly, acid insoluble ash and plant waxes such as n-alkanes can be used as markers of diet intake and digestibility (Mayes 2006; Mayes and Dove 2000).

When it is not possible to estimate diet digestibility using markers, it is nonetheless important to consider the extent of fiber digestion. In many cases, captive studies can provide estimates of digestibility. For example, Campbell and colleagues (Campbell et al. 2000; Campbell et al. 2004) conducted a series of studies that were used to describe the gastrointestinal tract, transit time, and fiber digestibility in a variety of captive lemurs. Because the fiber concentrations of the captive lemur diets were similar to their wild diets, these data on fiber digestibility could be applied to estimate wild lemur nutrition (Irwin et al. 2014). Conklin-Brittain, Knott, and Wrangham (2006) provide an excellent protocol for estimating energy digestibility that is focused on apes but can easily be modified and used for all primates.

Sample Collection and Processing

Determining the nutritional composition of primate diet requires analysis of the food items eaten (typically plant foods and insects). Obtaining the food items that primates consume can be logistically challenging depending on where the primates feed. Researchers often need to collect food samples from high in the tree canopy because that is where the primates feed. There are various methods to climb trees for primate research (Houle, Chapman, and Vickery 2004). For small trees, a tree saw with extender poles can be used to collect fruits and leaves. Terrestrial vegetation can be obtained by using plant pruners and handpicking foods from where the primates are eating. Gums, mushrooms, and berries can be collected by hand (the collector's hands should always be clean and sweat-free to avoid contamination). Methods for capturing and preserving insects include trapping, fogging, and opportunistic collection (Ozanne, Bell, and Weaver 2011). For nutritional analysis, researchers should aim to obtain at least 30–50 g of dry weight of material, depending on the number of analyses to be done. For some succulent plants, this may require collecting up to 500 g of wet weight of a sample, as some plant parts are quite high in water content. Samples should be weighed to 0.01 g immediately after collection, and then weighed again when they are at a constant dry weight in the field.

To get an accurate estimate of what the primate is consuming, the sample collected must be at the same stage as what the primate consumed. For example, if young leaves are eaten, then young leaves, not mature ones, should be collected. Furthermore, the samples should be processed in the same manner in which the primate eats them. For example, if a monkey spits out the seeds of a fruit and ingests only the pulp, then after collection the pulp should be separated from the seed and analyzed. Timely collection after observation is essential. Not only are fruiting and leafing phenology irregular and foods vulnerable to depletion by consumers, but food items can also vary tremendously in their nutritional composition according to differences in season, rainfall, and the specific habitat where the food item is located. Consequently, it is important to collect the samples in the exact location and same time frame as when the animals were eating it (Chapman et al. 2003).

Once primate food samples are collected, the best way to preserve them is to immediately place them in liquid nitrogen, transport them using a dry shipper, and then freeze-dry them. However, obtaining and transporting liquid nitrogen is difficult in field situations. In the absence of liquid nitrogen, samples should be dried as quickly as possible. Optimally, they are dried out of sunlight at 40–50°C using a food dehydrator or propane-powered field oven, or in an enclosed tent. Quick drying of samples prevents mold and halts the continuing enzymatic processes within the plant. Once the samples are completely dry, they should be weighed and stored in sufficiently labeled plastic or paper bags until they can be milled. Most assays require that samples be milled using a cutting mill (Wiley Mill) through a 1 mm screen. Nutritional analyses require a standard particle size because size affects surface area (Rothman et al. 2012; Van Soest 1994).

Nutrient Analysis

Specialized instruments are needed for nutritional analysis, so researchers need to collaborate with a suitable laboratory. Within university settings, animal science and veterinary departments often have animal nutrition labs. Commercial forage laboratories also provide standard nutritional analyses, but these laboratories usually conduct analyses on domestic animal feeds that differ significantly in their structural and chemical properties from the diverse array of fruits, leaves, gums, and insects eaten by primates. Thus, beginners in primate nutrition should additionally consult specialists in wildlife nutritional ecology for advice on how to analyze specific samples of interest. A variety of analytical methods can be used, each with merits and limitations. The Association of Official Analytical Chemists (AOAC) regularly produces handbooks of nutritional protocols. The most recent versions of these texts should be consulted to obtain protocols for various techniques. In addition, a variety of recent publications provide guides and directions for specifically analyzing primate foods (Conklin-Brittain et al. 2006; NRC 2003; Ortmann et al. 2006; Rothman et al. 2012; Rothman, Vogel, and Blumenthal 2013).

A basic nutritional analysis contains information about the carbohydrates, fats, and protein in primate diets. Nonstructural carbohydrates and fats are the main sources of energy, and as described above, fiber can be a substantial energy source depending on physiology. Minerals and vitamins in the diets of primates can also be assessed and may provide important baseline data in healthy populations or information on potential deficiencies where malnutrition is suspected. We do not outline methods for their measurement here, but they can be measured using standard analyses for human and domestic animal foods as outlined by the AOAC handbooks.

Here we provide basic information on the different analytical methods used to estimate the nutrients in primate foods. New methods are available to rapidly assess primate foods using near infrared spectroscopy, and we would encourage researchers who are analyzing large numbers of samples to investigate this method (Ortmann et al. 2006; Rothman, Chapman, et al. 2009). We would also like to mention that a number of methods for procedures to assess the energetic status and protein balance of primates using physiological measures are detailed in other publications (Emery Thompson and Knott 2008; Emery Thompson, Muller, and Wrangham 2012; Higham et al. 2011; Vogel et al. 2012).

Dry Matter

The first step in analyzing samples is to determine dry weight by removing moisture. This step is critical: nutrients are present only in the dry portion, so results of analysis should be expressed on a dry matter basis. To calculate a sample's moisture and dry matter we recommend that the sample be weighed immediately after collection in the field and that later a portion of this sample be dried to constant weight at 105°C. Nutritional results could also be expressed on an organic matter basis, accounting for the ash, or inorganic matter, of the sample (Rothman et al. 2012).

Protein

Proteins may be composed of hundreds of different amino acids that exist in plants. However, only twenty of these amino acids serve a function in animals, ten of which are essential to primates (though it is not known whether colobines may be able to synthesize some amino acids similarly to ruminants; see Milton 1998). The best way to estimate the protein quality is to assess the amino acid composition of primate foods through high-performance liquid chromatography (HPLC).

When this is not possible, it is important to also consider the components of protein that are unavailable for digestion, along with total protein content.

Two procedures are widely used to estimate protein content: the Kjeldahl procedure and the Dumas combustion method. Both of these methods measure the total amount of nitrogen (N) in a sample. Because protein in typical animal feed ingredients contains 16 percent nitrogen, multiplying N x 6.25 roughly estimates the protein composition. However, the nitrogen in wild plants may also be in different forms, such as alkaloids, cyanides, and glucosinolates, which are secondary metabolites of plants. In addition, some of the nitrogen may also be bound to the plant cell wall and unavailable for digestion. Consequently, some authors have proposed using lower conversion factors that account for this unavailable protein, such as 4.3 (Conklin-Brittain et al. 1999; Levey et al. 2000; Milton and Dintzis 1981; Rothman, Chapman, and Pell 2008). The estimates of usable protein can be further refined through an in vitro digestibility assay (DeGabriel et al. 2008), and/or by estimating the amounts of fiber-bound protein (Rothman, Chapman, and Pell 2008).

Fat

At 9 kilocalories per gram (kcal/g), fats are an excellent energy source for primates, which additionally require essential fatty acids, linoleic and linolenic acid. Fat is typically low in primate diets because the primary components—fruit and vegetation—are low in fat (typically 1–5% of the dry weight of a food item), though some fruits can be fatty (e.g., avocados). Seed-eating primates like saki monkeys have a fat-rich diet because seeds in their diets are especially high in fat (Norconk and Conklin-Brittain 2004). Similarly, insectivorous primates' diets are relatively high in fat because insects are fatty compared to plant foods.

The best way to estimate the fat content of primate diets is to quantify the amounts and types of different fatty acids using gas chromatography, but few studies have measured the fatty acid composition of primate diets because this technique is expensive. Most studies use an ether extraction, which is a simple weight-based procedure whereby weighed food samples are placed in hot ether and then removed and re-weighed; the amount of fat is calculated by difference. Although ether extraction provides a good estimate of the fats in animal foods, plants have nonfat components that are also extracted in ether, such as wax, cutin, essential oils, chlorophyll, glycerol, and other compounds. Correction factors can be used to account for these nonfat substances (Palmquist and Jenkins 2003).

Carbohydrates

Nonstructural carbohydrates (NSC) make up a large portion of primate foods and contribute about 4 kcal/g of energy. The NSC are diverse: they can be simple sugars, such as glucose and fructose, or storage compounds such as starch. High-sugar fruits are at a premium and are often highly sought food sources that primates compete over (Chapman, Rothman, and Lambert 2012). There are a number of methods for measuring sugars in primate foods. The most sophisticated method, involving HPLC, separates and quantifies different sugars. Using HPLC is expensive, however, so crude measurements of total sugars are more common: sugars are extracted into a hot water or alcohol solution and assessed via a colorimetric assay. The most popular of these methods are the anthrone method and the phenol sulfuric acid assay (Hall et al. 1999; Rothman et al. 2012). The type of assay chosen should reflect the nature of the samples under study. For example, Chow and Landhausser (2004) developed a method for woody plant tissues that uses different concentrations of reagents to prevent interference with compounds more commonly found in woody plants. These very broad-spectrum assays provide a rough estimate of the sugars in the sample based on a standard like glucose or sucrose. Starches are not commonly found in primate foods except in cases where seeds or underground storage organs are eaten. The concentration of starch in a food is determined by converting the starch to glucose via enzymes and measuring the glucose that is liberated (Hall 2009). A common method for estimating the "total" nonstructural carbohydrates (TNC) is to estimate them by difference. Here, percentages of protein, fat, neutral detergent fiber, and ash are subtracted from 100 percent. This very crude estimation should be avoided where possible because it compounds the inevitable errors associated with each of the other estimations. We suggest that primate researchers follow the methods of Hall and colleagues to determine the NSC in their samples (Hall 2009; Hall et al. 1999).

Animal enzymes cannot digest structural carbohydrates, so any fiber digestion is through fermentation by symbiotic bacteria to provide energy to the host. The digestibility of fiber varies according to digestive strategy. Soluble fiber, which includes the pectins in fruit, is easily digested by symbiotic microbes. Soluble fiber is rarely measured in primate food and is usually lumped into the same measure as TNC because it represents an easily digestible carbohydrate (but see Isbell et al. 2013; Milton 1991). Insoluble fiber, which is more difficult for primates to digest, is more commonly measured by primatologists. There are various ways to measure the insoluble fiber in primate foods, but the standard method is the Van Soest detergent analyses, which measure hemicellulose, cellulose, and lignin (Van Soest, Robertson, and Lewis 1991). This is a useful measurement in relation to primate digestion because hemicellulose and cellulose are usually partially digested, and lignin is indigestible. Out of the various compounds that are recovered in the assays (Van Soest 1994), neutral detergent fiber (NDF) provides a good estimate of the hemicellulose, cellulose and lignin in the sample; acid detergent fiber (ADF) is mainly cellulose and acid detergent lignin (ADL), and the final step in digestion is determining the amount of ADL. The hemicellulose, cellulose and lignin can be estimated by difference (i.e., NDF - ADF = hemicellulose, ADF - ADL = cellulose).

Energy

Primates with a greater net energy gain have increased indices of reproductive success, and energy acquisition is likely an important driver of female social relationships in primates (Borries, Gordon, and Koenig 2013; Koenig 2002). It is essential to consider digestible or metabolizable energy rather than gross energy because gross energy does not consider the portions of energy that can actually be digested by primates. We recommend that primatologists estimate metabolizable energy gains through equations, using an estimated 4 kcal/g for nonstructural carbohydrates and protein, and 9 kcal/g for fats (NRC 2003). The energetic contribution from fiber should be estimated as described above and in Conklin-Brittain et al. (2006).

Secondary Compounds

Secondary compounds or allelochemicals produced by plants are often considered a part of plant herbivory defenses (Waterman et al. 1984). Plant secondary compounds may have costs for primate consumers—including toxic properties in the diet—or benefits like antibacterial and antiparasitic properties. For example, specific bitter-tasting plants that chimpanzees seldom consume unless they have diarrhea are known to have anti-parasitic properties (Huffman 2003). Despite their common occurrence in primate plant foods, such compounds are difficult to measure, and little is known about their effects on primate feeding patterns. Condensed and hydrolyzable tannins, which have the potential to decrease protein digestibility, have been investigated more than other secondary compounds, probably because they are prevalent in primate foods.

To estimate tannins in primate diets, we suggest a three-step method (Rothman, Dusinberre, and Pell 2009). First, for screening samples to see if tannins are present, we suggest extraction in 70 percent aqueous acetone (v/v), and then using the acid butanol assay for condensed tannins and a potassium-iodate assay to screen for hydrolyzable tannins. Second, tannin purification via Sephadex can be used to quantify the amounts of tannins in primate diets. Last, estimations of the biological activity of tannins (e.g., protein-binding ability) could be obtained using the assay described by DeGabriel et al. (2008). A very useful handbook of tannin protocols is available from Ann Hagerman (2011).

Nutritional Frameworks

Animals, including primates, make food choices based on their nutritional needs, their ability to access and digest foods, and the availability of foods in the environment. A number of theoretical nutritional frameworks have attempted to understand, quantify, and predict the ways in which animals interact with their environment through food. One of the most classic means of examining these interactions is optimal foraging theory (OFT; see Stephens and Krebs 1986). OFT models fitness through feeding, whereby animals attempt to maximize their energy intake per unit of time while minimizing potential fitness costs (e.g., predation or toxins in food). OFT assumes that a single food component, usually energy, drives the foraging decisions of animals and acts as a proxy for fitness. OFT has been successfully applied to animals that consume a limited diversity of foods, in which case the rate of energy intake can be a good predictor of diet and foraging behavior. However, examining and predicting nonhuman primate foraging through OFT has been difficult, as primates tend to consume diverse foods with varied spatial abundance, nutrient composition, processing time, and digestibility (Garber 1987). Primate foraging may therefore be better understood when factors such as digestive limitations are taken into account, as well as the multiple fluctuating nutrient needs of the animal, beyond energy (Felton et al. 2009).

Although rarely applied in primate ecology, ecological stoichiometry (ES) is another way for ecologists to study interactions between consumers, food, and the environment (Elser 2006; Sterner and Elser 2002). ES looks at how organisms balance and exchange energy and elements (e.g., carbon, nitrogen, phosphorus) with the environment through ecological interactions such as feeding or decomposition. ES has been used successfully to study many aspects of energy and elemental flow in ecosystems (e.g., nutrient cycling). However, the framework may be difficult to apply to studies of animal nutrition, largely because animals do not interact with foods in their environment based on the balance of individual elements (e.g. carbon : nitrogen) in food, but through nutrient compounds like sugars and proteins (Raubenheimer, Simpson, and Mayntz 2009).

The Geometric Framework of Nutrition (GF) is a graphical approach that identifies how an animal solves the problem of balancing nutrient demands when faced with variation in food availability and composition. The GF may provide a more accurate representation of animal foraging than models that look at how an animal prioritizes one nutritional item (e.g., energy) as this framework can take into account multiple relevant nutrients. A helpful way to visually account for multiple nutrients in foods or the diet of animals, developed for the GF, is the right-angled mixture triangle (Raubenheimer 2011) (Figure 6.2). The GF models the amount of nutrients that an animal must ingest in order to meet its nutrient demands. Where an animal cannot gain all nutrients simultaneously, it may regulate the intake of some nutrients, and thereby "prioritize." For example, mountain gorillas prioritize nonprotein energy rather than available protein when faced with changes in food availability (Rothman, Raubenheimer, and Chapman 2011), and chacma baboons apparently regulate the balance of protein to energy in their diets (Johnson et al. 2013). We suggest that the GF is a useful approach

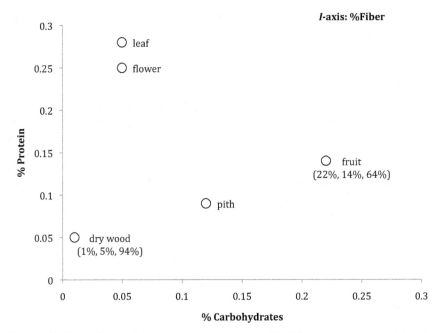

Figure 6.2. Example of a right-angled mixture triangle (RMT) showing three nutritional components of food types eaten by mountain gorillas in Bwindi Impenetrable National Park, Uganda (Rothman, et al. 2006). Protein and carbohydrates are the explicit axes, while fiber is the implicit axis. Protein is estimated from crude protein, non-structural carbohydrates from water soluble carbohydrates and fiber from NDF (see text body for discussion of nutritional measures); percentages are based on % dry matter. Each point represents a nutritional mixture e.g., fruits from the study are proportionally composed of 22% carbohydrates, 14% protein, and the remaining proportion: 100% – (22% +14%) = 64% fiber. The RMT is a simple way to visualize multiple nutrients in graphical space. For example, as predicted for these food types dry wood is low in protein and carbohydrates, but high in fiber. Leaves and flowers are high in protein, and fruit is high in carbohydrates. For more information on RMTs see Raubenheimer (2011).

for exploring the interactive effects of nutrients and understanding how primates balance their diets nutritionally (Raubenheimer et al. 2009).

Jessica Rothman is Professor at Hunter College of the City University of New York. Her research focuses on the nutritional ecology of primates. She is interested in how primates meet their nutritional needs through their environment under a variety of ecological and social constraints.

Caley Johnson is a PhD candidate at the Graduate Center of the City University of New York. Her dissertation focuses on the comparative nutrition of wild baboons in the forest and savannah. She is interested in the intricacies of plant-animal interactions.

References

Blumenthal, Scott A., Kendra L. Chritz, Jessica M. Rothman, and Thure E. Cerling. 2012. Detecting Intraannual Dietary Variability in Wild Mountain Gorillas by Stable Isotope Analysis of Feces. *Proceedings of the National Academy of Sciences of the United States of America* 109: 21277–21282.

Borries, Carola, Adam D. Gordon, and Andreas Koenig. 2013. Beware of Primate Life History Data: A Plea for Data Standards and a Repository. *Public Library of Science One* 8: e67200.

Campbell, Jennifer L., Joan H. Eisemann, Cathy V. Williams, and Kelly M. Glenn. 2000. Description of the Gastrointestinal Tract of Five Lemur Species: *Propithecus tattersalli, Propithecus verreauxi coquereli, Varecia variegata, Hapalemur griseus*, and *Lemur catta. American Journal of Primatology* 52: 133–142.

Campbell, Jennifer L., Cathy V. Williams, and Joan H. Eisemann. 2004. Use of Total Dietary Fiber across Four Lemur Species (*Propithecus verreauxi coquereli, Hapalemur griseus griseus, Varecia variegata*, and *Eulemur fulvus*): Does Fiber Type Affect Digestive Efficiency? *American Journal of Primatology* 64: 323–335.

Chapman, Colin A., Lauren J. Chapman, Lisa Naughton-Treves, Michael J. Lawes, and Lee R. McDowell. 2004. Predicting Folivorous Primate Abundance: Validation of a Nutritional Model. *American Journal of Primatology* 62: 55–69.

Chapman, Colin A., Lauren J. Chapman, Karyn D. Rode, Erin M. Hauck, and Lee R. McDowell. 2003. Variation in the Nutritional Value of Primate Foods among Trees, Time Periods, and Areas. *International Journal of Primatology* 24: 317–333.

Chapman, Colin A., Jessica M. Rothman, and Joanna E. Lambert. 2012. Food as a Selective Force. In *The Evolution of Primate Societies*, ed. John Mitani, Joseph Call, Peter M. Kappeler, Ryne Palombit, and Joan Silk, 149–168. Chicago: University of Chicago Press.

Chow, Pak S., and Simon M. Landhausser. 2004. A Method for Routine Measurements of Total Sugar and Starch Content in Woody Tissues. *Tree Physiology* 24: 1129–1136.

Conklin-Brittain, Nancy L., Ellen S. Dierenfeld, Richard W. Wrangham, Marilyn Norconk, and Scott C. Silver. 1999. Chemical Protein Analysis: A Comparison of Kjeldahl Crude Protein and Total Ninhydrin Protein from Wild, Tropical Vegetation. *Journal of Chemical Ecology* 25(12): 2601–2622.

Conklin-Brittain, Nancy L., Cheryl D. Knott, and Richard W. Wrangham. 2006. Energy Intake by Wild Chimpanzees and Orangutans: Methodological Considerations and a Preliminary Comparison. In *Feeding Ecology in Apes and Other Primates: Ecological, Physical and Behavioral Aspects*, ed. G. Hohmann, M. M. Robbins, and C. Boesch, 445–571. Cambridge: Cambridge University Press.

DeGabriel, Jane L., Ian R. Wallis, Ben D. Moore, and William J. Foley. 2008. A Simple, Integrative Assay to Quantify Nutritional Quality of Browses for Herbivores. *Oecologia* 156: 107–116.

Edwards, Mark S., and Duane E. Ullrey. 1999. Effect of Dietary Fiber Concentration on Apparent Digestibility and Digesta Passage in Non-human Primates II: Hindgut and Foregut Fermenting Folivores. *Zoo Biol.* 18(6): 537–549.

Elser, James. 2006. Biological Stoichiometry: A Chemical Bridge between Ecosystem Ecology and Evolutionary Biology. *American Naturalist* 168: S25–S35.

Emery Thompson, Melissa, and Cheryl D. Knott. 2008. Urinary C-peptide of Insulin as a Non-invasive Measure of Energy Balance in Wild Orangutans. *Hormones and Behavior* 53: 526–535.

Emery Thompson, Melissa, Martin N. Muller, and Richard W. Wrangham. 2012. Variation in Muscle Mass in Wild Chimpanzees: Application of a Modified Urinary Creatinine Method. *American Journal of Physical Anthropology* 149: 622–627.

Fahey, G. C., and H. G. Jung. 1983. Lignin as a Marker in Digestion Studies: A Review. *Journal of Animal Science* 57: 220–225.

Felton, Annika M., Adam Felton, David B. Lindenmayer, and William J. Foley. 2009. Nutritional Goals of Wild Primates. *Functional Ecology* 23: 70–78.

Garber, Paul A. 1987. Foraging Strategies Among Living Primates. *Annual Review of Anthropology* 16: 339–364.

Hagerman, Ann E. 2011. The Tannin Handbook. http://www.users.muohio.edu/hagermae Accessed on September 5, 2016

Hall, Mary Beth. 2009. Determination of Starch, Including Maltooligosaccharides, in Animal Feeds: Comparison of Methods and a Method Recommended for AOAC Collaborative Study. *Journal of AOAC International* 92: 42–49.

Hall, Mary Beth, William H. Hoover, Jocelyn P. Jennings, and Tammy K. Miller Webster. 1999. A Method for Partitioning Neutral Detergent-Soluble Carbohydrates. *Journal of the Science of Food and Agriculture* 79(15): 2079–2086.

Higham, James P., Cedric Girard-Buttoz, Antje Engelhardt, and Michael Heistermann. 2011. Urinary C-peptide of Insulin as a Non-invasive marker of Nutritional Status: Some Practicalities. *PloS One* 6: e22398.

Houle, Alain, Colin A. Chapman, and William L. Vickery. 2004. Tree Climbing Strategies for Primate Ecological Studies. *International Journal of Primatology* 25(1): 237–260.

Huffman, Michael A. 2003. Animal Self-Medication and Ethno-medicine: Exploration and Exploitation of the Medicinal Properties of Plants. *Proceedings of the Nutrition Society* 62(2): 371–381.

Irwin, Mitchell T., Jean-Luc Raharison, David Raubenheimer, Colin A. Chapman, and Jessica M. Rothman. 2014. Nutritional Correlates of the "Lean Season": Effects of Seasonality and Frugivory on the Nutritional Ecology of Diademed Sifakas. *American Journal of Physical Anthropology* 153: 78–91.

Isbell, Lynne A., Jessica M. Rothman, Peter J. Young, and Kathleen Rudolph. 2013. Nutritional Benefits of *Crematogaster mimosae* Ants and *Acacia drepanolobium* Gum for Patas Monkeys and Vervets in Laikipia, Kenya. *American Journal of Physical Anthropology* 150: 286–300.

Johnson, Caley A., David Raubenheimer, Jessica M. Rothman, David Clarke, Larissa Swedell. 2013. 30 Days in the Life: Daily Nutrient Balancing in a Wild Chacma Baboon. *Public Library of Science One* e70383.

Kay, Richard F. 1984. On the Use of Anatomical Features to Infer Foraging Behavior in Extinct Primates. In *Adaptations for Foraging in Nonhuman Primates,* ed. P. S. Rodman and G. H. Cant, 21–53. New York: Columbia University Press.

Kay, Richard F., and A. Glyn Davies. 1994. Digestive Physiology. In *Colobine Monkeys,* ed. A. G. Davies and J. F. Oates, 229–250. Cambridge: Cambridge University Press.

Koenig, Andreas. 2002. Competition for Resources and Its Behavioral Consequences among Female Primates. *International Journal of Primatology* 23(4): 759–783.

Levey, Douglas J., Heidi A. Bissell, and Sean F. O'Keefe. 2000. Conversion of Nitrogen to Protein and Amino Acids in Wild Fruits. *Journal of Chemical Ecology* 26: 1749–1763.

Mayes, Richard W. 2006. The Possible Application of Novel Marker Methods for Estimating Dietary Intake and Nutritive Value in Primates. In *Feeding Ecology in Apes and Other Primates,* ed. G. Hohmann, M. M. Robbins, and C. Boesch, 421–444. Cambridge: Cambridge University Press.

Mayes, Richard W., and H. Dove. 2000. Measurement of Dietary Nutrient Intake in Free-Ranging Mammalian Herbivores. *Nutrition Research Reviews* 13: 107–138.

Milton, Katharine. 1980. *The Foraging Strategies of Howler Monkeys: A Study in Primate Economics.* New York: Columbia University Press.

———. 1981. Food Choice and Digestive Strategies of Two Sympatric Primate Species. *American Naturalist* 117: 496–505.

———. 1991. Pectic Substances in Neotropical Plant Parts. *Biotropica* 23(1): 90–92.

———. 1998. Physiological Ecology of Howlers (*Alouatta*): Energetic and Digestive Considerations and Comparison with the Colobinae. *International Journal of Primatology* 19(3): 513–548.

Milton, Katharine, and Frederick R. Dintzis. 1981. Nitrogen-to-Protein Conversion Factors for Tropical Plant Samples. *Biotropica* 12: 177–181.

Norconk, Marilyn A., and Nancy L. Conklin-Brittain. 2004. Variation on Frugivory: The Diet of Venezuelan White-Faced Sakis. *International Journal of Primatology* 25(1): 1–26.

NRC (National Research Council). 2003. *Nutrient Requirements of Nonhuman Primates.* Washington, DC: The National Academic Press.

Ortmann, Sylvia, Brenda A. Bradley, Caroline Stolter, and Jorg U. Ganzhorn. 2006. Estimating the Quality and Composition of Wild Animal Diets: A Critical Survey of Methods. In *Feeding Ecology in Apes and Other Primates,* ed. G. Hohmann, M. M. Robbins, and C. Boesch, 396–420. Cambridge: Cambridge University Press.

Ozanne, Claire M. P., James R. Bell, and D. G. Weaver. 2011. Collecting Arthropods and Arthropod Remains for Primate Field Studies. In *Field and Laboratory Methods in Primatology,* ed. Joanna M. Setchell and Deborah J. Curtis, 271–285. Cambridge: Cambridge University Press.

Palmquist, D. L., and T. C. Jenkins. 2003. Challenges with Fats and Fatty Acid Methods. *Journal of Animal Science* 81: 3250–3254.

Pickett, Sarah B., Christina M. Bergey, and Anthony Di Fiore. 2012. A Metagenomic Study of Primate Insect Diversity. *American Journal of Primatology* 74: 622–631.

Raubenheimer, David. 2011. Towards a Quantitative Nutritional Ecology: The Right Angled Mixture Triangle. *Ecological Monographs* 81: 407–427.

Raubenheimer, David, Stephen J. Simpson, and David Mayntz. 2009. Nutrition, Ecology and Nutritional Ecology: Toward an Integrated Framework. *Functional Ecology* 23: 4–16.

Rothman, Jessica M., Colin A. Chapman, Julie L. Hansen, Deborah J. Cherney, and Alice N. Pell. 2009. Rapid Assessment of the Nutritional Value of Mountain Gorilla Foods: Applying Near-Infrared Reflectance Spectroscopy to Primatology. *International Journal of Primatology* 30: 729–742.

Rothman, Jessica M., Colin A. Chapman, and Alice N. Pell. 2008. Fiber-Bound Protein in Gorilla Diets: Implications for Estimating the Intake of Dietary Protein by Primates. *American Journal of Primatology* 70: 690–694.

Rothman, Jessica M., Colin A. Chapman, and Peter J. van Soest. 2012. Methods in Primate Nutritional Ecology: A User's Guide. *International Journal of Primatology* 33: 542–566.

Rothman, Jessica M., Ellen S. Dierenfeld, Harold F. Hintz, and Alice N. Pell. 2008. Nutritional Quality of Gorilla Diets: Consequences of Age, Sex and Season. *Oecologia* 155: 111–122.

Rothman, Jessica M., Ellen S. Dierenfeld, Denis O. Molina, Andrea V. Shaw, and Alice N. Pell. 2006. Nutritional Chemistry of Foods Eaten by Gorillas in Bwindi Impenetrable National Park, Uganda. *American Journal of Primatology* 68: 675–691.

Rothman, Jessica M., Kathy Dusinberre, and Alice N. Pell. 2009. Condensed Tannins in the Diets of Primates: A Matter of Methods? *American Journal of Primatology* 71: 70–76.

Rothman, Jessica M., David Raubenheimer, and Colin A. Chapman. 2011. Nutritional Geometry: Gorillas Prioritize Non-protein Energy while Consuming Surplus Protein. *Biology Letters* 7: 847–849.

Rothman, Jessica M., Erin R. Vogel, and Scott A. Blumenthal. 2013. Diet and Nutrition. In *Primate Ecology and Conservation: A Handbook of Techniques,* ed. Eleanor Sterling, Nora Bynum, and Mary Blair, 196–212. Oxford: Oxford University Press.

Stephens, David W., and John R. Krebs. 1986. *Foraging Theory.* Princeton: Princeton University Press.

Sterner, Robert W., and James J. Elser. 2002. *Ecological Stoichiometry: The Biology of Elements from Molecules to the Biosphere.* Princeton: Princeton University Press.

Van Soest, Peter J. 1994. *Nutritional Ecology of the Ruminant.* Ithaca, NY: Cornell University Press.

Van Soest, Peter J., James B. Robertson, and Bertha A. Lewis. 1991. Methods for Dietary Fiber, Neutral Detergent Fiber, and Non-starch Polysaccharides in Relation to Animal Nutrition. *Journal of Dairy Science* 74: 3583–3597.

Vogel, Erin R., Brooke E. Crowley, Cheryl D. Knott, Melissa D. Blakely, Michael D. Larsen, and Nathaniel J. Dominy. 2012. Non-invasive Method for Quantifying Nitrogen Balance in Free-Ranging Primates. *International Journal of Primatology* 33: 567–587.

Waterman, Peter G. 1984. Food Acquisition and Processing as a Function of Plant Chemistry. In *Food Acquisition and Processing by Primates,* David J. Chivers, Bernard A. Wood, Alan Bilsborough eds. 177–211. New York: Plenum Press.

Wrangham, Richard W. 1980. An Ecological Model of Female-Bonded Primate Groups. *Behaviour* 75: 262–300.

CHAPTER 7

Food Episodes/Social Events: Measuring the Nutritional and Social Value of Commensality

Janet Chrzan

> It is perhaps not too much to say that a dinner party, thoroughly good
> in menu, cookery, service ... and in the guests with educated palates,
> affords altogether the strongest everyday evidence of high civilization.
> Brutes feed. The best barbarian only eats. Only the cultured man can
> dine.
>
> —Mallery, "Manners and Meals" (1888)

In the very first volume of The American Anthropologist, Mallery, clearly under the influence of Lewis Henry Morgan, suggests that the essence of civilized
behavior (and thus civilization) is defined by commensality. He argues that the
highest functions of social life (diplomacy, negotiations, and construction of alli-
ances) are conducted while dining with others, and that the amicable and shared
meal is a preeminent sign that a society has reached the state of civilization. Today
we regard the shared meal as the ultimate symbol of the culturally good family
and social life, and the primary space in which to educate children into their roles
as civilized beings (Story and Neumark-Sztainer 2005; Weinstein 2005; Wills et
al. 2013; Skafida 2013). The importance of the shared meal as a cultural symbol
is undisputed and well researched by anthropologists, sociologists and psychologists, but the importance of food sharing to nutritional intake and dietary health
has been of interest for only the last few decades. Most research that examines
commensality, diet, and nutrition has been instigated by psychologists, sociologists, and nutritionists working in teams to measure multiple variables of social
life, economics, and food intake. Food marketers are very interested in how social
eating affects food choice, but that research will not be examined in this chapter

because it assumes an individualistic food choice model that often presupposes adult autonomy in food decision-making. It should be noted that much of the research conducted by non-anthropologists is often part of larger studies designed to examine family life, socioeconomic, and/or health-related barriers to optimal food choice. As a result, there is much room for anthropologists to conduct studies of commensality and diet, either as small-scale fieldwork or in team research on medical and health behaviors.

This chapter examines methods used for measuring the relationships between food sharing, dietary intakes, and other variables in free-living populations. Most research can be grouped into several broad categories, including social facilitation studies, correlation studies, food mapping, and dietary intake studies. Additionally, while conceptual tools to understand food choice and commensality are often focused on macro, meso, and micro social/environmental influences (see Belk 1975; Prattala and Roos 1999; Herman, Roth, and Polivy 2003; Wansink and Sobal 2007; Brug et al. 2008; Larson and Story 2009; De Castro 2010; Fischler 2011), this review concentrates on the micro level to explore how sociality directly affects diet.

Commensality has been demonstrated to influence food intake (De Castro 1990; De Castro and Brewer 1992; De Castro and Plunkett 2002; Herman et al. 2003), especially in families and among friends (De Castro 1994a; Kemmer, Anderson, and Marshall 1998; Sobal and Nelson 2003; Bove, Sobal, and Rauschenbach 2003; Ahye, Devine, and Odoms-Young 2006; Hendy et al. 2009; Pliner and Bell 2009; Pachucki, Jacques, and Christakis 2011; Williams, Veitch, and Ball 2011). Among people who eat together, mechanisms that influence intake include social facilitation, modeling, and impression management, most cogently summed up by Herman and colleagues (2003: 893):

> With only a modest degree of oversimplification, we may conclude that (a) when people eat in groups, they tend to eat more than they do when alone (social facilitation); (b) when individuals eat in the presence of models who consistently eat a lot or a little, these individuals likewise tend to eat a lot or a little, respectively (modeling); and (c) when people eat in the presence of others who they believe are observing or evaluating them, they tend to eat less than they do when alone (impression management).

This text is particularly telling because it embeds a central tenet of social eating research: that individuals choose their foods, and that such choice is deliberate, rational, and knowable to the investigator. In other words, the non-anthropologist's assumption is that individuals choose their foods for specific reasons that accord with a set of food beliefs, goals, and habits, and that the presence of other people somehow warps or alters this purely individualistic, rational, natural process.

The concept of commensality can be roughly reduced to three arenas of variables that include the microsocial, environmental, and macrosocial (Brug et al. 2008; Larson and Story 2009). "Micro-environments are defined as environmental settings in which groups of individuals meet and gather. Such settings are usually geographically distinct and provide opportunities for direct interaction between individuals and the environment. Examples of micro-environments are homes, schools, workplaces, supermarkets, bars and restaurants, recreational facilities, and neighborhoods. Macro-environments encompass the more anonymous infrastructure that may support or hinder energy-balance behaviors. Examples of macro-environments are national or international food and nutrition policies, and the ways food products are marketed, taxed, and distributed" (Brug et al. 2008: 308). Brug and colleagues suggest that four environments (physical, economic, political, and sociocultural) can each be divided into micro and macro-environments depending on the scope of the variable. While the scope and size of such an analysis render it impossible, the suggestion does provide a beginning for characterizing the potential variables for measurement. The authors further propose that each individual whose food choices are affected by environment (in their conceptualization, the environment contains the social world as well) is also governed by moderators, including the social environment (other people's habits and expectations), cognitive characteristics (internal cues, e.g., attitude, perceived control, behaviors, and expectations), and physical satiety. And, as might be expected, in many studies these variables are examined to measure the strength of their influence on food choices made by individuals when they eat with others or when others influence their eating habits. Larson and Story (2009: S57) define these environments similarly: "factors having an influence on food choices in (1) social environments, such as family, peers, and social networks; (2) physical environments (settings), including schools and child care, worksites, retail food stores, and restaurants; and (3) macro-environments, such as socioeconomic status, cultural norms, food marketing, and food and agriculture policy."

These examples demonstrate how some non-anthropologists think through the variables that influence social eating, which clearly arise from a sociological and/or psychological framework. This is due, in part, to seminal articles on consumer behavior by R. W. Belk, who argued that situational choice mechanisms are governed by objective rather than purely psychological variables. Belk (1975: 159) defined five categories of objective variables: physical environment (the built environment), social surroundings (including "other persons present, their characteristics, their apparent roles, and interpersonal interactions"), temporal parameters (season of the year, day of the week, time of day, etc.), task definition (what the person was doing or needed to do that would affect food choice), and antecedent characteristics such as mood and immediately previous experience. More recently, the Hartman Group (2011) and the Cornell Food Choice Research Group (see Sobal et al. 2012) have simplified these fields further, defining the variables as "Where we eat, What we eat, When we eat, Who we eat with and Why we eat." While these broad groupings contextualize the individual within a built and social environment, they also still assume that the individual is making rational choices within a social and environmental framework that influences decision making.

The Anthropology of Commensality

Anthropologists are aware that commensality affects intake—not just because it alters individual choice, but because eating together makes specific foods, in specific quantities, tied to specific social rules about "how to eat," available to members of food-sharing social groups. The study of food sharing is well established in the anthropological literature, but it is often in the abstract rather than the particular. For instance, an established body of research has explored the role of food sharing in evolutionary development (e.g., Hawkes 2003; Lovejoy 2009), and the understanding of food sharing rules as they affect sociality is very robust (e.g., Douglas 1972). Biocultural studies of intake often focus on individual diet to analyze nutritional content of particular meals in relation to overall health. The methods that enable these kinds of research are detailed elsewhere in this volume.

Four examples of food provisioning research illustrate the broader social implications of commensality. In *Foods of Association,* Nina Etkin (2009) reviews the food items that are eaten specifically in shared meals and rituals. She includes ritual foods, medicinal foods, and foods used as a part of temporal or ceremonial celebrations. Many food items are specific to social occasions, either as something intrinsic to such occasions (e.g., a birthday cake) or as a negotiated and habitual part of the larger social rituals (e.g., roast turkey and pumpkin pie at Thanksgiving). Given that many of these foods are high in fats, proteins, and sugars, they usually have some biological importance to dietary health and may contribute significant nutrients. Most importantly, they are often items that are usually eaten in a social setting; one rarely roasts a turkey for oneself, for instance. As a result these festival foods almost always influence dietary intake because they are eaten with others.

A second classic example of food sharing is provided by Miriam Kahn's (1994) ethnography *Always Hungry, Never Greedy,* about the Wamira of New Guinea. The Wamira farm taro and pigs, and like many New Guinea societies have strict rules about food distribution. To be a proper Wamiran person one must share food if asked (ibid.: 41) and portions must be equal (ibid.: 42). The expectation of sharing occurs daily as well as during feasts; it could be argued that hunger cannot exist among the Wamira when food is available because villagers have the right to ask for food when they see a meal being eaten. As in many New Guinea societies, foods have deep and specific symbolic meanings, and different types of feasts—feasts with different social goals—provide specific foods, albeit within the pork/taro/vegetable triad. Kahn documented the foods each person brought to a feast as well as how they were shared and eaten. She was also able to triangulate individual intakes, health/weight status, and portions provided in exchanges. Because the Wamiran people have strong social customs governing food sharing, these exchanges were visible rather than hidden, making the measurement of intakes easier than it might be in many societies. This kind of observation and measurement is standard research protocol for most nutritional and biocultural anthropologists interested in food sharing, but the Wamiran example demonstrates how sociality affects intake because many foods, such as pork, are rarely eaten outside of the social setting, and portions are regulated by social custom.

A third example is foraging, time allocation, and food sharing among the Hadza of Tanzania collected by Kristen Hawkes, James O'Connell, and Nicholas Blurton Jones (1997, 2001a). This comprehensive study generated an enormous amount of information using activity scans of village residents. Visual scans recorded the activities of each person under observation, producing information about what they were doing and with whom, including food sharing and provisioning. Weights of food collected and distributed were recorded, just as they were by Kahn in her study of the Wamira. Weights of all individuals, particularly children, allowed for analyses of weight in relation to food provisioning. This research demonstrated the importance of provisioning by grandmothers and other family members (besides the mother) to the health and well-being of children (Hawkes 2003) as well as the contribution of food sharing to household food provisioning (Weismantel 1989; Hawkes et al. 2001b).

Finally, anthropologists and other investigators recently have been creating food maps to better understand how people navigate physical and social space when acquiring food. Lidia Marte (2007, 2011) mapped spatial and temporal food acquisition and use on both macro (global, regional) and micro (household) levels, using individual cooks as a starting point (Marte 2007: 268). Other researchers have used food maps to illustrate nutrient intakes and the ways they are affected by the presence of other people and by the environment of home, school, work, and so forth (Sevenhuysen and Gross 2003; Albon 2007; Jaeger, Marshall, and Dawson 2009; Sobal et al. 2012). Most of these maps use the meal as a starting point, so as to contextualize each food event with people, place, time, recipes, et cetera. De Castro and his team also used 24-hour recalls and an early form of food mapping to explore mood and situational antecedents to food choice (De Castro et al. 1986; De Castro et al. 1987). They used an enhanced food diary to connect variables to meal events; their methods are outlined in the 1986 article. Food mapping is a robust means to identify the variables that affect food intake, especially when the physical sites are contextualized by linkages with persons or situations, or enhanced through a thick description of the subject's understanding of the food event.

Nutritional and Sociological Studies of Commensality

Social Facilitation

Psychologists have conducted a great many laboratory studies on social facilitation and how the presence of others influences intake (Brian Wansink and the Cornell Food and Brand Lab and the Cornell Food Choice Research Group have provided many of these excellent studies; see Wansink 2006; Wansink and Sobal 2007), but those studies, though interesting as a theoretical understanding of how sociality might affect intake, do not consistently generate information about the specific nutritional consequences of dining with others or being provisioned on a daily basis.

John De Castro has studied the effects of commensality using a diary method to link food events to people, place, and time. He asserts that social eating increases intake primarily because it increases the length of time spent eating (De Castro 1990, 1991, 1994a and b; De Castro and Plunkett 2002; Bell and Pliner 2003), although the number of people at table also increases intake (De Castro and Brewer 1992; Clenenen, Herman, and Polivy 1994). De Castro's methods are best described in his 1986 and 1990 articles, especially since the original study measured macronutrient intakes. The subjects were given "a small pocket sized diary and were instructed to record every item that they either ate or drank, the time they ate it, the amount they ate, and how the food was prepared ... [and] to estimate the amounts that they ate" (De Castro et al. 1986: 26; De Castro 1990). De Castro and his team have since used this diary method (as have many others; see Bellisle and Dalix 1999) to examine a number of variables that relate to eating in groups and alone. Obviously, subjects must be carefully tutored in how to keep an accurate diary (especially if measurement of quantities is required), and all diaries are likely to distort intakes either directly, by altering what people eat in order to look good for the research, or secondarily, by failing to record amounts and food events accurately.

Correlation Studies

Many social eating studies are designed to establish a correlation between a chosen dependent variable and social eating (the independent variable). Such studies are best known for measuring how family meals affect child well-being and health. Unfortunately, establishing causation through such studies is difficult unless the dependent variables are intrinsic to the independent variable, such as dietary intake of macro or micro nutrients. Most studies of this sort run tests for differing variables and then use statistics to see if the correlation is robust. Too often this correlation is then considered causative, especially when trying to establish the positive outcomes of regular family meals. Correlation studies are also found in research designed to elucidate how healthier eating patterns are established, maintained, or implemented.

One of the better known correlation studies is Project EAT (Eating Among Teens), which focused on teenagers to better determine how sociodemographic and behavioral variables affect health and social development. Project EAT measured the number of times a family ate together during the week as well as the frequency of particular meals and fast food meals in relation to dependent variables such as behavioral problems and daily intakes of fruits, vegetables, and nutrients (Neumark-Sztainer et al. 2003; Story and Neumark-Sztainer 2005; Burgess-Champeau et al. 2009; Larson et al. 2009; Neumark-Sztainer et al. 2010). This project was an important and valuable study, but the measurements were largely perceptual: food frequencies were used to establish dietary habits, and potential nutrient intakes and meals were measured; however, their components were not concretely linked to specific meals or social gatherings.

Social eating or the family meal is often considered a variable that promotes healthy eating and is tested against other variables assumed to promote healthy behaviors. It is not uncommon for correlation studies to analyze two perceptual measurements, such as a Likert scaling for choosing low-fat dairy and an estimation of the number of weekly family dinners. One study, for instance, measured the meal preparer's estimated intake of healthy foods against the same person's perception of the meals of other family members, to come to the unsurprising conclusion that the health-related choices of the primary food preparer were similar to the intakes of other family members, and that child fruit and vegetable intakes were influenced by shared meals (Hannon et al. 2003). Another study (Stanton, Green, and Fries 2007) used self-reported food frequency questionnaires to estimate fat and fiber intakes in twelve-year-olds and analyzed them in relation to a Likert scale of perception of family and friend support for healthy eating behaviors. Surprisingly, social support for healthy behaviors was correlated with fiber intake (and inversely correlated with fat intake). That these measures were perceptual rather than a measure of habit and intake was not discussed. Other studies measure sociodemographic or social support variables in relation to dietary behaviors such as fruit and vegetable intake (Videon and Manning 2003; Fowles, Murphey, and Ruiz 2011; Hermstad et al. 2010). Certainly there are well-designed studies demonstrating correlations between family meal frequencies and higher dietary quality among adolescents (Gillman, Rifas-Shiman, and Frazier 2000; Gross, Pollack, and Braun 2010; Skafida 2013), often through a correlation between food frequency data and social variables. There is nothing inherently wrong with correlation studies, but their limitations—that they usually do not measure social eating or provisioning directly—must be fully recognized. The range of variables measured and methods used in correlation studies is listed in Table 7.1.

Methods that Directly Link Social Eating with Outcome Variables

At this point it should be obvious that a large variety of measures and methods are available for examining the dimensions of social eating—and the social and health-related consequences of shared foods. Some direct measurements have already been discussed, particularly those of De Castro, Hawkes et al., and Kahn. However, a few more notable studies provide insight into direct measurement methods. In addition, many of the methods in this volume can be used to measure intake in relation to sociality by collecting data on who, where, and when in tandem with data on the what. One could certainly examine the number of people present at meals per day or week, but this would result in a correlation study. As a result, researchers have struggled to define the optimal unit central to a series of linkages. The Cornell Food Choice Research Group suggests that the best way to organize these data and include situational factors is to isolate what they label a "food event," that is, each time an individual eats or drinks something (Bisogni, Falk, and Madore 2007). By contrast, most nutrition intake information is organized by day or individual food item rather than meal. By focusing on the food event, the researcher is able to create a thick description that includes who, when, where, and what as well as more qualitative information such as why. The report by Bisogni and colleagues provides a comprehensive diagram (ibid.: 221) that maps out almost all of the possible variables available from a food event. Obviously, these data can then be aggregated to provide daily, weekly, or other averages; or they can be coded to provide analyzable numbers that can be compared with the findings of other studies that use daily, weekly, or other frequency measures. For instance, the Cornell team used consecutive 24-hour recalls contextualized with open-ended interviews. Individual methods for the studies discussed in this section can be found in Table 7.2.

De Castro provided some of the earliest and most workable methods for studies of direct commensality by championing a diary method backed by in-depth interviews (De Castro et al. 1986; De Castro and De Castro 1989; De Castro and Brewer 1992; De Castro 1987, 1990, 1991, 1994a, 1994b, 2010; Bellisle and Dalix 1999; Bellisle, Dalix, and Mennen 2003). Though his team's initial interest was in how mood affected food intake, they have since reported on how the number of co-eaters influences intake as well as how intervals between meals affect amounts eaten. Their diary method allows the investigator to aggregate data in various ways, from meal event to daily intake, which can provide more robust analytical opportunities. De Castro provides thoughtful analysis about how researchers can "get at" these kinds of data given the inherent problems of accuracy and analysis (De Castro 1994b, 2010).

The Cornell Food Choice Research Group has been particularly effective in measuring the variables associated with social eating. Their website (http://www.human.cornell.edu/dns/foodchoice/index.cfm) provides a comprehensive set of methods (http://www.human.cornell.edu/dns/foodchoice/frameworks.cfm). The Cornell team has recently published studies that measure food intakes in relation to social context, and their methods include qualitative seven-day, consecutive 24-hour recalls contextualized by interviews and consultations with subjects (Bisogni et al. 2007; Sobal et al. 2012).

Other non-anthropological studies have used similar methods, primarily relying on diary and recalls to generate social eating and dietary intake data. Most also identify the food event as the central node for linkage to social activities and analysis. Jaeger et al. (2009) used online 24-hour recalls to study how place affected intakes of specific types of foods. They also used canonical correspondence analysis to link event categories to other variables for analysis. Canonical correspondence analysis is a form of correspondence analysis that relates one set of categories (e.g., types of foods eaten) to another set of categories (e.g., contextual characteristics of meal occasions). Patel and Schlundt (2001) used diaries to explore how overweight women were affected by environmental cues, specifically those relating to mood and social presence. Similarly, the Ireland Food Consumption Survey (Harrington et al. 2001; Kiely et al. 2001; O'Dwyer, Gibney, and McCarthy 2005) examined adults' eating patterns to examine how location affects intake. They did not examine social eating directly, but they did analyze how the built social environment (workplace, pub, home, friends' homes, etc.) influenced intakes; thus, the social was assumed through location, especially for eating with friends or family. The Stanislaus Family study examined dietary concordance between pairs of children and adults in relation to location, family environment, and shared meals (Vauthier et al. 1996). Similarly, another study correlated shared meals with healthier food intakes by using 24-hour recalls linked to social data (Woodruff et al. 2010). And finally, Makela, Kjernes, and Pipping-Ekstro (1999) used food events as the central data point to elicit how the "eating system" affects intake. Their model includes the "eating pattern (the rhythm and the number of eating events, the alternations of hot and cold eating events), the meal format (the composition of the main course, the sequence of the whole meal) and the social organization of eating (where and with whom people are eating, who did the cooking)" (ibid.: 75). All these studies linked social data to a food event elicited via recall, diary, or interview.

These are, no doubt, only a few of the studies that have examined how social eating influences diet, and they are notably not anthropological studies. They are referenced here because their methods can be adapted for anthropological study and render qualitative/quantitative anthropological studies comparable to studies published in medical and nutrition journals. All link foods eaten to people present, either directly, as in the case of eating together, or indirectly, via provisioning or a social environment such as workplaces and schools. Because of the larger number of subjects in these studies, the researchers tended not to use direct observation, a method preferred in anthropology. Direct observation has been used in many biocultural studies to successfully examine social eating and its consequences, most notably in the anthropological studies described earlier in this chapter. Alternately, a combination of direct observation, diary, recall, and interviews can effectively link eating episodes, social life, and nutritional intakes and outcomes.

A Case Study Example: Dietary Intake, Provisioning, and Maternal and Child Outcomes

To better explore how provisioning from family and friends affects dietary intakes and outcomes during pregnancy, I designed a qualitative/quantitative study of diet, health care, and social life among pregnant teens. I was particularly interested in how provisioning contributed to maternal health and functioning during pregnancy. The core of the study relied on 24-hour recalls that were contextualized by provisioning and commensality data to link the what (food and food event) to the where, when, who (commensality), and how (who provided and/or cooked). See Table 7.3 for a full list of variables.

The "what"—the foods eaten—was queried using standard practices for recalls and coded using the USDA National Nutrient Database. I included food groups as well - and added categories of national and independent fast food restaurants as well as food trucks. The where was open-ended: subjects provided their own interpretation of place, from "school lunchroom" to "grandma's house." These variables were further coded as public sphere, school, work, friends' or family homes, and so on. The when was characterized by time, date, and weekday/weekend. The who, defined as everyone with whom the subject dined, was further contextualized to test the effects of specific social and familial relationships on food intake. For each person, I wanted to know the exact relationship, their generation in relation to the subject, how often they saw or talked to the person, and whether the person lived close to the subject. Later these categories were coded as friend or relative, maternal or paternal, generations up or down, and level of intimacy. Almost all these people were further queried about residency, social support measurements, and provisioning of money, housing, and other goods or services. The how was the person or persons who prepared or provided the meal, and was categorized in the same manner as the who; indeed, there were many overlaps between them.

All data were organized using Access, with the Subject as the connecting node. However, in order to include both the social data and the food data, I embedded an Access database inside another Access database because there was no other way to correctly model the one-to-many and one-to-one relationships. The food events had an Access database that was then linked with the larger database of subject, social, and medical information.

Finally, because this was a qualitative/quantitative study, I also embedded field notes about the subjects and their interviews in Access to make a solid qualitative analysis possible, especially when using the food event as the organizing node. And since Access allows such ease in slicing and dicing the data, the quantitative queries can be repurposed to run a number of different statistics tests.

Janet Chrzan is Adjunct Assistant Professor of Nutrition at the University of Pennsylvania. She received her PhD in physical/nutritional anthropology from the University of Pennsylvania. Her research explores the connections between social activities, nutritional intakes, and maternal and child health outcomes in pregnant teens. She is also interested in the dietary consequences of culinary tourism and the social and nutritional contexts of alcohol intake.

Appendix of Tables

Table 7.1. Correlation Studies

Variables	Methods	Study
Home cooked meals per week, place eaten, missed meals, meal strategies, food choice coping, cluster analysis of eating styles and planning methods	Guided Interview Likert scaling and clustering Subsampled 24 hour recalls, interviews	Blake et al., 2011
Daily servings of F&V, fast food meals/week, snack food frequencies, health efficacy and knowledge, social support for healthy eating from friends and family; barriers to healthy eating	Questionnaires with frequency questions, Likert scaling; all answers relied on subject perceptions	Williams et al., 2011 Williams et al., 2012
Food frequencies, frequencies of family meals, fast food/takeaway, food shopping with family; money spent on food, dieting and smoking behaviors. Body composition.	Self-administered written questionnaire Body Composition (ht, wt, skinfolds) Self-administered food frequency questionnaire	Barker et al., 2000
Food preparers were asked to estimate intake frequencies of high-fat foods, F&V and shared meal frequencies for themselves and their family members	Self-administered food frequency questionnaires Shared meals per week	Hannon et al., 2003
Family social support Food frequencies for fat and fiber	Self-administered healthy eating social support questionnaire Self-administered food frequency questionnaire	Stanton et al., 2007
Dietary intake using FFQ and 24 hour recalls (for validation), Tanner stages, weight and height, behavioral issues, health self-efficacy	Self-administered food frequency questionnaire 24 hour recall Family meal frequencies	Gillman et al., 2000
Average daily F&V consumption, child participation in menu planning and food selection at home, parental modeling, school environment, peer influences	Self-administered food frequency questionnaire Self-administered questionnaire about personal and family food behaviors and attitudes Family structure F&V available in the home	Gross et al., 2010

Variables	Methods	Study
Frequency of family meals Frequency of specific meals and fast food meals	Self-Administered mailed survey Self-administered food frequency questionnaire Self-reported weights, heights, etc.	Project EAT
BMI (Dependent), Weekly frequency of family meals "Quality" of meals – quality conceived of an absence of distractions rather than as dietary quality	Self-reported telephone survey; height and weight were asked to calculate BMI Self-reported weekly frequency of family meals (note: this includes take out and restaurant meals) Self-reported amount of distractions at table (TV, smart phones, etc.)	Berge et al., 2012
Breakfast consumption, frequencies of dairy and F&V, frequency of parental presence at dinner, body perceptions	Intake of F&V and dairy foods were assessed by eliciting recall self-reported frequencies for the previous day Self-reported breakfast frequency and breakfast foods Self-reported weekly numbers of dinners with parent; self-reported parental presence in the home Self-reported body perception	Videon et al., 2003
Meta-analysis of studies with family meal frequencies and outcome variables including weight status, consumption data and/or 'unhealthy eating'	Meta-analysis of 17 studies that reported OR for family meal frequency in relation to the targeted outcome variables	Hammons and Friese, 2011
Food frequencies Shared meal frequencies	Self-reported FFQ plus self - reported estimates of shared meals frequencies; these were dichotomized to construct ratios	Haapalahti et al., 2003
F&V intakes Perceived value of healthy eating, self-efficacy for healthy eating, social support, and home availability and accessibility of foods	Web-based self-reported questionnaire with social support questions, food frequencies and questions about sharing healthy meals and support for healthy eating from friends and family	Youth Eating Patterns (Pearson et al., 2011)
Married mens' perceptions of the family food environment and how their wives influence their diet	Thematic Content Analysis of focus group sessions	Allen et al., 2012
Frequency of consumption of fruit, vegetables, fatty snacks, sweets and fizzy drinks, frequency of snacks of crisps, fruit or sweets between meals. Maternal recall of where, when and with whom children eat	Longitudinal cohort study: structured interviews with mothers at 58 months	Skafida, 2013

(note: not all variables are listed in the table, only those relating to diet and food behavior.
Socio-demographic information was collected by all studies)

Table 7.2. Direct Commensality Methods

Variables	Methods	Study
Foods and beverages consumed, day and hour of consumption, location (where food and beverages were obtained/prepared/consumed), people present, food choice goals, feelings, other activities, and how the participant perceived his/her role in the situation. See Tables 1 and 2 of this report for a full listing of all variables.	Consecutive, qualitative 24-h recalls using a multiple pass approach with open ended questions about each eating or drinking episode. First recall conducted in person and subsequent recalls were done by telephone.	Cornell Food Choice Research Group (Bisogni et al., 2007; Sobal et al., 2012)
All foods and liquids, time ingested, recipes, amount eaten, how food was prepared, co-eaters, number of males and females and their relation with the subject, affective emotional physical states, hunger levels, mood, perception of palatability, place of eating, supplements taken	Seven-day food diary (small, pocket-sized) Photos were taken of meals before and after to estimate amounts eaten Food measurements (cups, grams, liters, etc.) Open-ended, in depth interviews about the diary entries	De Castro et al.
Subjects' food event naming categories, primary, secondary and tertiary foods eaten plus all liquids, and for each food event the following where elicited: time, number of previous meals eaten that day, whether the meal was cold, warm or 'a mix', location in general, specific location (e.g., kitchen, living room, bedroom), specific circumstances of the meal (e.g., on foot, watching TV, sitting by a computer) and who prepared the meal	Online 24 hour recall with open-ended categories for subjects to include qualitative information	Jaeger et al., 2009
Type of meal, with whom they ate, place, time, date and day. Subjects checked any of 18 possible adjectives to indicate how they felt physically and emotionally during each eating episode.	Eating Diaries: subjects were given booklets containing pages for recording information about their food intake. Subjects were trained to measure and record properly by a nutritionist prior to using the diaries.	Patel and Schlundt (2001)
Foods eaten, where eaten, who prepared the food, the day, date, time, location and meal type of each food event. Respondents provided a description of the food, quantity, cooking method and recipes	7 day food diary Questionnaires on socio-demographic information, activity levels, and attitudes toward food	Ireland Food Consumption Survey

Foods eaten, meal type, location, schedules of meals, social environment of meals, number of meals per week shared by each pair of relatives	3 day food diary (children and parents), followed by review by dietician. Open-ended interviews with families about meal habits in relation to the diary records	The Stanislas Family Study
Foods eaten, meal type, people present during meals, self-reported height and weight	Single 24 hour recall with multiple choice questionnaire to elicit social data	Woodruff et al., 2010
Foods eaten including meal composition and sequences, location, with whom people ate, who cooked and open ended questions about food culture	24 hour recalls with questionnaires conducted via telephone and computer	Makela et al., 1999

Table 7.3. Chrzan Study

Variable	Method
What (food)	24 hour recall (7-10 per subject)
When: time of day	Meal and hour
Where: subject's categories, further coded as home, work, school, friends' houses, family members' houses (maternal, paternal relatives and their degree of kinship), restaurant, types of restaurant	Open ended Questionnaire, later coded
Time: meal event name, time of day, day of week and calendar date, subject's name for the time/event	Open ended Questionnaire, later coded
Who: name, relationship, gender, proximity (kinship), proximity (degree of friendship), generation, frequency of contact	Open ended Questionnaire, later coded
How: who prepared or paid for the meal; name, relationship, gender, proximity (kinship), proximity (degree of friendship), generation, frequency of contact. Also monetary support in general that might be used for food	Open ended Questionnaire, later coded
Height, weight, skinfolds	Standard anthropometry

References

Ahye, Brenda, Carol Devine, and Angela Odoms-Young. 2006. Values Expressed through In-
    tergenerational Family Food and Nutrition Management Systems among African Ameri-
    can Women. *Family and Community Health* 29(1): 5–16.
Albon, Deborah. 2007. Exploring Food and Eating Patterns Using Food-Maps. *Nutrition &*
    Food Science 37(4): 254–259.
Belk, Russell W. 1975. Situational Variables and Consumer Behavior. *Journal of Consumer*
    Research 2(3): 157–164.
Bell, R., and P. L. Pliner. 2003. Time to Eat: The Relationship between the Number of People
    Eating and Meal Duration in Three Lunch Settings. *Appetite* 41: 215–218.
Bellisle, F., and A.-M. Dalix. 1999. Eating Patterns in French Subjects Studied by the "Weekly
    Food Diary" Method. *Appetite* 32: 46–52.
Bellisle, F., A.-M. Dalix, and L. Mennen, 2003. Contribution of Snacks and Meals in the Diet
    of French Adults: A Diet-Diary Study. *Physiology and Behavior* 79: 183–189.
Bisogni, Carol, Laura Winter Falk, Elizabeth Madore, et al. 2007. Dimensions of Everyday
    Eating and Drinking Episodes. *Appetite* 48: 218–231.
Bove, Caron F., Jeffery Sobal, and Barbara Rauschenbach. 2003. Food Choices among Newly
    Married Couples: Convergence, Conflict. *Appetite* 40: 25–41.
Brug, Johannes, Stef Kremers, Frank van Lenthe, and David Crawford. 2008. Environmental
    Determinants of Healthy Eating: In Need of Theory and Evidence. *Proceedings of the Nu-
    trition Society* 67: 307–316.
Burgess-Champoux, Teri, Nicole Larson, Dianne Neumark-Sztainer, and Mary Story. 2009.
    Are Family Meal Patterns Associated with Overall Diet Quality during the Transition from
    Early to Middle Adolescence? *Journal of Nutrition Education and Behavior* 41(2): 79–86.
Clenenen, Vanessa I., C. Peter Herman, and Janet Polivy. 1994. Social Facilitation of Eating
    among Friends and Strangers. *Appetite* 23: 1–13.
Cornell Food and Brand Lab. http:// foodpsychology.cornell.edu
Cornell Food Choice Research. http://www.human.cornell.edu/dns/foodchoice/index.cfm.
De Castro, John. 1987. Macronutrient Relationships with Meal Patterns and Mood in the
    Spontaneous Feeding Behavior of Humans. *Physiology and Behavior* 39: 561–569.
———. 1990. Social Facilitation of Duration and Size but Not Rate of the Spontaneous Meal
    Intake of Humans. *Physiology and Behavior* 47: 1129–1135.
———. 1991. Social Facilitation of the Spontaneous Meal Size of Humans Occurs on Both
    Weekdays and Weekends. *Physiology and Behavior* 49: 1289–1291.
———. 1994a. Family and Friends Produce Greater Social Facilitation of Food Intake than
    Other Companions. *Physiology and Behavior* 56: 445–455.
———. 1994b. Methodology, Correlational Analysis, and Interpretation of Diet Diary Re-
    cords of the Food and Fluid Intake of Free-Living Humans. *Appetite* 23: 179–192.
———. 2010. The Control of Food Intake of Free-Living Humans: Putting the Pieces Back
    Together. *Physiology and Behavior* 100: 446–453.
De Castro, John, and E. M. Brewer. 1992. The Amount Eaten in Meals by Humans Is a Power
    Function of the Number of People Present. *Physiology and Behavior* 51: 121–125.
De Castro, John, and Elizabeth De Castro. 1989. Spontaneous Meal Patterns of Humans:
    Influence of the Presence of Other People. *American Journal of Clinical Nutrition* 50:
    237–247.

De Castro, John, Judith McCormick, Margaret Pedersen, and Stephen Kreitzman. 1986. Spontaneous Human Meal Patterns Are Related to Preprandial Factors Regardless of Natural Environmental Constraints. *Physiology and Behavior* 38: 25–29.

De Castro, John, and Stephanie Plunkett. 2002. A General Model of Intake Regulation. *Neuroscience and Biobehavioral Reviews* 26: 581–595.

Douglas, Mary. 1972. Deciphering a Meal. *Daedalus* 101(1): 61–81.

Etkin, Nina. 2009. *The Foods of Association.* Tucson: University of Arizona Press.

Fischler, Claude. 2011. Commensality, Society and Culture. *Social Science Information* 50: 528–550.

Fowles, Eileen, Christina Murphey, and Roberta Jeanne Ruiz. 2011. Exploring Relationships among Psychosocial Status, Dietary Quality, and Measures of Placental Development during the First Trimester in Low-Income Women. *Biological Research for Nursing* 13(1): 70–79.

Gillman, Matthew, Sheryl Rifas-Shiman, and Lindsey Frazier. 2000. Family Dinner and Diet Quality among Older Children and Adolescents. *Archives of Family Medicine* 9: 235–240.

Gross, Susan, Elizabeth Davenport Pollack, and Bonnie Braun. 2010. Family Influence: Key to Fruit and Vegetable Consumption among Fourth- and Fifth-Grade Students. *Journal of Nutrition Education and Behavior* 42: 235–241.

Hannon, Peggy, Deborah Bowen, Carol Moinpour, and Dale McLerran. 2003. Correlations in Perceived Food Use between the Family Food Preparer and Their Spouses and Children. *Appetite* 40: 77–83.

Harrington, K. E., P. J. Robson, M. Kiely, J. Lambe, and M. J. Gibney. 2001. The North/South Ireland Food Consumption Survey: Survey Design and Methodology. *Public Health Nutrition* 4(5A): 1037–1042.

Hartman Group. 2011. *How America Eats: The Crucial Role of Food Culture Inside Weight Management; Overview.* Bellevue, WA: The Hartman Group.

Hawkes, K. 2003. Grandmothers and the Evolution of Human Longevity. *American Journal of Human Biology* 15: 380–400.

Hawkes, K., J. O'Connell, and N. Blurton Jones. 1997. Hadza Women's Time Allocation, Offspring Provisioning, and the Evolution of Long Postmenopausal Lifespans. *Current Anthropology* 38: 551–577.

———. 2001a. Hadza Meat Sharing. *Evolution and Human Behavior* 22: 113–142.

———. 2001b. Hunting and Nuclear Families. *Current Anthropology* 42(5): 681–709.

Hendy, Helen, Keith Williams, Thomas Camise, Nicholas Eckman, and Amber Hedemann. 2009. The Parent Mealtime Action Scale (PMAS): Development and Association with Children's Diet and Weight. *Appetite* 52: 328–339.

Herman, C. Peter, Deborah A. Roth, and Janet Polivy. 2003. Effects of the Presence of Others on Food Intake: A Normative Interpretation. *Psychological Bulletin* 129(6): 873–886.

Hermstad, April, Deanne Swan, Michelle Kegler, J. K. Barnette, and Karen Glamz. 2010. Individual and Environmental Correlates of Dietary Fat Intake in Rural Communities: A Structural Equation Model Analysis. *Social Science and Medicine* 71: 93–101.

Jaeger, Sara, David Marshall, and John Dawson. 2009. A Quantitative Characterization of Meals and Their Contexts in a Sample of 25- to 49-Year-Old Spanish People. *Appetite* 52: 318–327.

Kahn, Miriam. 1994. *Always Hungry, Never Greedy,* 2nd ed. Long Grove, IL: Waveland Press.

Kemmer, Debbie, A. S. Anderson, and D. W. Marshall. 1998. Living Together and Eating Together: Changes in Food Choice and Eating Habits during the Transition from Single to Married/Cohabiting. *Sociological Review*: 46 (1): 48–72.

Kiely, M., A. Flynn, K. E. Harrington, P. J. Robson, and G. Cran. 2001. Sampling Description and Procedures Used to Conduct the North/South Ireland Food Consumption Survey. *Public Health Nutrition* 4(5A): 1029–1035.

Larson, Nicole, Melissa Nelson, Dianne Neumark-Sztainer, Mary Story, and Peter Hannan. 2009. Making Time for Meals: Meal Structure and Associations with Dietary Intake in Young Adults. *Journal of the American Dietetic Association* 109: 72–79.

Larson, Nicole, and Mary Story. 2009. A Review of Environmental Influences on Food Choices. *Annals of Behavioral Medicine* 38(Suppl. 1): 56–S73.

Lovejoy, C. Owen. 2009. Reexamining Human Origins in Light of *Ardipithecus ramidu*. *Science* 326: 74–81.

Makela, J., U. Kjernes, and M. Pipping-Ekstro, et al. 1999. Nordic Meals: Methodological Notes on a Comparative Survey. *Appetite* 32: 73–79.

Mallery, Garrick. 1888. Manners and Meals. *The American Anthropologist* 1(3): 193–208.

Marte, Lidia. 2007. Foodmaps: Tracing Boundaries of "Home" through Food Relations. *Food and Foodways* 15(3–4): 261–289.

———. 2011. Afro-Diasporic Seasonings. *Food, Culture and Society* 14(2): 181–204.

Neumark-Sztainer, Dianne, Peter Hannan, Mary Story, Jillian Croll, and Cheryl Perry. 2003. Family Meal Patterns: Associations with Sociodemographic Characteristics and Improved Dietary Intake among Adolescents. *Journal of the American Dietetic Association* 103: 317–322.

Neumark-Sztainer, Dianne, Nicole Larson, Jayne Fulkerson, Marla Eisenberg, and Mary Story. 2010. Family Meals and Adolescents: What Have We Learned from Project EAT (Eating Among Teens)? *Public Health Nutrition* 13(7): 1113–1121.

O'Dwyer, N. A., M. J. Gibney, and S. N. McCarthy. 2005. The Influence of Eating Location on Nutrient Intakes in Irish Adults: Implications for Developing Food-Based Dietary Guidelines. *Public Health Nutrition* 8(3): 258–265.

Pachucki, Mark, Paul Jacques, and Nicholas Christakis. 2011. Social Network Concordance in Food Choice among Spouses, Friends, and Siblings. *American Journal of Public Health* 101(11): 2170–2177.

Patel, K. A., and D. G. Schlundt. 2001. Impact of Moods and Social Context on Eating Behavior. *Appetite* 36: 111–118.

Pliner, P., and R. Bell. 2009. A Table for One: The Pain and Pleasure of Eating Alone. In *Meals in Science and Practice: Interdisciplinary Research and Business Applications*, ed. H.L. Meiselman: 169–189. Oxford: Woodhead Publishing Limited.

Prattala, R., and E. Roos. 1999. From Regional Ethnographies to Interdisciplinary Approaches: Research on Meals in Finland. *Appetite* 32: 66–72.

Project EAT (Eating Among Teens). http://www.sphresearch.umn.edu/epi/project-eat

Sevenhuysen, Gustaaf, and Ursula Gross. 2003. Documenting the Reasons People Have for Choosing Their Food. *Asia Pacific Journal of Clinical Nutrition* 12(1): 30–37.

Skafida, Valeria. 2013. The Family Meal Panacea: Exploring How Different Aspects of Family Meal Occurrence, Meal Habits and Meal Enjoyment Relate to Young Children's Diets. *Sociology of Health and Illness* 35(6): 906–923.

Sobal, et al. 2012. Eating Maps: Places, Times, and People in Eating Episodes. *Ecology of Food and Nutrition* 51(3): 247–264.

Sobal, Jeffery, and Mary K. Nelson. 2003. Commensal Eating Patterns: A Community Study. *Appetite* 41: 181–190.

Stanton, Cassandra, Scott Green, and Elizabeth Fries. 2007. Diet-Specific Social Support among Rural Adolescents. *Journal of Nutrition Education and Behavior* 39: 214–218.

Story, Mary, and Dianne Neumark-Sztainer. 2005. A Perspective on Family Meals: Do They Matter? *Nutrition Today* 40(6): 261–266.

Vauthier, Jean-Michel, Ann Lluch, Edith Le Comte, Yves Artur, and Bernard Herbeth. 1996. Family Resemblance in Energy and Macronutrient Intakes: The Stanislas Family Study. *International Journal of Epidemiology* 25(5): 1030–1037.

Videon, Tami, and Carolyn Manning. 2003. Influences on Adolescent Eating Patterns: The Importance of Family Meals. *Journal of Adolescent Health* 32: 365–373.

Wansink, Brian. 2006. *Mindless Eating: Why We Eat More than We Think.* New York: Bantam Books.

Wansink, Brian, and Jeffrey Sobal. 2007. Mindless Eating: The 200 Daily Food Decisions We Overlook. *Environment and Behavior* 39: 106–124.

Weinstein, Miriam. 2005. *The Surprising Power of Family Meals: How Eating Together Makes Us Smarter, Stronger, Healthier, and Happier.* Hanover, NH: Steerforth Press.

Weismantel, Mary. 1989. *Food, Gender and Poverty in the Ecuadorian Andes.* Philadelphia: University of Pennsylvania Press.

Williams, Lauren K., Jenny Veitch, and Kylie Ball. 2011. What Helps Children Eat Well? A Qualitative Exploration of Resilience among Disadvantaged Families. *Health Education Research* 26(2): 296–307.

Wills, Wendy, Kathryn Backett-Milburn, Mei-Li Roberts, and Julia Lawton. 2013. The Framing of Social Class Distinctions through Family Food and Eating Practices. *Sociological Review* 59(4): 725–740.

Woodruff, S. J., R. M. Hanning, K. McGoldrick, and K. S. Brown. 2010. Healthy Eating Index-C Is Positively Associated with Family Dinner Frequency among Students in Grades 6–8 from Southern Ontario, Canada. *European Journal of Clinical Nutrition* 64: 454–460.

SECTION
III

Archaeological Study of Food and Food Habits

CHAPTER 8

Archaeological Food and Nutrition Research

Section Introduction

Patti J. Wright

Introduction

Food is a biological necessity, yet for humans it is and always has been a key part of our cultural expression as well. Food is transformed by and transforms the human situation. What people choose to eat is due to a range of decisions. Decisions can be based on economics: What is the cost of obtaining a specific food item? Aspects of social and political organization can dictate how food is acquired, distributed, consumed, and disposed of. Religion and rituals influence the choice of food and how that food is transformed from the raw resources into the consumed meal. The archaeology of diet and nutrition has great potential to contribute to our understanding of not only past behaviors and beliefs associated with food, but also the food systems of today. The enormous yet fruitful (pun intended) task of understanding food systems within an ancient culture has propelled diet and nutrition studies and the quest for new methods to the forefront of archaeological inquiry.

Archaeologists who study past diet and nutrition traditionally have focused their research on ingredients: the plant and animal remains that make up food. Analyses of these kinds of remains date to the latter half of the nineteenth century. Early on, plant macroremains like seeds, and fruits, and the bones of large animals formed the basis of most dietary studies, and these kinds of remains continue to be significant sources of information today. As archaeological research has matured, new kinds of evidence and new methods and technologies have been added to the researcher's toolkit. Analyses of tiny remains like starch grains or pollen, and of molecular and chemical evidence like DNA or lipid residues, have greatly enhanced the researchers ability to interpret diets that transcend millennia. Ancillary data can be derived from grinding stones, pans, bowls, and other kinds of artifacts that were used in the procurement, preparation, and consumption of foods. Human skeletal remains also provide evidence in the form of tooth wear and trace elements found within the bone. Correspondingly, the aim of this chapter is to briefly introduce the reader to these key kinds of evidence and their associated methodologies, thus setting the stage for upcoming chapters.

Animal and Plant Remains

Before proceeding with the discussion, a brief clarification of terminology is necessary. Europeans often refer to the study of animal or *faunal* remains from archaeological contexts as *archaeozoology* (Lyman 2005: 836). American researchers more often use the term *zooarchaeology*. There are also two common terms to denote the study of plant or floral remains: *archaeobotany* and *paleoethnobotany*. Some use the terms interchangeably. Others often apply the latter to culturally engaged studies, such as using plant remains to study past human diets, economics, rituals, and so on, and reserve the former for studies that are more technical and botanical in nature, such as using archaeologically derived plant remains to infer past patterns of vegetation (Ford 1979: 299; Fritz 2005: 773). To avoid any confusion, I will limit my use of the terms to animal remains, plant remains, zooarchaeology, and paleoethnobotany. It also should be noted that plant remains are frequently subdivided into two major classes: *macroremains* (remains of seeds, nutshells, fruits, or other large parts that are visible to the naked eye or with low-power magnification) and *microremains* (remains of pollen, phytoliths, and starch grains that are identifiable only with high-power magnification). These two terms will be used to speak more broadly about the respective plant parts.

Most plant and animal remains are recovered from what archaeologists call *secondary deposits,* loci away from the primary location where the plants were used. Plant remains found in secondary deposits represent debris that was discarded (e.g., bone remains from a meal dumped in a trash heap) or lost (e.g., tiny grains blown away during winnowing). Animal remains typically retrieved from archaeological contexts consist of hard parts like bone, teeth, antler, horn, and shell as opposed to softer tissues like muscle or organ meat, which not only tend to be consumed but also do not preserve well (Peres 2010). The calcium contained within the so-called hard parts aids in their preservation, making such remains especially durable when they become buried in alkaline sediments. In addition, the preservation of bone can vary within and across taxa. For example, the soft, spongy bones of very young animals are less likely to be preserved than are adult bones, and the bones of large mammals are likelier to survive than those of tiny reptiles. These kinds of preservation differences result in skewing of the faunal data. Studies of taphonomic processes and how they potentially affect quantitative and distributional properties of the archaeozoological record have produced invaluable information that has strengthened interpretations of past human as well as early hominid subsistence practices (see Behrensmeyer and Hill 1980; Lyman 1987; Meehan 1977a, 1977b; Pickering, Schick, and Toth 2007; and Moore this volume).

Plant data is also skewed but in different ways (Wright 2010 and Wright this volume). Macrobotanical remains are found in trash deposits or less frequently in primary deposits such as storage containers or structures. Mostly they are preserved by carbonization. In other words, the tissues of grains, nutshells, seeds, and the like that were fortuitously thrown into a campfire or stored in house that burned were converted to inorganic carbon and hence preserved for millennia. The carbonization process thwarts decomposition and deters consumption of the residual plant tissues by the decomposers and scavengers that thrive in most archaeological contexts. Certain plant parts are more likely to become carbonized than others; for example, a hickory nutshell is more likely to survive thermal exposure than consumable greens. Microremains are relatively durable and have different preservational trajectories. Taking the lead from some archaeozoologists, paleoethnobotanists have experimented with plant remains to better understand the biases of their preservation (e.g., Wright 2010).

The very phenomenon that allows for the preservation of certain animal and certain plant remains at the expense of others also means that recovery, processing, identification, and quantification strategies that tend to be used to analyze animal remains differ from those used for plant remains. These differences are too great to be discussed in much detail in this short, introductory section. In general, animal bones and plant macroremains are collected by hand or more systematically by the screening of archaeological sediments. The widespread use of the flotation method resulted in revolutionary recovery of information relevant to dietary changes and agricultural origins (Watson 1976). Plant microremains require more specialized sampling and recovery methods that are best described in Pearsall (2000) and Piperno (2006). As previously mentioned, plant and animal remains can be identified using the naked eye or a light microscope. Paleoethnobotanical studies since the 1980s have increasingly employed scanning electron microscopy (SEM) to detect minute structural details that differentiate wild from domesticated species. Differences in the preservation and recovery of plant and animal remains also influence they ways in which researchers quantify their assemblages. Tabulations of counts and weights are common to both, but that basic information is then used in different ways. Archaeozoologists may use these raw measures to calculate minimum numbers of individuals (MNI) or biomass that can then be used to assess relative representation of different species or groups of species (Grayson 1984). There is no MNI equivalent in paleoethnobotany; nor do paleoethnobotanists attempt to reconstruct biomass. Rather, they calculate ubiquity measures and/or standardize measures against sample volume or plant counts and weights (Pearsall 2000).

For more detailed information about the methods and techniques used in archaeozoology and paleoethnobotany I refer the reader to other chapters in this volume as well as few key texts mentioned in the following sentences. A forthcoming work, *Method and Theory in Paleoethnobotany* (Marston, D'alpoim Guedes, and Warinner 2014) contains numerous chapters describing various methods and techniques as well as case studies to demonstrate the value of analyzing macrobotanical and microbotanical remains to interpret past human diets. Chapters by Henry and Pearsall are especially useful for those who want to incorporate microremains like starch grains and pollen into their research. Works such as Fritz (2005) and Miller (2002) use case studies to provide brief but thorough descriptions of how paleoethnobotanists analyze macrobotanical remains to help understand past diet. Redding (2002) does the same for archaeozoological remains. Additional archaeozoological information is contained in Reitz and Wing's 1999 classic, *Archaeozoology.* Thus far little mention has been made of the use of shell to discuss diet, but Meehan's (1977a, 1977b) contributions to the study of shell middens both model the incorporation of ethnographic studies and provide unique insights on the gathering of shellfish by coastal hunters and gatherers of northern Australia. The reader should also look to peer-reviewed international journals such as American Antiquity, Journal of Archaeological *Science*, and *Journal of Ethnobiology* for articles containing information about methods, research designs, and case studies.

The kinds of animal and plant remains described above, which have been the traditional source of dietary studies, are by-products of human consumption. Seldom do researchers find a Tollund Man that gives them the chance to examine stomach and intestinal contents and determine with some specificity a meal—in this case, a porridge made from vegetables, grains of barley, and linseed (Silkeborg Public Library 2004–2005). The occasional find of paleofecal material in guts and in dry caves or other desiccated contexts has allowed researchers to study diet and parasitic diseases (Reinhard et al. 2006; Reinhard and Bryant 1996, 2008).

At this point it is worth reiterating that preservation biases make it impossible to extrapolate absolute representation of different plants and animals in past diets. The researcher can, however, consider changes in the relative importance of those plant or animal species when recovered from archaeological contexts. Most remains recovered from archaeological contexts represent byproducts of food preparation and consumption. Analyzing human gut contents or paleofeces allows discussion of what was actually consumed by past peoples, but because those sources represent only one or a few meals eaten by one person or a small, select group of individuals, they may not be representative of the entire population or the foods consumed on a daily basis.

Chemical and Molecular Evidence

The process of understanding past diet and nutrition based on archaeological remains has been enhanced by the adoption of new methods such as DNA and isotopic analyses. These analyses rely on evidence recovered from sediment, the pores of ceramic vessels, crevices in stone tools and teeth, human skeletal remains, or the vestiges of surviving animal and plant tissues (Pearsall 2000; Reitz and Wing 1999). Dietary contributions can be accessed through ratios of isotopes of carbon and of nitrogen, and through the proportions of strontium and calcium in human bone. Compounds such as proteins and lipids also enhance our understanding of human diet and the origins of food production. In addition, DNA can survive in animal and plant remains and aid in precisely identifying remains. For information about how these kinds of analyses can be used to understand diet and nutrition, among other topics of studies, good overviews are provided in Brown and Brown (2011), Evershed (2008), and Pollard et al. (2007). Given that molecular and chemical studies require not only specialized knowledge but also highly costly and specialized equipment and lab spaces, archaeozoologists and paleoethnobotanists often call on professionals in the fields of histology, immunology, molecular testing, chemistry or biochemistry to perform the actual work.

Integration of Data

Holistic approaches to understanding past human diets and nutrition are perhaps the most fruitful. The idea of holistic approaches has been around for since at least the 1990s (e.g., Crane and Carr 1994; Spielmann and Angstadt-Leto 1996). At the April 2000 meeting of the Society for American Archaeology, the symposium "Integrating Plants, Animals, and People in Archaeological Interpretation" was devoted to data integration. A discussant for the symposium, Patty Jo Watson, pointed out the critical need for good communication and coordination between all members of the archaeological team. It is advisable that specialists and the principal investigator(s) work together from the outset to ensure optimal recovery of the archaeological materials. Optimal recovery can be easier said than done. Despite their potential, holistic approaches have not been common, as animal and plant assemblages each have unique preservational and taphonomic biases. Advances are being made in understanding those biases (see Peres 2010 and Wright 2010, respectively). Through ongoing discussions of ways to preserve, recover, and analyze archaeological traces, revise traditional methods, and generate new methods, researchers' abilities to integrate quantitative and qualitative data have improved.

One of the more recent and more thorough works to discuss holistic approaches is VanDerwarker and Peres's edited volume *Integrating Zooarchaeology and Paleoethnobotany: A Consideration of Issues, Methods, and Cases.* Early in the volume, the editors (VanDerwarker and Peres 2010: 2) frame three broad steps that they deem necessary to successful integration:

(1) acknowledgement of the different taphonomic and recovery histories,
(2) development of methods for integrating data, and
(3) testing the interpretive value of any given method by implementing it within the context of a case study.

Moreover, the subsequent chapters of the volume provide the reader with a diversity of useful approaches and methods that can be integrated or can stand alone to provide highly insightful information about past human diet and nutrition.

Patti J. Wright is Associate Professor at the University of Missouri, St. Louis in the Department of Anthropology, Sociology, and Languages. She is an archaeologist with research interests in paleoethnobotany, early agriculture, archaeological methods and techniques, and site formation studies.

References

Behrensmeyer, A. K. and A. Hill, eds. 1980. *Fossils in the Making: Vertebrate Paleoecology and Taphonomy.* Chicago: University of Chicago Press.
Brown, Terry, and Keri Brown. 2011. *Biomolecular Archaeology: An Introduction.* Malden, MA: Wiley and Blackwell.
Crane, Cathy and H. Sorayya Carr. 1994. Integration and Quantification of Economic Data from a Late Preclassic Maya Community in Belize. In *Paleonutrition: The Diet and Health of Prehistoric Americans,* ed. K. D. Sobolik, 66–79. Carbondale: Center for Archaeological Investigations, Southern Illinois University.
Evershed, R. P. 2008. Organic Residue Analysis in Archaeology: The Archaeological Biomarker Revolution. *Archaeometry* 50: 895–924.
Ford, Richard I., ed. 1979. Paleoethnobotany in American Archaeology. In *Advances in Archaeological Method and Theory,* vol. 2, ed. Michael B. Schiffer, 285–336. New York: Academic Press.
Fritz, Gayle J. 2005. Paleoethnobotanical Methods and Applications. In *Handbook of Archaeological Methods,* vol. 2, ed. Herbert D. G. Maschner and Christopher Chippindale, 773–834. New York: Altamira Press.
Grayson, Donald K. 1984. *Quantitative Zooarchaeology.* New York: Academic Press.
Lyman, R. Lee. 1987. Zooarchaeology and Taphonomy: A General Consideration. *Journal of Ethnobiology* 7: 93–117.
———. 2005. Zooarchaeology. *In Handbook of Archaeological Methods,* vol. 2, ed. Herbert D. G. Maschner and Christopher Chippindale, 835–870. New York: Altamira Press.
Marston, John M., Jade D'Alpoim Guedes, and Christina Warinner, eds. 2014. *Method and Theory in Paleoethnobotany.* Boulder: University of Colorado Press.
Meehan, B. 1977a. Hunters by the Seashore. *Journal of Human Evolution* 6: 363–370.

————. 1977b. Man Does Not Live by Calorie Alone: The Role of Shellfish in a Coastal Cuisine. In *Sunda and Sahul,* ed. J. Allen, J. Golson, and R. Jones, 493–531. London: Academic Press.

Miller, Naomi F. 2002. The Analysis of Archaeological Plant Remains. In *Archaeology: Original Readings in Method and Practice,* ed. Peter N. Peregrin, Carol R. Ember, and Melvin Ember, 81–91. Upper Saddle River, NJ: Prentice Hall.

Pearsall, Deborah M. 2000. *Paleoethnobotany: A Handbook of Procedures,* 2nd ed. San Diego: Academic Press.

Peres, Tanya M. 2010. On Methodological Issues in Zooarchaeology. In *Integrating Zooarchaeology and Paleoethnobotany: A Consideration of Issues, Methods, and Cases,* ed. Amber M. VanDerwarker and Tanya M. Peres, 15–37. New York: Springer.

Piperno, Dolores R. 2006. *Phytoliths: A Comprehensive Guide for Archaeologists and Paleoecologists.* Lanham, MD: Altamira Press.

Pollard, Mark, Catherine Batt, Benjamin Stern, and Suzanne M. M. Young. 2007. *Analytical Chemistry in Archaeology.* Cambridge: Cambridge University Press.

Redding, Richard W. 2002. The Study of Human Subsistence Behavior Using Faunal Evidence from Archaeological Sites. In *Archaeology: Original Readings in Method and Practice,* ed. Peter N. Peregrin, Carol R. Ember, and Melvin Ember, 92–110. Upper Saddle River, NJ: Prentice Hall.

Reinhard, Karl J., Sherrian Edwards, Teyona R. Damon, and Debra K. Meier. 2006. Pollen Concentration Analysis in Ancient Pueblo Dietary Variation. *Paleogeography, Paleoclimatology, and Paleoecology* 237: 92–109.

Reitz, Elizabeth J., and Elizabeth S. Wing. 1999. *Archaeozoology.* Cambridge: Cambridge University Press.

Silkeborg Public Library. 2004-5. The Tollund Man. http://www.tollundman.dk/. Accessed January 2, 2014.

Spielmann, Katherine A., and Eric A. Angstadt-Leto. 1996. Hunting, Gathering, and Health in the Prehistoric Southwest. In *Evolving Complexity and Environmental Risk in the Prehistoric Southwest,* ed. J. Tainter and B. B. Tainter, 79–106. Madison, PA: Addison-Wesley Press.

VanDerwarker, Amber M., and Tanya M. Peres, eds. 2010. *Integrating Zooarchaeological and Paleoethnobotany: A Consideration of Issues, Methods, and Cases.* New York: Springer.

Watson, Patty Jo. 1976. In Pursuit of Prehistoric Subsistence: A Comparative Account of Some Contemporary Flotation Techniques. *Midcontinental Journal of Archaeology* 1: 77–100.

Wright, Patti J. 2010. On Methodological Issues in Paleoethnobotany. In *Integrating Zooarchaeology and Paleoethnobotany: A Consideration of Issues, Methods, and Cases,* ed. Amber M. VanDerwarker and Tanya M. Peres, 37–64. New York: Springer.

CHAPTER 9

Researching Plant Food Remains from Archaeological Contexts

Macroscopic, Microscopic, Chemical, and Molecular Approaches

Patti J. Wright

Information about past diet and nutrition lies buried beneath our feet in archaeological remains of seeds, tubers, leaves, pollen, and phytoliths. Recovery of these traces through excavations and various analyses reveals dynamics of human diet that span millennia. Recognition of the potentials of archaeological plant remains has resulted in a wealth of literature including several texts that present general information on the methods used to collect, analyze, and interpret plant remains retrieved from archaeological sites. The "go to" book is Deborah Pearsall's 2000 edition of *Paleoethnobotany: A Handbook of Procedures.* Examples of published works reporting over the years on the current status of archaeobotanical research have included Beck (2006), Ford (1978, 1979), Fritz (2005), Hastorf and Popper (1988), and Marston, D'Alpoim Guedes, and Warinner (2014).

Researching past diets based on plant remains recovered from archaeological contexts presents many challenges. The first emerges during the design of the research. Following excavation, it is not uncommon for an archaeobotanist to be added to the research team. To make the most of the available plant data, it is crucial that the archaeobotanist have input in (1) decisions about when, where, and how to field sample for plant remains, (2) the technique(s) used to collect the samples, (3) methods used to process the samples, (4) subsampling in the lab, (5) equipment and supplies, (6) budgets, (7) time tables, and (8) storage of the remains.

Sampling for macroremains (tubers, seeds, and other plant parts that can be identified with the naked eye or the use of a low-power microscopic) and for microremains (pollen, phytoliths, and starch grains that can only be identified using high-power magnification) has been thoroughly discussed in the literature (M. Jones 1991; Lennstrom and Hastorf 1995; Lepofsky and Lertzman 2005; Pearsall 2000: 66–76, 270–289, 399–410; Piperno 2006: 81–88). The sampling strategies keep processing and analysis from reaching unmanageable proportions, while affording an assemblage that is representative of the total population of plant remains at a site. Prior to excavation, decisions need to be made on how many samples will be collected, and from what contexts. A thorough consideration of research questions should guide the choices. As Delores Piperno (2006: 81–86) points out, sampling strategies can be combined into two groups: sediment column sampling, and horizontal sampling of sediments and artifacts. Whether sampling for macroremains or microremains, the former strategy is used to establish broad diachronic trends, whereas the latter can be used to answer synchronic questions about diet and nutrition. Authors such as Heidi Lennstrom and Christine Hastorf (1995) and Deborah Pearsall (2000: 66–76) discuss sampling techniques for collecting macrobotanical remains and present good discussions of their respective impacts on densities and assemblage composition. G. E. M. Jones (1991) and Martin Jones (1991) examine sampling strategies for taking macrobotanical or flotation samples at site and intra-site levels as above and also present information about sampling at regional levels.

The technique(s) used to recover samples will depend on the kind of remains that are being collected. For example, macroremains can be retrieved by hand, in a screen, or via flotation samples, which are block units of sediment that are removed and taken to the lab for processing (Fritz 2005; Pearsall 2000: 12–64; Wright 2005). Hand collection and screening are biased toward larger, readily visible plant remains; specifically in the case of field screening, the collected remains will be those pieces with a minimum dimension greater than the size of the mesh. Flotation, although not without its own biases (see Wagner 1988; Wright 2005), provides the most exhaustive assemblages, as this method makes it possible to collect even the tiniest of macroremains. It should be recognized that macrobotanical remains can preserve in several different states: carbonized, desiccated, frozen, waterlogged, and so on. Preservation is an additional criterion that needs to be considered when planning for the collection of remains. For instance, it may be perfectly acceptable to "float" carbonized, macrobotanical remains, but the water used in the flotation process may cause desiccated tissues to expand and fracture. To facilitate the separation of the desiccated plant remains from their dirt matrix, it is probably wiser to dry-screen samples through a nest of progressively smaller geological sieves.

Microremains like pollen, phytoliths, and starch grains can be extracted from sediments, vessels, the guts of preserved bodies, and paleofecal materials, among other contexts. Detailed information about strategies for collecting and sampling microremains can be found in both Pearsall (2000) and Piperno (2006). Additional works addressing the recovery of pollen are Davis (1994), Faegri, Kaland, and Krzywinski (1989), Gorham and Bryant (2001), and Lentifer and Boyd (2000). Piperno's 2006 volume *Phytoliths* includes information about field and laboratory techniques as well as research designs. Both Pearsall (2000) and Piperno (2006) specify techniques for extracting microbotanical remains from artifacts, dental remains, paleofeces, and sediments. Coil et al. (2003) propose a technique for extracting multiple kinds of microbotanical remains from a single sample. Whereas most of the above literature focuses on methods and techniques for the recovery of microbotanical remains from artifacts or terrestrial settings; Gorham and Bryant (2001) discuss underwater sites' potential to yield micro-remains, and in turn recover information about a ship's food supply. They also include information about how and where to sample shipwrecks and on the con-servation of waterlogged samples.

A number of natural and cultural processes can impact the likelihood of recov-ering plant remains (Wright 2010). Plant use, discard patterns, pedoturbation, recovery techniques, and a host of other processes may mask or exaggerate dietary patterns or even suggest change in diet where none occurred. Pearsall (2000: 349) and others (e.g., Davis 1994; Faegri et al. 1989) also recognize that working with pollen, phytoliths, and starch grains is complex. Ultimately, more defensible interpretations require understanding of pre-depositional processes. Prior to em-barking on an archaeobotanical study, it is worth considering the growing litera-ture designed to understand the taphonomic history of surviving plant remains. One might ask, for example, whether a grain found in a hearth is a by-product of humans' processing grain for food, or a product of burning dung as fuel (Miller and Smart 1984). While pollen can enter the archaeological record as a result of human activity or as a result of pollen rain, phytoliths and starch grains derive largely from on-site plant discard as a result of human activity (Piperno 2006).

Understanding post-depositional processes is also important. Once macrore-mains become a part of archaeological contexts, they may survive physical and chemical decomposition over hundreds or even thousands of years via processes of carbonization, desiccation, quick-freezing, mineralization, waterlogging, and preservation in coprolites. These processes inhibit the growth of decomposers like bacteria or saprophytic fungi, slow the rate of enzyme action, and/or lower the speed at which chemical reactions occur (Bryant 1989). Like macroremains, microremains can fall prey to a host of biological organisms as well as to chemi-cal and physical erosion (Bryant 1989; Pearsall 2000; Piperno 2006). Rowe and Kershaw (2008: Table 42.1) summarize the preservation characteristics of pollen, phytoliths, and starch grains and provide useful information about their deposi-tion, applications, advantages, and limitations. For example, pollen is more likely to survive under acidic or anaerobic conditions than in sandy sediments or open-air sites that expose them to oscillating conditions of wet and dry and hot and cold. Starch grains may be the most vulnerable of the microbotanical remains, while phytoliths are considered the most durable of all plant remains.

The plant evidence that has survived the ravages of natural processes is then subjected to G. Jones 1991; Kadane 1988; Miller 1988; Pearsall 2000: 191, 302–318; 444–491; Popper 1988: 115–125). Counts and weights are often used, despite the fact that absolute measures are heavily influenced by factors such as preservation and sampling (Popper 1988). Though they do not necessarily alleviate all the biases, manipulations of counts and weights like conversion factors, diversity indices, rankings, ratios, and ubiquity measure do help to standardize the remains. Even more sophisticated statistics like those obtained through multivariate analysis, while useful, do not preclude the conditioning of the assemblage by cultural, natural, or analytical processes that may ultimately influence interpretations.

To this point, I have discussed macro- and microremains. In recent years, methods to extract chemical and molecular evidence have greatly broadened and strengthened discussions of past human diet and nutrition. These kinds of evidence are found in sediments, the pores of ceramic vessels, crevices in stone tools and teeth, within human skeletal remains, or the vestiges of surviving plant tissues (Ford 1979; Pearsall 2000). Dietary contributions of plants can be assessed based on ratios of isotopes of carbon and of nitrogen and the proportions of strontium and calcium in human bone (Ambrose and DeNiro 1986; Boyd et al. 2008). Compounds such as proteins and lipids that survive in macroremains provide an alternative basis for their identification and can enhance our understanding of human diet and the origins of food production (Lombard and Wadley 2000; Malainey, Przybylski, and Sherriff 1999; Rottlander 1990). In addition, DNA can survive in charred and uncharred plant remains. Giles and Brown (2008) report on improved methods for extracting and amplifying DNA. Equally interesting is Poinar et al.'s 2001 discussion about the dietary diversity of three archaic Native Americans based on molecular analysis. These studies and other potential synergies frequently require collaborations with experts in the fields of histology, immunology, molecular testing, chemistry or biochemistry. They can entail the use of microscopy, mass spectrometry, or high-temperature gas chromatography and demand costly and specialized instruments and spaces. Evershed (2008) presents a wealth of information on the "archaeological biomarker revolution."

Problem orientation and subsequent interpretations are project-specific and are structured as much by theoretical perspectives as available time and money. We may never realize all the nuances of past human diets, but studies of archaeologically derived plant remains, especially those combining different methods of analyses, deserve recognition and can result in sophisticated understandings of the dynamic relationship between people and plant foods.

Patti J. Wright is Associate Professor at the University of Missouri, St. Louis in the Department of Anthropology and Archaeology. She is an archaeologist with research interests in paleoethnobotany, early agriculture, archaeological methods and techniques, and site formation studies.

References

Ambrose, Stanley H., and Michael J. DeNiro. 1986. Reconstruction of African Human Diet Using Bone Collagen, Carbon and Nitrogen Isotope Ratios. *Nature* 319: 321–324.

Beck, Wendy. 2006. Plant Remains. In *Archaeology in Practice: A Student Guide to Archaeological Analyses,* ed. Jane Balme and Alistair Paterson, 296–315. Malden, MA: Blackwell.

Boyd, Matthew, T. Varney, C. Surette, and J. Surette. 2008. Reassessing the Northern Limit of Maize Consumption in North America: Stable Isotope, Plant Microfossil, and Trace Element Content of Carbonized Food Residue. *Journal of Archaeological Science* 35: 2545–2556.

Bryant, Vaughn M., Jr. 1989. Botanical Remains in Archaeological Sites. In *Interdisciplinary Workshop on the Physical-Chemical-Biological Processes Affecting Archaeological Sites,* comp. Christopher C. Mathewson, 85–115. Environmental Impact Research Program.

Coil, James, M., Alejandra Korsanje, Steven Archer, and Christine A. Hastorf. 2003. Laboratory Goals and Considerations for Multiple Microfossil Extraction in Archaeology. *Journal of Archaeological Science* 30: 991–1008.

Davis, Owen K. 1994. Aspects of Archaeological Palynology: Methodology and Applications. *AASP Contributions* 29: 1–5.

Evershed, R. P. 2008. Organic Residue Analysis in Archaeology: The Archaeological Biomarker Revolution. *Archaeometry* 50: 895–924.

Faegri, Knut, Peter E. Kaland, and Knut Krzywinski, eds. 1989. *Textbook of Pollen Analysis,* 4th ed. London: Wiley.

Ford, Richard I., ed. 1978. *The Nature and Status of Ethnobotany.* Anthropological Papers No. 67, Museum of Anthropology. Ann Arbor: University of Michigan Press.

———. 1979. Paleoethnobotany in American Archaeology. In *Advances in Archaeological Method and Theory,* vol. 2, ed. Michael B. Schiffer, 285–336. New York: Academic Press.

Fritz, Gayle J. 2005. Paleoethnobotanical Methods and Applications. In *Handbook of Archaeological Methods,* vol. 2, ed. Herbert D. G. Maschner and Christopher Chippindale, 773–834. New York: Altamira Press.

Giles, Rachel J., and Terence A. Brown. 2008. Improved Methodology for Extraction and Amplification of DNA from Single Grains of Charred Wheat. *Journal of Archaeological Science* 35: 2585–2588.

Gorham, Dillon, and Vaughn M. Bryant. 2001. The Role of Pollen and Phytoliths in Underwater Archaeology. *International Journal of Nautical Archaeology* 30(2): 299–305.

Hastorf, Christine A. 1999. Recent Research in Paleoethnobotany. *Journal of Archaeological Research* 7: 55–103.

Hastorf, Christine, and Virginia S. Popper, eds. 1988. *Current Paleoethnobotany: Analytical Methods and Cultural Interpretations of Archaeological Plant Remains.* Chicago: University of Chicago.

Jones, G. E. M. 1991. Numerical Analysis in Archaeobotany. In *Progress in Old World Paleoethnobotany,* ed. Willem Van Zeist, Krystyna Wasylikowa, and Karl Ernst Behre, 63–80. Rotterdam: A.A. Balkema.

Jones, Martin. 1991. Sampling in Paleoethnobotany. In *Progress in Old World Paleoethnobotany,* ed. Willem Van Zeist, Krystyna Wasylikowa, and Karl Ernst Behre, 53–62. Rotterdam: A.A. Balkema.

Kadane, Joseph B. 1998. Possible Statistical Contributions to Paleoethnobotany. In *Current Paleoethnobotany: Analytical Methods and Cultural Interpretations of Archaeological Plant Remains,* ed. Christine A. Hastorf and Virginia S. Popper, 206–222. Chicago: University of Chicago Press.

Lennstrom, Heidi A., and Christine A. Hastorf. 1995. Interpretation in Its Context: Sampling and Analysis in Paleoethnobotany. *American Antiquity* 60: 701–721.

Lentifer, Carol J., and William E. Boyd. 2000. Simultaneous Extractions of Phytoliths, Pollen and Spores from Sediments. *Journal of Archaeological Science* 27: 363–372.

Lepofsky, Dana, and Ken Lertzman. 2005. More on Sampling for Richness and Diversity in Archaeobiological Assemblages. *Journal of Ethnobiology* 25: 175–188.

Lombard, Marlize, and Lyn Wadley. 2007. The Morphological Identification of Micro-residues on Stone Tools Using Light Microscopy: Progress and Difficulties Based on Blind Tests. *Journal of Archaeological Science* 34: 155–165.

Malainey, Mary E., Roman Przybylski, and Barbara L. Sherriff. 1999. The Effects of Thermal and Oxidative Degradation on the Fatty Acid Composition of Food Plants and Animals of Western Canada: Implications for the Identification of Archaeological Vessel Residues. *Journal of Archaeological Science* 26: 95–103.

Marston, John M., Jade D'Alpoim Guedes, and Christina Warinner, eds. 2014. *Method and Theory in Paleoethnobotany.* Boulder: University of Colorado Press.

Miller, Naomi F. 1988. Ratios in Paleoethnobotanical Analysis. In *Current Paleoethnobotany: Analytical Methods and Cultural Interpretations of Archaeological Plant Remains,* ed. Christine A. Hastorf and Virginia S. Popper, pp. 72–85. Chicago: University of Chicago Press.

Miller, Naomi F., and Tristine L. Smart. 1984. Intentional Burning of Dung as Fuel: A Mechanism for the Incorporation of Charred Seeds into the Archaeological Record. *Journal of Ethnobiology* 4: 15–28.

Pearsall, Deborah M. 2000. *Paleoethnobotany: A Handbook of Procedures,* 2nd ed. San Diego: Academic Press.

Piperno, Dolores R. 2006. *Phytoliths: A Comprehensive Guide for Archaeologists and Paleoecologists.* Lanham, MD: Altamira Press.

Poinar, Hendrik N., Melanie Kuch, Kristin D. Sobolik, Ian Barnes, Artur B. Stankiewicz, Tomasz Kuder, W. Geoffrey Spaulding, Vaughn M. Bryant, Alan Cooper, and Svante Pääbo. 2001. A Molecular Analysis of Dietary Diversity for Three Archaic Native Americans. *Proceedings of the National Academy of Sciences of the United States of America* 98: 4317–4322.

Popper, Virginia S. 1988. Selecting Quantitative Measurements in Paleoethnobotany. In *Current Paleoethnobotany: Analytical Methods and Cultural Interpretations of Archaeological Plant Remains,* ed. Christine A. Hastorf and Virginia S. Popper, 53–71. Chicago: University of Chicago Press.

Rottlander, R. C. A. 1990. Lipid Analysis in the Identification of Vessel Content. In *Organic Contents of Ancient Vessels,* ed. William R. Biers and Patrick E. McGovern, 37–40. MASCA Research Papers in Science and Archaeology, vol. 7. Philadelphia: University of Pennsylvania Press.

Rowe, Cassandra, and Peter Kershaw. 2008. Microbotanical Remains in Landscape Archaeology. In *Handbook of Landscape Archaeology*, ed. Bruno David and Julian Thomas, 430–441. Walnut Creek, CA: Left Coast Press.

Wagner, Gail E. 1988. Comparability among Recovery Techniques. In *Current Paleoethnobotany: Analytical Methods and Cultural Interpretations of Archaeological Plant Remains*, ed. Christine A. Hastorf and Virginia S. Popper, 17–35. Chicago: University of Chicago Press.

Wright, Patti J. 2005. Flotation Samples and Some Paleoethnobotanical Implications. *Journal of Archaeological Science* 32: 19–26.

———. 2010. On Methodological Issues in Paleoethnobotany. In *Integrating Zooarchaeology and Paleoethnobotany: A Consideration of Issues, Methods, and Cases*, ed. Amber M. VanDerwarker and Tanya M. Peres, 37–64. New York: Springer.

CHAPTER **10**

Methods for Reconstructing Diet

Bethany L. Turner and Sarah V. Livengood

Introduction

The study of paleodiet is perhaps the most critical component of research on past populations. The fundamental, daily necessity of procuring and/or producing food items from the surrounding environment provides clues about not only the environment itself and its changes through time, but also the particular techno-logical, economic, behavioral, and cultural characteristics of small groups and large populations alike. Because subsistence and diet are critical to the well-being and adaptive success of human biological populations and to cultures as well (Roosevelt 1987), it is prudent to utilize an explicitly biocultural focus when reconstructing adaptive or maladaptive aspects of paleodiet (Armelagos 1987, 1994). Moreover, the rapid rates of dietary change seen over the past fifteen mil-lennia have had significant effects on population health and cultural dynamics (Eaton, Eaton, and Cordain 2002; Eaton, Eaton and Konner 1997; Nestle 1999; Turner and Thompson 2013); therefore, the study of paleodiet is a useful way to interpret modern diets and their health effects within broader temporal and cross-cultural frameworks.

The methods available for investigating questions of ancient subsistence, diet, and nutritional status can be broadly separated into two categories: *indirect* meth-ods for estimating or reconstructing resources that were available or utilized but not what or how much was actually eaten, and *direct* methods that estimate or characterize the types and relative proportions of resources that were actually consumed. Each broad category contains a suite of methods; indirect methods include the archaeological study of subsistence tools, site features, and physical remains such as food residues in soils (Carbone and Keel 1985; Ishige 2001; Knudson et al. 2004; Webb, Schwarcz, and Healy 2004) and preserved plant and animal remains (Balasse and Tresset 2002; Bokyoni 1975; Fritz 1994; Gu-merman IV 1994). Although these techniques have contributed significantly to advancing what is known of past resource bases and subsistence, reconstructions of resource *availability* cannot be used alone to confidently predict the degree or frequency of resource *use* among the members of archaeological groups (Parmalee 1985; Styles 1994).

Complementing many of these archaeological approaches is the study of morphological changes and pathological conditions related to diet and nutrition in archaeological human remains. Chronic nutritional stress and/or dietary monotony often leads to skeletal and dental involvement through disrupted growth, oral disease, cranial lesions, and other such features (Goodman et al. 1984), while variations in patterns of tooth wear are often used to identify various food processing techniques (Irish and Turner 1997). Bioarchaeological research therefore utilizes separate but complementary approaches to reconstructing diet on the one hand and nutritional status on the other, and analyzes these data in concert with archaeological evidence of subsistence behaviors to better understand ancient health and well-being.

A discussion of reconstructing and inferring nutritional status can be found elsewhere in this volume (Goodman). The present chapter, however, focuses on reconstructing aspects of dietary intake. These are not mutually exclusive endeavors, as some skeletal features are used to infer aspects of diet from the resulting effects on nutrition, for example using the frequency and severity of tooth carious lesions to infer diets heavy in maize versus meat (Turner 2013); however, skeletal lesions are *indirect* indicators of diet. This chapter describes three common methodologies for *directly* assessing diet, independent of food resource availability or nutritional status: dental microscopy, stable isotope analysis, and trace element analysis.

Dental Microscopy: Microwear Analysis

Dental microwear studies look at direct data about past behaviors by observing the microscopic markings that food leaves behind on the occlusal (top, cuspal) surfaces of enamel crowns (Teaford 2007). Microwear analysis was applied to bioarchaeological populations following the discovery by Baker, Jones, and Wardrop (1959) that the phytoliths on grasses and soil grit were the cause of scratches on the enamel of sheep's teeth, revealing a direct relationship between what was being eaten and the evidence left behind on the enamel. The main focus of microwear research during the 1970s was reconstructing the diets of ancestral hominins (Grine 1977; Puech 1979; Puech and Prone 1979) and the relationship between different diets and variations in microwear (Rensberger 1978; Ungar et al. 2008; Walker, Hoeck, and Perez 1978).

When the conclusions drawn in the 1970s about dental microwear and diet were re-evaluated in the ensuing decades, concern arose about the lack of standardized methods (Ungar et al. 2008). Researchers wondered whether diet could actually be directly concluded from microwear patterns. For example, Peters (1982) argued that chert pieces and phytoliths made the same striations, making it hard to tell whether grit or the actual food caused microwear. It was obvious that controls were needed to allow for comparison, and scanning electron microscope (SEM) settings needed to be standardized, down to the positioning of the tooth under the microscope (Ungar et al. 2008). This set the stage for new quantitative analyses confirming that microwear does in fact reveal diet, and there has been a re-demonstration of seasonal and ecological variation (Ungar et al. 2008). For instance, Covert and Kay (1981) suggested opossums showed no difference in dental microwear when they ate plant fibers versus when they ate the exoskeleton of insects. Gordon and Walker (1983) later argued that these two food substances leave behind similar microwear because of the grit that can be found in plant matter. Gordon (1984, 1988) also countered that there needed to be a larger focus on standardizing dental microwear methods, such as the SEM settings, position of tooth under the microscope, and which tooth facet to analyze. This need for standardized methods brought about a resurgence in low-magnification light microscopy (see below). More recently, Peter Ungar's Paleoanthropology Lab at the University of Arkansas has developed a methodology that supersedes SEM analysis of dental microwear. Dental microwear textural analysis reduces some of the limitations associated with feature-based dental microwear studies by offering a repeatable, interobserver-error free way to analyze the texture of a tooth's occlusal surface. Scanning a tooth cast with a white-light confocal microscope creates a digital copy of the tooth and maps its three-dimensional surfaces. Surface analysis software is used to analyze surface features including anisotropy, complexity, the scale of maximum complexity, textural fill volume, and heterogeneity of complexity (see Scott et al. 2005 for in-depth description). All of these characterizations have been successfully used to separate groups of nonhuman primates, fossil hominins, and bioarchaeological populations in predictable ways.

Dental microwear analysis has had limited applications in bioarchaeological populations, and is more widely used to reconstruct broad diet patterns in living and extinct nonhuman primates and fossil hominins (species ancestral to modern humans). Many studies that have utilized microwear analyses in archaeological human remains have focused on how maize processing techniques and consumption affect microwear features (Organ, Teaford, and Larsen 2005; Schmidt 2001; Teaford and Lytle 1996), sometimes in concert with isotopic data (Hogue and Melsheimer 2008; Livengood 2012). Microwear features associated with maize are typically characterized by a high frequency of "large" scratches and "large" pits (Gordan 1986; Teaford and Lytle 1996), discussed in more detail below. Often, this association is based on the fact that maize processed on grinding stones incorporates grit and other abrasives that produce these larger microwear features when the processed maize is consumed (Livengood 2012; Organ et al. 2005;

Teaford and Lytle 1996). Textural analysis has similarly been limited in its applications to human populations; recently Krueger and Ungar (2010) provided insights into bioarchaeological groups that use their teeth as tools in a variety of contexts, associating lower values of anisotropy with holding materials during hide preparation. High values for textural fill volume are associated with larger pits and scratches from heavy loads; in this case the high values are related to activities that would flake the enamel. The heterogeneity values, however, have been attributed to varying amounts of grit in the diet (Krueger and Ungar 2010). Researchers have applied dental microwear texture analysis to various bioarchaeological groups from sites in North America, Europe, the Levant, and China (Beach and Schmidt 2013; Chiu et al. 2012; Schmidt et al. 2011; Van Sessen et al. 2013). Others (El-Zaatari 2008) have focused exclusively on museum collections of teeth from modern hunter-gatherers with differing proportions of meat and plant parts in their diets, finding significant variation between groups related to both diet and food preparation techniques.

New methodological controls and an increase in studies using multivariate statistical techniques such as principal components analysis (PCA) have pushed the dental microwear field forward, making it a more integral part of reconstructing dietary patterns. Past dental microwear studies have used low-magnification stereomicroscopy and scanning electron microscopy to provide direct evidence about diet (Grine 1986; Ryan and Johanson 1989; Ungar and Grine 1991). Recently developed texture analysis techniques are able to quantify even subtler differences in microwear patterns to reveal information about diet variability and the frequency of consumption of different foods, with less inter-observer error and high repeatability (Scott et al. 2005).

Isotope Analysis

Isotopic reconstructions of diet in archaeological samples constitute an important and now common area of bioarchaeological research, studying the relative importance of constituent food types to individual diets. Briefly, isotopes are variants of a given element that differ in the number of neutrons in their atomic nuclei; this difference has no effect on the charge of the element, but does influence its atomic weight. In biological systems, lighter isotopes of common elements such as carbon, nitrogen, oxygen, and sulfur more easily enter into physical or chemical reactions such as digestion, tissue formation, and respiration, but while the heavier isotopes do not. This results in differing abundances of different isotopes of a given element that can be modeled and predicted in the food webs of various ecosystems. Many of the elemental isotopes in food webs undergo predictable changes in their relative abundances as plants are consumed by animals that are then in turn consumed by other animals: as more of the light isotope is consumed by processes of metabolism and excretion at every step of the food web, the relative abundance of the heavier isotope increases (except in the case of stable strontium isotopes; see below). This enrichment of the heavier isotope is referred to as fractionation. The relative abundances of different isotopes in the tissues of different plants and consumers can be used to study existing food webs and reconstruct ancient ones as well. Because the absolute differences in the stable (nonradioactive) isotopes of carbon, nitrogen, and other elements relevant to reconstructing diet are extremely small, the ratios of these isotopes are typically expressed in parts per thousand, or per mil (‰), in delta (δ) notation relative to established geological or environmental standards (reviewed in Ambrose 1993; Schwarcz and Schoeninger 1991).

Paleodietary analyses using stable isotopes have grown increasingly sophisticated with the refinement of analytical techniques, increased resolution, and greater understanding of the complex and variable cycling of stable isotopes in biological systems. These include controlled feeding studies of laboratory animals (Ambrose and Norr 1993; Tieszen and Fagre 1993) and studies that include reference data from local floral and faunal food sources (Iacumin et al. 1998; Schoeninger and DeNiro 1984; Tieszen and Chapman 1993; White and Schwarcz 1994). There are two main categories of preserved tissue that contain elemental isotope ratios useful in reconstructing *in vivo* diet: the *organic* components, including collagen and keratin from bone, dentin, hair, fingernails, and soft tissues; and the *inorganic* components, specifically carbonate and phosphate in bone and enamel hydroxyapatite ($Ca_{10}(CO_4)_6(OH)_2$). The two most commonly utilized elemental isotope ratios are carbon-13 relative to carbon-12 ($\delta^{13}C$), and nitrogen-15 relative to nitrogen-14 ($\delta^{15}N$). Less commonly used isotope ratios include sulfur-34 relative to sulfur-32 ($\delta^{34}S$) and stable strontium-88 relative to strontium-86 ($\delta^{88/86}Sr$).

Stable Carbon Isotopes

Isotopic ratios of carbon in the carbonate and phosphate portions of bone and enamel hydroxyapatite represent carbon drawn from all sources in the diet. These sources include terrestrial or marine animals, and plants with C_3 versus C_4 photosynthetic pathways; humans less commonly consume plants with crassulean-acid metabolism photosynthetic pathways, whose $\delta^{13}C$ values are between the lower average C_3 and higher average C_4 isotopic values (~ -22‰ and -12‰, respectively). As such, carbonate and phosphate isotopic values represent a composite dietary signal representing carbohydrates, fats, and protein. In bone and dentin collagen and hair keratin, the same $\delta^{13}C$ values appear to disproportionately represent the contribution of carbon found in dietary protein (Ambrose and Norr 1993); however, if an individual's diet was low in protein overall, these $\delta^{13}C$ values will likely include a significant contribution of carbon found in lipids and carbohydrates (Schwarcz 2000). Carbon isotopic values are expressed relative to the PeeDee Belemite geological standard (vPDB), and in organismic food webs these values are almost universally negative integers.

Comparing organic (collagen, keratin) and inorganic (carbonate, phosphate) $\delta^{13}C$ values characterized in the same individual can provide some insights into the different sources of energy and protein in the diet. Traditionally, this was accomplished using carbonate – collagen spacing, or $\Delta^{13}C_{ap\text{-}col}$, to estimate the type and proportion of protein in the overall diet (Ambrose 1993; Ambrose and Norr 1993). However, recent research suggests that *in vivo* metabolic routing of dietary components to different bodily tissues in humans is more complex, so regression formulae have been proposed to accurately estimate different dietary components in archaeological samples (Froehle, Kellner, and Schoeninger 2012; Kellner and Schoeninger 2007). Importantly, bone/dentin collagen and hair/nail keratin have distinct fractionation effects resulting in different diet-tissue spacing, largely due to different amino acid profiles among the two protein types. Because over 30 percent of collagen is composed of glycine, which has a higher $\delta^{13}C$ value than most other essential amino acids, diet – tissue spacing of $\delta^{13}C_{collagen}$ is approximately +5‰, while controlled feeding experiments suggest a diet – tissue spacing of $\delta^{13}C_{keratin}$ is +3.5‰ (O'Connell et al. 2001).

Stable Nitrogen Isotopes

Isotopic nitrogen ratios ($\delta^{15}N$) are found in bone and dentin collagen and hair and nail keratin, and are metabolized from the nitrogen consumed in dietary protein. Similar to $\delta^{13}C$, the base values of $\delta^{15}N$ in food webs depend on the types of plants consumed. Some plants, such as legumes, fix nitrogen from the atmosphere via symbiotic bacteria living in their roots, and have lower $\delta^{15}N$ values than plants that uptake nitrogen from nitrates and nitrites in surrounding soils (DeNiro 1987). Marine plants such as seaweeds and phytoplankton fix nitrogen from dissolved nitrates and ammonium in seawater, and tend to have higher $\delta^{15}N$ values than both nitrogen-fixing and non–nitrogen-fixing terrestrial plants (Schoeninger and DeNiro 1984). Among the animals in food webs, $\delta^{15}N$ represents trophic-level effects in protein intake associated with consumed organisms' positions within food webs, namely the types of plants or plant-consuming animals that they themselves consume (Ambrose et al. 1997; Ambrose and Norr 1993; Lee-Thorp, Sealy, and van der Merwe 1989). The nitrogen that is incorporated into bodily tissues is drawn primarily from metabolized dietary proteins; tissue $\delta^{15}N$ values are therefore useful in estimating the types of protein (e.g., animal, vegetable, leguminous, terrestrial versus marine) incorporated into the diet (Ambrose 1991; DeNiro and Schoeninger 1983). Nitrogen isotope values are expressed relative to atmospheric nitrogen (vAIR) and in organismic food webs are universally positive integers.

Unlike carbon isotope values, $\delta^{15}N$ shows little to no difference in diet – tissue spacing between bone collagen and hair keratin, as both show approximately 3–4‰ in controlled feeding studies (DeNiro and Epstein 1978; O'Connell et al. 2001). However, $\delta^{15}N$ values are also influenced by the overall concentration of nitrogen in consumed dietary protein (O'Connell and Hedges 1999). They can also increase due to a number of physiological factors, including water conservation in arid climates through excretion of ^{14}N-concentrated urine (Ambrose 1991), and lean tissue catabolism for gluconeogenesis during bouts of starvation (Fuller et al. 2005); they can also decrease due to differential routing of nitrogen in the body when an individual is pregnant (Fuller et al. 2004) or suffering from a wasting disease (Katzenberg and Lovell 1999). For these reasons, it is important to consider not only the environmental context in which the individuals of interest lived, but also osteological indicators of malnutrition or severe, chronic infection (see Goodman's chapter).

Other Diet-Related Stable Isotopes

While isotope ratios of carbon and nitrogen are most commonly analyzed in paleodiet research, sulfur isotope analysis has also been employed to distinguish between terrestrial and marine food sources in the diets of humans and other animals (Hobson 1999). Sulfur isotopes are studied in the organic portions of tissues such as bone collagen and hair keratin, and $\delta^{34}S$ values in these tissues reflect those of consumed plants and animals. Terrestrial plants have significantly lower $\delta^{34}S$ values than do marine plants, resulting in clear differences in the tissue $\delta^{34}S$ values of consumers who consume sulfur sources from terrestrial versus marine food webs, and have been used to infer diet composition related to movement between coastal and inland regions (Fernández, Panarello, and Schobinger 1999). Sulfur isotope values are expressed relative to the Canyon Diablo troilyte geological standard (vCDT).

A recent addition to the biochemical toolkit in bioarchaeology, proposed by Knudson and colleagues (2010), is the analysis of stable strontium isotopes (which differs from the more widespread analysis of radiogenic ^{87}Sr relative to ^{86}Sr to estimate residential origin and regional migration; see Knudson and Price [2007] for a review of this area of research). In contrast with "light" isotopes like carbon, nitrogen, and sulfur, the stable "heavy" isotopes ^{88}Sr and ^{86}Sr in food webs, when fractionated, show a systematic depletion of $\delta^{88/86}Sr$ values rather than an enrichment. There is also a slight difference in notation: stable strontium isotope values are expressed relative to the NBS-987 strontium carbonate geological standard; a positive value indicates that the tissue ratio of ^{88}Sr to ^{86}Sr is greater than that of the NBS-987 standard, while a negative value indicates that the former is smaller than the latter (Knudson et al. 2010: 3). Values of $\delta^{88/86}Sr$ show promise in distinguishing diets according to trophic levels in food webs, similar to $\delta^{15}N$ and particularly so for marine food webs. However, since the $\delta^{88/86}Sr$ values in soils and bedrock vary slightly depending on the age and composition of the bedrock itself, the absolute values of these isotopes are not directly comparable between different geologic regions without controlling for geologic variability. An advantage is that the same preparation techniques employed for radiogenic $^{87}Sr/^{86}Sr$ characterization will also accommodate slight modifications for $\delta^{88/86}Sr$ analysis (see below), making this technique particularly useful for maximizing the amount of data produced from relatively small samples of bone or enamel hydroxyapatite (Knudson et al. 2010).

Trace Element Analysis

In addition to characterizing isotope ratios in preserved archaeological tissues, it is also possible to reconstruct aspects of diet by measuring the concentrations of certain trace elements incorporated into the mineral structures of bones and teeth. The underlying assumption of this form of paleodiet estimation is that these elements are incorporated into bodily tissues from the diet, and that understanding the natural abundances of these elements in various plant and animal tissues makes it possible to estimate the relative proportions of meat and plants in the diet of ancient humans. The first and most commonly studied trace elements are strontium and calcium. In measuring the ratio of strontium to calcium (Sr/Ca) in food webs, early researchers revealed a predictable "biopurification" effect whereby strontium levels decrease with each successive step in a trophic web (see Burton and Price 2000; Pate 1994 for extensive reviews). This relationship prompted an expansion of elemental studies to include ratios of barium to calcium (Ba/Ca), and levels of zinc (Zn), copper (Cu), iron (Fe), magnesium (Mg), manganese (Mn), and other elements to infer the quantities of meat versus plants, or terrestrial versus marine foods, in human diets (Burton and Price 2000; Sandford 1992; Sillen and Kavanagh 1982).

However, the measurement and analysis of trace elements in bones and teeth has become less common in bioarchaeological research, due in large part to issues involving the interpretation of these data (Sillen, Sealy, and van der Merwe 1989). Studies in the 1990s demonstrated that that the relationship between element and diet is far more complex than straightforward meat/plant or terrestrial/marine comparisons, and that several key premises must be satisfied in order to accurately interpret diet using trace element data: the elements in question must be incorporated into bones and teeth, and their levels in skeletal tissues should be determined by the diet and not by other metabolic or diagenetic processes (Ezzo 1994), the latter having long been of concern (reviewed in Pate 1994). In applying these criteria, Burton (1996; Burton and Wright 1995) argues that strontium and barium are the only trace elements that provide accurate information on dietary composition; however, rather than differentiating between meat and plant foods in the diet, the concentrations of these elements appear to reflect the type of calcium-rich foods consumed, no matter how abundant they were in the overall diet. The authors argue that it is therefore more reasonable to use Sr and Ba elemental concentrations to distinguish between consumption of leafy green vegetables, which are high in calcium, and consumption of lower-calcium foods like grains, regardless of whether they were minor or major dietary components. Recent trace element studies have also inferred different diets among subsets of skeletal populations using Sr (János et al. 2011) and both Sr and Zn (Safont et al. 1998). This makes trace element analysis particularly useful in combination with stable isotope analysis, as many plants exhibit similar $\delta^{13}C$ and/or $\delta^{15}N$ values despite being nutritionally quite different.

Methodologies

Dental Microscopy

Before the 1970s, low-magnification stereomicroscopy was the only method used to analyze dental microwear (Ungar et al. 2008). This method was surrounded by controversy because it left out microwear that could be seen on a submicron level. Then the 1970s saw the development of scanning electron microscope (SEM) analysis (Ungar et al. 2008), which allows wear patterns to be seen on curved aspects or the rough topography of the tooth. Low-magnification microscopy can be done at low cost and fairly quickly, which means a larger number of individuals can be analyzed; low-magnification microscopy also uses an external light source that can be manipulated to see features that are not immediately apparent. However, extensive training is necessary to recognize microwear features at a lower magnification, and this technique misses submicron microwear, which can only be seen with SEM (Teaford 2007). Conversely, SEM analysis of microwear provides more feature detail but is significantly more expensive and time- consuming, and has high inter-observer error rates even with the assistance of a computer (Semprebon et al. 2004; Teaford 2007). Positively, postmortem wear does not pose a problem because wear patterns during life are in specific locations on the tooth surface (Ungar, Grine, and Teaford 2006).

    Lower-magnification microscopy requires a dental cast from every individual studied, preferably of the same tooth type, such as a permanent, left mandibular (lower jaw) second molar (Semprebon et al. 2004). The individual's teeth are first cleaned with 95 percent alcohol (Semprebon et al. 2004) or a piece of cotton soaked in acetone (Ungar et al. 2008). Impressions of the occlusal surface of the tooth are made using the high-resolution, self-curing polysiloxane impression material commonly used in modern clinical dentistry. High-quality, clear epoxy-resin casts are made from these impressions (Semprebon et al. 2004; Ungar et al.

2008) and examined for microwear, typically at 35x magnification under a stereomicroscope with an external fiber optic light source (Semprebon et al. 2004). The external fiber optic light source casts shadows, which can help discern the size of pits and scratches; this external oblique illumination can be moved into different angles and positions when examining features in order to elucidate more subtle manifestations of surface pits and scratches (ibid.).

Pits are classified as large, small, or puncture, while scratches are classified as fine, coarse, or hypercoarse. Pits look like compression fractures, and have a length-to-width ratio less than 4:1, while scratches are linear with a length-to-width ratio that exceeds 4:1. Pits and scratches come in different sizes. Small pits look shiny and white because they are shallower, which allows them to refract more light, and a large pit or scratch looks darker and less shiny because it is deeper (Semprebon et al. 2004). Puncture pits are the largest of the pits with a deep, symmetrical appearance; they also appear darker than large pits because of low refractivity (ibid.). Scratches can be fine and appear shiny because they are shallow and narrow; indeed, sometimes they are barely observable (ibid.). Scratches can also be coarse and thus wider and more easily observed. The largest scratches are hypercoarse scratches, which appear dark because they are etched deep into the enamel (ibid.). On occasion, puncture pits occur at the end of a hypercoarse scratch where an object was dragged across the enamel (ibid.).

Recently, researchers have developed an additional technique for studying microwear patterns: dental microwear texture analysis (Scott et al. 2005). Tooth casts are made the same way as in low-magnification analysis (see above). Teeth are then mounted on non-drying clay so that a Phase II facet is flat under the microscope (see Krueger et al. 2008 for a description of facets related to mastication and resultant microwear). A white-light scanning confocal profiler (microscope) scans the facet with a 100x objective lens to generate a 3-D picture of the tooth's surface topography. Four adjacent scans are taken to cover an area of 276µm x 204µm. Scans are then normalized and edited to remove defects, such as dust particles, using Solarmap Universal Software (Solarius, Inc., http://www.solarius-inc.com/solarmap). The scans are then analyzed using Toothfrax (Surfract 2007, http://www.surfract.com/products.html) and SFrax (ibid.) scale-sensitive fractal analysis software. This software is based on the principle that surface texture features' size (volume and length) change with the scale of observation, much in the way an impressionist painting looks like a collection of blobs of paint when viewed from one inch away, compared to the actual image when viewed from five feet away.

The information gathered typically concerns complexity and anisotropy, but Scott et al. (2005) suggest also looking at other parameters, such as heterogeneity, scale of maximal complexity, and textural fill volume. All these variables measure different components of change in surface texture across a tooth's surface, and associated diets (see Scott et al. 2005 for a detailed description of these measurements).

Isotopic and Trace Elemental Analysis

Regardless of the specific chemical signature to be studied and the precise methods employed to do so, the researcher must address several key questions when undertaking biochemical analyses.

How much tissue is needed for each analysis?

Tissue sampling is a crucial concern associated with these biochemical techniques, because isotope and trace element analyses are, to varying degrees, intrusive in that material is removed from the remains being studied and is then consumed entirely by the ensuing analysis. It is therefore important to know the smallest amount of bone or other preserved tissue needed for different types of analysis, so as to minimize damage to the skeleton and dentition. As mass spectrometry technology and preparation methods have improved over the past several decades, that minimum amount has steadily decreased; now, where a gram of bone was once needed, a few milligrams will produce the same quality of data. Indeed, for most isotopic and trace element analyses no more than 20 mg of tooth enamel or 150 mg of bone is needed; with the application of laser ablation and x-ray fluorescence (XRF) techniques to both trace element and isotopic research, researchers have the ability to generate accurate chemical data while leaving little or no macroscopically visible traces on the bone or teeth being studied. However, these latter two technologies are less commonly employed because they are expensive; in addition, the data resulting from analysis of minute samples of tissue material can have higher error ranges, which can affect interpretations of diet variation. Consequently, the majority of biochemical paleodiet research relies on more traditional sampling techniques.

What in vivo developmental period(s) is the focus of this analysis?

One of the most exciting aspects of the direct methods discussed here is that dietary information can be characterized in multiple preserved tissues that reflect diet composition at different points in an individual's lifespan, allowing a researcher to reconstruct longitudinal dietary data sets in addition to cross-sectional ones. This is because some tissues—hair, fingernails, and tooth crowns—become metabolically inert once they have formed, while others—skin, organs, and bones—remain continuously metabolically active throughout life. Deciduous tooth crowns form in utero, while permanent tooth crowns form during the first decade or so of life, and different tooth types (incisors, first molars, second premolars, and the like) form at different developmental periods within this first decade (Hillson 1996). Isotope and trace element signatures in tooth enamel and, barring remodeling from breakage or other trauma, dentin will thus reflect diet composition during the specific period in infancy or childhood in which the tooth crown formed, regardless of how old an individual was when she or he died. Similarly, hair grows incrementally at roughly 1cm per month during life, and hair strands that have ceased growth will often remain in the follicle for several months. Consequently, isotope and trace element signatures in hair segments reflect diet resources consumed in the weeks or months prior to death, depending on a hair segment's distance from the scalp and whether a hair strand was actively growing at the time of death (Nakamura et al. 1982; O'Connell and Hedges 1999). Bone cells undergo metabolic turnover continuously during life, at different rates depending on the specific bone type and bone structure. Isotopic and trace element signatures in bone therefore represent an average of dietary resources over the last decade or more of an individual's life (Manolagas 2000). Finally, dental microfeatures and microwear patterns have a "Last Supper" effect where only the last few meals are etched into the enamel or left as microbotanical residues (Teaford 2007), providing additional measures of late-life diet.

What larger interpretive questions form the basis of this study?
This question is arguably the most important, as it determines one's research design, methods, and sampling strategy. It is also most important because of the inherently destructive nature of most biochemical techniques; given the relative rarity of archaeological human remains and the ethical issues surrounding their excavation and study, the removal of tissue samples should serve to provide insights into ancient diet and nutrition that would be otherwise unobtainable, and to inform a larger understanding of cultural behavior and overall ways of life. Isotopic studies of ancient populations have provided critical insights into prehistoric subsistence related, for example, to movement between regions (Aufderheide et al. 1994; Turner, Kingston, and Armelagos 2010; White et al. 2009) and shifts from nomadism to sedentism (Benfer 1990). Changes in subsistence have also been related to aspects of state formation and consolidation, including increased maize production and consumption (Finucane, Agurto, and Isbell 2006; Sandness 1992), access to meat (Hastorf 2001a), gendered and status-based access to high-status foods (Hastorf 2001b; Ubelaker, Katzenberg, and Doyon 1995), and shifting relationships between subject groups and imperial cores over time (Slovak 2007). Carbon isotope analyses have been useful in reconstructing diet and mobility in a number of archaeological (Knudson et al. 2012; Turner, Kingston, and Milanich 2005; Wright and Schwarcz 1998) and paleoanthropological (Lee-Thorp et al. 2010; Sponheimer and Lee-Thorp 1999) contexts. Trace element studies (reviewed in Katzenberg and Harrison 1997; Pate 1994; Pollard et al. 2007) have similarly been used to infer differences in diets mediated by different subsistence regimes, social stratification, and resource specialization.

The combination of trace element and stable isotopic characterizations provides fruitful opportunities to refine dietary estimates and relate them to larger social processes such as social status (Schutkowski et al. 1999), maize intensification, and culture change (White and Schwarcz 1989), and to better estimate geological regions of residence that would result in differing subsistence patterns (Hooge-werff et al. 2001).

Preparing Samples and Conducting Analyses

The methods for preparing preserved tissues for isotopic or trace elemental analysis vary according to the type of tissue being studied, but an underlying commonality is that an isolate tissue substrate (such as bone collagen or enamel phosphate) is processed through a mass spectrometer. The sample is either combusted or digested in acid, and the gases released through this process are then separated molecularly by their atomic weights for isotope analysis, or measured in their entirety for trace elemental analysis.

Human remains with preserved soft tissues are relatively rare in bioarchaeological research, but should the opportunity to analyze archaeological hair, muscle, or skin present itself, preparing these tissues is simple and straightforward. Often, soft tissue samples are simply cleaned ultrasonically with a sequence of distilled water, ethanol, and distilled water to remove surface contaminants, though samples may also be rehydrated with a dimethyl sulfoxide (DMSO) solution for additional microscopic analyses prior to isotope or elemental analysis (Williams, White, and Longstaffe 2011). Sample preparation techniques for isotope analysis of skeletal material generally involve the removal of lipid components (particularly in bone samples that are very well preserved), and either all of the lipids and proteins in order to isolate the mineral fraction, or the removal of all lipid and mineral components to isolate the protein components. The tissue is first cleaned, often using a combination of surface abrasion with a rotary tool and/or acid leaching followed by ultrasonic cleaning in distilled water. To isolate the collagen-dominated protein components of bone or tooth dentin, samples are crushed, treated with a solution of methanol, chloroform, and water, and then demineralized in a dilute hydrochloric acid solution, followed by treatment with a basic solution of sodium hydroxide or potassium hydroxide to remove humic acids and other contaminants from the interment environment (Ambrose 1993). Samples are then gelatinized in a very dilute hydrochloric acid solution, and sometimes passed through ultrafine mesh filters to remove any remaining microscopic contaminants, then freeze-dried. These prepared samples are then digested or combusted in a mass spectrometer (a variety of mass spectrometry options are available; see Price and Burton 2011).

Methods to isolate the mineral components of bone and tooth enamel depend on whether one seeks to isolate carbonate or phosphate apatite. Methods to isolate carbonate are simpler and less costly, involving ultrasonic cleaning in distilled water followed by treatment with a bleach/distilled water solution and a further treatment with dilute acetic acid; the isolated carbonate is then freeze-dried and digested on a mass spectrometer (Price and Burton 2011). Methods to isolate phosphate hydroxyapatite are more complex: the bonds between phosphorous and oxygen are much stronger than those between carbon and oxygen, so harsher chemical treatments are required to break those bonds (Sponheimer and Lee-Thorpe 1999). Because of its weaker chemical bonds and more loosely packed mineral matrix, bone carbonate is considered more prone to postmortem diagenetic alteration of its crystalline structure than enamel carbonate or bone phosphate is (Koch, Tuross, and Fogel 1997); however, the extent to which increased crystallinity has any effect on isotopic values is unclear (Lee-Thorp and Sponheimer 2003; Metcalfe, Longstaffe, and White 2009), particularly in arid environments with excellent preservation (Ugan et al. 2012).

Trace elements are typically characterized by leaching or digesting the bone or tooth sample in an acidic solution in an apparatus interfaced with a mass spectrometer (Price and Burton 2011). It is also common to analyze duplicate samples using x-ray fluorescence analysis (Hoogewerff et al. 2001), and use of handheld XRF machines is increasingly common as a noninvasive technique for measuring the relative ratios of different trace elements in skeletal tissues (Gonzalez-Rodriguez and Fowler 2013; János et al. 2011). Trace elemental data are typically analyzed through multivariate statistical methods such as principal components analysis (PCA), given the size of the resulting data set; PCA can also be used to correct for the likelihood of diagenetic contamination (Shafer et al. 2008).

With all of these methods, it is necessary to assess the extent to which the elemental concentrations or isotope ratios represent the elements that were consumed and metabolized during an individual's life, versus elements in the surrounding environment that intruded into the tissue during postmortem decomposition. Such an intrusion, which results from elemental exchange between preserved tissue cells and the soils and water of different burial environments, is known as diagenesis. Diagenetic alteration is typically estimated rather than demonstrated conclusively, and these chemical data should always be analyzed and interpreted with caution. For example, it is common to calculate percent yield and the ratio of percent carbon to percent nitrogen (C/N) in assessing the integrity of collagen and keratin, whereas percent carbon and a measure of crystallinity are commonly used in assessing the integrity of carbonate and phosphate. In addition, samples of surrounding burial soils and water sources are commonly taken as a way to estimate the degree of elemental exchange in the burial environment (Price and Burton 2011). Tooth enamel is considered highly resistant to diagenesis because enamel is composed almost entirely of carbonate and phosphate hydroxyapatite, and its tightly packed crystalline structure makes it highly impervious to intrusive compounds during life and in the burial environment.

Limitations: What Direct Methods Cannot Say About Diet

There are a lot of questions about the effects specific foods have on the enamel surface, especially when food preparation techniques are involved (Teaford 2007). According to Lucas (1991), most foods in the human diet are not hard enough to leave behind microwear, but preparation of foods can introduce abrasives that cause microwear. Dental microwear also has a "Last Supper" effect where only the last few meals are etched into the enamel, but it is still useful for assessing large dietary differences (Teaford 2007). Analyzing human diet can be problematic because of food processing as well as seasonal, geographic, and annual variation in dietary patterns (ibid.). Microwear analysis has been useful in discerning dietary shifts among human populations; for example, cereals leave distinct patterns that may start to appear in populations depending more on agriculture, and hunter-gatherer groups have a tougher diet that leaves behind more pits and larger scratches (Mahoney 2006). New method controls, such as uniform magnification and use of the hypocone of the maxillary first molar for most studies, increase the accuracy of quantitative analysis and advance the dental microwear field, which plays an integral part in reconstructing dietary patterns.

Previous dental microwear studies (Bullington 1991; Molleson and Jones 1991; Organ et al. 2005; Schmidt 2001; Sołtysiak 2011; Teaford et al. 2001; Ungar and Spencer 1999) that looked at diet in bioarchaeological populations are limited, as previously stated, by inter- observer error and lack of repeatability (Scott et al. 2005). There is also a limit to the conclusions that can be drawn with feature-based microwear studies; this has been addressed somewhat by integrating multiple dietary analyses (see above). Meanwhile, future studies aim to better understand the forces affecting the enamel of a tooth.

What chemical methods cannot tell a researcher about ancient diets is as important what they can, since recognizing the inherent limitations of these methods is essential to properly interpreting the results. Of chief importance is the fact that isotopic and trace elemental analyses cannot be used to estimate the absolute quantities of different resources consumed by individuals, but only their relative proportions based on the types of resources available. It is also difficult to estimate specific foods that were consumed, as many food resources have similar isotopic values and/or elemental concentrations despite being very different in nutritional content and often necessarily obtained through different subsistence regimes. The best way to accurately estimate dietary components from isotopic data is to define as clearly as possible what the available food resources are at a given site, and what the range of isotopic values is for each of them (and their different edible parts). It is also important to consider the possibility or likelihood of imported foods that might not otherwise have been present in the local environment but may nonetheless have been important in local diets. Because of these main limitations, it is also difficult to infer nutritional status from isotopic and elemental data; however, studies have analyzed trace element and isotope data together to more accurately characterize the sources of calcium in the diet and thus distinguish between plants that would be indistinguishable using only isotopic values (Burton and Price 2000). Moreover, recent studies have analyzed isotopic data in concert with the frequencies and severities of pathological conditions in bones and teeth (see Goodman this volume) to estimate the relationships between diet composition and signs of malnutrition or chronic disease (Turner 2013; Turner and Armelagos 2012).

Conclusion

Reconstructing ancient diets is a complicated endeavor, but one that has demonstrated tremendous and far-reaching success in helping researchers to better understand lifeways, overall health and health disparities, cultural norms, and ritual practices in ancient societies. The methods described here are not the only ones proven useful in reconstructing subsistence and diet composition in archaeological populations. However, as the ones most commonly employed to directly estimate dietary intake, they can provide insights into diet composition among individuals, and at different points in one individual's lifetime. Using individuals as the units of analysis, it is then possible to reconstruct larger group-level trends that permit a researcher to take a "bottom-up" approach and appreciate the variation in diets between populations, within populations, and within individual lifespans. It has been the aim of this chapter to provide a basic conceptual framework and outline of laboratory methods for these types of direct analysis, and highlight some of the extensive literature available to those interested in pursuing these analyses in their own research.

Bethany L. Turner is Associate Professor in the Department of Anthropology at Georgia State University, where she also directs the Bioarchaeology Laboratory. Dr. Turner's research centers on multi-isotopic analysis of human remains from populations in Peru associated with the Inca Empire and Spanish Conquest. In addition to these Peruvian contexts, she has also analyzed human remains from medieval Mongolia, Sudanese Nubia, and the southeastern United States, often in collaboration with her students. Her research has been published in sources including *Journal of Archaeological Science, American Journal of Physical Anthropology,* and *International Journal of Osteoarchaeology,* and has been funded by the National Science Foundation and Wenner-Gren Foundation for Anthropological Research.

Sarah V. Livengood is currently a PhD student at the University of Arkansas, where she is also Lab Coordinator for the Ungar Lab (ungarlab.uark.edu). She began her lab experience in the Bioarchaeology Lab at Georgia State University, prepping hair, bone, and teeth for isotopic analysis. Sarah's research combines microwear analysis with various methodologies, including work with the Hadza, in order to understand the role of different dietary components in the evolution of early *Homo*. She is also involved in research to better understand the etiology of noncarious cervical lesions (NCCLs) in modern dentistry.

References

Ambrose, Stanley H. 1991. Effects of Diet, Climate and Physiology on Nitrogen Isotope Abundances in Terrestrial Food Webs. *J Archaeol Sci* 18(3): 293–317.

———. 1993. Isotopic Analysis of Paleodiets: Methodological and Interpretive Considerations. In *Investigations of Ancient Human Tissue: Chemical Analyses in Anthropology*, ed. M. Sandford, 59–130. Langhorne, PA: Gordon and Breach Science Publishers.

Ambrose, Stanley H., Brian M. Butler, Douglas B. Hanson, Rosalind L. Hunter-Anderson, and Harold W. Krueger. 1997. Stable Isotopic Analysis of Human Diet in the Marianas Archipelago, Western Pacific. *American Journal of Physical Anthropology* 104(3): 343–361.

Ambrose, Stanley H., and Lynette Norr. 1993. Experimental Evidence for the Relationship of the Carbon Isotope Ratios of Whole Diet and Dietary Protein to Those of Bone Collagen and Carbonate. In *Prehistoric Human Bone: Archaeology at the Molecular Level*, ed. J. B. Lambert and Gisela Grupe, 1–37. Berlin: Springer-Verlag.

Armelagos, George J. 1987. Biocultural Aspects of Food Choice. In *Food and Evolution: Toward a Theory of Human Food Habits*, ed. Marvin Harris and E. B. Ross, 579–594. Philadelphia: Temple University Press.

———. 1994. "You Are What You Eat". In *Paleonutrition: The Diet and Health of Prehistoric Americans*, ed. K. D. Sobolik, 235–244. Center for Archaeological Investigations, Southern Illinois University Occasional Paper No 22. Carbondale: Board of Trustees, Southern Illinois University.

Aufderheide, Arthur C., Mark A. Kelley, Mario Rivera, Luz Gray, Larry L. Tieszen, Elysha Iversen, H. Roy Krouse, and Alvaro Carevic. 1994. Contributions of Chemical Dietary Reconstruction to the Assessment of Adaptation by Ancient Highland Immigrants (Alto-Ramirez) to Coastal Conditions at Pisagua, North Chile. *Journal of Archaeological Science* 21(4): 515–524.

Baker, G., L. H. P. Jones, and I. D. Wardrop. 1959. Cause of Wear in Sheep Teeth. *Nature* 184: 1583–1584.

Balasse, Marie, and Anne Tresset. 2002. Early Weaning of Neolithic Domestic Cattle (Bercy, France) Revealed by Intra-tooth Variation in Nitrogen Isotopic Ratios. *Journal of Archaeological Science* 29: 853–859.

Beach, Jeremy J., and Christopher W. Schmidt. 2013. Foodways and Polity Formation: A Bioarchaeological Analysis of the Xiognu Using Dental Microwear Texture Analysis and Pathological Conditions. *American Journal of Physical Anthropology* 150: 76.

Benfer, Robert A. 1990. The Preceramic Period site of Paloma, Peru: Bioindications of Improving Adaptation to Sedentism. *Latin American Antiquity* 1(4): 284–318.

Bökönyi, Sandor. 1975. Effects of Environmental and Cultural Changes on Prehistoric Faunal Assemblages. In *Gastronomy: The Anthropology of Food and Food Habits,* ed. M. L. Arnott, 3-12. The Hague: Mouton.

Bullington, Jill. 1991. Deciduous Dental Microwear of Prehistoric Juveniles from the Lower Illinois River Valley. *American Journal of Physical Anthropology* 84(1): 59–73.

Burton, James H. 1996. Trace Elements in Bone as Paleodietary Indicators. *ACS Symposium Series,* 327–333. Oxford: Oxford University Press.

Burton, James H., and T. Douglas Price. 2000. The Use and Abuse of Trace Elements for Paleodietary Research. In *Biogeochemical Approaches to Paleodietary Analysis,* ed. S. H. Ambrose and M. A. Katzenberg, 159–171. New York: Kluwer.

Burton, James H., and Lori E. Wright. 1995. Nonlinearity in the Relationship between Bone Sr/Ca and Diet: Paleodietary Implications. *American Journal of Physical Anthropology* 96(3): 273–282.

Carbone, Victor A., and Bennie C. Keel. 1985. Preservation of Plant and Animal Remains. In *The Analysis of Prehistoric Diets,* ed. R. I. Gilbert Jr. and J. H. Mielke, 1–19. Orlando: Academic Press.

Chiu, Laura W., Christopher W. Schmidt, Patrick Mahoney, and Jaqueline I. McKingley. 2012. Dental Microwear Texture Analysis of Bronze and Iron Age Agriculturalists from England. *American Journal of Physical Anthropology* 147: 115.

Covert, Herbert H., and Richard F. Kay. 1981. Dental Microwear and Diet: Implications for Determining the Feeding Behaviors of Extinct Primates, with a Comment on the Dietary Pattern of *Sivapithecus. American Journal of Physical Anthropology* 55: 331–336.

DeNiro, Michael J. 1987. Stable Isotopy and Archaeology. *American Scientist* 75(2): 182–191.

DeNiro, Michael J., and Samuel Epstein. 1978. Influence of Diet on the Distribution of Carbon Isotopes in Animals. *Geochimica et Cosmochimica Acta* 42(5): 495–506.

DeNiro, M. J., and M. J. Schoeninger. 1983. Stable Carbon and Nitrogen Isotope Ratios of Bone-Collagen: Variations within Individuals, between Sexes, and within Populations Raised on Monotonous Diets. *Journal of Archaeological Science* 10(3): 199–203.

Eaton, S. Boyd, S. Boyd Eaton III, and Loren Cordain. 2002. Evolution, Diet, and Health. In *Human Diet: Its Origin and Evolution,* ed. P. S. Ungar and M. F. Teaford, 7–17. Westport, CT: Bergin & Garvey.

Eaton, S. Boyd, S. Boyd Eaton III, and Melvin J. Konner. 1997. Paleolithic Nutrition Revisited: A Twelve-Year Retrospective on Its Nature and Implications. *European Journal of Clinical Nutrition* 51: 207–216.

El-Zaatari, Sireen 2008. Occlusal Molar Microwear and the Diets of the Ipiutak and Tigara Populations (Point Hope) with Comparisons to the Aleut and Arikara. *J Archaeol Sci* 35: 2517–2522.

Ezzo, Joseph A. 1994. Putting the "Chemistry" Back into Archaeological Bone Chemistry Analysis: Modeling Potential Paleodietary Indicators. *Journal of Anthropological Archaeology* 13(1): 1–34.

Fernández. Jorge, Héctor O. Panarello, and Juan Schobinger. 1999. The Inka Mummy from Mount Aconcagua: Decoding the Geographic Origin of the "Messenger to the Deities" by Means of Stable Carbon, Nitrogen, and Sulfur Isotope Analysis. *Geoarchaeology: An International Journal* 14(1): 27–46.

Finucane, Brian, Patricia Maita, and William H. Isbell. 2006. Human and Animal Diet at Conchopata, Peru: Stable Isotope Evidence for Maize Agriculture and Animal Management Practices during the Middle Horizon. *Journal of Archaeological Science* 33: 1766–1776.

Fritz, Gayle J. 1994. The Value of Archaeological Plant Remains for Paleodietary Reconstruction. In *Paleonutrition: The Diet and Health of Prehistoric Americans,* ed. K. D. Sobolik, 21–33. Center for Archaeological Investigations, Southern Illinois University at Carbondale Occasional Papers 22. Carbondale: Board of Trustees, Southern Illinois University.

Froehle, Andrew W., Corrina M. Kellner, and Margaret J. Schoeninger. 2012. Multivariate Carbon and Nitrogen Stable Isotope Model for the Reconstruction of Prehistoric Human Diet. *American Journal of Physical Anthropology* 147(3): 352–369.

Fuller, Benjamin T., James L. Fuller, Nancy E. Sage, David A. Harris, Tamsin C. O'Connell, and Robert E. M. Hedges. 2004. Nitrogen Balance and δ15N: Why You're Not What You Eat During Pregnancy. *Rapid Communications in Mass Spectrometry* 18: 2889–2896.

———. 2005. Nitrogen Balance and d15N: Why You're Not What You Eat during Nutritional Stress. *Rap Comm Mass Spec* 19: 2497–2506.

González-Rodriguez, Jose, and Gillian Fowler. 2013. A Study on the Discrimination of Human Skeletons Using X-Ray Fluorescence and Chemometric Tools in Chemical Anthropology. *Forensic Science International* 231(1–3): 407e.401–407e.406.

Goodman, Alan H., Debra L. Martin DL, and George J. Armelagos. 1984. Indicators of Stress from Bone and Teeth. In *Paleopathology at the Origins of Agriculture,* ed. Mark N. Cohen and George J. Armelagos, 13–49. Orlando: Academic Press.

Gordon, Kathleen D. 1984. Hominoid Dental Microwear: Complications in the Use of Microwear Analysis to Detect Diet. *Journal of Dental Research* 63: 1043–1046.

———. 1986. Dental Microwear Analysis to Detect Human Diet. *American Journal of Physical Anthropology* 69: 206–207.

———. 1988. A Review of Methodology and Quantification in Dental Microwear Analysis. *Scanning Microscopy* 2: 1139–1147.

Gordon, Kathleen D., and Alan C. Walker. 1983. Playing "Possum": A Microwear Experiment. *American Journal of Physical Anthropology* 60: 109–112.

Grine, Frederick E. 1977. Analysis of Early Hominid Deciduous Molar Wear by Scanning Electron Microscopy: A Preliminary Report. *Proceedings of the Electron Microscopy Society of South Africa* 7: 157–158.

———. 1986. Dental Evidence for Dietary Differences in *Australopithecus* and *Paranthropus*: A Quantitative Analysis of Permanent Molar Microwear. *Journal of Human Evolution* 15(8): 783–822.

Gumerman, George. 1994. Feeding Specialists: The Effect of Specialization on Subsistence Variation. In *Paleonutrition: The Diet and Health of Prehistoric Americans,* ed. Kristin D. Sobolik, 80–97. Center for Archaeological Investigations, Southern Illinois University at Carbondale Occasional Paper No 22. Carbondale: Board of Trustees, Southern Illinois University.

Hastorf, Christine A. 2001a. Agricultural Production and Consumption. In *Empire and Domestic Economy,* ed. T. N. D'Altroy and C. A. Hastorf, 155–178. New York: Kluwer Academic/Plenum Publishers.

———. 2001b. Gender, Space and Food in Prehistory. In *Contemporary Archaeology in Theory,* ed. R. W. Preucel and I. Hodder, 460-484. Oxford: Blackwell.

Hillson, Simon 1996. *Dental Anthropology.* Cambridge: University Press.

Hobson, Keith A. 1999. Tracing Origins and Migration of Wildlife Using Stable Isotopes: A Review. *Oecologia* 120: 314–426.

Hogue, S. Homes, and Rebecca Melsheimer. 2008. Integrating Dental Microwear and Isotopic Analyses to Understand Dietary Change in East-Central Mississippi. *Journal of Archaeological Science* 35: 228–238.

Hoogewerff, Jurian, Wolfgang Papesch, Martin Kralik, Margit Berner, Pieter Vroon, Hermann Miesbauer, Othmar Gaber, Karl-Heinz Künzel, and Jos Kleinjans. 2001. The Last Domicile of the Iceman from Hauslabjoch: A Geochemical Approach Using Sr, C, and O Isotopes and Trace Element Signatures. *Journal of Archaeological Science* 28: 982–989.

Iacumin, Paola, Helene Bocherens, Louis Chaix, and A. Marioth. 1998. Stable Carbon and Nitrogen Isotopes as Dietary Indicators of Ancient Nubian Populations (Northern Sudan). *Journal of Archaeological Science* 25(4): 293–301.

Irish, Joel D., and Christy G. Turner. 1997. Brief Communication: First Evidence of LSA-MAT in Non-Native Americans: Historic Senegalese from West Africa. *American Journal of Physical Anthropology* 102(1): 141–146.

Ishige, Naomichi 2001. *The History and Culture of Japanese Food.* London: Kegan Paul.

János, István, Lázló Szathmáry, A. Nádas, Z. Béni, and E. Máthé. 2011. Evaluation of Elemental Status of Ancient Human Bone Samples from Northeastern Hungary Dated to the 10th Century AD by XRF. *Nuclear Instruments and Methods in Physics Research Section B: Beam Interactions with Materials and Atoms* 269(21): 2593–2599.

Katzenberg, M. Anne, and Roman G. Harrison. 1997. What's in a Bone? Recent Advances in Archaeological Bone Chemistry. *Journal of Archaeological Research* 5(3): 265–293.

Katzenberg, M. Anne, and Nancy C. Lovell NC. 1999. Stable Isotope Variation in Pathological Bone. *International Journal of Osteoarchaeology* 9(5): 316–324.

Kellner, Corrina, and Margaret Schoeninger. 2007. A Simple Carbon Isotope Model for Reconstructing Prehistoric Human Diet. *Am J Phys Anthropol* 133: 1112–1127.

Knudson, Kelly J., Lisa Frink, Brian W. Hoffman, and T. Douglas Price. 2004. Chemical Characterization of Arctic Soils: Activity Area Analysis in Contemporary Yup'ik Fish Camps Using ICP-AES. *Journal of Archaeological Science* 31: 443–456.

Knudson, Kelly J., Barra O'Donnabhain, Charisse Carver, Robin Cleland, and T. Douglas Price. 2012. Migration and Viking Dublin: Paleomobility and Paleodiet through Isotopic Analyses. *Journal of Archaeological Science* 29: 308–320.

Knudson, Kelly J., and T. Douglas Price. 2007. Utility of Multiple Chemical Techniques in Archaeological Residential Mobility Studies: Case Studies from Tiwanaku- and Chiribaya-Affiliated Sites in the Andes. *American Journal of Physical Anthropology* 132(1): 25–39.

Knudson, Kelly J., Hope M. Williams, Jane E. Buikstra, Paula D. Tomczak, Gwyneth W. Gordon, and Ariel D. Anbar. 2010. Introducing $\delta^{88/86}$Sr Analysis in Archaeology: A Demonstration of the Utility of Strontium Isotope Fractionation in Paleodietary Studies. *Journal of Archaeological Science* 37(9): 2352–2364.

Koch, Paul L., Noreen Tuross N, and Marylin L. Fogel. 1997. The Effects of Sample Treatment and Diagenesis on the Isotopic Integrity of Carbonate in Biogenic Hydroxylapatite. *Journal of Archaeological Science* 24: 417–429.

Krueger, Kristin L., Jessica R. Scott, Richard F. Kay, and Peter S. Ungar. 2008. Technical Note: Dental Microwear Textures of "Phase I" and "Phase II" Facets. *American Journal of Physical Anthropology* 137(4): 485–490.

Krueger, Kristin L., and Peter S. Ungar. 2010. Incisor Microwear Textures of Five Bioarchaeological Groups. *International Journal of Osteoarchaeology* 20(5): 549–560.

Lee-Thorp, Julia, and Matt Sponheimer. 2003. Three Case Studies Used to Reassess the Reliability of Fossil Bone and Enamel Isotope Signals for Paleodietary Studies. *Journal of Anthropological Archaeology* 22: 208–216.

Lee-Thorp, Julia A., Judith C. Sealy, and Nikolaas van der Merwe. 1989. Stable Carbon Isotope Ratio Differences between Bone-Collagen and Bone Apatite, and Their Relationship to Diet. *Journal of Archaeological Science* 16(6): 585–599.

Lee-Thorp, Julia A., Matt Sponheimer, Benjamin H. Passey, Darryl J. de Ruiter, and Thure E. Cerling. 2010. Stable Isotopes in Fossil Hominin Tooth Enamel Suggest a Fundamental Dietary Shift in the Pliocene. *Philosophical Transactions of the Royal Society B: Biological Sciences* 365(1556): 3389–3396.

Livengood, Sarah V. 2012. *Refining Dietary Estimates at Machu Picchu Using Combined Dental Macro/Microwear and Isotopic Analyses.* Atlanta: Georgia State University.

Lucas, Peter W. 1991. Fundamental Physical Properties of Fruits and Seeds in the Diet of Southeast Asian Primates. In *Primatology Today,* ed. Akiyoshi Ehara, Tasuku Kimura, Osamu Takenaka, and Mitsuo Iwamoto, 125–128. Amsterdam: Elsevier Science Limited.

Mahoney, Patrick 2006. Dental Microwear from Natufian Hunter-Gatherers and Early Neolithic Farmers: Comparisons Within and Between Samples. *American Journal of Physical Anthropology* 130(3): 308–319.

Manolagas, Stavros C. 2000. Birth and Death of Bone Cells: Basic Regulatory Mechanisms and Implications for the Pathogenesis and Treatment of Osteoporosis. *Endocrine Reviews* 21: 115–137.

Metcalfe, Jessica Z., Fred J. Longstaffe, and Christine D. White. 2009. Method-Dependent Variations in Stable Isotope Results for Structural Carbonate in Bone Bioapatite. *Journal of Archaeological Science* 36: 110–121.

Molleson, Theya, and Karen Jones. 1991. Dental Evidence for Dietary Change at Abu Hureyra. *Journal of Archaeological Science* 18(5): 525–539.

Nakamura, K., D. A. Schoeller, F. J. Winkler, and Hanns-Ludwig Schmidt. 1982. Geographical Variations in the Carbon Isotope Content of the Diet and Hair of Contemporary Man. *Biomedical Mass Spectrometry* 9: 390–394.

Nestle, Marion 1999. Animal vs. Plant Foods in Human Diets and Health: Is the Historical Record Unequivocal? *Proceedings of the Nutrition Society* 58: 211–218.

O'Connell, Tamsin C., and Robert E. M. Hedges. 1999. Investigations into the Effect of Diet on Modern Human Hair Isotopic Values. *American Journal of Physical Anthropology* 108: 409–425.

O'Connell, Tamsin C., Robert E. M. Hedges, M. A. Healey, and A. H. R. W. Simpson. 2001. Isotopic Comparison of Hair, Nail and Bone: Modern Analyses. *Journal of Archaeological Science* 28(11): 1247–1255.

Organ, Jason M., Mark F. Teaford, and Clark S. Larsen. 2005. Dietary Inferences from Dental Occlusal Microwear at Mission San Luis de Apalachee. *American Journal of Physical Anthropology* 128: 801–811.

Parmalee, Paul W. 1985. Identification and Interpretation of Archaeologically Derived Animal Remains. In *The Analysis of Prehistoric Diets,* ed. Robert I. Gilbert Jr. and James H. Mielke, 61–95. Orlando: Academic Press.

Pate, F. Donald 1994. Bone Chemistry and Paleodiet. *Journal of Archaeological Method and Theory* 1(2): 161–209.

Peters, Charles R. 1982. Electron-Optical Microscopic Study of Incipient Dental Microdamage from Experimental Seed and Bone Crushings. *American Journal of Physical Anthropology* 57: 283–301.

Pollard, Mark, Catherine Batt, Ben Stern and Suzanne M. M. Young. 2007. *Analytical Chemistry in Archaeology.* Cambridge: Cambridge University Press.

Price, T. Douglas, and James H. Burton. 2011. An Introduction to Archaeological Chemistry. New York: Springer.

Puech, Pierre-François. 1979. Diet of Early Man: Evidence from Abrasion of Teeth and Tools. *Current Anthropology* 20: 590–592.

Puech, Pierre-François, and A. Prone. 1979. Mechanical Process of Dental Wearing Down by Abrasion, Reproduced by Experimentation and Applied to Fossil Man and His Paleoecological Surroundings. *CR Academy of Science D Nat* 289: 895.

Rensberger, J. M. 1978. Scanning Electron Microscopy of Wear and Occlusal Events in Some Small Herbivores. In *Development, Function, and Evolution of Teeth,* ed. P. M. Butler, and K. A. Joysey, 415–438. New York: Academic Press.

Roosevelt, Anna. 1987. The Evolution of Human Subsistence. In *Food and Evolution: Toward a Theory of Human Food Habits,* ed. Marvin Harris and Eric B. Ross, 565–578. Philadelphia: Temple University Press.

Ryan, Alan S., and Donald C. Johanson. 1989. Anterior Dental Microwear in *Australopithecus afarensis*: Comparisons with Human and Nonhuman Primates. *Journal of Human Evolution* 18(3): 235–268.

Safont, S., A. Malgosa, M. E. Subirá, and J. Gilbert. 1998. Can Trace Elements in Fossils Provide Information About Paleodiet? *International Journal of Osteoarchaeology* 8: 23–37.

Sandford, Mary K. 1992. A Reconsideration of Trace Element Analysis in Prehistoric Bone. In *Skeletal Biology of Past Peoples: Research Methods,* ed. S. R. Saunders and M. A. Katzenberg, 79–104. New York: Wiley-Liss.

Sandness, Karin L. 1992. Temporal and Spatial Dietary Variability in the Prehistoric Lower and Middle Osmore Drainage: The Carbon and Nitrogen Isotope Evidence. MA thesis. Lincoln: University of Nebraska at Lincoln.

Schmidt, Christopher W. 2001. Dental Microwear Evidence for a Dietary Shift Between Two Nonmaize-Reliant Prehistoric Human Populations from Indiana. *American Journal of Physical Anthropology* 114: 139–145.

Schmidt, Christopher W., Laura W. Chiu, Lindsy Frazer, Claire Barrett, and Patrick Mahoney. 2011. Dental Microwear Texture Analysis of Natufian Hunter-Gatherers and Neolithic Farmers from Northern Israel. *American Journal of Physical Anthropology* 144: 265.

Schoeninger, Margaret J., and Michael J. DeNiro. 1984. Nitrogen and Carbon Isotopic Composition of Bone-Collagen from Marine and Terrestrial Animals. *Geochimica Et Cosmochimica Acta* 48(4): 625–639.

Schutkowski, H., B. Herrmann, F. Wiedemann, Helene Bocherens, and Gisela Grupe. 1999. Diet, Status and Decomposition at Weingarten: Trace Element and Isotope Analyses on Early Mediaeval Skeletal Material. *Journal of Archaeological Science* 26(6): 675–685.

Schwarcz, Henry P. 2000. Some Biochemical Aspects of Carbon Isotopic Paleodiet Studies. In *Biogeochemical Approaches to Paleodietary Analysis,* ed. S. H. Ambrose and M. A. Katzenberg, 189–209. New York: Kluwer.

Schwarcz, Henry P., and Margaret J. Schoeninger. 1991. Stable Isotope Analyses in Human Nutritional Ecology. *Yearbook of Physical Anthropology* 34: 283–321.

Scott, R. S., Peter S. Ungar, T. S. Bergstrom, C. A. Brown, F. E. Grine, Mark F. Teaford, and Alan Walker. 2005. Dental Microwar Texture Analysis Shows Within-Species Diet Variability in Fossil Hominins. *Nature* 436(7051): 693–695.

Semprebon, Gina M., Laurie R. Godfrey, Nikos Solounias, Michael R. Sutherland, and William L. Jungers. 2004. Can Low Magnification Stereomicroscopy Reveal Diet? *Journal of Human Evolution* 47: 115–144.

Shafer, Martin M., Malika Siker, Joel T. Overdier, Peter C. Ramsi, Maria Teschler-Nicola, and Philip M. Farrell. 2008. Enhanced Methods for Assessment of the Trace Element Composition of Iron Age Bone. *Science of the Total Environment* 401(1–3): 144–161.

Sillen, Andrew, and Maureen Kavanagh. 1982. Strontium and Paleodietary Research: A Review. *American Journal of Physical Anthropology* 25(S3): 67–90.

Sillen, Andrew, Judith C. Sealy, and Nikolaas J. van der Merwe. 1989. Chemistry and Paleodietary Research: No More Easy Answers. *American Antiquity* 54(3): 504–512.

Slovak, Nicole M. 2007. Examining Imperial Influence on Peru's Central Coast: Isotopic and Cultural Analyses of Middle Horizon Burials at Ancon. Unpublished PhD dissertation. Stanford, CA: Stanford University.

Sołtysiak Arkadiusz. 2011. Cereal Grinding Technology in Ancient Mesopotamia: Evidence from Dental Microwear. *Journal of Archaeological Science* 38(10): 2805–2810.

Sponheimer, Matt, and Julia A. Lee-Thorp. 1999. Alteration of Enamel Carbonate Environments During Fossilization. *Journal of Archaeological Science* 26: 143–150.

———. 1999b. Oxygen Isotopes in Enamel Carbonate and Their Ecological Significance. *Journal of Archaeological Science* 26: 723–728.

Styles, Bonnie W. 1994. The Value of Archaeological Faunal Remains for Paleodietary Reconstruction: A Case Study for the Midwestern United States. In *Paleonutrition: The Diet and Health of Prehistoric Americans,* ed. Kristin D. Sobolik, 34–54. Center for Archaeological Investigations, Southern Illinois University at Carbondale Occasional Paper No 22. Carbondale: Board of Trustees, Southern Illinois University.

Surfract. 2007. Surface Metrology and Fractal Analysis. http://www.surfract.com

Teaford, Mark F. 2007. What Do We Know and Not Know about Dental Microwear and Diet? In *Evolution of the Human Diet,* ed. Peter S. Ungar, 106–131. Oxford: Oxford University Press.

Teaford, Mark F., Clark S. Larsen, Robert F. Pastor, and V. E. Noble. 2001. Dental Microwear and Diet in La Florida. In *Bioarchaeology of La Florida,* ed. Clark S. Larsen, 82–112. Gainesville: University Press of Florida.

Teaford Mark F., and James D. Lytle. 1996. Brief Communication: Diet-Induced Changes in Rates of Human Tooth Microwear; A Case Study Involving Stone-Ground Maize. *American Journal of Physical Anthropology* 100: 143–147.

Tieszen, Larry L., and Michael Chapman. 1993. Carbon and Nitrogen Isotopic Status of the Major Marine and Terrestrial Resources in the Atacama Desert of Northern Chile. In *First World Congress on Mummy Studies,* ed. A. Aufderheide, 409–426. Santa Cruz, Tenerife, Canary Islands: World Congress on Mummy Studies.

Tieszen, Larry L., and Tim F. Fagre. 1993. Carbon Isotopic Variability in Modern and Archaeological Maize. *Journal of Archaeological Science* 20: 25–40.

Turner, Bethany L. 2013. Interpreting Oral Pathology at Machu Picchu, Peru. *International Journal of Osteoarchaeology* 25(4): 502–514 .

Turner, Bethany L., and George J. Armelagos. 2012. Diet, Residential Origin, and Pathology at Machu Picchu, Peru. *American Journal of Physical Anthropology* 149(1): 71–83.

Turner, Bethany L., John D. Kingston, and George J. Armelagos. 2010. Variation in Dietary Histories among the Immigrants of Machu Picchu: Carbon and Nitrogen Isotope Evidence. *Chungara: Revista de Antropología Chilena* 42(2): 515–524.

Turner, Bethany L., John D. Kingston, and Jerald T. Milanich. 2005. Isotopic Evidence of Immigration Linked to Status during the Weeden Island and Suwanee Valley Periods in North Florida. *Southeastern Archaeology* 24(2): 121–136.

Turner, Bethany L., and Amanda L. Thompson. 2013. Beyond the Paleolithic Prescription: Incorporating Diversity and Flexibility in the Study of Human Diet Evolution. *Nutrition Reviews* 71(8): 501–510.

Ubelaker, Douglas H., M. Anne Katzenberg, and Leon G. Doyon. 1995. Status and Diet in Precontact Highland Ecuador. *American Journal of Physical Anthropology* 97(4): 403–411.

Ugan, Andrew, Gustavo Neme, Adolfo Gil, Joan Coltrain, Robert Tykot, and Paula Novellino. 2012. Geographic Variation in Bone Carbonate and Water $\delta^{18}O$ values in Mendoza, Argentina and Their Relationship to Prehistoric Economy and Settlement. *Journal of Archaeological Science* 39: 2752–2763.

Ungar, Peter S., and Frederick E. Grine. 1991. Incisor Size and Wear in *Australopithecus africanus* and *Paranthropus robustus*. *Journal of Human Evolution* 20(4): 313–340.

Ungar, Peter S., Frederick E. Grine, and Mark F. Teaford. 2006. Diet in Early Homo: A Review of the Evidence and a New Model of Adaptive Versatility. *Annual Review of Anthropology* 35: 209–228.

Ungar, Peter S., Robert S. Scott, Jessica A. Scott, and Mark F. Teaford. 2008. Dental Microwear Analysis: Historical Perspectives and New Approaches. In *Technique and Applications in Dental Anthropology*, ed. Joel D. Irish and G. C. Nelson, 389–425. Cambridge: Cambridge University Press.

Ungar, Peter S., and Mark A. Spencer. 1999. Incisor Microwear, Diet, and Tooth Use in Three Amerindian Populations. *American Journal of Physical Anthropology* 109: 387–396.

Van Sessen, Rebecca, Christopher W. Schmidt, Susan G. Sheridan, Jaime Ullinger, and Matthew Grohovsky. 2013. Dental Microwear Texture Analysis at Tell Dothan. *American Journal of Physical Anthropology* 150: 276.

Walker, Alan, Hendrick N. Hoeck, and Linda Perez. 1978. Microwear of Mammalian Teeth as an Indicator of Diet. *Science* 201: 908–910.

Webb, Elizabeth A., Henry P. Schwarcz, and Paul F. Healy. 2004. Detection of Ancient Maize in Lowland Maya Soils Using Stable Carbon Isotopes: Evidence from Caracol, Belize. *Journal of Archaeological Science* 31: 1039–1052.

White, Christine D., Andrew J. Nelson, Fred J. Longstaffe, Gisela Grupe, and A Jung. 2009. Landscape Bioarchaeology at Pacatnamu, Peru: Inferring Mobility from $\delta^{13}C$ and $\delta^{15}N$ Values of Hair. *Journal of Archaeological Science* 36(7): 1527–1537.

White, Christine D., and Henry P. Schwarcz. 1989. Ancient Maya Diet as Inferred from Istopic and Elemental Analysis of Human Bone. *Journal of Archaeological Science* 16(5): 451–474.

———. 1994. Temporal Trends in Stable Isotopes for Nubian Mummy Tissues. *American Journal of Physical Anthropology* 93(2): 165–187.

Williams, Lana J., Christine D. White, and Fred J. Longstaffe. 2011. Improving Stable Isotopic Interpretations Made from Human Hair Through Reduction of Growth Cycle Error. *American Journal of Physical Anthropology* 145(1): 125–136.

Wright, Lori E., and Henry P. Schwarcz. 1998. Stable Carbon and Oxygen Isotopes in Human Tooth Enamel: Identifying Breastfeeding and Weaning in Prehistory. *American Journal of Physical Anthropology* 106(1): 1–18.

CHAPTER **11**

Nutritional Stress in Past Human Groups

Alan H. Goodman

Introduction and Purpose

Human skeletal remains are the most direct means for assessing malnutrition and particularly undernutrition in past populations. Despite the many serious scientific challenges to reconstructing past nutrition from bones and teeth, interdisciplinary collaborations are making it possible to infer the general nutritional status of past individuals and groups. This chapter's purpose is to provide a theoretical and methodological introduction to the study of the nutritional status of past populations, a major component of paleonutrition—the study of the diet (Turner and Livengood, this volume) and nutritional status (this chapter) of past populations. I begin by outlining how the skeleton responds generally to physiological perturbations or stress. Against this background, I review three of the most common and accepted paleonutrition indicators: linear bone growth, linear enamel hypoplasias, and porotic hyperostosis. Specific attention is paid to the "state of the art": what has been established for each nutritional stress indicator, and what additional knowledge is most essential. Where possible, I focus on the possible adaptive and functional implications of these nutritional stress indicators, inferred from their study in contemporary contexts.

The Systemic (Nutritional) Stress Perspective

A stress model (Figure 11.1) focuses on skeletal manifestations of physiological perturbation (or stress) (Goodman and Armelagos 1989; Goodman and Martin 2002). The model is useful for illustrating connections between systemic etiology and skeletal manifestations of undernutrition on the one hand, and the adaptive and functional consequences of these stress indicators on the other hand.

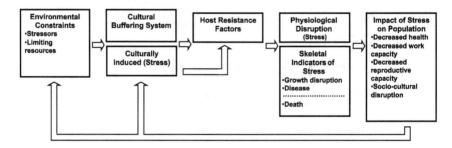

Figure 11.1. Stress model adapted for use in skeletal series. Although stress as a physiological disruption cannot be directly measured, various skeletal changes may be used to infer stress and its impact on individual and population adaptation (from Goodman and Armelagos 1989).

The left side of the model starts with environmental constraints to adaptation: limiting resources and stressors. Stressors may be related to climatic extremes, such as excesses of heat and cold, or low partial pressure of oxygen. The most important limiting resources are likely to be basic ones: water, shelter, and nutrients.

Cultural systems are generally effective in buffering environmental constraints and stressors. Agriculture, for example, is an economic adjustment that brings about a number of changes in a culture's ability to buffer stresses. Energetic efficiency and the amount of food produced per unit area are greater for agriculture than for hunting and gathering. Thus, agriculture would seem to provide a buffer against caloric insufficiency. However, greater population density and socioecological changes are frequent covariates of agricultural intensification that may have unforeseen consequences for health and nutrition (Cohen and Armelagos 1984). Thus, culture acts to both buffer stress and produce new stressors and constraints (Goodman and Armelagos 1989).

Both environmental constraints that are not well buffered by the cultural system and newly produced cultural stressors reach individuals. From then on, the degree of adaptation to these stressors and constraints depends on the individual's level of host resistance, a function of genetic, developmental, and physiological statuses. Unfortunately, chronic stressors and limiting resources often overwhelm adaptive systems. Individuals who have poor nutrition, for example, are less resistant to infectious diseases, and infectious disease further lowers nutritional status (Allen 1984; Martorell 1980; Mata Urrutia, and Lechtig 1971).

The severity and duration of the stress response may be viewed as a function of the degree of cultural and environmental constraints and stressors, balanced against the adequacy of the cultural buffering system and individual resistance resources. Fortunately for the paleo-epidemiologist, the stress response, a stereotypic physiological change resulting from the struggle to adjust, is frequently manifested in relatively permanent skeletal changes. Because bone and teeth are limited in their response repertoire, less is known of the stressors that were the cause of the struggle, but fortunately one finds clear evidence of a struggle to adapt.

The significance of health and adaptation extends beyond the individual to the population and society. Undernutrition, for example, has a negative effect on work capacity, fertility, morbidity, and mortality, causing secondary disruptions to the social, political, and economic structure of a community (Allen 1984). The following section provides information on three main indicators of nutritional health status.

The Evidence of Nutritional Stress in Skeletal Tissues

A wealth of indicators have been developed to gain insight into stress, disease, and nutrition from the skeleton (Goodman and Martin 2002). In this section I highlight three main indicators of nutritional status.

Linear Bone Growth and Adult Stature

Introduction: Contemporary studies and functional interpretations
Because growth is sensitive to a wide range of environmental conditions, studies of human growth and development have long been key tools for the analysis of stress and adaptation in past and present groups. Growth in parameters such as height, weight, and arm circumference are sensitive indicators of nutritional status (Sutphen 1985; Eveleth and Tanner 1976), defined as "the state resulting from the balance between the supply of nutrients on the one hand and the expenditure of the organism on the other" (McLaren 1976: 3).

The most important distinction to be made in paleonutrition is between studies of subadults and adults (Johnston and Zimmer 1989). The main advantage of studies of subadults is that they provide the most sensitive measures of changes in nutritional status, whereas studies of adults provide an index of the cumulative genetic and environmental conditions during all of development. Adult size and shape is subject to catch-up growth, the increase in growth rate following recovery from growth-dampening conditions. Catch-up growth can obscure the effects of transient but significant growth variations. Furthermore, variation in subadults is likely due to immediate conditions, whereas size variation in adults is more likely to reflect chronic conditions.

Because growth is rather quickly affected by nutrient deficiency, it is a sensitive indicator of nutritional stress. Acheson (1960) suggests that growth's sensitivity to poor nutrition is logical when interpreted in adaptive terms. The growing organism can usually catch up, once adequate nutrition is restored. However, if deprivation is severe or long-lasting, then a short-term adaptation can become a warning sign of impairment of critical functions such as disease resistance and reproductive capacity. In this regard, growth may also be used to infer deficits in other critical functions (Allen 1984). Chavez and Martinez (1982) have found that mild-to-moderate malnutrition in Mexican peasant children has a profound effect on their activity levels, social behavior, learning patterns, and disease resistance. For example, those children who are most malnourished (and show the greatest deficiencies in growth) tend to be far less exploratory, cry more often, are less interactive with their parents, and are ill for longer periods of time compared to their better nourished peers (ibid.).

Because of its sensitivity and nonspecificity, Tanner (1986) has proposed that growth variation is useful as a measure of equality of conditions within a society. He suggests that when variation in growth between socioeconomic groups disappears, one may be able to say that in that society, all individuals have equal access to resources. In summary, the anthropometric status of living individuals and groups provides insight into their adaptation to environmental influences affecting diet.

Anthropometric studies of skeletal populations
Subadult growth. Despite the potential of studies of subadult growth in prehistoric populations, several practical factors have limited their development (Goodman and Martin 2002; Johnston and Zimmer 1989). First, prehistoric series are frequently plagued by small sample size, particularly after five years of age. This is the primary reason for the paucity of comparative studies of growth of prehistoric subadults. Second, there is a technical problem of measuring long bones with and without epiphyses (the unattached growing ends of long bones), which are frequently destroyed or otherwise lost to archaeological recovery. This irregularity has the potential of adding considerable measurement error. Third, because the archaeological sample is cross-sectional (in fact, a death assemblage), the results can be used to infer periods of peak stress only when demographic parameters are relatively stable. Furthermore, cemetery-based studies represent not the healthy or even the "average" child, but those who died (Wood et al. 1992).

Fourth, dental age is the best known proxy for chronological age. This can be considered a potential source of error in that a bias arises toward a more conservative estimation of growth failure, as dental age (based on calcification and eruption times) is also likely to be somewhat affected by environmental conditions (Garn, Rohmann, and Guzman 1963). Similarly, inability to distinguish sex of subadults disallows comparisons between boys and girls. And fifth and finally, we have only limited ability to compare growth in prehistory directly to that of contemporary groups. The only sample from which longitudinal growth of long bones is well established is that of the childhood growth study conducted in

Denver, Colorado (Maresh 1955). Despite these limitations, a number of useful paleoepidemiological studies have focused on subadult growth (e.g., Armelagos et al. 1972; Cook 1971; Jantz and Owsley 1984; Johnston 1962).

Anthropometry of adults. Studies of adults are less constrained by problems of assignment of age and sex or small sample sizes than are subadult samples. In addition to separate study of male and female growth, adult samples allow for comparison of patterns of growth (sexual dimorphism studies) between males and females. Small sample sizes, which frequently limit the power of analysis of subadult growth, are less of a factor in analysis of adult growth.

The largely technical advantages of studying adults are unfortunately offset by disadvantages. As in studies of adult anthropometry of living populations, the main drawback to studies in prehistory revolves around the loss of sensitivity for clarifying underlying processes affecting growth and ultimate size at adulthood. The loss of the most stressed segment of the population (subadults) due to death before adulthood, coupled with the ability to catch up in growth, renders adult morphology less sensitive to environmental variation when compared to subadult growth and development.

Nonetheless, comparisons of adult stature can be very informative, and a wide variety of studies of adult anthropometry have been performed. In a review of stature (derived from long-bone lengths) in prehistoric populations from Mesoamerica, Genoves (1967: 76; also Bass 1971; Brothwell 1981; Ubelaker 1981) has found that female stature decreased from a mean of around 62 inches in northern Mesoamerica and the American Southwest to about 58 inches in southern Mesoamerica. Male stature also declined from around 66 inches in the north to around 62 inches in the south. Genoves suggests that subsistence differences may be responsible for the gradient in heights from the north to the south.

Summary
Anthropometric studies of living populations have profoundly influenced similar studies of prehistoric populations. Studies of adult stature and subadult long-bone lengths are best regarded as nonspecific indicators of stress. Because the consequence of growth faltering looks the same regardless of specific stressor or limiting resources, contextual information is needed to interpret the cause of the growth faltering. Some sense of the severity and temporal pattern of stress may be inferred from the pattern of disruption. Like studies of mortality, studies of subadult growth are frequently hampered by imprecision in estimation of age and small sample sizes. Despite these limitations, anthropometric studies of past populations continue to yield valuable information, which is perhaps a testament to the vigor of this indicator. Our ability to assess subadult growth and adult morphology from skeletal remains provides a powerful tool for the assessment of nutritional status in prehistoric humans.

Linear Enamel Hypoplasias

Pathophysiology and etiology

Linear enamel hypoplasias (LEH) are a class of developmental enamel defects (DED). Visibly recognizable as transverse or linear deficiencies in enamel thickness, they are the permanent end result of a disruption during the enamel secretion stage of tooth crown development (Suckling 1989; Goodman and Rose 1990). The importance of these defects rests in the fact that they provide an indelible indicator of periods of stress during early life and tooth crown development (prenatally to twelve months for deciduous teeth, and birth to seven years for permanent teeth).

Enamel hypoplasias vary from light multiple and single pits to lines of increased enamel thickness and thick bands of missing enamel. Based on the pattern of defects within and among teeth, hypoplasias can reliably be distinguished as resulting from one of three conditions: (1) a hereditary anomaly, (2) a localized trauma, or (3) a systemic metabolic stress (Shawashy and Yaeger 1986). Although enamel hypoplasias due to systemic stresses are common and easily discerned from defects due to non-systemic factors, it is difficult to attribute them to a more exact cause (Pindborg 1982). Cutress and Suckling (1982) compiled a list of nearly a hundred factors considered to be possible causes of enamel defects. The list of potential causes, which includes many nutritional insufficiencies as well as drug toxicities and almost any disease that severely stresses metabolism, gives credence to the view that enamel defects are highly sensitive to physiological and metabolic changes and are best considered to be indicators of nonspecific stress.

Perhaps the most important characteristic of LEHs is that an estimation is possible of the developmental age of the individual at the time of their formation. This information may be inferred from the location of enamel defects on tooth crowns. Thus, by locating LEHs on tooth crowns, one can begin to develop a chronological record of physiological stress experienced by individuals (Kreshover 1960; Sarnat and Schour 1941). For example, Swardstedt (1966) compared the prevalence of enamel defects by half-year developmental periods in "social groups" at Westerhus in medieval Sweden.

Because a number of issues influence the accurate estimation of age at development of a defect (see Goodman and Rose 1990, 1991 for reviews), it should be kept in mind that developmental age is not exactly equal to chronological age. Nonetheless, this methodology provides a very useful and unique understanding of stress experienced by adolescents and adults during infancy and childhood.

Enamel hypoplasias in contemporary and prehistoric populations

Epidemiological studies of the frequency of enamel hypoplasias in contemporary populations find an association between the prevalence of enamel hypoplasias and general living conditions. Though direct comparison is difficult due to differences in method of diagnosis and sampling of individuals and teeth (Goodman and Armelagos 1985a, 1985b), individuals in developed countries tend to have lower rates of enamel defects than do individuals from underdeveloped areas. The frequency of individuals with one or more hypoplasias on permanent teeth is generally less than 10 percent in most populations from developed, industrialized countries (Cutress and Suckling 1982) and is usually over 50 percent in developing countries (Goodman and Rose, 1990, 1991).

The pioneering work of Sweeney (Sweeney and Guzman 1966; Sweeney et al. 1969; Sweeney, Saffir, and de Leon 1971) firmly established an association between enamel hypoplasias and malnutrition. Sweeney and co-workers (1971) found an increase in enamel hypoplasias of the deciduous upper central incisor (teeth whose crowns develop from about 6 months prenatally to about 3 months postnatally) and with severity of malnutrition in Guatemalan children: 43 percent of the children aged two to seven with second-degree malnutrition (61% to 75% weight-for-age) had hypoplasias, whereas 73 percent of children with the more severe third-degree malnutrition (60% or less weight-for-age) had enamel hypoplasias.

Goodman and colleagues (1987) studied the frequency and chronological distribution of enamel hypoplasias in Mexican children from five rural communities selected because of the presence of endemic mild-to-moderate malnutrition (children at 60%–95% weight for age). They found one or more hypoplasias on 46.7 percent of 300 children examined. As weaning generally takes place in the second year in these Mexican communities, they suggest that the increased frequency of hypoplasias may result from undernutrition and infectious diseases associated with weaning. A prospective study in Tezonteopan, another town in highland Mexico, found that LEHs are about half as frequent in children who were provided nutrient supplements (Goodman, Martinez, and Chavez 1991). The supplement, which contained over twenty nutrients (calories, proteins, and a soup of micronutrients), also reduced the incidence and severity of respiratory and diarrheal diseases in the children that took them, so the reduction in LEH frequency cannot be attributed to a single nutritional factor (ibid.).

LEHs have frequently been used to compare stress levels among different prehistoric populations. Numerous authors, including Cassidy (1984); Goodman and co-workers (1984); Perzigian, Tench, and Braun (1984); and Smith, Bar-Yosef, and Sillen (1984) have noted an increased frequency of defects in agriculturalists versus hunting and gathering groups. Goodman, Armelagos, and Rose (1984) also note that the peak period of stress tends to be earlier in the agriculturalists versus gatherer-hunters.

Hutchinson and Larsen (1988) found a greater frequency of hypoplasias in individuals from the Georgia coast post-European contact as compared with pre-contact individuals. Corruccini, Handler, and Jacobi (1985) evaluated the chronological distribution of enamel defects in enslaved Africans from Barbados. They found a relatively late peak age at development of defects (around 3.5 to 4.0 years) and attribute this peak to a historically documented late age at weaning and post-weaning stress.

Summary

Linear enamel hypoplasias are one of the most frequently studied skeletal manifestations of stress. In comparison to measures of completed growth, which tend to signify chronic stress, these measures of growth disruption are time-specific and may indicate more acute periods of stress. Like growth status, they are best thought of as nonspecific (general) indicators of stress. However, when combined with measures of achieved growth they can help to provide information on the severity and temporal pattern of stress.

Enamel hypoplasias are a well-studied paleo-epidemiological tool. They have been subject to strict tests of reliability, and their etiology has been studied through ecological, case-control, and prospective designs (Goodman and Rose 1991). These studies have helped sharpen our understanding of the utility of these defects, but they have not answered all questions. Among a few concerns needing further attention are the best means of estimating an individual's age at development of defects, the best set of teeth for evaluation of stress in survey studies, and the way to interpret variations in the size and shape of enamel defects.

Without doubt a great deal of recent work has gone into understanding the cause of LEH and possible functional inferences to be derived from LEH studies. Studies of contemporary populations have shown a consistent increase in the prevalence of enamel hypoplasias for groups that live in poorly nourished and underdeveloped communities. Though the association of enamel defects with weaning suggests a strong role for a nutritional cause, it is not clear how important nutrition is, which nutrients are most critical, and how nutrition interacts with other factors such as infectious and parasitic diseases.

Porotic Hyperostosis and Anemia

Background: Pathophysiology, etiology, and functional inferences

Anemias potentially affect bones involved in the production of red blood cells. While the possible etiologies of anemia include discrete genetic traits (Mensforth et al. 1978), hereditary hemolytic anemia (Angel 1964, 1966, 1967), or some form of nutritional disorder (Nathan and Haas 1966), nutritional anemia has been suggested as the primary factor in the etiology of porotic hyperostosis for the vast majority of the documented cases in prehistory (Mensforth et al. 1978; Mensforth 1991; Stuart-Macadam 1987).

Porotic hyperostosis is a descriptive term for lesions on the cranium, the roof of the eye orbits, and the ends of long bones. These lesions are produced by bone marrow proliferation that is diagnostic of anemia. As the name implies, the lesion has a very porous (coral-like) appearance that develops when the diploe (the trabecular portion of the cranial bone that separates the inner and outer surfaces) expands. With the expansion of the diploe, the outer layer of bone becomes thinner and may eventually disappear, exposing the inner trabecular bone, which is quite porous.

The lesions of porotic hyperostosis typically involve thinning and destruction of the outer tables of the cranial vault, accompanied by thickening and exposure of the deeper diploic tissue. Porotic hyperostosis is usually symmetrically distributed and presents as a tight cluster of small porous openings that are visible to the naked eye. The lesion is typically exhibited on bones of the cranial (frontal, temporals, parietals, occipital) and the superior border of the eye orbits. Many researchers have given the expression of the disease as it appears in the orbits the label "cribra orbitalia," because for many years it was not clear that the two locations (vault and orbit) had the same etiology. There is now overwhelming evidence that both types of lesions are part of the same disease process (see Stuart-Macadam 1987, 1989) and should be referred to as porotic hyperostosis.

In a review of the literature on clinical evidence of bone changes in anemic individuals, Stuart-Macadam (1987) provided compelling evidence that bony lesions are a product of iron-deficiency anemia. In addition to a thickening of the diploe of cranial and orbital bones in anemia patients, the lesion is usually distributed in a symmetrical pattern on the cranium. In her analysis of clinical data combined with X-ray and skeletal observations of the disease, Stuart-Macadam demonstrated that anemia is responsible for the lesion seen on bones.

Consensus has developed that porotic hyperostosis in the New World is most likely related to iron-deficiency anemia (Mensforth et al. 1978). This view, according to Mensforth and co-workers (1978: 7), developed from three lines of evidence. First, iron-deficiency anemia and porotic hyperostosis are widespread throughout the New and the Old Worlds. Second, the distribution of porotic hyperostosis corresponds to the distribution of dietary staples that are low in utilizable iron. Finally, there is no pre-Columbian evidence to support the occurrence of skeletal changes that are characteristically found in the hemolytic anemias associated with hemoglobin variants. Some sense of the functional meaning of these porotic lesions may be estimated from studies of anemia in contemporary populations. Iron-deficiency anemia is one of the most widespread and common nutritional problems in the contemporary world (Dallman, Yip, and Johnson 1984). It is particularly pronounced in children, adolescents, and women during child-bearing years (Dallman, Simes, and Stekel 1980).

Indeed, the functional consequences of mild anemia are well understood and have been shown to be profound (Scrimshaw 1991). Iron deficiency—even at levels where the most common measures of iron status, hemoglobin and hematocrits, are normal, that is, iron deficiency without anemia—can lead to a suite of functional costs. Various organs and systems show structural changes with borderline iron deficiency. Vyas and Chandra (1984: 45) note that the multiple consequences of iron deficiency are not surprising because iron is "an essential cofactor of several enzyme systems that play an important role in metabolic processes and cell proliferation." Many of these enzymes are involved in vital functions such as DNA synthesis, mitochondrial electron transport, and catecholamine metabolism.

The organism-level consequences of iron deficiency are typically divided into three areas: (1) disease resistance, (2) activity/work capacity, and (3) cognition and behavior. Mild iron deficiency, without low hemoglobin, is associated with learning deficiencies (Howell, 1971). Of particular note are changes in attention and memory control processes. Howell (1971) showed that 3- to 5-year-old anemic children had decreased attention spans, and Sulzer, Wesley, and Leonig (1973) illustrated that anemic children of the same age had lower IQ measures and impaired associative reactions.

The effects of iron deficiency and anemia on work capacity are particularly profound (Scrimshaw 1991). Anemic subjects cannot maintain the same pace and duration of work as can non-anemic subjects, and they reach a lower mean maximal workload. Anemic Guatemalan laborers performed much worse on the Harvard Step Test (a measure of moderate exertion) than their non-anemic peers, and the work output and pay of Indonesian rubber tappers correlates almost perfectly with their hemoglobin levels (ibid.). Decreased oxygen affinity and increased cardiac output are the "adaptive" responses to anemia (Vyas and Chandra 1984). However, these adaptations can only cover for deficiency when the organism is sedentary or at rest. The example of the Indonesian rubber tappers suggests a troubling synergy: iron deficiency leads to less pay, and less pay further erodes diets.

Iron deficiency has a variety of effects on immunocompetence and infection. Experimentally induced iron deficiency results in a reduction in lymphocyte proliferation, the production of rosette-forming T-cells, and the microbicidal capacity of neutrophils (Dallman 1987; Vyas and Chandra 1984). In humans, iron supplements have led to a decreased prevalence of diarrhea and upper- and lower-respiratory infections. Thus, lesions indicative of porotic hyperostosis and anemia in prehistory have potential to provide insights as to how well children and adult performed in terms of cognitive tasks, work capacity, and infection resistance.

Paleoepidemiology

Several examples serve to highlight the complexity of interpreting rates of porotic hyperostosis in past groups. Lallo, Armelagos, and Mensforth (1977) and Mensforth et al. (1978) recorded the frequency and distribution of lesions by age. Using very small age group categories, Lallo and colleagues (1977) demonstrated that the clustered lesions in younger children reflected an increased need for iron metabolism during growth and development at Dickson Mounds, Illinois. An analysis of the relationship between porotic hyperostosis and infectious diseases strongly suggested that the two occurred together and acted in a synergistic fashion, with porotic hyperostosis increasing the likelihood of infectious disease. Porotic hyperostosis had an earlier age of onset than did infection, and the diseases co-occur with high frequency at subsequent ages. Thus, Lallo and colleagues (1977) were able to document their claim that iron deficiency predisposed children to infectious disease, possibly by lowering their resistance.

On the other hand, Mensforth et al. (1978) showed the reverse process for a prehistoric population from Libben, Ohio: infectious diseases predisposed children to iron-deficiency anemia. By distinguishing between healed and unhealed lesions, the researchers revealed a synergistic relationship whereby infectious disease acted as the initial stress that predisposed Libben individuals to iron deficiency (ibid.). The importance of these two studies is that different ecological and cultural variables worked to cause the same lesion (porotic hyperostosis) in each archaeological population, even though different underlying conditions precipitated the response.

Summary and epidemiological considerations

In order to better understand the functional consequences of porotic hyperostosis, it would be useful to have more precise information on the severity and duration of anemia necessary to cause the osseous changes. My assumption is that porotic hyperostosis is a relatively severe and chronic manifestation of iron deficiency. However, this point has not been well documented by studies that directly compare standard measures of iron status (such as hemoglobin, hematocrit, and plasma transferrin) with skeletal changes. Also, although it is now fairly standard to record the severity and extent of porotic lesions as well as the degree of remodeling, there is no reference standard for evaluation of degree of involvement or degree of remodeling, nor is there a set method for classification of pattern of involvement or choice of bone(s) for evaluation in incomplete skeletons.

The above epidemiological issues notwithstanding, tremendous advancements in the study of porotic hyperostosis have been made thanks to the detailed research of Mensforth (1991; Mensforth et al. 1978), Stuart-Macadam (1987, 1989), and others. Today we have a fairly well developed understanding of how porotic lesions are formed, and we are relatively confident about differential diagnosis. It bears repeating that iron deficiency is not the only cause of anemia and seldom occurs without other nutrient deficiencies. In all, though, understanding the functional significance of iron status in contemporary populations and the severity of porotic hyperostosis in some past populations can lead to a sense of how infirmity may have affected the lives and livelihood of past peoples.

Conclusions

Many of the most exciting developments in anthropology have come in the over-lapping fields of paleonutrition, paleopathology, and paleodemography. These fields, which respectively focus on the nutrition, health, and demography of past populations, have all enjoyed promising advancements in methodology. Even more consequentially, improved understanding of the context, causes, and consequences of morbidity and mortality in individuals and groups has led to new inferences and research directions. The human skeleton found in the archaeological context is now widely understood to hold key historical and human ecological information.

This chapter has provided a current assessment of the toolkit for measurement and analysis of nutrition from skeletal remains. For illustrative purposes, I have focused on three commonly used, well accepted indicators of nutritional status. All indicators suffer from incomplete understanding of the biological processes leading to their formation. Still, when studied together and with data archaeological information on diets, these data can provide critical insights as to nutritional status and adaptation in past populations.

Alan Goodman is Professor of Biological Anthropology at Hampshire College in Amherst, Massachusetts. His interests focus on the intersections of biology and culture, and particularly on the health and nutritional consequences of political-economic processes. Goodman is the editor or author of seven books and numerous articles including *Race: Are We So Different?* (co-authored with Moses and Jones) and *Nutritional Anthropology* (co-edited with Dufour and Pelto). He received his PhD in anthropology from the University of Massachusetts and was a postdoctoral fellow in international nutrition at the University of Connecticut. Formerly Vice President for Academic Affairs and Dean of Faculty at Hampshire College, he is also a past President of the American Anthropological Association.

Acknowledgements

This chapter updates and abstracts from a prior chapter (Goodman and Martin 2002). This chapter is dedicated to George Armelagos (1936–2014), who taught me many of the specifics of paleonutrition as well as how to think like an anthropologist and a scientist.

References

Acheson, R. M. 1960. Effect of Nutrition and Disease on Human Growth. In *Human Growth*, ed. J. M. Tanner, 73–92. New York: Pergamon Press.

Allen, Lindsay. H. 1984. Functional Indicators of Nutritional Status of the Whole Individual or the Community. *Clinical Nutrition* 3(5): 169–175.

Angel, J. Lawrence. 1964. Osteoporosis: Thalassemia? *American Journal of Physical Anthropology* 22: 369–374.

———. 1966. Porotic Hyperostosis, Anemias, Malarias, and Marshes in Prehistoric Eastern Mediterranean. *Science* 153: 760–763.

———. 1967. Porotic Hyperostosis or Osteoporosis Symmetrica. In *Diseases in Antiquity*, ed. D. R. Brothwell and A. T. Sandison, 378–389. Springfield, IL: Charles C Thomas.

Armelagos, George J., J. H. Mielke, H. O. Kipling, D. P. Van Gerven, J. R. Dewey, and P. E. Mahler. 1972. Bone Growth and Development in Prehistoric Populations from Sudanese Nubia. *Journal of Human Evolution* 1: 89–119.

Bass, William M. 1971. *Human Osteology: A Laboratory and Field Manual of the Human Skeleton*. Columbia, Missouri: University of Missouri Archaeological Museum Society.

Brothwell, Don R. 1981. *Digging Up Bones*. Ithaca, NY: Cornell University Press.

Cassidy, Claire M. 1984. Skeletal Evidence for Prehistoric Subsistence Adaptation in the Central Ohio River Valley. In *Paleopathology at the Origins of Agriculture*, ed. M. N. Cohen and G. J. Armelagos, 307–346. New York: Academic Press.

Chavez, Adolfo, and C. Martinez. 1982. *Growing Up in A Developing Community*. Mexico City: Instituto Nacional de la Nutricion.

Cohen, Mark N., and G. J. Armelagos, eds. 1984. *Paleopathology at the Origins of Agriculture*. New York: Academic Press.

Cook, Della C. 1971. Patterns of Nutritional Stress in Some Illinois Woodland Populations. Unpublished thesis. Department of Anthropology, University of Illinois.

Corruccini, Robert S., J. S. Handler, and K. P. Jacobi. 1985. Chronological Distribution of Enamel Hypoplasias and Weaning in a Caribbean Slave Population. *Human Biology* 57: 699–711.

Cutress, Terry W., and G. W. Suckling. 1982. The Assessment of Non-carious Defects of Enamel. *International Dental Journal* 32: 117–122.

Dallman, P. 1987. Iron Deficiency and the Immune Response. *American Journal of Clinical Nutrition* 46: 329–334.

Dallman, P., R. Simes; A. Stekel. 1980. Iron Deficiency in Infancy and Childhood. *American Journal Clinical Nutrition* 33: 86–118.

Dallman, P. R., R. Yip, and C. Johnson. 1984. Prevalence and Causes of Anemia in the United States, 1976 to 1980. *American Journal of Clinical Nutrition* 39: 437–445.

Eveleth, Philis B., and J. M. Tanner. 1976. *Worldwide Variation in Human Growth*. International Biological Programme 8. Cambridge University Press.

Garn, Stanley M., C. G. Rohmann, and M. A. Guzman. 1963. Genetic, Nutritional and Maturational Correlates of Dental Development. *Journal of Dental Research* 44: 228–242.

Genoves, Santiago. 1967. Proportionality of the Long Bones and Their Relation to Stature among Mesoamericans. *American Journal of Physical Anthropology* 26: 67–78.

Goodman, Alan H., L. H. Allen, G. P. Hernandez, A. Amador, L. V. Arriola, A. Chavez, and G. H. Pelto. 1987. Prevalence and Age at Development of Enamel Hypoplasias in Mexican Children. *American Journal of Physical Anthropology* 72: 7–19.

Goodman, Alan H., and G. J. Armelagos. 1985a. Factors Affecting the Distribution of Enamel Hypoplasias within the Human Permanent Dentition. *American Journal of Physical Anthropology* 68: 479–493.

———. 1985b. The Chronological Distribution of Enamel Hypoplasia in Human Permanent Incisor and Canine Teeth. *Archives of Oral Biology* 30: 503–507.

———. 1989. Infant and Childhood Morbidity and Mortality Risks in Archaeological Populations. *World Archaeology* 21(2): 225–243.

Goodman, Alan H., G. J. Armelagos, and J. C. Rose. 1984. The Chronological Distribution of Enamel Hypoplasias from Prehistoric Dickson Mounds Populations. *American Journal of Physical Anthropology* 65: 259–266.

Goodman, Alan H., and Martin, D. L. 2002. Reconstructing Health Profiles from Skeletal Remains. In *The Backbone of History*, ed. R. H. Stekel and J. C. Rose, 11–60. Cambridge University Press.

Goodman, Alan H., C. Martinez, and A. Chavez. 1991. Nutritional Supplementation and the Development of Linear Enamel Hypoplasias in Children from Tezonteopan, Mexico. *American Journal Clinical Nutrition* 53: 773–781.

Goodman, Alan H., and J. C. Rose. 1990. Assessment of Systemic Physiological Perturbations from Dental Enamel Hypoplasias and Associated Histological Structures. *Yearbook of Phys. Anthropol.* 33: 59–110.

———. 1991. Dental Enamel Hypoplasias as Indicators of Nutritional Status. In *Advances in Dental Anthropology*, ed. M. Kelley and C. Larsen, 279–293. New York: Wiley-Liss.

Howell, D. 1971. *Significance of Iron Deficiencies: Consequence of Mild Deficiency in Children; Extent and Meaning of Iron Deficiency in the United States.* Washington, DC: National Academy of Sciences.

Hutchinson, Dale L., and C. P. Larsen. 1988. Determination of Stress Episode Duration from Linear Enamel Hypoplasias: A Case Study from St. Catherine's Island, Georgia. *Human Biology* 60: 93–110.

Jantz, Richard L., and D. W. Owsley. 1984. Temporal Changes in Limb Proportionality among Skeletal Samples of Arikara Indians. *Annals of Human Biology* 11(2): 157–163.

Johnston, Frank E. 1962. Growth of the Long Bones of Infants and Young Children at Indian Knoll. *American Journal of Physical Anthropology* 20: 249–254.

Johnston, Frank E., and L. O. Zimmer. 1989. Assessment of Growth and Age in the Immature Skeleton. In *Reconstruction of Life from the Skeleton,* ed. M. Y. Iscan and K. A. Kennedy, 11–22. New York: Alan R Liss.

Kreshover, S. 1960. Metabolic Disturbances in Tooth Formation. *Annals of the New York Academy of Science* 85: 161–167.

Lallo, John, G. J. Armelagos, and R. P. Mensforth. 1977. The Role of Diet, Diseases and Physiology in the Origin of Porotic Hyperostosis. *Human Biology* 49: 471–483.

Maresh, M. M. 1955. Linear Growth of Long Bones of Extremities from Infancy through Adolescence. *American Journal of Diseases of Children* 89: 725–742.

Martorell, Reynaldo 1980. Interrelationships between Diet, Infectious Disease, and Nutritional Status. In *Social and Biological Predictors of Nutritional Status, Physical Growth, and Neurological Development,* ed. L. Greene, 81–106. New York: Academic Press.

Mata, L., J. Urrutia, and A. Lechtig. 1971. Infection and Nutrition of Children of a Low Socioeconomic Rural Community. *American Journal of Clinical Nutrition* 24: 249–259.

McLaren, D. 1976. Concepts and Context of Nutrition. In *Nutrition in the Community,* ed. D. McLaren, 3–12. London: John Wiley and Sons.

Mensforth, Robert P. 1991. Paleoepidemiology of Porotic Hyperostosis in the Libben and BT-5 Skeletal Populations. *Kirtlandia* 46: 1–47.

Mensforth, Robert P., C. O. Lovejoy, J. W. Lallo, and G. J. Armelagos. 1978. The Role of Constitutional Factors, Diet and Infectious Disease on the Etiology of Porotic Hyperostosis and Periosteal Reactions in Prehistoric Infants and Children. *Medical Anthropology* 2(1): 1–59.

Nathan, H., and N. Haas. 1966. "Cribra orbitalia": A Bone Condition of the Orbit of Unknown Nature. *Israel Journal of Medical Sciences* 2: 171–191.

Perzigian, Anthony J., P. A. Tench, and D. J. Braun. 1984. Prehistoric Health in the Ohio River Valley. In *Paleopathology at the Origins of Agriculture,* ed. M. N. Cohen and G. J. Armelagos, 347–366. New York: Academic Press.

Pindborg, J. J. 1982. Aetiology of Developmental Enamel Defects Not Related to Fluorosis. *International Dental Journal* 32: 123–134.

Sarnat, Bernard G., and I. Schour. 1941. Enamel Hypoplasias (Chronic Enamel Aplasia) in Relationship to Systemic Diseases: A Chronological, Morphological and Etiological Classification. *Journal of the American Dental Association* 28: 1989–2000.

Scrimshaw, Nevin 1991. Iron deficiency. *Scientific American* (October): 46–52.

Shawashy, M., and J. Yaeger. 1986. Enamel. In *Orban's Oral Histology and Embryology,* ed. S. N. Behaskar, 45–100. St. Louis: CV Mosby.

Smith, P., O. Bar-Yosef, and A. Sillen. 1984. Archaeological and Skeletal Evidence for Dietary Change during the Late Pleistocene/Early Holocene in the Levant. In *Paleopathology at the Origins of Agriculture,* ed. M. N. Cohen and G. J. Armelagos, 101–127. New York: Academic Press.

Stuart-Macadam, Patricia 1987. Porotic Hyperostosis: New Evidence to Support the Anemia Theory. *American Journal of Physical Anthropology* 74(4): 521–526.

———. 1989. Nutritional Deficiency Disease: A Survey of Scurvy, Rickets and Iron Deficiency Anemia. In *Reconstruction of Life from the Skeleton*, ed. M. Y. Iscan and K. A. R. Kennedy, 201–222. New York: Alan R. Liss.

Suckling, Grace 1989. Developmental Defects of Enamel: Historical and Present-Day Perspectives on Their Pathogenesis. *Advances in Dental Anthropology* 3(2): 87–94.

Sulzer, J. L., H. H. Wesley, and F. Leonig. 1973. Nutrition and Behavior in Head Start Children: Results from the Tulane Study. In *Nutrition, Development and Social Behavior,* ed. D. J. Kallen, 73–242. DHEW publication no. Washington, DC: NIH.

Sutphen, J. L. 1985. Growth as a Measure of Nutritional Stress. *Journal of Pediatric Gastroenterology and Nutrition* 4: 169–181.

Swardstedt, Torsten 1966. *Odontological Aspects of a Medieval Population from the Province of Jamtland/Mid-Sweden.* Stockholm: Tiden Barnangen, AB.

Sweeney, E. A., J. Cabrera, J. Urritia, and L. Mata. 1969. Factors Associated with Linear Hypoplasia of Human Deciduous Incisors. *Journal of Dental Research* 48: 1275–1279.

Sweeney, E. A., and M. Guzman. 1966. Oral Conditions in Children from Three Highland Villages in Guatemala. *Archives of Oral Biology* 11: 687–698.

Sweeney, E. A., J. A. Saffir, and R. de Leon. 1971. Linear Enamel Hypoplasias of Deciduous Incisor Teeth in Malnourished Children. *American Journal of Clinical Nutrition* 24: 29–31.

Tanner, James M. 1986. Growth as a Mirror of the Condition of Society: Secular Trends and Class Distinctions. In *Human Growth: A Multidisciplinary Review,* ed. A. Demirjian, 3–34. London: Taylor and Francis.

Ubelaker, Douglas H. 1981. *Human Skeletal Remains: Excavation, Analysis, Interpretation.* Chicago: Aldine.

Vyas, D., and R. K. Chandra. 1984. Functional Implications of Iron Deficiency. In *Iron Nutrition in Infancy and Childhood,* ed. A. Stekel, 45–59. New York: Raven Press.

Wood, James W., G. R. Milner, H. C. Harpending, and K. M. Weiss. 1992. The Osteological Paradox: Problems of Inferring Prehistoric Health from Skeletal Samples. *Current Anthropology* 33: 343–358.

CHAPTER **12**

Research on Direct Food Remains

Katherine M. Moore

Introduction

Animal foods are the earliest known direct food remains of hominin ancestors. Animal foods are nutrient-dense and satisfying; in addition, they are a common focus of social and ceremonial behavior. Foods from animals have played a central role in nutrition over the course of hominin evolution. Hard animal parts like bone, shell, and exoskeleton are durable and visible; bones have been collected from thousands of sites. Such remains document the persistent importance of animal foods in hominization (Braun et al. 2010; Stanford and Bunn 2001), the spread of humans to landmasses beyond Africa, the appearance of modern faunas, and the organization of sedentary societies in villages and cities (deFrance 2009). The methods used to study zooarchaeological remains draw on analogies with contemporary animals, animal tissues, and people. In each of the methodological approaches mentioned below, similar comparisons are used: archaeological assemblages of animals are compared to modern animal communities, to the behavior and anatomy of living animals, and to observations of decay and destruction of animal tissue. The most powerful insights from zooarchaeological analysis result from integrating evidence of use of animals with evidence for plant use, the technology of food production, and the bioarchaeology of food habits from human remains.

The nutritional value of animal food is broadly similar across the animals used as food, compared to the diversity of nutritional profiles of, for example, grains, tubers, fruits, and nuts. Meat is generally rich in protein and iron, potentially limiting nutrients for humans. Because of this similarity, the nutritional impact of using one animal species rather than another might be minor, though the differences in technology, social organization, or ecological impact over another might be great. The amount of meat available to a family or group at a particular time is an important variable in nutritional modeling, though it is quite difficult to approach zooarchaeologically. Herd animals are effectively stored "on the hoof" while being cared for before slaughter. Without refrigeration, technologies for storing animal products are limited to drying and salting. Zooarchaeologists have developed measures of food utility for individual skeletal elements that suggest meat drying (Friesen 2001). The most significant nutritional variable tracked by zooarchaeologists is fat—both the fat visible on meat and organs and the fat sequestered within marrow spaces and spongy bone tissue. Because of the nutrient density of fat (at least twice as much energy per gram as protein and carbohydrate), small decisions about choosing animals or animal parts bearing different amounts of fat could make big differences in the energy intake of individuals and families (Speth 1989, 2010).

Research Design in Zooarchaeology

Most archaeological animal remains come from deposits representing household trash. (Rarely, archaeologists have a chance to recover direct dietary remains from intact containers in offerings or from fecal deposits, or coprolites [Reinhard and Bryant 1992]. Fecal deposits can yield bone, muscle, skin, hair, and insect parts in addition to abundant plant material.) Animal bones from sites may be food remains, but archaeologists must first exclude the possibility that bones could be incidental additions to a bone collection (Lyman 1994). Traces used to confirm that animal bones or shells are discarded food remains include indications from archaeological context (the order and arrangement of archaeological deposits), associated plant remains, and microscopic and chemical aspects of soils (Goldberg, Nash, and Petraglia 1993).

Bones can be picked out by hand during excavation of archaeological deposits, but repeated experiments have shown that hand collection biases the sample of larger fragments and under-collects or misses the remains of small animals such as rodents, fish, and birds (Payne 1972; Shaffer 1992). Screening (sieving) and water flotation (Pearsall 2000) allow archaeologists to collect a more representative sample of animal remains. Such systematic recovery is now standard to estimate dietary intake from archaeological remains. The use of screens at archaeological sites in the past thirty years has changed our view of the importance of fish in particular to prehistoric diets (Partlow 2006).

Archaeologists create the zooarchaeological record as they excavate, discarding sediment and small fragments while they save and organize larger fragments. As field archaeologists choose between parts of a site or different chronological periods to excavate, they control once and for all the assemblage that zooarchaeologists (and other scholars) will have to study. In a best-case scenario, sampling and recovery decisions result from a dialogue between excavators and all those who will be studying the excavated remains. That best-case scenario also includes appropriate and mutually agreed-upon decisions about how to clean, stabilize, organize, pack, and store the remains as they await study. Some assemblages of zooarchaeological remains have waited for study for decades in museums and other storage areas. When older assemblages are approached for new research initiatives, methods must take into account sampling and storage decisions that may have been made under outdated research protocols. Even with some limitations, significant findings have emerged from such restudy projects (Stiner 1994; Zeder 2003). In addition, zooarchaeological material may be an important source of molecules for isotopes or genetic analysis, or as a source of intact material for absolute dating.

Taphonomy in Zooarchaeology

Archaeologists pay careful attention to the taphonomic signatures of food use on animal bones; these may include traces from dismemberment and butchering, cooking, serving, consumption, and disposal (Lyman 1994; O'Connor 2005). Generally, taphonomy refers to any change that takes place in an animal's remains after death. This covers any physical change from the time of slaughter to the moment when an archaeological assemblage is studied in the laboratory. The predictable but irregular progress of destruction and decay has come to organize archaeological research on animal bone (Lyman 1994). Experiments and field research on bone destruction in natural settings (known as actualistic research) have refined understanding of many steps in the process (Binford 1978, 1981; O'Connor 2005). The taphonomic damage that comes from food use can be obvious (sharp broken edges from blows to release marrow, narrow traces of cut marks); or more subtle (changes in bone composition from heat applied during cooking) (Outram et al. 2005; Roberts et al. 2002). Taphonomic changes on several scales can affect the interpretation of how the remains were altered after burial. Modifications of bone surfaces and broken edges from food preparation can be examined under magnification to distinguish cut marks, tooth marks, and traces of trampling damage, as well as the sequence in which the traces were made. Such analysis placed early hominin food use in a regional food web in which hominins were only a minor agent (Bunn and Ezzo 1993; Selvaggio 1998).

The possible importance of cooking in hominid evolution has been noted by scholars interested in the dietary shifts that may have accompanied the decrease in hominin cheek tooth area. According to one argument, cooking plant and animal foods would allow improved nutrient density with fewer anatomical specializations for feeding (Wrangham 2009). Very little positive zooarchaeological evidence supports this argument, despite abundant animal food remains. Damage from heat treatment to bone can be difficult to separate from the effect of weathering and soil microorganisms (Alhaique 1997; Lupo and Schmitt 1997; Roberts et al. 2002). Depending on climate, the effects of cooking can be similar to the taphonomic changes resulting from burial. Currently, there are few approaches that could suggest or exclude the possibility that a bone was heated as part of cooking, particularly for very early sites with extensive fossilization of bone material.

Burned and blackened or calcined (completely whitened) bone is often observed in prehistoric sites (Shipman, Foster, and Schoeninger 1984; Stiner et al. 1995.) (Staining with minerals also blackens bone but is usually distinguishable on close inspection (Weiner 2010.)) At one time this charring was thought to be evidence of cooking; certainly it is evidence of heat exposure. Experiments and careful observations of traditional cooking show that the temperatures used in cooking (100–200 °C) are well below those needed to produce such burned bone (400–600 °C) (Stiner et al. 1995; Nicholson 1993). Burned bone, though it may be common and is evidence of the control of fire by a site's occupants, probably most often resulted from clean-up activities or the re-use of an occupation surface where bone had been buried, rather than being directly relating to cooking (Moore et al. 2010; Stiner et al. 1995; Weiner 2010).

Zooarchaeology shares the insights of taphonomy with anthropologists who study human skeletal remains, but two the fields overlap directly in the study of cannibalism. In this case, human skeletal remains are both social individuals and food remains. Earlier applications of taphonomy to cannibalism tended to focus on human remains as a special case unto itself, using taphonomic traces to study dismemberment, breakage, and scattering of human remains (Hurlbut 2001; White 1992). More recently, research on the archaeology of survival cannibalism has been placed in the context of research on dietary stress, directly comparing evidence for using both animals and humans as food (Ellis et al. 2011; Novak 2011). The analogy between the taphonomy of humans and that of other large mammal prey deserves careful evaluation as methods become increasingly detailed and informative.

Identification of Bones and Other Animal Remains

Identification of zooarchaeological remains to genus or species is a routine part of archaeological analysis. Identifications link food remains with modern biological information on those animals (Reitz and Wing 2006; Wolverton 2012). Identification takes place in laboratories where archaeological specimens and modern skeletons can be compared side by side. Rare specimens are often taken to natural history museums when zooarchaeological reference collections cannot provide a match. Increasingly, photographs and 3-D images of unidentified bones are posted online so that many "eyes" can judge their characters. This detailed biological work is only the first step in reconstructing a past diet, however.

Not all animal foods came from vertebrates or produced bones. For example, vessels storing pure rendered fat ("bog butter") have been found archaeologically and characterized based on their chemical composition (Berstan et al. 2004). Insects and other invertebrates are uncommon foods in industrialized diets, but their abundance and high protein and fat content make up for their tiny body size in some ecological settings (Sutton 1995). Insect life cycles may include brief seasons where abundant insects attract human foragers for only a few weeks. Understanding the scheduling of such resource use can let zooarchaeologists pinpoint vulnerable times of a foraging or farming year. The most durable invertebrate food remains are mollusk shells (Claassen 1998). Shell can be a bulky, conspicuous part of midden deposits, so much so that shell heaps may have acted as a social beacon for ritual behavior (Luby and Gruber 1999; Moore and Thompson 2012). Details of shell microstructure sometimes can reveal the season of harvest, suggesting the scheduling of shellfishing. Mollusks tend to be nutritionally inferior to meat, but their predictable locations have made them a key resource (Andrus and Crowe 2000; Claassen 1986).

Preservation of insect, crustacean, and echinoderm parts in archaeological deposits occurs in soil conditions different from those that lead to the preservation of bone, and methods for recovering and studying them are much less developed than those for bone (Reitz and Wing 2006; Kenward and Large 1997). Except for dry deposits like caves, samples for recovering insects in the archaeological record demand special processing and analysis. Coprolites often offer information about consumption of insects and other invertebrates, but these samples are difficult to generalize to overall dietary intake (Reinhard and Bryant 1992). Bird eggshell is often found in fine-mesh screen samples but is seldom integrated into a proportional reconstruction of dietary intake (Sargeantson 2009). More often, such records serve to remind archaeologists of the wide range of high-quality foods that might have been used in the past, and how likely it was that prehistoric people would have used such foods when available. A similar status might be mentioned in regard to honey, an iconic high-quality food wherever available. Faint evidence for the use of honey comes from residues of beeswax and concentrations of flower pollen, but these signs come much later in the archaeological record than the probable first use of honey itself (Needham and Evans 1987; Crittenden 2011).

Animal Remains in Nutritional Context

Zooarchaeological analysis considers animal bones and how they are broken to infer the way that an animal "became" food in the course of butchering, preparation, storage, and serving; and how they then stopped being food at the point of discard. Detailed recording of which body parts are present in the assemblage can be combined with information about how meat and fat are distributed on an animal carcass. Zooarchaeologists have calculated values to express the food yield of mammal skeletal elements (so called utility indices) in terms of meat, marrow, and residual grease, using determinations from modern carcasses (Binford 1978; Lyman 1994; Metcalfe and Jones 1988). Parts of the animal body bearing abundant meat and fat are assumed to have had intrinsic high cultural value, based on their nutrient density; and the distribution of those parts is examined for inferences of where, or to whom, these parts of a carcass went after dismemberment. Plotting the representation of bone elements against utility indices for an assemblage could indicate that less meaty and less fatty sections of the body are underrepresented in an assemblage. This might be attributed to the missing elements having been discarded off-site, fed to animals, or intensively consumed in a situation of resource scarcity. The critical importance of fat in early forager diets has been documented by careful bone-by-bone calculations of the yield of meat and fat from each element. Combining evidence for seasonal patterns in animal use and evidence for fat selectivity has allowed fine-grained reconstructions of how hunters might have chosen particular animals based on their own nutritional needs at the particular time of year (Speth 1983).

Zooarchaeology would be straightforward indeed, if such principles could be applied directly. In practice, scavengers, weathering, and soil compression destroy less dense bones faster than they destroy sturdy bones, altering the representation of different types of bones in a deposit (Jans 2006; Lyman 1994). Physical attrition progresses more quickly faster in less sturdy bones than in dense bones, regardless of whether the less-dense bones were high food-value parts or low-value parts liable to be discarded in any case (Lyman 1994, 2008). The density of bones in terms of their mineral content (originally referred to as bulk density) for each skeletal element has been generated to help predict taphonomic patterns (Lyman 1994). Bone mineral values come from densiometry scans or CT scans of bones, but these measures obscure some important variation in bone shape and thickness (Lam et al. 2003).

Two cascades of taphonomic destruction, one from cultural behavior and one from physical and biological damage, may combine to obscure the original behavioral signature in body part representation. Damage resulting from food choice and preparation, as opposed to noncultural ravaging and weathering, is continually monitored as zooarchaeological analysis progresses (Marean and Frey 1997; Marom and Bar-Oz 2008). Not only does taphonomic bias affect estimates of which body parts were preferred, but it can also act to bias estimates of the usual age of slaughter since the bones of young animals are destroyed more readily than those of adults (Munson and Garniewicz 2003).

Using the Archaeological Record to Study Ancient Animal Food

Archaeological finds of animal bones are not a direct measure of dietary intake. Meat science data can be used to calculate the amount of meat, fat, and blood obtainable from an average carcass as outlined above. The question of how many animals were used has been a long-running problem for zooarchaeologists (Lyman 2008). When archaeological bones were compared to historical records of how much food was available at a site, it was shown that the archaeological remains documented only a tiny sample of the original food (Guilday 1970). Zooarchaeologists always count the identified bone fragments as a basic measure of abundance (NISP or the number of identified specimens), but the significance of this measure in terms of meat can be unclear. The most abundant bone element in an assemblage can be used to estimate how many animals were represented (the so-called minimum number of individuals, or MNI). More precise measures are obtained by estimating the segments of animals (such as the hindquarter) that were recovered in a particular deposit. These calculations involve numerous judgment calls on how to count and group various body parts, so MNI estimates are always reported along with NISP (Reitz and Wing 2006). In some animal groups (particularly ones like fish that grow throughout life), the body sizes of individual animals vary enough for age variation to have significant impact on nutritional reconstructions. Where body size varies widely, measurements of a skeletal element can be used to track the use of large versus small members of one species.

Zooarchaeologists can discern when some parts of some animals were discarded or abandoned before all possible nutrients had been used. In some cases, intense breakage indicates that cooks had wrung every bit of separable fat from already cleaned bone before fragments were discarded (Outram 2003, 2004). In seasonal environments, the nutritional status of animals themselves could have declined at some period (during the winter or during the dry season), and different nutrients would have been available from the same individual animal depending on the time of hunt or slaughter (Ervynk 2005). Slaughtering a stressed animal might indicate local resource depletion; to monitor this, techniques have been borrowed from wildlife management to estimate the season of death for individual skeletons (Lieberman 1994; Monks 1981; Wilson, Grigson, and Payne 1982).

Estimating overall intake of nutrients from animal food involves combining the dietary contributions of all the animals eaten in the rough proportion in which they were found: mammals, birds, fish, and the many invertebrate animals such as mollusks, crabs, urchins, grubs, and insects. The multiple sources of bias in assessing the nutrients obtained by a set of remains of different kinds of animals have been overwhelming for archaeologists (Reitz and Wing 2006). Even coming up with a meaningful comparison of the importance of fishing to hunting, using fish bones and mammal bones as primary data, has demanded assumptions about bone-to-food and bone-to-bone relationships that some archaeologists feel are questionable. One streamlined approach to estimating animal biomass represented by an assemblage calculates the food value predicted from the weight of archaeological remains for individual species. For example, the weight of sea urchin testae and fish bone would be used to estimate the amount of food contributed by urchins vs. fish (Jackson 1989; Reitz et al. 1987).

Attempts to reconstruct the relative proportion of plant food and animal food in a prehistoric diet using direct archaeological remains have been even less productive. To better approach this question, zooarchaeologists have sought to integrate their results with those from stable isotope dietary analysis from human and animal skeletal remains (see Turner, this volume). Dietary intake estimated using isotopic signatures comes from individual skeletal remains, whereas archaeological remains reflect combined dietary intakes of many people over an unknowable period of time. Combining skeletal isotope data with direct food remains in the context of well-dated artifactual remains of food production activities allows the fullest picture of ancient food. A related approach is to quantify the organic residues of different animal foods absorbed into a sample of pottery shards (Evershed et al. 2008.)

Herds of cattle, sheep, goats, horses, camels, reindeer, and yaks are kept for milk production today, but dairy foods are a relatively recent addition to the human diet (Greenfield 2010). Dairy production was a revolution in the relationship between humans and animals, resulting in distinct herd compositions, distinct animal types, and altered landscapes. The rapid geographic expansion of dairy animals and the technology for keeping them suggests these foods have profoundly affected recent human evolution in Eurasia and Africa (see Monge, this volume). The first archaeological evidence for this development came from images of milking, from the expansion of dairy animals beyond their original home in the Near East, and from the demographic composition of herds dominated by older females and many young animals (Sherratt 1983). These traditional archaeological data have been superseded by abundant and compelling direct evidence of dairy fats in materials scraped from ancient ceramic pots. This work uses profiles of fatty acids and stable carbon isotopes from each fatty acid (Evershed 2008). The residue evidence shows that archaeological estimates of early dairy foods based on bone remains have been too late, lagging by as much as two thousand years (Evershed et al. 2008). Evidently, dairy foods moved into Neolithic Europe as a package with grains and other agricultural foods.

The Social Archaeology of Animal Food

Understanding the meaning of food use in the past demands careful study of the entire archaeological record along with direct remains of a particular food.

Iconography, inscriptions, and historical records are used to understand the significance of food choices, the nature of a cuisine, and the ways that food is used to claim or experience a particular social status (Russell 2012). Archaeological excavations of a place of ceremony or mortuary ritual often include whole animals or parts of animals that appear to be the remains of food offerings, sometimes involving massive numbers of animals (Kansa et al. 2009). Archaeologists speculate about the special nature of the animals involved in these ritual and feast events, trying to connect ritually loaded special events with the everyday events of slaughter and meat eating (or milk drinking) (Dietler and Hayden 2001; Kelly 2001). Reconstructions of social value based on intrinsic biological criteria (dangerous animals, fatty animals, etc.) are challenged, though, by the variation in specific historically known food traditions (Bartosiewicz 1997).

Using communal contexts to study ancient ritual practice around food often assumes that such practice was generally shared (Russell 2012). Yet, anthropologists constantly find that smaller social groups define themselves in terms of food choice, or food prohibition. Given the role of taphonomic processes in destroying food remains, it may be difficult to make a convincing case for a food prohibition using the absence of remains of a particular animal; there are just too many other explanations for why some animal is missing from an archaeological assemblage. Even so, prohibitions on using animals such as pigs are some of the most strongly held food practices known, and the archaeology of pig use has been carefully examined through this lens (Nelson 1998). The archaeology of social and ethnic food traditions in multiethnic situations is methodologically challenging. Ideally it would require that a social group discarded or interred its remains in a specific deposit with other evidence of social identity. Special cases from Europe and the eastern Mediterranean show the promise of such careful analysis in suggesting dietary prohibitions and even cuisine practices within those traditions (Jones O'Day, Van Neer, and Ervynk 2004; Marom and Zuckerman 2012). Archaeologists also know that discard itself is a culturally loaded act, and must keep in mind the range of meanings incorporated into discard, ranging potentially from veneration to disgust (Bartosiewicz 2003). The archaeological record of food discard in the twentieth century United States, made famous as "garbology" by Rathje (1977), demonstrated the impact of signaling via discard with records of fresh meat, still in its store wrapper, discarded in household trash.

Summary

Zooarchaeological remains are coarse evidence at best for specific dietary intake in past communities. They are, though, evocative and detailed evidence of the role of animal foods in prehistoric diets in time periods and places for which no other evidence is as good and analogies with modern environments are inappropriate. Zooarchaeological remains from settlements and urban contexts have considerable potential to reveal the development of food patterns such as local cuisine and cultural proscriptions. At the community level, animal bone deposits have shown long-term patterns of animal production and the relationship of meat and dairy production to crops and other plant foods. Remains from feasts and mortuary deposits allow archaeologists to see very specific one-time consumption of animals in highly charged social contexts. Taking zooarchaeological remains together with bioarchaeological data on individuals allows us to estimate the impact of gender, sex, age, and social status on dietary intake, health, and well-being.

Katherine M. Moore received her PhD in anthropology at the University of Michigan in 1989. She has conducted zooarchaeological research in North America, South America, and Central Asia, working on prehistoric hunting, fishing, and the origins of pastoralism. She is particularly interested in integrating insights about ancient food that come from animal bones with information gained from studying plant remains and human skeletal remains. She is a consulting scholar at the University of Pennsylvania Museum and the Mainwaring Teaching Specialist in the Center for the Analysis of Archaeological Materials.

Key Basic References

Binford, Lewis R. 1978. *Nuniamuit Ethnoarchaeology.* New York: Academic Press
deFrance, Susan. D. 2009. Zooarchaeology in Complex Societies: Political Economy, Status, and Ideology. *Journal of Archaeological Research* 172: 105–168.
Lyman, R. Lee. 1994. *Vertebrate Taphonomy.* Cambridge Manuals in Archaeology. New York: Cambridge University Press.
————. 2008. *Quantitative Paleozoology.* Cambridge: Cambridge University Press.
Mulville, Jacqui, and Alan Outram. 2005. *Zooarchaeology of Fats, Oils, Milk and Dairying.* Oxford: Oxbow Books.
Reitz, Elizabeth, and Elizabeth Wing. 2006. *Zooarchaeology,* 2nd ed. Cambridge: Cambridge University Press.
Ruscillo, Deborah, ed. 2006. *Recent Advances in Ageing and Sexing Animal Bones.* Oxford. Oxbow Books.
Russell, Nerissa. 2012. *Social Zooarchaeology: Humans and Animals in Prehistory.* Cambridge University Press.
Wilson, Bob, Caroline Grigson, and Sebastian Payne, eds. 1982. *Aging and Sexing Bones from Archaeological Sites.* Oxford: British Archaeological Reports British Series 109.

References

Alhaique, Francesca. 1997. Do Patterns of Bone Breakage Differ Between Cooked and Uncooked Bones? *Anthropozoologia* 25–26: 49–56.

Andrus, C. Fred T., and Douglas E. Crowe. 2000. Geochemical analysis of *Crassostrea virginica* as a Method to Determine Season of Capture. *Journal of Archaeological Science* 27: 33–42.

Bartosiewicz, Laszlo. 1997. This Little Piggy Went to Market... An Archaeozoological Study of Modern Meat Values. *European Journal of Archaeology* 51: 170–182.

———. 2003. "There's Something Rotten in the State...": Bad Smells in Antiquity. *European Journal of Archaeology* 62: 175–195.

Berstan, R., S. N. Dudd, M. S. Copley, E. D. Morgan, A. Quye, and Richard Evershed. 2004. Characterisation of "Bog Butter" Using a Combination of Molecular and Isotopic Techniques. *Analyst* 1293: 270–275.

Binford, Lewis R. 1978. *Nuniamuit Ethnoarchaeology.* New York: Academic Press.

———. 1981. *Bones: Ancient Men and Modern Myths.* Orlando: Academic Press.

Braun, D. R., J. W. Harris, N. E. Levin, J. T. McCoy, A. I. R. Herries, M. K. Bamford, L. C. Bishop, B. G. Richmond, and M. Kibunjia. 2010. Early Hominin Diet Included Diverse Terrestrial and Aquatic Animals 1.95 Ma in East Turkana, Kenya. *Proceedings of the National Academy of Sciences* 107(22): 10002–10007.

Bunn, Henry T., and J. A. Ezzo. 1993. Hunting and Scavenging by Plio-Pleistocene Hominids: Nutritional Constraints, Archaeological Patterns, and Behavioural Implications. *Journal of Archaeological Science* 204: 365–398.

Claassen, Cheryl. 1986. Shellfishing Seasons in the Prehistoric Southeastern United States. *American Antiquity* 51: 21–37.

———. 1998. *Shells.* Cambridge Manual in Archaeology. New York: Cambridge University Press.

Crittenden, A. N. 2011. The Importance of Honey Consumption in Human Evolution. *Food and Foodways* 19: 257–273.

Dietler, Michael, and Brian Hayden. 2001. *Feasts: Archaeological and Ethnographic Perspectives on Food, Politics and Power.* Washington, DC: Smithsonian Institution Press.

Ellis, Meredith A. B., Christopher Merritt, Shannon Novak, and Kelly J. Dixon. 2011. The Signature of Starvation: A Comparison of Bone Processing at a Chinese Encampment in Montana and the Donner Party Camp in California. *Historical Archaeology* 45: 97–112.

Ervynck, Anton. 2005. Detecting the Seasonal Slaughtering of Domestic Mammals: Inferences from the Detailed Recording of Tooth Eruption and Wear. *Environmental Archaeology* 10: 153–169.

Evershed, Richard P. 2008. Organic Residue Analysis in Archaeology: The Archaeological Biomarker Revolution. *Archaeometry* 50: 895–924.

Evershed, Richard P., Sebastian Payne, Andrew Sherratt, M. S. Copley, J. Coolidge, D. Urem-Kotsu, and M. Ö. G. Kostas Kotsakis. 2008. Earliest Date for Milk Use in the Near East and Southeastern Europe Linked to Cattle Herding. *Nature* 4557(212): 528–531.

Friesen, T. M. 2001. A Zooarchaeological Signature for Meat Storage: Re-thinking the Drying Utility Index. *American Antiquity* 66: 315–331.

Goldberg, Paul, D. T. Nash, and M. D. Petraglia, eds. 1993. Formation Process in Archaeological Context. Monograph no. 17. Madison: Prehistory Press.

Greenfield, Haskel J. 2010. The Secondary Products Revolution: The Past, the Present and the Future. *World Archaeology* 421: 29–54.

Guilday, John E. 1970. Animal Remains from Archaeological Excavations at Fort Ligonier. *Annals of the Carnegie Museum* 42: 177–186.

Hurlbut, S. A. 2001. The Taphonomy of Cannibalism: A Review of Anthropogenic Bone Modification in the American Southwest. *International Journal of Osteoarchaeology* 10: 4–26.

Jackson, H. Edwin. 1989. The Trouble with Transformations: Effects of Sample Size and Sample Composition on Meat Weight Estimates Based on Skeletal Mass Allometry. *Journal of Archaeological Science* 166: 601–610.

Jans, Miranda. 2006. Histological Characterisation of Diagenetic Alteration of Archaeological Bone. Geoarchaeological and Bioarchaeologial Studies 4. Amsterdam: Vrije Universiteit.

Jones O'Day, Sharon, Wim Van Neer, and Anton Ervynk, eds. 2005. *Behaviour Behind Bones: The Zooarchaeology of Ritual, Religion, Status and Identity.* Oxford: Oxbow.

Kansa, Sarah W., S. C. Gauld, S. Campbell, and Elizabeth E. Carter. 2009. Whose Bones Are Those? Preliminary Comparative Analysis of Fragmented Human and Animal Bones in the "Death Pit" at Domuztepe, a Late Neolithic Settlement in Southeastern Turkey. *Anthropozoologica* 441: 159–172.

Kelly, Lucretia. 2001. A Case of Ritual Feasting at the Cahokia Site. In *Feasts: Archaeological and Ethnographic Perspectives on Food, Politics and Power,* ed. Michael Dietler and Brian Hayden, 334–367. Washington, DC: Smithsonian Institution Press.

Kenward, Henry, and F. Large. 1997. Recording the Preservational Condition of Archaeological Insect Fossils. *Environmental Archaeology* 21: 49–60.

Lam, Yin M., O. M. Pearson, Curtis W. Marean, and X. Chen. 2003. Bone Density Studies in Zooarchaeology. *Journal of Archaeological Science* 30: 1701–1708.

Lieberman, Daniel E. 1994. The Biological Basis for Seasonal Increments in Dental Cementum and Their Application to Archaeological Research. *Journal of Archaeological Science* 21: 525–539.

Luby, E. M., and M. F. Gruber. 1999. The Dead Must be Fed: Symbolic Meanings of the Shellmounds of the San Francisco Bay Area. *Cambridge Archaeological Journal* 9: 95–108.

Lupo, Karen D., and Dave N. Schmitt. 1997. Experiments in Bone Boiling: Nutritional Returns and Archaeological Reflections. *Anthropozoologica* 25–26: 137–144.

Marean, Curtis W., and Carol J. Frey. 1997. Animal Bones from Caves to Cities: Reverse Utility Curves as Methodological Artifacts. *American Antiquity* 62: 698–711.

Marom, Nimrod, and Guy Bar-Oz. 2008. "Measure for Measure": A Taphonomic Reconsideration of the Kebaran Site of Ein Gev I, Israel. *Journal of Archaeological Science* 352: 214–227.

Marom, Nimrod, and Sharon Zuckerman. 2012. The Zooarchaeology of Exclusion and Expropriation: Looking Up from the Lower City in Late Bronze Age Hazor. *Journal of Anthropological Archaeology* 31: 573–585.

Metcalfe, Duncan, and Kevin T. Jones. 1988. A Reconsideration of Animal Body-Part Utility Indices. *American Antiquity* 53: 486–504.

Monks, Gregory. G. 1981. Seasonality Studies. *Studies in Archaeological Method and Theory* 4: 177–240.

Moore, C. R., and V. D. Thompson. 2012. Animism and Green River Persistent Places: A Dwelling Perspective of the Shell Mound Archaic. *Journal of Social Archaeology* 12: 264–284.

Moore, Katherine M., Maria Bruno, Jose M. Capriles, and Christine A. Hastorf. 2010. Integrated Contextual Approaches to Understanding Past Activities Using Plant and Animal

Remains from Kala Uyuni, Lake Titicaca, Bolivia. In *Integrating Zooarchaeology and Paleoethnobotany,* ed. Amber Vanderwerker and Tanya Perez, 173–203. New York: Springer.

Munson, Patrick J., and R. C. Garniewicz. 2003. Age-Mediated Survivorship of Ungulate Mandibles and Teeth in Canid-Ravaged Faunal Assemblages. *Journal of Archaeological Science* 304: 405–416.

Needham, Stuart, and John Evans. 1987. Honey and Dripping: Neolithic Food Residues from Runnymede Bridge. *Oxford Journal of Archaeology* 61: 21–28.

Nelson, Sarah. M., ed. 1998. Ancestors for the Pigs: Pigs in Prehistory. MASCA Papers Vol. 15. Philadelphia: University of Pennsylvania Museum Press.

Nicholson, Rebecca A. 1993. A Morphological Investigation of Burnt Animal Bone and an Evaluation of Its Utility in Archaeology. *Journal of Archaeological Science* 20: 411–428.

Novak, Shannon A. 2011. [Wo]man and Beast: Skeletal Signatures of a Starvation Diet. In *An Archaeology of Desperation: Exploring the Donner Party's Alder Creek Camp,* ed. Kelly J. Dixon, Julie Schablitsky, and Shannon A. Novak, 185–218. Norman: University of Oklahoma.

O'Connor, Terry, ed. 2005. *Biosphere to Lithosphere: New Studies in Vertebrate Taphonomy.* Oxford: Oxbow.

Outram, Alan K. 2003. Comparing Levels of Subsistence Stress amongst Norse Settlers in Iceland and Greenland Using Levels of Bone Fat Exploitation as an Indicator. *Environmental Archaeology* 82: 119–128.

———. 2004. Identifying Dietary Stress in Marginal Environments: Bone Fats, Optimal Foraging Theory and the Seasonal Round. In *Colonisation, Migration, and Marginal Areas: A Zooarchaeological Approach,* ed. Mariana Mondini, Sebastian Munoz, and S. Wickler, 74–85. Oxford: Oxbow.

Outram, Alan. K., C. J. Knüsel, S. Knight, and A. F. Harding. 2005. Understanding Complex Fragmented Assemblages of Human and Animal Remains: A Fully Integrated Approach. *Journal of Archaeological Science* 32: 1699–1710.

Partlow, M. A. 2006. Sampling Fish Bones: A Consideration of the Importance of Screen Size and Disposal Context in the North Pacific. *Arctic Anthropology* 431: 67–79.

Payne, Sebastian. 1972. Partial Recovery and Sample Bias: The Results of Some Sieving Experiments. In *Papers in Economic Prehistory,* ed. Eric. S. Higgs, 49–64. Cambridge: Cambridge University Press.

Pearsall, Deborah M. 2000. *Paleoethnobotany: A Handbook of Procedures,* 2nd ed. Walnut Creek, CA: Left Coast Press.

Rathje, William L. 1977. In Praise of Archaeology: Le Projet du Garbage. In *Historical Archaeology and the Importance of Material Things,* ed. Leyland Ferguson, 36–42. Lansing, MI: Special Publication Series-*Society for Historical Archaeology* no. 2.

Reinhard, Karl J., and Vaughn M. Bryant. 1992. Coprolite Analysis: A Biological Perspective on Archaeology. *Archaeological Method and Theory* 4: 245–288.

Reitz, E. J., I. R. Quitmyer, H. S. Hale, S. J. Scudder, and E. S Wing. 1987. Application of Allometry to Zooarchaeology. *American Antiquity* 52: 304–317.

Roberts S. J., C. I. Smith, A. Millard, and M. J. Collins. 2002. The Taphonomy of Cooked Bone: Characterizing Boiling and Its Physico–chemical Effects. *Archaeometry* 44: 485–494.

Sargeantson, Dale. 2009. *Birds.* Cambridge Manual in Archaeology. Cambridge: Cambridge University Press.

Selvaggio, Marie. 1998. Evidence for a Three-Stage Sequence of Hominid and Carnivore Involvement with Long Bones at FLK Zinj, Olduvai Tanzania. *Journal of Archaeological Science* 25: 191–202.

Shaffer, Brian S. 1992. Quarter-Inch Screening: Understanding Biases in Recovery of Vertebrate Faunal Remains. *American Antiquity* 57: 129–136.

Sherratt, Andrew. 1983. The Secondary Exploitation of Animals in the Old World. *World Archaeology* 15: 90–104.

Shipman, Patricia, G. Foster, and Margaret Schoeninger. 1984. Burnt Bones and Teeth: An Experimental Study of Color, Morphology, Crystal Structure and Shrinkage. *Journal of Archaeological Science* 114: 307–332.

Speth, John D. 1983. *Bison Kills and Bone Counts: Decision Making by Ancient Hunters.* Chicago: University of Chicago Press.

———. 1989. Early Hominid Hunting and Scavenging: The Role of Meat as an Energy Source. *Journal of Human Evolution* 184: 329–343.

———. 2010. *The Paleoanthropology and Archaeology of Big-Game Hunting: Protein, Fat, Or Politics?* New York: Springer.

Stanford, Craig. B., and Henry T. Bunn, eds. 2001. *Meat-Eating and Human Evolution.* New York: Oxford University Press.

Stiner, Mary C. 1994. *Honor Among Thieves: A Zooarchaeological Study of Neandertal Ecology.* Princeton: Princeton University Press.

Stiner, Mary C., Steven L. Kuhn, Stephen Weiner, and Ofer Bar-Yosef. 1995. Differential Burning, Recrystallization, and Fragmentation of Archaeological Bone. *Journal of Archaeological Science* 22: 223–237.

Sutton, Mark. 1995. Archaeological Aspects of Insect Use. *Journal of Archaeological Method and Theory* 2: 253–298.

Weiner, Steven. 2010. *Microarchaeology: Beyond The Visible Archaeological Record.* Cambridge: Cambridge University Press.

White, Tim. 1992. *Prehistoric Cannibalism at Mancos 5MTUMR-2346.* Princeton, NJ: Princeton University Press.

Wolverton, Steve. 2012. Data Quality in Zooarchaeological Faunal Identification. *Journal of Archaeological Method and Theory* 20: 1–16.

Wrangham, Richard. 2009. *Catching Fire: How Cooking Made Us Human.* New York: Basic Books.

Zeder, Melinda. 2003. Hiding In Plain Sight: The Value of Museum Collections in the Study of the Origins of Animal Domestication In *Documenta Archaeobiologiae 1: Deciphering Ancient Bones; The Research Potential of Bioarchaeological Collections,* ed. Gisela Grupe and Joris Peters, 125–138. Rahden and Westfalia: Verlag M. Leidorf.

CHAPTER 13

If There Is Food, We Will Eat

An Evolutionary and Global Perspective on Human Diet and Nutrition

Janet M. Monge

Introduction

The diversity of diet across evolutionary time and over the expanse of the globe today highlights the range of tolerated and consumed foods that characterize humans as a species. The range, as it is often times quoted, includes almost exclusive animal food consumption to diets virtually completely devoid of any animal sources of nourishment (except for the incidental ingestion of insect residua). This diversity underscores the issues and problems in defining what constitutes an "optimal" diet for all humans. Indeed it appears that there is no optimal diet, although there are dietary guidelines that minimize a host of diet-mediated illnesses including many manifestations of cardiovascular disease, many types of cancers, and systemic metabolic imbalances (Lindeberg 2010).

Many lines of evidence bear on the issues associated with the adequacy of diet and the nutritional needs of humans in the modern world. Many studies relevant to this issue regard patterns of nutritional disease as a baseline for understanding what is normal, necessary, or optimal. Because of different genetic substrates, the necessary analyses are quite complex. Nevertheless, there appears to be a general agreement, reflected well in the nutrition reports by the WHO (World Health Organization), that human nutritional requirements are best fulfilled by taking in calories and nutrients from a maximal variety of food sources. In addition, an evolutionary perspective confirms that it is best to choose foods from the vegetable and fruit categories with limited quantities of fats. It is also good practice to minimize the quantity of salt and simple carbohydrates in the diet (*http://www.who.int/features/factfiles/nutrition/facts/en/index9.html*). In addition, an evolutionary perspective appears to indicate that to maximize long-term health, that an increased amount of foods rich in both calcium and potassium be consumed in all life stages.

On a globe where approximately 180 million children are without adequate calories and nutrients to maintain an optimal potential for growth and development, it is ironic that in many nations, especially the United States, overconsumption of calories has produced the public health problem of obesity—most alarmingly, from a public health perspective, in childhood. In addition, the incidence of obesity is rising in many nations. In fact, in virtually all areas of the world a subset of the population with access to greater resources is overweight or obese (for the actual statistics see: *http://www.who.int/dietphysicalactivity/publica tions/facts/obesity/en/*). Similarly, within the confines of the richest nations in world there are individuals or entire populations that are under- or malnourished. No one research field of inquiry can possibly address all the issues associated with nutritional adequacy and inadequacy. All else being equal, however, it does appear that whenever there is available food and the necessary means to acquire it, humans will eat it.

The evolutionary perspective, however, does give us a fruitful way to understand the baseline of some of the broad issues addressed within the related fields of the nutritional sciences. Simply addressed, the question is, can an understanding of the diet of our ancestors give us insights into modern human diets and the adequacy of these diets for the maintenance of long-term health?

The Evolutionary Perspective

The evolutionary study of diet and nutrition has been invaded by a plethora of books that feed often times into the popular "diet craze" that exists in our weight-conscious society (see, e.g., Cordain 2002; Cordain and Friel 2005; De Vany 2010; Wolf 2010; Audette and Gilchrist 1999). The first serious synopsis focused on an evolutionary perspective on diet and nutrition, published in 1985 by Eaton and Konner, was expanded into a book (Eaton, Shostak, and Konner 1988) that emphasized the use of recent gatherer/hunter studies. In this same time period, two other edited volumes set the stage for the analysis of diet from an evolutionary perspective (Harding and Teleki 1981; Harris and Ross 1989). Since that time, the accumulation of new data, along with exponential expansion in techniques of analysis used to test these data sets, has further refined and reintegrated this research agenda.

The basic premise of the evolutionary perspective as applied to an understanding of diet and human evolution is that all forms of life are adapted to the consumption of an optimal combination of foods and that selection has operated over time to produce not only the means to acquire these foods but also the means to extract nutrients from food once it is ingested. Interest has recently expanded to the analysis of food sources that are used only under conditions where optimal food sources are no longer available. These are called "fallback foods" (Constantino and Wright 2009). These adaptations can be behavioral, biological, and in the case of humans and perhaps other animals as well, cultural or social. Tracking the dietary course of human evolution, it seems apparent that the major shifts in food acquisition and consumption can be broken down into the following stages (at least it is often presented in this way).

Stages In Human Dietary Evolution

1. Generalized omnivory as part of our primate ancestry;
2. A shift in the emphasis on particular food types, based on movements of hominid ancestors into novel environments early in the history of humans;
3. An economic adjustment that expands hominid-food interactions into a social, at least familial networks. Also marking this stage of human evolution is an increase in food preparation including cooking and the integration of higher quality protein into the diet, primarily from animal sources;
4. A dramatic shift to food production associated with the origin of agriculture and the domestication of animals;
5. An expansion of global economies related to food production and distribution that allow food resources to be transferred over ever expanding distances and introduce humans to a unique range of foodstuffs.

Stage 1: General Omnivory

Primates

Although it is difficult to know just how far to extend living primate studies to human evolution, it seems safe to assume that the general pattern of omnivory can be applied to even the very earliest phases of human evolution. Primates appear to be generalized feeders responding to food availability opportunistically and when foods are seasonally available, including animal-source foods. Omnivory refers to a general trophic level within the food web, and not to particular foods consumed by animals on this level.

Since the hominoids, especially the large-bodied African chimpanzee, bonobo, and gorilla, are our closest relatives, much attention has focused on these animals' diets. Beyond the general statement that their diet varies both between and within species, and that it is best described as omnivorous, are there any statements that pertain to the question of the origin of human diet? Studies of the microwear (an indicator of abrasive elements in the food consumed, oftentimes used for comparison to fossil forms in the human lineage) on the dentition of the African hominoids illustrates the diversity of diets consumed by even individual animals and highlights that nonfood items might be a contributor to their dietary strategies (Galbany et al. 2009). It is essential at this junction to state that although we are close relatives to these other hominoid species, they are not our ancestors; indeed, their evolutionary history as distinct from our common ancestor is as long as that of humans. The usefulness of these comparative studies of living primates is therefore probably of limited value.

It is generally assumed that the chimpanzee is the best model for comparison to early human ancestors. Living chimpanzees are best categorized as ripe-fruit frugivores. If these animals are good models for the last common ancestor of the chimp and human lineages, then we can hypothesize that this last ancestor was an opportunistic feeder but with an emphasis on ripe fruit. Comparison of the earliest known members of our lineage, *Ardipithecus ramidus* and *Australopithecus anamensis,* using both microstructural analysis and overall dental morphology, indicate that at the origin of our lineage, dietary choices were distinct from any of the living hominoids (Suwa et al. 2009; Macho and Shimizu 2010). Thus, it appears that an adaptive shift occurred at the very inception of our lineage and that this shift, reflected in both ecology and diet, set the stage for future changes in our evolutionary line.

Rodman (2002) summarizes much of the ecological and food-related behaviors associated with diet in the living hominoids. The conclusion, which can be applied to hominid ancestors, is that food choices among the apes encompass a broad spectrum of edible elements and that across this spectrum choices are varied and random in respect to individuals and populations as well as between species. In addition, many primates including hominoids engage in extra-oral food processing and food sharing (Hohmann 2009), making a wider range of foods more available. Although not a perfect model for understanding diets in our ancestors, the commonalities across this broad range of nonhuman hominoids allow us to assume that this pattern was part of the common ancestry of all hominoids, including humans.

Similarly, the anatomy of the alimentary canal below the oral cavity, the basic nutrient requirements, and the food transit times (an aspect of digestion influenced by individual and dietary difference in some populations) within the GI tract are similar across all hominoid species (Milton 1999). Differences in dietary composition across these varied species apparently can be tolerated within these anatomical and thus evolutionarily constrained digestive tubes. Although the parts of the digestive system can be somewhat modulated during life based on the diversity of consistent dietary choices over a long term, these represent only small fluctuations from this basic design. For the most part, humans have a somewhat expanded small intestine accommodating a greater proportion of animal foods within the diet; gorillas, on the other hand, with their heavy concentration of low nutrient-quality leaves and high fiber concentration as a portion of diet, have larger segments of the GI tract devoted to the colon (ibid.). Similarly, Lambert

(1998) refers to these alterations within the compartments of the gastrointestinal system as "modularity" and that the basic composition of the GI tract does not limit the types and varieties of foods that compose the hominoid diet.

This type of research is of course constrained by the inability to derive appropriate soft tissue data from the fossil record of human evolution. Another limitation is that measurements of the area devoted to each segment of the digestive canal give no actual data on the histomorphology of the gut and microorganisms that are a necessary component of digestion (Walker 2007). Thus, animals with virtually identical digestive compartments may indeed have differing diets and different mechanisms for processing and extracting the nutrients from that food (Vrieze et al. 2010), possibly reflecting individual or population differences and not necessarily species-wide evolutionary adaptations.

Thus, although not very fulfilling in a number of ways, the phenomenon of worldwide variation in human diets is heavily based on the primate pattern of nutrient acquisition and food exploitation. There are really no limitations in the types of food consumed by humans, and humans are very much opportunistic eaters. One essential limitation to understanding the evolution of the human diet based on models derived from primate studies is the absolute dearth of data on the micronutrient components of primates' diets. Most studies factor in only broad categories of diet components like "meat," "leaves," or "fiber" (see, e.g., Conklin-Brittain, Wrangham, and Smith 2002). The sustainability of particular diets does not rest on these overarching components alone but on what the actual sources of nourishment contained within these foods (Eaton and Eaton 2000) are, beyond protein for tissue building, carbohydrates for energy, and fiber for altering transit times and the potential for nutrient absorption.

Gatherer-Hunters
Nutritional studies of modern gathering-hunting peoples (sometimes also referred to as foraging peoples) have also contributed to the understanding of baseline human diets. Like primate models, gathering-hunter models are also inadequate in some respects. The question is, do modern (at least until very recently, when many of these groups were subsumed within the economy of nation-states) gatherer-hunters reflect a more "natural" human dietary condition? At least, is this type of resource extraction strategy more similar to the ways our early ancestors collected resources? Modern gatherer-hunters are not our ancestors. With several caveats, the use of this model, at least as far as dietary information is concerned, is probably more informative than models based on agricultural peoples. Modern gathering-hunting peoples have very sophisticated technologies for extracting resources from the environment that were not part of the distant evolutionary past of humans. In addition, the fossil record shows clearly that our early ancestors had relatively small brain sizes that probably translated to differing behavioral complexity, here associated with differences in resource extraction behaviors.

The systematic application of gatherer-hunter studies to diet and human evolution began with data compiled as part of the Harvard Kalahari Research Project (1963–1976) on food, diet, nutrition, and health (summarized in Lee and DeVore 1968; Lee 1979) on the Dobe Ju/'hoansi (!Kung language speakers, also called the Bushmen). Aware that the emphasis was traditionally on meat and the acquisition of animal resources, Dahlberg (1981) amassed a series of articles in an edited volume on the role of women in traditional gathering-hunting societies. The most recent synopsis of the Dobe Ju/'hoansi research, including analysis of life history, diet and disease, is contained within the work of Nancy Howell (2010). Other strategic early work on diet includes seven articles on forager and/ or gatherer-hunter food strategies and subsistence in Harris and Ross (1987: part 4, "Pre-State Foodways: Past and Present") and Hayden (1981). A more recent summary volume of foraging societies is the *Cambridge Encyclopedia of Hunter-Gatherers* (Lee and Daly 2004).

Gatherer-hunter societies exhibit a broad range in the quantity and proportion of animal and plant materials in the diet. A major component of dietary choice is based on availability, most often associated with seasonality and latitude (Kelly 1995, 2007). In all human groups, the proportion of foods from animal sources outstrips the quantity of meat (including insects) found in nonhuman primate diets. Thus, discussions of dietary changes in human evolution tend to emphasize the role of "meat" in the diet. Though it is true that sources of animal protein and fat are important in the gathering-hunting diet, the importance of meat has traditionally been overemphasized (Fiddes 1991; Stanford and Bunn 2001), and the role of gathering downplayed. It does appear that gathered foods (of plant or animal origin) were the base of virtually all gathering-hunting groups' diets in tropical and subtropical areas (the origin place of the human evolutionary lineage), which in turn allowed for the riskier behaviors associated with hunting the relatively rare animal (Zihlman and Tanner 1978).

Many primate groups show behaviors described as food sharing, and the point in human evolution when an economic shift occurred towards resource extraction specialization (based on sex and perhaps age-groups) and resource sharing is debated. Certainly the necessary tools for effective gathering-hunting do not make an appearance in the very earliest stages of human evolution, although, as with our primate cousins, tool use certainly occurred in the common ancestry of at least the apes and humans. It is also possible that even the simple digging stick could have significantly altered the types and quantities of foodstuffs accessible to the typical clawless, pawless, bipedal hominid (Mann 1981). The dietary shift associated with gathering-hunting is one of the most important in all of human evolution. That this technique survives today (of course in a modified form, since modern gatherer-hunters interact with neighboring societies of all sorts and have been incorporated politically into nation-states) is a testament to its effectiveness as a good extraction method.

In addition, gathering-hunting group diets give insights into the overall pattern of diet-mediated health issues in human evolution. The general pattern is that gathering-hunting groups experience times of low caloric extraction and intake, and at certain times of the year could be considered deficient in calories—what nutritionists call calorie-restricted—but rarely suffer from malnutrition (Cohen 1989). Thus, seasonality and low caloric consumption may be part of a healthy human dietary pattern that comes in part from our gatherer-hunter past, and the benefits of calorie-restrictive diets are now being explored within the framework of biomedical research on modern human populations regarding their influence on disease and patterns of aging (Hursting et al. 2010; Fontana 2009).

Stage 2: Beyond Omnivory

What do we know about the earliest deviations from the common ancestor, dietary or otherwise, in our lineage? We have some fossils extending as far back as six million years that are purported to be members of our lineage, but the first large, more extensive sample and more thoroughly published species, *Ardipithecus ramidus,* is dated to approximately 4–5 million years BP (before present). Although chimpanzees are often used to model the earliest members of our lineage, it seems apparent that even at this early (and possibly inceptive) date, *Ardipithecus* reflects not only a host of morphological differences from chimps, but also a substantive break from the environmental and behavior features, including dietary ones, of both the living chimp and the last common ancestor of chimps and humans. (The journal *Science* devoted the full issue of 2 October 2009, volume 326, to analysis of these fossils and to reconstructions of the behavior and biology of this species).

Lovejoy (2009) has argued cogently that this early member of our lineage, with its unique morphology including bipedalism and notable changes in dentition (i.e., in the orifice associated with the beginnings of food processing), shows a substantive adaptive shift from earlier forms as reconstructed from models of the last common ancestor of chimps and humans. Others have argued, in theoretical terms not based on fossil evidence, that at this early junction, chimpanzee behavioral and morphological models for this evolutionary transition would, based on the general principles of evolutionary thought, have dictated a total adaptive shift, with a distinct and unique combination of changes occurring early in our lineage (Hohmann 2009).

Of most importance are the shifts that Lovejoy proposes in male-female interactions, moving from the confines of the occasional food sharing and provisioning seen among living chimps, to full-blown provisioning of females by males as well as a series of cascading changes that would have ensued, including the inception of male-female pair bonding and possible economic alterations in the ways that the sexes independently procure foods from the environment.

Thus, it is possible that at this early junction in human evolutionary history, one of the key components of unique human ecological (including food) extraction behaviors emerged alongside social features like pair-bonding. That key component would be what Kaplan, Hooper, and Gurven (2009: 3289) refer to as changes in "the degree of complementarity in male and female inputs into production." From there, other unique or defining features of human social organization and food production would have emerged within our lineage. It is often argued that the shift to pair-bonding, based on primate models, is best illustrated in the fossil record by a reduction in the degree of sexual dimorphism. Plavcan (2001) aptly illustrates the complexity of ecological, social, and evolutionary factors that influence the degree and manifestation of sexual dimorphism. There is no real evidence that the large degree of sexual dimorphism shown in the fossil record within species in the hominid lineage in the early phases of human evolution obviates discussions of pair-bonding and provisioning as models for this first in a series of adaptive shifts.

Stage 3: Meat and Food Acquisition and Preparation

At some time in human evolution, and perhaps at multiple points, dietary composition was altered significantly to involve the exploitation of new environmental niches. When did this occur, and how do we accumulate the data from the fossil evidence with reconstructed environments to build a greater understanding of these shifts?

After about 3 million years BP, the fossil record indicates that multiple species composed the human lineage. Their relationship to each other and to later forms in that lineage is not completely clear. These early forms are all generally placed into the genus *Australopithecus*. This genus is generally broken into gracile and the more specialized robust types. At about 2 million years BP the genus *Homo* emerged, defined primarily by increases in brain size. It is at this junction that most researchers recognize a substantive change in the quality of food resources, which may have been fueled by competition with multiple other species, including members of *Australopithecus*. One of the most significant changes occurs upon the transition to a greater quantity of meat, which is generally considered to have accompanied our ancestors' ability to accumulate and consume a greater quantity of animal foods in the diet (some have argued for the role of scavenging of animal carcasses in human evolution; see Shipman 1986). A second significant change, perhaps occurring at about the same time, is the beginning of more elaborate tool technologies and eventually cooking.

Cooking and other types of food preparation

Although there is no general consensus on the earliest habitual use and control of fire, it is possible that the first members of our lineage placed into the genus *Homo*, specifically *Homo erectus*, made use of fire in the preparation of foods

(Karkanas et al. 2007; Clark and Harris 1985; Brain and Sillen 1988; Weiner et al. 1998). Whenever the habitual use of fire for roasting and/or cooking became established, the process appears to have yielded great dietary benefits for our ancestors. Carmody and Wrangham (2009a, 2009b) list the major net positive changes effected by this alteration in technology: (1) chemical changes in the starch content of particular foods; (2) changes in the structure of proteins; (3) detoxification of foods containing pathogens and various other toxins. In addition, and very importantly, cooking might improve the taste of foods, especially animal proteins and fats (Wobber, Hare, and Wrangham 2008).

Beyond cooking, direct preparation of vegetable foods could also change the digestibility and toxicity of many foods. Other preparation techniques using simple tools include peeling, soaking, and crushing. These alterations change the digestibility, content, and toxicity of especially many roots and tubers.

Luca, Perry, and Di Rienzo (2010) also note that cooking would have reduced the extent of, and time spent on, processing food in the mouth. This might be associated with changes in not only the size of the dentition macroscopically but also the types of wear on the individual teeth microscopically, and could also be related to dimensions of the face and skull associated with the musculature of mastication and/or to the bony buttressing of skull.

Back to meat

As stated before, with the origin of the genus *Homo,* there is an expansion in brain size that is easy to document from the fossil evidence. This increase occurs beginning at about 2 million years BP. Although we can plot the occurrence of this increase, the reason(s) for the expansion is(are) contentious. One theoretical method used to understand brain size increase in the *Homo* lineage rests firmly on models that use dietary assumptions. Perhaps the best accepted, put forward by Aiello and Wheeler (1995), was called the expensive tissue hypothesis. Metabolically the brain is a very expensive tissue, using approximately 15 to 20 percent of all of the energy consumed by modern humans. In order to support selection for increases in neurological tissues, dietary quality would necessarily have to increase so as to maintain other energy-consuming activities, including digestion, and keep overall metabolic costs stable. Since animal foods are easier to digest, the proportion of body size occupied by the gastrointestinal system reduces, as do energy consumptive costs, allowing for potential increases in brain size. In this model and other proposed models based on meat consumption (Milton 2003; Leonard and Robertson 1994 with many earlier references), the acquisition and consumption of meat is the substrate underpinning increases in brain size concomitant with expansions in brain size and the origin of the genus *Homo.*

Is there evidence that perhaps other dietary or life-history changes (an evolution-based way to study times frames in the life courses of animals within the species, e.g., infancy or childhood) are associated with the evolution of the genus

Homo? Isotope studies (see below) on fossil bones do not seem to confirm a dietary shift to the consumption of more animal products at the junction with the origin of the genus *Homo* in the fossil record (Sponheimer and Dufour 2009). O'Connell, Hawkes, and Blurton Jones (2002) propose a model of the evolution of the genus *Homo* that does not require a dietary shift in this surviving branch of our lineage. Thus, there are alternative viewpoints on the expanded exploitation of animal products in the diet of our ancestors.

Micro and macro anatomy related to diet
An extensive body of literature exists on topics related primarily to the dentition and overall cranial anatomy of hominid ancestors. The range of morphological, biomechanical, and enamel structure and microwear studies that explore the topic of diet in human evolution have often produced conflicting results that are difficult to synthesize. These research studies are typically based on the use of different samples and/or species, distinct protocols of data collection, and the use of very different statistical analytic tools (for an example of one meta-analysis study, see Grine et al. 2010). Does this avenue of research give us any insights into the evolution of diet in our lineage?

Dental microwear studies are difficult to interpret because there is a great deal of individual variation in the appearance of microabrasive patterns on the dentition of fossil forms and on the living forms that set the comparative and experimental base to which fossils are compared. Moreover, these abrasion patterns might derive from nonfood sources like dust and dirt, and micro changes in the enamel that occur after the death of the individual, which all become part of the postmortem microwear patterning (Galbany et al. 2009). When it is possible to distinguish between pre- and postmortem influences on the appearance of these marks, microwear probably reflects only the last few days or weeks of the animal's life, and not the full range of possible dietary elements processed by that animal—especially over different seasons and through the exploitation of differing environments. Also confounding dietary interpretations are some aspects of dental microstructure that may reflect the use of "fallback" foods rather more than other, more consistent aspects of the diet (Ungar 2009). Thus, it is difficult to interpret the meaning of the patterns observed in the range of fossil specimens that have been analyzed using this technique to infer dietary composition of extinct species (Teaford 2007).

Likewise, studies of tooth size and shape, enamel structure, and biomechanical analyses of fossils oftentimes result in conflicting conclusions about the diets of fossil species (for a summary study, see Teaford, Ungar, and Grine 2002). Furthermore, these studies can come into direct conflict with studies of microstructure and isotope composition (see below).

Based on these studies, it appears that the early *Australopithecus* members of our lineage were in all likelihood able to consume a broad-based diet with a possible shift towards the ability to process hard objects like large nuts and seeds, if not as a major component in the diet then perhaps as "fallback" foods (Strait et al. 2009; Teaford et al. 2002; Ungar, Grine, and Teaford 2008; Ungar 2009). With the appearance of the genus *Homo,* the broad dietary base is maintained but with a reduced emphasis on hard foods (which are crushed or cracked) to an increased consumption of tougher foods (e.g., foods that have thicker skins or even animal [muscle] foods) (Constantino et al. 2010). In addition, the reduction in overall jaw size and shape, and changes in molar tooth size and in occlusal surface relief—and perhaps in the microstructure of the enamel itself—are all perhaps associated with extra-oral food processing due to increased use of tools and an increased variety of tool types used to process foods.

Isotopic studies

Isotopic studies, as applied in all varieties of fossil bone analysis, rely upon the extraction from these ancient tissues of chemical signature information that reflects the chemical elements that were absorbed into the bony structural component of what once were living animals. Some of these extracted chemicals have been related to diet. Several different chemical profiles are used to reconstruct past diets. These include carbon isotopes, oxygen isotopes, strontium/calcium ratios, and strontium isotope studies, all of which rely upon the ability to distinguish the original chemical components of the bone as it once was present and preserved in the living animal, from the chemical alterations that are part of the fossilization process (for an excellent recent review of the literature, see Lee-Thorp 2008).

Isotopic studies also present a complex picture of past hominid-diet interactions. Can these studies illuminate and clarify other sources of information on the dietary composition of members of our evolutionary lineage? Again, the emerging picture is in fact quite complex. From the summative studies of isotopes and unique hominid lineages, it seems apparent that the isotopic shift is reflective—at least in South Africa, where many australopithecine-grade fossils have been found—of a dietary shift toward exploitation of grassy, open patches for a variety of foods (Lee-Thorp 2002). The lack of significant dietary distinctiveness between *Australopithecus* forms and early members of the genus *Homo* is counterintuitive to other biologically and morphologically distinctive features of these genera (as explored above). Sponheimer and Dufour (2009) come to much the same conclusion.

As the final word, an isotopic signature found in australopithecines distinguishes them from chimpanzees. The data from chemical analysis are not as easy to interpret, primarily because of small sample size. It does appear, though, that in conjunction with the other lines of evidence directed toward this issue, early *Homo* demonstrates a shift in emphasis but not an alteration in the dietary composition of earlier and contemporaneous australopithecine species. Some of this is probably best understood and mediated by changes in extra-oral food preparation and probably the incorporation of a repertoire of tools that can be brought to food preparation tasks.

Stage 4: The Origin of Agriculture and Animal Domestication

The origins of agriculture, in many geographic areas of both the Old and the New World, altered the course of human diet and evolution forever. Humans have been experimenting with sources of plant and animal food for many thousands of years. These experiments culminated in the almost total manipulation of these food sources and over time have come to achieve complete control of the places where the foods are grown as well as the genetic composition of these foods through the process of artificial selection (Ross 1987). The most recent manifestation of this control is the production of genetically modified foods, a part of biotechnology applied to the food industry that alters the genetic composition of plants in a single generation (an accelerated version of genetic changes fostered by artificial selection). The initial transition to agriculture and animal domestication occurred over millennia, with the first recognition of this transition in the archaeological record at about ten thousand years BP. Not all populations are part of this transition, although all populations are probably affected by proximity to agricultural groups. This includes living populations of gatherer-hunters.

Up to this point, ever expanding populations of members of our lineage developed tool technologies to more effectively exploit diverse food sources. Although archaeologists have tracked the course of increases in complexity in technologies for resource extraction, this is probably, like all patterns of material cultural complexity, a function of both innovation and necessity and manifests as diversity rather than a steady transition to more and more complex cultural elements (for a discussion of technologies and resource exploitation in Upper Pleistocene populations, see Shea 2009 and Churchill and Rhodes 2009). The first stone tools make an appearance at about 2.5 million years BP. Early stone tool technologies as part of the Early and Middle Pleistocene are more difficult to associate with particular patterns of resource extraction and in fact seem more conservative and generalized (Klein 2009). With the origins of agriculture, tool technologies reflect the function as extraction devices for horticultural products.

What happens to the human-food interaction at the beginnings of agriculture? This is probably the greatest alteration in all human environmental interactions in the whole of human history. Not only do patterns of diet change, but the entire dynamic of human populations is altered, as are the disease patterns that characterize our species. In a series of innovative papers, Eaton and Konner outline the dietary changes associated with the origin of agriculture as well as the changes in the nutritionally mediated diseases that occur as human populations diverge from our evolutionary dietary needs (for a subset of these, see Eaton and Konner 1985; Eaton et al. 1988; Eaton, Eaton, and Cordain 2002; Eaton 2007).

The primary disjoint between pre- and post-agricultural peoples is represented by a move away from the broad-based feeding strategy that is part of the omnivory pattern of humans, to a more mono-product diet based on one of the high starch-content grains. Indeed, most of the world's population today subsists on a diet composed of over 90 percent of one of these grains.

Stage 5: Diet And Nutrition in the Globalized World

It is increasingly clear that the genome of our species contains much variation. More importantly, from the perspective of diet, many of these gene changes are results of recent adaptations that have occurred since the origin of agriculture and thus extend into the not-so-distant past (at least from the perspective of the entire course of human evolution) (Cochran and Harpending 2009; Luca et al. 2010). Of significance beyond mere discussions of diet, these genetic adaptations illustrate the profound relationship between culture, here represented by the domestication of plants and animals, and the genetic foundation that allows for the maximum extraction of nutrients from those food resources.

Two examples of the coevolution of genes and culture illustrate this point well. The first is the relationship between cultures that have a long history of using domesticated animals for milk (Campbell and Tishkoff 2009; Itan et al. 2009); the second, an association between cruciferous vegetables (bitter-tasting to many humans) and malaria (Krebs 2009). In a general overview article, Hancock et al. (2010) demonstrated the relationship between the pattern of SNPs (single nucleotide polymorphism) and specific environmental, and possibly dietary, ecozones. While their focus was specifically on genetic signals associated with starch and sucrose metabolism and diets dominated by the use of roots and tubers as staples, and with energy metabolic pathway genes in polar ecozone populations, the possibility exists that many other types of genetic variants can be associated with particular foods and diet.

This may explain some of the worldwide variation in the tolerance of such varied diets as the ones seen around the globe today, and it might also explain why, under globalization and the widespread transport of foodstuffs, all foods cannot be utilized equally well by all humans. The food industrial complex with its globally based distribution networks may not be in the best interest of the diet and health of humans. As importantly, when foods are distributed by multinational corporations, little attention is paid to the cultural content of food choices, food preparation techniques, or ways of integrating foods into local cuisines. Certainly the genetic contributions to tolerance and digestion are also not transported. This highlights yet another lesson from the evolutionary history of humans: that food is best utilized when grown and eaten locally (World Health Organization: WHA57.17 Global Strategy on Diet, Physical Activity and Health, 2004).

Summary and Best Guess for the Present and Future

From an evolutionary perspective, a few general dietary guidelines emerge:

1. Broad-based feeding is a long-term evolutionary pattern of food acquisition and consumption in the order primates.
2. In addition, seasonal use of resources is common among primates and also in foraging/gatherer-hunting societies.
3. Along with the seasonal availability of resources, the evolutionary history of our lineage seems to indicate that at points in time, foods were either abundant or scarce. It makes sense that humans will eat when food is available and move into caloric-restrictive patterns at other times. In addition, human evolutionary history indicates that members of our lineage were very active and rarely if ever moved out of metabolic energy balance.
4. High-quality protein and fat parceled in a variety of ways, such as animal meat (vertebrates and invertebrates from the land and sea, including insects) and nuts, were a much sought-after food resource.
5. Local combinations and distribution networks of foods as part of a "cuisine" are central to understanding humans' relationship to their food. This includes food-processing techniques that can alter the mechanical and chemical properties of food and change patterns of digestion.
6. As nutrition science develops other strategies to understand the components of food, micro elements and phytochemicals will become increasingly important to understanding what constitutes an optimal diet for humans.
7. A clearly emerging pattern is that there exist genetic adaptations to particular foods and diet in general. Thus, any nutritionally mediated disease will involve multi-causal factors that may not apply across population boundaries.

Janet Monge has done fieldwork in many locations in Europe, Kenya, and Australia. Her primary interest is in the development of methodologies to preserve and broadcast data sets to the physical anthropology community using computed tomography, traditional radiology, and human dental micro-anatomy, and in the distribution of the highest quality castings of human fossils to universities and museums all over the world. An example of this work is *The Radiographic Atlas of the Krapina Neandertals,* which she published with Alan Mann. Dr. Monge is also Keeper of Skeletal Collections at the University of Pennsylvania Museum of Archaeology and Anthropology in Philadelphia. Her dedication to undergraduate research was rewarded with a grant to develop the Museum in Philadelphia as a national center for Native American student research.

References

Aiello, L. C., and P. Wheeler. 1995. "The Expensive Tissue Hypothesis." *Current Anthropology* 36: 199–221.

Audette, R., and T. Gilchrist. 1999. *NeanderThin: Eat Like a Caveman to Achieve a Lean, Strong, Healthy Body.* New York: St. Martin's Press.

Brain, C. K., and A. Sillen. 1988. "Evidence from Swartkrans Cave for the Earliest Use of Fire." *Nature* 336: 464–466.

Campbell, M. C., and S. A. Tishkoff. 2008. "African Genetic Diversity: Implications for Human Demographic History, Modern Human Origins, and Complex Disease Mapping." *Annual Review Genomics Human Genetics* 9: 403–433.

Carmody, R. N., and R. W. Wrangham. 2009a. "The Energetic Significance of Cooking." *Journal of Human Evolution* 57: 379–391.

———. 2009b. "Cooking and the Human Commitment of a High-Quality Diet." *Cold Spring Harbor Symposium of Quantitative Biology* 74: 427–434.

Churchill, S. E., and J. A. Rhodes. 2009. "The Evolution of the Human Capacity for 'Killing at a Distance': The Human Fossil Evidence for the Evolution of Projectile Weaponry." In *The Evolution of Hominin Diets: Integrating Approaches to the Study of Palaeolithic Subsistence,* ed. J.-J. Hublin and M.P. Richards, 201–210. Chicago: Springer Science.

Clark, J. D., and W. K. Harris. 1985. "Fire and Its Roles in Early Hominid Lifeways." *African Archaeology Review* 3: 3–27.

Cochran, G., and H. Harpending. 2009. *The 10,000 Year Explosion: How Civilization Accelerated Human Evolution.* New York: Basic Books.

Cohen, N. N. 1989. *Health and the Rise of Civilization.* New Haven, CT: Yale University Press.

Conklin-Brittain, M. L, R. W. Wrangham, and C.C. Smith. 2002. "A Two-Stage Model of Increased Dietary Quality in Early Hominid Evolution: The Role of Fiber." In *Human Diet: Its Origin and Evolution,* ed. P. S. Unger and M. F. Teaford, 61–76. Westport, CT: Bergin & Garvey.

Constantino, P. J., and B. W. Wright. 2009. "The Importance of Fallback Foods in Primate Ecology and Evolution." *American Journal of Physical Anthropology* 140: 599–602.

Constantino, P. J., J. J. Lee, H. Chai, B. Zipfel, C. Ziscovici, B. R. Lawn, and P. W. Lucas. 2010. "Tooth Chipping Can Reveal the Diet and Bite Forces of Fossil Hominins." *Biology Letters* June 2010 (e-publication ahead of print).

Cordain, L. 2002. *The PaleoDiet: Lose Weight and Get Healthy by Eating the Food You Were Designed to Eat.* Hoboken, NJ: John Wiley & Sons.

Cordain, L., and J. Friel. 2005. *The PaleoDiet for Athletes: A Nutritional Formula for Peak Athletic Performance.* St. Emmaus, PA: Rodale.

Dahlberg, F., ed. 1981. *Woman the Gatherer.* New Haven, CT: Yale University Press.

De Vany, A. 2010. *The New Evolution Diet: What Our Paleolithic Ancestors Can Teach Us about Weight Loss, Fitness, and Aging.* St. Emmaus, PA: Rodale.

Eaton, S. B. 2007. "Preagricultural Diets and Evolutionary Health Promotion." In *Evolution of the Human Diet: The Known, the Unknown, and the Unknowable,* ed. P. S. Ungar, 384–394. Human Evolution Series. New York: Oxford University Press.

Eaton, S. B., and S.B. Eaton III. 2000. "Consumption of Trace Elements and Minerals by Preagricultural Humans." In *Clinical Nutrition of the Essential Trace Elements and Minerals,* ed. J. D. Bogden and L. M. Klevay, 37–47. Totowa, NJ: Humana Press.

Eaton, S. B., S. B. Eaton III, and L. Cordain. 2002. "Evolution, Diet, and Health." In *Human Diet: Its Origin and Evolution*, ed. P. S. Ungar and M. F. Teaford, 7–17. Westport, CT: Bergin & Garvey.

Eaton, S. B., and M. Konner. 1985. "Paleolithic Nutrition: A Consideration of Its Nature and Current Implication." *New England Journal of Medicine* 312: 283–289.

Eaton, S. B., M. Shostak, and M. Konner. 1988. *The Paleolithic Prescription: A Program of Diet and Exercise for a Design for Living*. New York: Harper Collins.

Fiddes, N. 1991. *Meat: A Natural Symbol*. Routledge: London.

Fontana, L. 2009. "The Scientific Basis of Caloric Restriction Leading to Longer Life." *Current Opinion Gastroenterology* 25: 144–150.

Galbany, J., F. Estebaranz, L. M. Martinez, and A. Perez-Perez. 2009. "Buccal Dental Microwear Variability in Extant African Hominoidea: Taxonomy versus Ecology." *Primates* 50: 221–230.

Grine, F. E., S. Judex, D. J. Daegling, E. Ozcivici, P. S. Ungar, M. F. Teaford, M. Sponheimer, J. Scott, R. S. Scott, and A. Walker. 2010. "Craniofacial Biomechanics and Functional and Dietary Inferences in Hominin Paleontology." *Journal of Human Evolution* 58: 293–308.

Hancock, A. M., D. B. Witonsky, E. Ehler, G. Alkorta-Aranburu, C. Beall, A. Gebremedhin, R. Sukernik, G. Utermann, J. Pritchard, G. Coop, and A. DiRienzo. 2010. "Colloquium Paper: Human Adaptations to Diet, Subsistence, and Ecoregion Are Due to Subtle Shifts in Allele Frequency." *Proceedings of the National Academy of Sciences USA* 107, Suppl. 2: 8924–8930.

Harding, R. S. O., and G. Teleki, eds. 1981. *Omnivorous Primates: Gathering and Hunting in Human Evolution*. New York: Columbia University Press.

Harris, M., and E. B. Ross, eds. 1989. *Food: Toward a Theory of Human Food Habits*. Philadelphia: Temple University Press.

Hayden, B. 1981. "Subsistence and Ecological Adaptations of Modern Hunter/Gatherers." In *Omnivorous Primates: Gathering and Hunting in Human Evolution*, ed. R. S. O. Harding and G. Teleki, 344–421. New York: Columbia University Press.

Hohmann, G. 2009. "The Diets of Nonhuman Primates: Frugivory, Food Processing, and Food Sharing." In *The Evolution of Hominin Diets: Integrating Approaches to the Study of Palaeolithic Subsistence*, ed. J.-J. Hublin and M. P. Richards, 1–14. Chicago: Springer Science.

Howell, N. 2010. *Life Histories of the Dobe !Kung: Food, Fatness, and Well-Being over the Life-Span*. Berkeley: University of California Press.

Hursting, S. D., S. M. Smith, L. M. Lashinger, A. E. Harvey, and S. N. Perkins. 2010. "Calories and Carcinogenesis: Lessons Learned from 30 Years of Calorie Restriction Research." *Carcinogenesis* 31: 83–89.

Itan, Y., A. Powell, M. A. Beaumont, J. Burger, and M. G. Thomas. 2009. "The Origins of Lactase Persistence in Europe." *PLoS Computational Biology* 5(8): e1000491.

Kaplan, H. S., P. L. Hooper, and M. Gurven. 2009. "The Evolutionary and Ecological Roots of Human Social Organization." *Philosophical Transactions of the Royal Society, Series B* 364: 3289–3299.

Karkanas, P., R. Shahack-Gross, A. Ayalon, M. Bar-Matthews, R. Barkai, A. Frumkin, A. Gopher, and M. C. Stiner. 2007. "Evidence for Habitual Use of Fire at the End of the Lower Paleolithic: Site-Formation Processes at Qesem Cave, Israel." *Journal of Human Evolution* 53: 197–212.

Kelly, R. L. 1995. *The Foraging Spectrum: Diversity in Hunter-Gatherer Lifeways*. Washington, DC: Smithsonian Institution Press.

———. 2007. *The Foraging Spectrum: Diversity in Hunter-Gatherer Lifeways*. Clinton Corners, NY: Eliot Werner.

Klein, R. G. 2009. *The Human Career*, 3rd ed. Chicago: University of Chicago Press.

Krebs, J. R. 2009. "The Gourmet Ape: Evolution and Human Food Preferences." *American Journal of Clinical Nutrition* 90: 707S–711S.

Lambert, J. E. 1998. "Primate Digestion: Interactions among Anatomy, Physiology, and Feeding Ecology." *Evolutionary Anthropology* 7: 8–20.

Lee, R. B. 1979. *The !Kung San: Men, Women, and Work in a Foraging Society.* Cambridge: Cambridge University Press.

Lee, R. B., and R. Daly. 2004. *The Cambridge Encyclopedia of Hunters and Gatherers.* New York: Cambridge University Press.

Lee, R. B., and I. DeVore, eds. 1968. *Man the Hunter.* Chicago: Aldine.

Lee-Thorp, J. A. 2002. "Hominid Dietary Niches from Proxy Chemical Indicators in Fossils: The Swartkrans Example." In *Evolution of the Human Diet: The Known, the Unknown, and the Unknowable*, ed. P. S. Ungar, 123–141. Human Evolution Series. New York: Oxford University Press.

———. 2008. "On Isotopes and Old Bones." *Archaeometry* 50: 925–950.

Leonard, W. R., and M. Robertson. 1994. "Evolutionary Perspectives on Human Nutrition: The Influence of Brain and Body Size on Diet and Metabolism." *American Journal of Human Biology* 6: 77–88.

Lindeberg, S. 2010. *Food and Western Disease: Health and Nutrition from an Evolutionary Perspective.* West Sussex: Wiley-Blackwell.

Lovejoy, C. O. 2009. "Reexamining Human Origins in Light of *Ardipithecus ramidus.*" *Science* 326: 74, 74e1–74e8.

Luca, F., G. H. Perry, and A. Di Rienzo. 2010. "Evolutionary Adaptations to Dietary Change." *Annual Review of Nutrition* 30: 291–314.

Macho, G. A., and D. Shimzu. 2010. "Kinematic Parameters Inferred from Enamel Microstructure: New Insights into the Diet of *Australopithecus anamensis.*" *Journal of Human Evolution* 58: 23–32.

Mann, A. E. 1981. "Diet and Human Evolution." In *Omnivorous Primates: Gathering and Hunting in Human Evolution*, ed. R. S. Harding and G. Teleki, 10–36. New York: Columbia University Press.

Milton, K. 1999. "A Hypothesis to Explain the Role of Meat-Eating in Human Evolution." *Evolutionary Anthropology* 8: 11–21.

———. 2003. "The Critical Role Played by Animal Source Foods in Human (*Homo*) Evolution." *Journal of Nutrition* 133 (11 Suppl 2): 3886S–3892S.

O'Connell, J., K. Hawkes, and N. Blurton Jones. 2002. "Meat-Eating, Grandmothering, and the Evolution of Early Human Diets." In *Human Diet: Its Origin and Evolution*, ed. P. S. Ungar and M. F. Teaford, 48–60. Westport, CT: Bergin & Garvey.

Plavcan, J. M. 2001. "Sexual Dimorphism in Primate Evolution." *Yearbook of Physical Anthropology* 44: 25–53.

Rodman, P. S. 2002. "Plants of the Apes: Is There a Hominoid Model for the Origins of the Hominid Diet?" In *Human Diet: Its Origin and Evolution*, ed. P. S. Ungar and M. F. Teaford, 77–109. Westport, CT: Bergin & Garvey.

Ross, E. B. 1987. "An Overview of Trends in Dietary Variation from Hunter-Gatherer to Modern Capitalist Societies." In *Food and Human Evolution: Towards a Theory of Human Food Habits*, ed. M. Harris and E. B. Ross, 7–55. Philadelphia: Temple University Press.

Shea, J. J. 2009. "The Impact of Projectile Weaponry on Late Pleistocene Hominin Evolution." In *The Evolution of Hominin Diets: Integrating Approaches to the Study of Palaeolithic Subsistence*, ed. J.-J. Hublin and M. P. Richards, 189–200. Chicago: Springer Science.

Shipman, P. 1986. "Scavenging or Hunting in Early Hominids: Theoretical Framework and Tests." *American Anthropologist* 88: 27–43.

Sponheimer, M., and D. L. Dufour. 2009. "Increased Dietary Breadth in Early Hominin Evolution: Revisiting Arguments and Evidence with a Focus on Biogeochemical Contributions." In *The Evolution of Hominin Diets: Integrating Approaches to the Study of Palaeolithic Subsistence*, ed. J.-J. Hublin and M. P. Richards, 229–240. Chicago: Springer Science.

Stanford, D. B., and H. T. Bunn. 2001. *Meat-Eating and Human Evolution*. New York: Oxford University Press.

Strait, D. S., G. W. Weber, S. Neubauer, J. Chalk, B. G. Richmond, P. W. Lucas, M. A. Spencer, C. Schrein, P. C. Dechow, C. F. Ross, I. R. Grosse, B. W. Wright, B. Constantino, B. A. Wood, B. Lawn, W. L. Hylander, Q. Wang, D. E. Slice, and A. L. Smith. 2009. "The Feeding Biomechanics and Dietary Ecology of *Australopithecus africanus*." *Proceedings of the National Academy of Science USA* 106: 2124–2129.

Suwa, G., R. T. Kono, B. Asfaw, C. O. Lovejoy, and T. D. White. 2009. "Paleobiological Implications of the *Ardipithecus ramidus*." *Science* 326: 94–99.

Teaford, M. F. 2007. "What Do We Know and Not Know about Dental Microwear and Diet?" In *Evolution of the Human Diet: The Known, the Unknown, and the Unknowable*, ed. P. S. Ungar, 106–131. Human Evolution Series. New York: Oxford University Press.

Teaford, M. F., P. S. Ungar, and F. E. Grine. 2002. "Paleontological Evidence for the Diets of African Plio-Pleistocene Hominins with Special Reference to Early Homo." In *Human Diet: Its Origin and Evolution*, P. S. Unger and M. F. Teaford, 143–166. Westport, CT: Bergin & Garvey.

Ungar, P. S. 2009. "Tooth Form and Function: Insights into Adaptation through the Analysis of Dental Microwear." *Frontiers Oral Biology* 13: 38–43.

Ungar, P. S., F. E. Grine, and M. F. Teaford. 2008. "Dental Microwear and Diet of the Plio-Pleistocene Hominin *Paranthropus boisei*." *PLoS One* 3: e2044.

Vrieze, A., R. Holleman, E. G. Zoetendal, W. M. de Vos, J. B. L. Hoekstra, and M. Nieuwdorp. 2010. "The Environment Within: How Gut Microbiota May Influence Metabolism and Body Composition." *Diabetologia* 53: 606–613.

Walker, A. 2007. "Early Hominin Diets: Overview and Historical Perspectives." In *Evolution of the Human Diet: The Known, Unknown, and Unknowable*, ed. P. S. Ungar, 3–10. New York: Oxford University Press.

Weiner, S., Q. Xu, P. Goldberg, J. Liu, and O. Bar-Yosef. 1998. "Evidence for the Use of Fire at Zhoukoudian, China." *Science* 281: 251–253.

Wobber, V., B. Hare, and R. W. Wrangham. 2008. "Great Apes Prefer Cooked Foods." *Journal of Human Evolution* 55: 340–348.

Wolf, R. 2010. *The Paleo Solution: The Original Human Diet*. Auberry, CA: Victory Belt.

Zihlman, A., and N. Tanner. 1978. "Gathering and the Hominid Adaptation." In *Female Hierarchies*, ed. L. Tiger and H. Fowler, 163–194. Chicago: Beresford Books.

CHAPTER 14

Experimental Archaeology, Ethnoarchaeology, and the Application of Archaeological Data to the Study of Subsistence, Diet, and Nutrition

Karen Bescherer Metheny

Introduction

Subsistence has been a subject of archaeological inquiry since archaeology was first formalized as an academic discipline. The physical remains associated with food procurement, processing, consumption, and waste disposal constitute one of the largest categories of archaeological data available for study and include artifacts as diverse as hunting weapons, cooking utensils, and serving vessels, as well as the remnants of the plants and animals that were collected, hunted, grown, processed, and consumed as meals. A key concern of archaeologists is how to link these physical remains to past human behavior. To what extent do objects found in an archaeological context encode past human behavior, and how do we best interpret such activity from the inanimate and mute remains of the past? Further, though subsistence is a central economic activity, it is heavily intertwined with social systems and cultural practice that imbue particular foods, materials, behaviors, and spaces with significance. How do we work outward from material remains to questions of meaning?

Two areas of inquiry have emerged since the 1960s to address these questions: experimental archaeology and ethnoarchaeology. Ethnoarchaeological or actualistic studies involve the observation of human behavior in the present in order to formulate analogies that are used to understand behavior in the past, with particular emphasis on the material signatures of human actions. Experimental approaches, though not necessarily involving living systems (much research occurs as laboratory work), also require the use and study of material culture and technology in the present. Both approaches are grounded in the methods of scientific inquiry and hypothesis testing as a specific answer to this larger question about knowledge. Both rely upon empirical data as the basis of research and cross-cultural study. Through focused inquiry, archaeologists may observe, measure, compare and, through relational analogy, gain insight into past human activity.

The study of contemporary societies and of the material signatures created by human behavior *in the present* is especially important because the archaeological record contains only the "static" byproducts of past behavior (e.g., Binford 1980, 1981). Middle-range theory—that is, theory building that attempts to connect the static past with dynamic living systems—involves "experimental research with documented living systems" to lay the groundwork for analogy and inference (Binford 1981: 27). Though considerable debate has centered on the construction and validity of analogic models for interpretation (e.g., Binford 1980, 1981; Gould and Watson 1982; Kusimba 2005; O'Connell 1995; Roux 2007; Schiffer 1976; Schiffer and Skibo 1987; Schiffer et al. 2001; Skibo 2009; Wylie 1985, 1989), both experimental and ethnoarchaeological approaches have made substantive contributions to our understanding of the past, no more so than in subsistence and food-related studies.

Contributions of Food-Related Studies

Studies of food-related technologies and prehistoric subsistence practices are significant for several reasons. Ethnoarchaeological and experimental studies provide data that are often absent from the archaeological and written records. In proto- and historical cultures, textual sources frequently lack descriptions of daily activities and the material culture associated with food procurement, processing, and consumption, whether the tools used to plant crops and harvest grains, or the technologies used to bake bread. In the absence of documentary records, ethnoarchaeological and experimental studies are often the only source of analogs for interpreting the material remains and behaviors associated with prehistoric subsistence practices.

Experimental and ethnoarchaeological studies may also fill gaps in our knowledge about material culture forms that do not preserve well in the archaeological record (organic materials such as wood, bone, or fibers) or food remains (especially plants) that are perishable and may not leave an archaeological signature. Processes such as fermentation that may be inferred but are difficult to document archaeologically also may be studied through modern analogs.

Ethnoarchaeological and experimental approaches are particularly important for correcting and challenging Western-centric, androcentric, and essentialized models of the past. These studies contribute to our knowledge of the poorly documented and understudied domestic activities of women, for example, particularly those centered around food production. Lyons and D'Andrea (2003: 515) note that "most food-heating technologies are not studied in the detail necessary for archaeological analysis.... This is partly because women, who cross-culturally dominate food processing and preparation, are perceived by Westerners as nontechnical."

Finally, both types of research may provide analogs for behaviors that are not easily identified archaeologically (ritual, social, cultural, symbolic). The data obtained through such studies help archaeologists make analogies and inferences about the impact of social factors and cultural belief systems upon human behavior and the material world.

Food-Related Experimental Archaeology

Experimental approaches allow archaeologists to test some very basic assumptions about how prehistoric technologies worked, how material culture was used, and the relationship between material objects and their users. Gur-Arieh et al. (2012: 122) argue that "traditional [archaeological] methods based on visual observations of their forms" are inherently limited in what they can tell us because of the idiosyncratic nature of disposal behaviors, preservation bias and taphonomic factors, and the static nature of archaeological remains. Experimental data both supplement and fill in gaps in archaeological knowledge. As defined by Millson (2011: 3), experimental archaeology follows one of two approaches: experiments to test hypotheses about artifacts or sites, and experiments to test methods that archaeologists use to recover data. Both are grounded in the principles of scientific inquiry and rely upon hypothesis testing through repeated and replicable experimentation.

Reconstructing Methods of Food Production, Food Processing, and Cooking

Food-related experimentation has emphasized the reconstruction of ancient technologies related to food production and processing (e.g., tool manufacture or cooking technologies) and the behavioral aspects associated with those processes (how things work). Hunter-gatherer studies investigate hunting technologies, lithic manufacture, and butchering techniques, for example (e.g., Goren-Inbar et al. 2002; P. Jones 1980; Keeley 1980; Schick and Toth 1993, 2009; Shea 2007; Toth 1997). Indeed, experimentation constitutes one of the primary means of hypothesis testing concerning subsistence behaviors in the Paleolithic (e.g., Bettinger 1982, 1987; Ingersoll, Yellen, and MacDonald 1977; Shea 2007). Assessments of costs and benefits, carrying capacity, optimal foraging behavior, and other factors can contribute to the revision and refinement of subsistence models. Other subsistence-related studies have focused on agricultural practices, including crop rotation, plant-processing methods, and harvesting and threshing technologies (Anderson 1999); storage (Cunningham 2011; Forbes and Foxhall 1995); and methods of preservation such as fermentation (Arthur 2012). As traditional, nonindustrial farming practices die out, experimental work has become an important source of comparative information.

Considerable work has focused on the reconstruction of cooking technologies, particularly pyrotechnic methods (e.g., Nelson 2010; Thoms 2008, 2009; Wandsnider 1997). Researchers have tested the thermal properties of mud and rock, as well as different clays, vessel forms, tempers, and firing temperatures for their utility and suitability for cooking (e.g., Braadbaart et al. 2012; Gur-Arieh et al. 2012). Simms, Berna, and Bey (2013) have proposed, for example, that fired clay balls recovered at the site of Escalera al Cielo in the Yucatán are evidence of a previously undocumented cooking technology; though no hearths were located, the fired clay balls were clustered behind the back wall of a kitchen, and starch residues covered their surfaces. To test this hypothesis, clay balls were replicated and tested under varying conditions to determine their heating properties. Ceramic technology has also been the subject of extensive study (e.g., Schiffer and Skibo 1987; Schiffer et al. 2001; Skibo 1994).

Experimentation with ancient foods and technologies is widespread, but bread and alcoholic beverages, because of their ubiquity in past and present cultures, are particularly well studied. Researchers have experimented with brewing beer and baking bread using information gleaned from textual and ethnographic sources, material culture, and *in situ* archaeological remains. Analysis of residues found in storage jars and drinking vessels from archaeological contexts has even made it possible to identify specific ingredients in ancient beers and fermented beverages, allowing for their re-creation (e.g., Arthur 2012; Dineley 2011; Goulder 2010; Lehner 1994, 1997; McGovern 2007; Samuel 1999, 2010). Such studies provide much-needed understanding of *how* these processes worked—a counterpoint to the tendency of many archaeologists to "add nutrition and stir" without considering the physical, chemical, material, and sensory processes that are involved (Metheny 2012).

Experimental approaches allow us to move beyond replication, however, to explore the relationship between subsistence, technological change, and cognitive advances, such as the use of fire and the development of cooking. Such events may be seen as thresholds for social, cultural, and even evolutionary change (e.g., Wrangham and Carmody 2010; Carmody and Wrangham 2009). Thoms (2008, 2009), for example, has proposed that the spread of cook-stone technologies (griddle stones, earth ovens, and steaming and boiling pits) in western North America after 4000 BP was driven by the need to increase nutrition and digestibility of foods for an expanding population. Experimental data also contribute to our understanding of the relationship between material culture and population shifts, changes to subsistence patterns, nutrition, resource use, and food availability, as well as evolutionary changes to digestion, cognition, and social cooperation (Twomey 2013).

Experimental approaches also have applicability to questions about social organization and cultural practice. Researchers have experimented with Philistine pebble hearth constructions to determine the heating properties of this type of hearth, but have also used this study as the basis for investigating identity formation and boundary maintenance through a comparison of contemporary Iron Age hearth-building methods (e.g., Gur-Arieh et al. 2012; Maeir, Hitchcock, and Horwitz 2013). Researchers who focus on the use of beer and bread as worker rations in early complex societies have evaluated nutritional value and caloric content, shelf life, ease of distribution or storage, and the suitability of ancient grains like emmer or barley for bread or beer manufacture (Lehner 1994, 1997; Samuel 1999, 2010). Goulder (2010) created replicas of a mass-produced ceramic vessel, the bevel-rim bowl, which is found at numerous fourth-millennium BC sites in Mesopotamia, in order to test a range of hypotheses regarding its function. Though frequently linked to the distribution of grain, Goulder also tested the vessel's suitability for the production of bread, soft cheese, yoghurt, or salt. Though the testing was inconclusive, Goulder's experiments provide useful insight into the practical challenges of centralized food production and distribution, an emerging bureaucracy, urbanization, and other complex social forms during the Uruk period.

New Data Recovery Methods

Another major contribution of experimental approaches has been the discovery of new data recovery methods. Recent work has demonstrated that plant microfossils such as starches may be recovered from hearths, cooking implements, and other surfaces (Simms et al. 2013; Thoms 2009). Researchers also have experimented with different cooking techniques to document the unique changes to the micromorphology of phytoliths and starch grains that occur with heating, providing archaeologists with additional tools to discern ancient cooking techniques in desiccated food remains and archaeologically recovered plant microfossils (e.g., Gong et al. 2011; Henry, Hudson, and Piperno 2009).

Research Designs and Resources

Experimental archaeology often incorporates multi- and interdisciplinary approaches, and many of the best studies draw on cross-disciplinary research, involving not only experts in field archaeology and experimental and ethnoarchaeological approaches, but specialists in soil microtechniques, dating methods, zooarchaeology, paleoethnobotany, geoarchaeology, anthropology, and ethnography. Students interested in experimental research are encouraged to begin with a review of the literature, including Coles (1973, 1979) and Ingersoll et al. (1977); more recent publications by Ferguson (2010) and Outram (2008) reflect contemporary interests and debates. The proceedings from a number of experimental archaeology conferences have also been published (e.g., Cunningham, Heeb, and Paardekooper 2008). Volumes focused only on food, diet, and nutrition are still rare, however (cf. Anderson 1999).

Academic and scientific rigor is central to experimentation and will distinguish the best studies from less meticulous work. Institutional support is key; much experimental research emerges from programs with degrees in experimental archaeology. Practitioners stress the need for controlled conditions for experiments, replicability, measurement, standardized data collection, and rigorous documentation. Other considerations center on the practicalities of doing research (laboratory research vs. field research), including sample size, the control of variables, and the availability of funding. Publications that explicitly discuss the process of constructing a research design also emphasize the importance of discerning when and how certain research methods may be used and what questions can be asked and tested through experimentation (e.g., Ferguson 2010). A review of the literature will help to identify appropriate research questions. Ferguson (ibid.) also notes that experimental research has greater significance when it is theory-driven; thus a strong knowledge of anthropological and social theory is advisable.

A substantial body of experimental data amassed by academic and institutional researchers is available for study. Many resources are available online, such as DEXAR, a database on experimental archaeology maintained by the University of Glasgow (http://www.gla.ac.uk/schools/humanities/research/archaeology research/projects/dexar/). EXARC, which is affiliated with the International Council of Museums (ICOM), maintains a website (http://exarc.net/) that researchers use as a network and forum, and hosts the Experimental Archaeology Conference on a yearly basis. EXARC publishes an online journal by the same name, as well as a second journal, *euroRAE: (Re)construction and Experiment in Archaeology.* The *Journal of Archaeological Science,* the *Journal of Anthropological Archaeology,* and *World Archaeology* are key publishing venues. Students should review these publications to gain an overview of research designs, testing methodologies, data, and conclusions.

Ethnoarchaeological Approaches to Diet, Subsistence, and Foodways

Ethnoarchaeological studies have traditionally focused on subsistence practices among hunter-gatherers, herders/pastoralists, and preindustrial agriculturalists. Lewis Binford's work on Nunamiut ethnoarchaeology (1978) is an exemplar of this type of research. Hunter-gatherer studies from Africa and Australia are also primary contributions to the literature (e.g., Lee 1979, 1984; Lee and DeVore 1968, 1976; Yellen 1977). Over the last few decades, ethnoarchaeologists have compiled a substantial, cross-cultural database that can be used to interpret the archaeological record.

As a subfield of archaeology, the methods and theories informing ethnoarchaeology developed in tandem with the New Archaeology (also called processual archaeology) in the 1960s and 1970s, and ongoing debates over the role of analogy and inference reflect this relationship (e.g., Binford 1980, 2001; Gould 1978; Gould and Watson 1982; Skibo 2009; Tringham 1978). Though ethnographic observation has always been the core of ethnoarchaeological study, definitions of this subfield have ranged from "action archaeology in living communities" (Kleindienst and Watson 1956), "living archaeology" (Gould 1968, 1980), and what Stiles (1977: 88) refers to as archaeological ethnography—"direct observation field study" among "living, non-industrial peoples" for the purpose of creating explanatory models to "aid archaeological analogy and inference"—to the more encompassing "study of relationships between human behavior and its material consequences in the present" (O'Connell 1995: 205).

Ethnoarchaeology has been critiqued at times for its production of descriptive studies that do not attempt to explain observed behavior, and for failing to recognize variation and diversity in societies (e.g., Denbow 1984; Kusimba 2005; O'Connell 1995). Others have noted that archaeological models tend to obscure not only the considerable variation in subsistence practices among hunter-gatherers, but also change that occurs through contact with other groups. Nonetheless, O'Connell's definition reflects the maturation of this subfield even as archaeologists look to make stronger connections between the archaeological record and past behavior, and engage in ethnoarchaeological study of nontraditional study groups.

Contributions of Food-Related Ethnoarchaeological Studies

Ethnoarchaeology is a key source of evidence for archaeologists who study past subsistence practices associated with hunting and gathering, pastoralism, and agriculture. Studies of hunter-gatherers have been particularly significant for hominid research, especially in modeling resource procurement and food sharing strategies (e.g., Bettinger 1982, 1987; Binford 1980, 1981; Denbow 1984; Kusimba 2005; Lee 1979, 1984; Lee and DeVore 1968, 1976; O'Connell 1995). Ethnoarchaeological research also has helped to refine data collection methods and suggest new analytical tools. The use of phytolith assemblages, geoarchaeology, and isotopic analysis to identify livestock enclosures and other activity areas is such an example (e.g., Shahack-Gross, Marshall, and Weiner 2003; Shahack-Gross, Simons, and Ambrose 2008; Tsartsidou et al. 2008).

Ethnoarchaeology begins with ethnographic observations that produce relational analogies between what is observed and what is seen in the archaeological record. Correlations may be made between material forms that exist in largely identical form in past and present cultures, suggesting that the past form might operate in the same way as the present form. Tandir-style ovens, for example, are assumed to have worked the same way in the past as they do today and to have been used for a similar purpose—to bake flat or unleavened bread (Parker 2011; see also Mulder-Heymans 2002). Such functional analogies form a basis for inferences about past human behavior, and ethnoarchaeologists have examined a range of material culture forms, technologies, and food-related practices for this purpose. These include cooking, baking, and brewing; ceramic manufacture; lithic tool use and manufacture; food processing and preservation; and harvesting and threshing technologies (e.g., Anderson 1999; Harlan 1999; Kramer 1985; Mason 1995; Shea 2007; Skakun 1999; Stout 2002; van Gijn 1999; Vincent 1985; Weedman 2006; Whittaker 2000). Archaeologists also have examined salt production (Williams 1999, 2002; Yankowski and Kerdsap 2013); water usage (Grillo 2012; Jenkins, Baker, and Elliott 2011); irrigation (Harrower 2008); and trash disposal (Jones et al. 2012; Rathje et al. 1992). The study of subsistence-related activities within households and in domestic spaces is particularly strong (e.g., Efstratiou 2007; Kamp 2000; Kramer 1982; Ogundele 2005).

The construction of functional analogies has tended to dominate ethnoarchaeological studies, but researchers are increasingly using relational analogies to make inferences about social organization and cultural practice. Following the work of Brumbach and Jarvenpa (1997), ethnoarchaeologists have produced more nuanced studies of gender roles in subsistence-related activities (e.g., S. Jones 2009; Marshall and Weissbrod 2009; Parker 2011). Bird and Bird (2000) have documented the subsistence activities of children. Others have focused on status or hierarchy—gendered, economic, political, social, age-based, or other—as reflected in such activities as feasting and alcohol consumption (e.g., Adams 2004; Arthur 2003; Hayashida 2008; Hayden 2003), and their relevance to the construction and use of public/institutional and domestic spaces associated with food production and consumption.

Ethnoarchaeologists also have begun to examine past subsistence practices, technologies, and foods in terms of their broader implications for social organization and cultural practice. In a study comparing griddle technology in Ethiopia with bread baking in Africa and the Near East, for example, Lyons and D'Andrea (2003: 515) argue that the griddle was adapted to indigenous African cereals lacking in gluten, a "technical choice … constrained by social factors involved in producing bread and by the physical properties of the starchy foods available." The authors further conclude that these constraints shaped not only the food preparation methods and preferences associated with this grain complex, but also the social aspects of domestic labor associated with food production. In another example, Kalentzidou (2000) uses pottery manufacture to look at the relationship between material culture attributes and usage, identity, and ethnicity. Haaland's (2007) study of porridge and bread complexes in Africa and the Near East explores food as a medium for communication and symbolism associated with the transformation of raw or natural ingredients to cultural product. Finally, Marshall and Weissbrod (2009) have explored the implications of donkey domestication for social organization and economic strategies among the Maasai. The authors studied environmental conditions, herd size and composition, and management practices, as well as household structure and gendered tasks ranging from the collection of water and firewood to livestock care and protection of the herd. They conclude that increasing sedentism has led to greater investment in livestock, including care and management of herds, but increased reliance on fixed water sources has left households vulnerable to drought and climate fluctuation. Such studies have implications for understanding the processes of domestication, migration, and population growth in the Holocene but also for the way we model subsistence practices in terms of costs and benefits.

Research Designs and Resources

There is an extensive literature on the methods and theory of ethnoarchaeology. David and Kramer's volume (2001) serves as a primer for field research, providing an overview of the origins and definitions of ethnoarchaeology, theoretical and methodological constructs, ethical issues in the field, and key research topics. As with most volumes, food-related studies are not encompassed within a single entry or chapter, but instead overlap with studies of material residues, subsistence strategies, exchange systems, and activity areas associated with food production, processing, and consumption.

As with experimental studies, a considerable body of data already exists. Students are advised to look at the Human Relations Area File (online as eHRAF, http://hraf.yale.edu/) and other compiled data sources (e.g., tDAR, the Digital Archaeological Record, http://www.tdar.org/). Researchers will also find many unpublished papers, articles, and dissertations online.

Again, ethnoarchaeologists stress the importance of a well-conceived research design, and students will find it useful to review the literature to determine what methods are best used to collect data and test hypotheses. Data recording, systematic inquiry, and replicability are key to successful research programs. Multiple forms of data collection and documentation are used, including ethnographic observation, interviews, census and survey techniques, photography, and mapping/spatial analysis. Sampling strategies should be clearly articulated. For example, in her ethnoarchaeological study of food and gender in Fiji (2009), Sharyn Jones offers a detailed discussion of her methods, including archaeological field standards and interview techniques, and the theoretical perspectives informing her project. Students will also find her observations on the practicalities of conducting an ethnoarchaeological study very useful (see also David and Kramer 2001). Considerations include access to a study group, funding, and obtaining permission from informants. Informed consent and the guarantee of anonymity are paramount.

Application of Ethnoarchaeological or Experimental Approaches to Contemporary Households and Communities

Studies such as those of cattle and donkey herders by Grillo (2012), Marshall and Weissbrod (2009), and Ryan et al. (1996) allow archaeologists to better understand pastoralism in a prehistoric context, but as these authors demonstrate, ethnoarchaeological studies often have application to contemporary society (Miller, Moore, and Ryan 2011). The documentation of herding practices reveals not only indigenous knowledge—for example, plants used for treating cattle (Ryan et al. 1996)—but also the social and economic significance of subsistence behaviors. Social relations that are encoded in cattle genealogy reveal the centrality of transactions involving animals relative to family, household, and community networks, but also their ritual significance and cultural meaning (ibid.). In addition, such studies document human responses to stress from climate change and from economic, social, or political pressures over centuries or even millennia. These data thus have implications for resource management, sustainability, population health, and food security in contemporary societies. Likewise, experimental data that permit the documentation and reconstruction of past agricultural practices or the use of plants or food processing methods that today are undervalued or have been lost (e.g., Anderson 1999) are potentially relevant to contemporary issues surrounding sustainability, loss of biodiversity, and climate change.

"Disaster ethnoarchaeology," the ethnoarchaeological study of the impact of disasters (man-made or natural) on social and economic structures, also has relevance to contemporary households and communities. Yazdi, Garazhian, and Dezhamkhooy's (2011) study of city of Bam in southeastern Iran examined short- and long-term impacts of a 1993 earthquake on market and exchange systems, including wholesale and resale markets for staple foods (e.g., butcheries, greengrocers, sandwich stands) both in the city and in the rural districts surrounding Bam. The authors documented the continued instability of the market; pressures on food purveyors to become mobile, relocate, or change their goods in response to declining sales; and the rise of informal exchange mechanisms such as the black market. Though collected for their applicability to ancient economic systems, these data have relevance to contemporary disaster responses and the stabilization of the community during rebuilding, underlining the potential for such research in the future.

Conclusion

As this overview demonstrates, the applications of experimental and ethnoar-chaeological approaches to the study of human diet, nutrition, and subsistence are diverse and relevant for understanding both past behavior and contemporary concerns. Archaeological, experimental, and ethnographic techniques may be equally valuable for studying the effects, past or present, of human migration, the spread of knowledge, and the impact of new technologies or foods on subsistence practices, diet and nutrition, social organization, and cultural practice, and for documenting human responses to cultural, social, political, economic, or environmental stress.

Karen Bescherer Metheny is Lecturer for the Master of Liberal Arts program in Gastronomy at Metropolitan College, Boston University, and Visiting Researcher in the Department of Archaeology, Boston University. She is co-editor with Mary Beaudry of *Archaeology of Food: An Encyclopedia* (2015) and is currently working on a multidisciplinary study of the cultural significance of maize in colonial New England. She has taught courses in the anthropology and archaeology of food, food history and food culture of New England, and method and theory in food studies.

References

Adams, Ron L. 2004. An Ethnoarchaeological Study of Feasting in Sulawesi, Indonesia. *Journal of Anthropological Archaeology* 23: 56–78.

Anderson, Patricia C., ed. 1999. *Prehistory of Agriculture: New Experimental and Ethnographic Approaches.* Los Angeles: Institute of Archaeology, University of California.

Arthur, John W. 2003. Brewing Beer: Status, Wealth and Ceramic Use Alteration among the Gamo of South-Western Ethiopia. *World Archaeology* 34(3): 516–528.

———. 2012. Bubbles, Beer, and Bread: An Ethnoarchaeological and Ethnographic Analysis of Fermented Foods in Ethiopia. Annual Meeting of the American Anthropological Association, San Francisco, 18 November 2012.

Bettinger, Robert L. 1982. Explanatory/Predictive Models of Hunter-Gatherer Adaptation. In *Advances in Archaeological Method and Theory: Selections for Students from Volumes 1 through 4,* ed. Michael B. Schiffer, 157–223. New York: Academic Press.

———. 1987. Archaeological Approaches to Hunter-Gatherers. *Annual Review of Anthropology* 16: 121–142.

Binford, Lewis R. 1978. *Nunamiut Ethnoarchaeology.* New York: Academic Press.

———. 1980. Willow Smoke and Dogs' Tails: Hunter-Gatherer Settlement Systems and Archaeological Site Formation. *American Antiquity* 45: 4–20.

———. 1981. *Bones: Ancient Men and Modern Myths.* New York: Academic Press.

———. 2001. Where Do Research Problems Come From? *American Antiquity* 66(4): 669–678.

Bird, Douglas W., and Rebecca Bliege Bird. 2000. The Ethnoarchaeology of Juvenile Foragers: Shellfishing Strategies among Meriam Children. *Journal of Anthropological Archaeology* 19: 461–476.

Braadbaart, Freek, Imogen Poole, Hans D. J. Huisman, and Bertil van Os. 2012. Fuel, Fire and Heat: An Experimental Approach to Highlight the Potential of Studying Ash and Char Remains from Archaeological Contexts. *Journal of Archaeological Science* 39: 836–847.

Brumbach, Hetty Jo, and Robert Jarvenpa. 1997. Ethnoarchaeology of Subsistence Space and Gender: A Subartic Dene Case. *American Antiquity* 62(3): 414–436.

Carmody, Rachel N., and Richard W. Wrangham. 2009. The Energetic Significance of Cooking. *Journal of Human Evolution* 57: 379–391.

Coles, John M. 1973. *Archaeology by Experiment.* London: Hutchinson.

———. 1979. *Experimental Archaeology.* London: Academic Press.

Cunningham, Penny. 2011. Cache or Carry: Food Storage in Prehistoric Europe. In *Experimentation and Interpretation: The Use of Experimental Archaeology in the Study of the Past,* ed. Dana C. E. Millson, 7–28. Oxford: Oxbow Books.

Cunningham, Penny, Julia Heeb, and Roeland Paardekooper, eds. 2008. *Experiencing Archaeology by Experiment: Proceedings of the Experimental Archaeology Conference, Exeter 2007.* Oxford: Oxbow Books.

David, Nicholas, and Carol Kramer. 2001. *Ethnoarchaeology in Action.* Cambridge: Cambridge University Press.

Denbow, James R. 1984. Prehistoric Herders and Foragers of the Kalahari: The Evidence for 1500 Years of Interaction. In *Past and Present in Hunter-Gatherer Studies,* ed. Carmel Schrire, 175–193. Orlando: Academic Press.

Dineley, Merryn. 2011. Experiment or Demonstration? Making Fermentable Sugars from the Grain and a Discussion of Some of the Evidence for This Activity in the British Neolithic. In *Experimentation and Interpretation: The Use of Experimental Archaeology in the Study of the Past,* ed. Dana C. E Millson, 96–108. Oxford: Oxbow Books.

Efstratiou, Nikos. 2007. Neolithic Households in Greece: The Contribution of Ethnoarchaeology. In *Building Communities: House, Settlement and Society in the Aegean and Beyond,* ed. Ruth Westgate, Nick Fisher, and James Whitley, 29–35. British School at Athens Studies 15. London: British School at Athens.

Ferguson, Jeffrey R., ed. 2010. *Designing Experimental Research in Archaeology: Examining Technology through Production and Use.* Boulder: University Press of Colorado.

Forbes, Hamish, and Lin Foxhall. 1995. Ethnoarchaeology and Storage in the Ancient Mediterranean: Beyond Risk and Survival. In *Food in Antiquity,* ed. John Wilkins, David Harvey, and Mike Dobson, 69–86. Exeter: University of Exeter Press.

Gong, Yiwen, Yimin Yang, David K. Ferguson, Dawei Tao, Wenying Li, Changsui Wang, Enguo Lü, and Hongen Jiang. 2011. Investigation of Ancient Noodles, Cakes, and Millet at the Subeixi Site, Xinjiang, China. *Journal of Archaeological Science* 38(2): 470–479.

Goren-Inbar, Naama, Gonen Sharon, Yoel Melamed, and Mordecai Kislev. 2002. Nuts, Nut Cracking, and Pitted Stones at Gesher Benot Yaa`qov, Israel. *Proceedings of the National Academy of Science* 99: 2455–2460.

Gould, Richard A. 1968. Living Archaeology: The Ngatatjara of Western Australia. *Southwestern Journal of Anthropology* 24(2): 101–122.

———. 1978. The Anthropology of Human Residues. *American Anthropologist* 80(4): 815–835.

————. 1980. *Living Archaeology.* New York: Cambridge University Press.

Gould, Richard A., and Patty Jo Watson. 1982. A Dialogue on the Meaning and Use of Analogy in Ethnoarchaeological Reasoning. *Journal of Anthropological Archaeology* 1: 355–381.

Goulder, Jill. 2010. Administrators' Bread: An Experiment-Based Re-assessment of the Functional and Cultural Role of the Uruk Bevel-Rim Bowl. *Antiquity* 84: 351–362.

Grillo, Katherine. 2012. The Materiality of Mobile Pastoralism: Ethnoarchaeological Perspectives from Samburu, Kenya. PhD dissertation. St. Louis: Department of Anthropology, Washington University. http://www.academia.edu/3268893/The_Materiality_of_Mobile _Pastoralism_Ethnoarchaeological_Perspectives_from_Samburu_Kenya_Ph.D._Disser tation_. Accessed 9 August 2013.

Gur-Arieh, Shira, Elisabetta Boaretto, Aren Maeir, and Ruth Shahack-Gross. 2012. Formation Processes in Philistine Hearths from Tell es Safi/Gath (Israel): An Experimental Approach. *Journal of Field Archaeology* 37(2): 121–131.

Haaland, Randi. 2007. Porridge and Pot, Bread and Oven: Food Ways and Symbolism in Africa and the Near East from the Neolithic to the Present. *Cambridge Archaeological Journal* 17(2): 165–182.

Harlan, Jack R. 1999. Harvesting of Wild Grass Seed and Implications for Domestication. In *Prehistory of Agriculture: New Experimental and Ethnographic Approaches,* ed. Patricia C. Anderson, 1–5. Los Angeles: Institute of Archaeology, University of California.

Harrower, Michael J. 2008. Hydrology, Ideology, and the Origins of Irrigation in Ancient Southwest Arabia. *Current Anthropology* 49(3): 497–510.

Hayashida, Frances M. 2008. Ancient Beer and Modern Brewers: Ethnoarchaeological Observations of *Chicha* Production in Two Regions of the North Coast of Peru. *Journal of Anthropological Archaeology* 27: 161–174.

Hayden, Brian. 2003. Were Luxury Foods the First Domesticates? Ethnoarchaeological Perspectives from Southeast Asia. *World Archaeology* 34(3): 458–469.

Henry, Amanda G., Holly F. Hudson, and Dolores R. Piperno. 2009. Changes in Starch Grain Morphologies from Cooking. *Journal of Archaeological Science* 36: 915–922.

Ingersoll, Daniel W., John E. Yellen, and William MacDonald, eds. 1977. *Experimental Archaeology.* New York: Columbia University Press.

Jenkins, Emma, Ambroise Baker, and Sarah Elliott. 2011. Past Plant Use in Jordan as Revealed by Archaeological and Ethnoarchaeological Phytolith Signatures. In *Water, Life and Civilisation: Climate, Environment and Society in the Jordan Valley,* ed. Steve Mithen and Emily Black, 381–400. Cambridge: Cambridge University Press.

Jones, Peter R. 1980. Experimental Butchery with Modern Stone Tools and Its Relevance for Palaeolithic Archaeology. *World Archaeology* 12: 153–165.

Jones, Sharyn. 2009. *Food and Gender in Fiji: Ethnoarchaeological Explorations.* New York: Lexington Books/Rowman & Littlefield.

Jones, Sharyn, Anna McCowan, Mallory Messersmith, Courtney Andrews, and Loretta Cormier. 2012. Talking Trash. *Ethnoarchaeology* 2: 148–184.

Kalentzidou, Olga. 2000. Pots Crossing Borders: Ethnic Identity and Ceramics in Evros, Northeastern Greece. *Near Eastern Archaeology* 63(2): 70–83.

Kamp, Katheryn. 2000. From Village to Tell: Household Ethnoarchaeology in Syria. *Near Eastern Archaeology* 63(2):84–93.

Keeley, Lawrence H. 1980. *Experimental Determination of Stone Tool Uses: A Microwear Analysis.* Chicago: University of Chicago Press.

Kleindienst, Maxine R., and Patty Jo Watson. 1956. "Action Archeology": The Archeological Inventory of a Living Community. *Anthropology Tomorrow* 5: 75–78.

Kramer, Carol. 1982. Ethnographic Households and Archaeological Interpretations. In Archaeology of the Household: Building a Prehistory of Domestic Life, ed. Richard R. Wilk and William J. Rathje. *American Behavioral Scientist* 25(6): 663–676.

———. 1985. Ceramic Ethnoarchaeology. *Annual Review of Anthropology* 14: 77–102.

Kusimba, Sibel B. 2005. What Is a Hunter-Gatherer? Variation in the Archaeological Record of Eastern and Southern Africa. *Journal of Archaeological Research* 13(4): 337–366.

Lee, Richard B. 1979. *The !Kung San: Men, Women and Work in a Foraging Society.* Cambridge: Cambridge University Press.

———. 1984. *The Dobe !Kung.* New York: Holt, Rinehart, and Winston.

Lee, Richard B., and Irven DeVore, eds. 1968. *Man the Mighty Hunter.* Chicago: Aldine.

———. 1976. *Kalahari Hunters and Gatherers: Studies of the !Kung San and Their Neighbors.* Cambridge: Harvard University Press.

Lehner, Mark. 1994. The Giza Mapping Project, 1993–94: Annual Report. Oriental Institute, University of Chicago. http://oi.uchicago.edu/research/pubs/ar/93–94/giza.html. Accessed 4 October 2013.

———. 1997. Replicating an Ancient Bakery. *Archaeology* 50(1): 36.

Lyons, Diane, and A. Catherine D'Andrea. 2003. Griddles, Ovens, and Agricultural Origins: An Ethnoarchaeological Study of Bread Baking in Highland Ethiopia. *American Anthropologist* 105(3): 515–530.

Maeir, Aren M., Louise A. Hitchcock, and Liora Kolska Horwitz. 2013. On the Constitution and Transformation of Philistine Identity. *Oxford Journal of Archaeology* 32(1): 1–38.

Marshall, Fiona, and Lior Weissbrod. 2009. *The Consequences of Women's Use of Donkeys for Pastoral Flexibility: Maasai Ethnoarchaeology.* In *Tracking Down the Past: Ethnohistory Meets Archaeozoology,* ed. Gisela Grupe, George McGlynn, and Joris Peters, 59–79. Documenta Archaeobiologiae No. 7. Rahden, Westphalia: Verlag Marie Leidorf GmbH.

Mason, Sarah. 1995. Acornutopia? Determining the Role of Acorns in Past Human Subsistence. In *Food in Antiquity,* ed. John Wilkins, David Harvey, and Mike Dobson, 12–24. Exeter: University of Exeter Press.

McGovern, Patrick E. 2007. A Beverage for King Midas and at the Limits of the Civilized World. In *Ancient Wine: The Search for the Origins of Viticulture,* 279–298. Princeton: Princeton University Press.

Metheny, Karen. 2012. "If the Flavour Be Agreeable": The Meal as Sensory Experience. Annual Meeting of the Council for Northeast Historical Archaeology, St. John's, Newfoundland, 6 October.

Miller, Naomi F., Katherine M. Moore, and Kathleen Ryan. 2011. *Sustainable Lifeways: Cultural Persistence in an Ever-Changing Environment.* Philadelphia: University of Pennsylvania, Museum of Archaeology and Anthropology.

Millson, Dana C. E. 2011. Introduction. In *Experimentation and Interpretation: The Use of Experimental Archaeology in the Study of the Past,* ed. Dana C. E. Millson, 1–6. Oxford: Oxbow Books.

Mulder-Heymans, Noor. 2002. Archaeology, Experimental Archaeology and Ethnoarchaeology on Bread Ovens in Syria. *Civilisations: Revue internationale d'anthropologie et de sciences humaines* 49: 197–221. http://civilisations.revues.org/1470. Accessed 21 January 2013.

Nelson, Kit. 2010. Environment, Cooking Strategies and Containers. *Journal of Anthropological Archaeology* 29: 238–247.

O'Connell, James F. 1995. Ethnoarchaeology Needs a General Theory of Behavior. *Journal of Archaeological Research* 3(3): 205–255.

Ogundele, Samuel Oluwole. 2005. Ethnoarchaeology of Domestic Space and Spatial Behavior among the Tiv and Ungwai of Central Nigeria. *African Archaeological Review* 22(1): 25–54.

Outram, Alan K. 2008. Introduction to Experimental Archaeology. *World Archaeology* 40(1): 1–6.

Parker, Bradley J. 2011. Bread Ovens, Social Networks and Gendered Space: An Ethnoarchaeological Study of Tandir Ovens In Southeastern Anatolia. *American Antiquity* 76(4): 603–627.

Rathje, W. L., W. W. Hughes, D. C. Wilson, M. K. Tani, G. H. Archer, R. G. Hunt, and T. W. Jones. 1992. The Archaeology of Contemporary Landfills. *American Antiquity* 57(3): 437–537.

Roux, Valentine. 2007. Ethnoarchaeology: A Non Historical Science of Reference Necessary for Interpreting the Past. *Journal of Archaeological Method and Theory* 14(2): 153–178.

Ryan, Kathleen, Karega Munene, Samuel M. Kahinju, and Paul N. Kunoni. 1996. Ethnoarchaeology in Kenya Maasailand: Managing Livestock. In *Aspects of African Archaeology: Papers of the 10th Congress of the PanAfrican Association for Prehistory and Related Studies*, ed. Gilbert Pwiti and Robert Soper, 745–754. Harare: University of Zimbawe.

Samuel, Delwen. 1999. A New Look at Old Bread: Ancient Egyptian Baking. *Archaeology International* 3: 28–31.

———. 2010. Experimental Grinding and Ancient Egyptian Flour Production. In *Beyond the Horizon: Studies in Egyptian Art, Archaeology and History in Honour of Barry J. Kemp*, ed. Salima Ikram and Aidan Dodson, 456–477. Cairo: American University in Cairo Press.

Schick, Kathy D., and Nicholas P. Toth. 1993. *Making Silent Stones Speak: Human Evolution and the Dawn of Technology.* New York: Simon & Schuster.

———, eds. 2009. *The Cutting Edge: New Approaches to the Archaeology of Human Origins.* Gosport, IN: Stone Age Institute Press.

Schiffer, Michael B. 1976. *Behavioral Archeology.* New York: Academic Press.

Schiffer, Michael B., and James M. Skibo. 1987. *Theory and Experiment in the Study of Technological Change. Current Anthropology* 28(5): 595–622.

Schiffer, Michael Brian, James M. Skibo, Janet L. Griffitts, Kacy L. Hollenback, and William A. Longacre. 2001. Behavioral Archaeology and the Study of Technology. *American Antiquity* 66(4): 729–737.

Shahack-Gross, Ruth, Fiona Marshall, and Steve Weiner. 2003. Geo-Ethnoarchaeology of Pastoral Sites: The Identification of Livestock Enclosures in Abandoned Maasai Settlements. *Journal of Archaeological Science* 30(4): 439–459.

Shahack-Gross, Ruth, Allison Simons, and Stanley H. Ambrose. 2008. Identification of Pastoral Sites Using Stable Nitrogen and Carbon Isotopes from Bulk Sediment Samples: A Case Study in Modern and Archaeological Pastoral Settlements in Kenya. *Journal of Archaeological Science* 35(4): 983–990.

Shea, John. 2007. Lithic Archaeology, or What Stone Tools Can (and Can't) Tell Us About Early Hominin Diets. In *Evolution of the Human Diet: The Known, the Unknown and the Unknowable*, ed. Peter Ungar, 212–229. Oxford: Oxford University Press.

Simms, Stephanie R., Francesco Berna, and George J. Bey III. 2013. A Prehispanic Maya Pit Oven? Microanalysis of Fired Clay Balls from the Puuc Region, Yucatán, Mexico. *Journal of Archaeological Science* 40: 1144–1157.

Skakun, Natalia N. 1999. Evolution of Agricultural Techniques in Eneolithic (Chalcolithic) Bulgaria. In *Prehistory of Agriculture: New Experimental and Ethnographic Approaches,* ed. Patricia C. Anderson, 199–210. Los Angeles: Institute of Archaeology, University of California.

Skibo, James M. 1994. The Kalinga Cooking Pot: An Ethnoarchaeological and Experimental Study of Technological Change. In *Kalinga Ethnoarchaeology: Expanding Archaeological Theory and Method,* ed. William A. Longacre and James M. Skibo, 113–126. Washington DC: Smithsonian Institution Press.

———. 2009. Archaeological Theory and Snake-Oil Peddling: The Role of Ethnoarchaeology in Archaeology. *Ethnoarchaeology* 1(1): 27–56.

Stiles, Daniel. 1977. Ethnoarchaeology: A Discussion of Methods and Applications. *Man* 12: 87–103.

Stout, Dietrich. 2002. Skill and Cognition in Stone Tool Production: An Ethnographic Case Study from Irian Jaya. *Current Anthropology* 43: 693–722.

Thoms, Alton. 2008. The Fire Stones Carry: Ethnographic Records and Archaeological Expectations for Hot-Rock Cookery in Western North America. *Journal of Anthropological Archaeology* 27: 443–460.

———. 2009. Rocks of Ages: Propagation of Hot-Rock Cookery in Western North America. *Journal of Archaeological Science* 31(2): 213–232.

Toth, Nicholas P. 1997. The Artifact Assemblages in the Light of Experimental Studies. In *Plio-Pleistocene Archaeology, vol. 5: Koobi Fora Research Project Series,* ed. Glynn L. Isaac and Barbara Isaac, 363–402. Oxford: Clarendon.

Tringham, Ruth. 1978. Experimentation, Ethnoarchaeology, and the Leapfrogs in Archaeological Methodology. In *Explorations in Ethnoarchaeology,* ed. Richard A. Gould, 169–199. Santa Fe: School for Advanced Research Press.

Tsartsidou, Georgia, Simcha Lev-Yadun, Nikos Efstratiou, and Steve Weiner. 2008. Ethnoarchaeological Study of Phytolith Assemblages from an Agro-Pastoral Village in Northern Greece (Sarakini): Development and Application of a Phytolith Difference Index. *Journal of Archaeological Science* 35: 600–613.

Twomey, Terrence. 2013. The Cognitive Implications of Controlled Fire Use by Early Humans. *Cambridge Archaeological Journal* 23(1): 113–128.

Van Gijn, Annelou. 1999. The Interpretation of Sickles: A Cautionary Tale. In *Prehistory of Agriculture: New Experimental and Ethnographic Approaches,* ed. Patricia C. Anderson, 254–259. Los Angeles: Institute of Archaeology, University of California.

Vincent, Anne S. 1985. Plant Foods in Savanna Environments: A Preliminary Report of Tubers Eaten by the Hadza of Northern Tanzania. *World Archaeology* 17(2): 131–148.

Wandsnider, LuAnn. 1997. The Roasted and the Boiled: Food Composition and Heat Treatment with Special Emphasis on Pit-Hearth Cooking. *Journal of Anthropological Archaeology* 16(1): 1–48.

Weedman, Katheryn J. 2006. An Ethnoarchaeological Study of Hafting and Stone Tool Diversity among the Gamo of Ethiopia. *Journal of Archaeological Method and Theory* 13(3): 189–238.

Whittaker, John C. 2000. *Alonia* and *Dhoukanes*: The Ethnoarchaeology of Threshing in Cyprus. *Near Eastern Archaeology* 63(2): 62–69.

Williams, Eduardo. 1999. The Ethnoarchaeology of Salt Production in the Lake Cuitzeo Bain, Michoacán, México. *Latin American Antiquity* 10(4): 400–414.

———. 2002. Salt Production in the Coastal Area of Michoacan, Mexico: An Ethnoarchaeological Study. *Ancient Mesoamerica* 13: 237–253.

Wrangham, Richard, and Rachel Carmody. 2010. Human Adaptation to the Control of Fire. *Evolutionary Anthropology* 19: 187–199.

Wylie, Alison. 1985. The Reaction Against Analogy. *Advances in Archaeological Method and Theory* 8: 63–111.

———. 1989. The Interpretive Dilemma. In *Critical Traditions in Contemporary Archaeology*, ed. Valerie Pinsky and Alison Wylie, 18–27. Cambridge: Cambridge University Press.

Yankowski, Andrea, and Puangthip Kerdsap. 2013. Salt-Making in Northeast Thailand: An Ethnoarchaeological Study in Tambon Phan Song Khram, Nakhon Rachasima Province, Northeast Thailand. *Silpakorn University Journal of Social Sciences, Humanities, and Arts* 13(1): 231–252.

Yazdi, Leila Papoli, Omran Garazhian, and Maryam Dezhamkhooy. 2011. Exchange System Patterns in Bam, Southeastern Iran, after the Earthquake (December 2003): An Ethnoarchaeological Study. *Ethnoarchaeology* 3(1): 29–62.

Yellen, John. 1977. *Archaeological Approaches to the Present: Models for Reconstructing the Past*. New York: Academic Press.

Index

Printed in the USA
CPSIA information can be obtained
at www.ICGtesting.com
LVHW081746031123
762986LV00046B/1039